# Guerrilla USA

The publisher gratefully acknowledges the generous
support of the Humanities Endowment Fund of
the University of California Press Foundation.

# Guerrilla USA

*The George Jackson Brigade and the
Anticapitalist Underground of the 1970s*

---

Daniel Burton-Rose

UNIVERSITY OF CALIFORNIA PRESS
*Berkeley   Los Angeles   London*

University of California Press, one of the most distinguished university presses in the United States, enriches lives around the world by advancing scholarship in the humanities, social sciences, and natural sciences. Its activities are supported by the UC Press Foundation and by philanthropic contributions from individuals and institutions. For more information, visit www.ucpress.edu.

University of California Press
Berkeley and Los Angeles, California

University of California Press, Ltd.
London, England

© 2010 by The Regents of the University of California

Library of Congress Cataloging-in-Publication Data

Burton-Rose, Daniel.
   Guerrilla USA : the George Jackson Brigade and the anticapitalist underground of the 1970s / Daniel Burton-Rose.
      p.    cm.
   Includes bibliographical references and index.
   ISBN 978-0-520-26428-1 (cloth : alk. paper)
   ISBN 978-0-520-26429-8 (pbk. : alk. paper)
    1. George Jackson Brigade—History—20th century.  2. Guerrillas—United States—History—20th century.  I. Title.

HV6432.5.G46B87  2010
322.4'20973—dc22
                                           2010004932

19  18  17  16  15  14  13  12  11  10
10  9  8  7  6  5  4  3  2  1

*To my father, Peter Rose, for raising me on Noam Chomsky and Che Guevara*

*To those who have contributed their personal memories to the collective one*

CONTENTS

*List of Illustrations* ix
*Acknowledgments* xi

Prelude 1

PART I. ORIGINS

1. Conceptions of Revolution and Violence, 1961–1967 9
2. A Cresting Wave, 1967–1970 20
3. Delivering on Threats, 1971–1975 30

PART IIa. CONSCIOUSNESS: COMRADE CRIMINAL

4. A Child Prodigy 41
5. Jailhouse Lawyer 46
6. Strike! 53
7. A Rebel and a Cause 66
8. The Destroyer's Creation 81

PART IIb. CONSCIOUSNESS: SISTER SUBVERTER

9. Woman over the Edge of Crime 91
10. Women's Work 101

| | |
|---|---:|
| 11. Inside Out | *110* |
| 12. Days and Nights of Love and War | *119* |
| 13. New York, New York | *127* |

## PART III. UNDERGROUND

| | |
|---|---:|
| 14. Liberating the New World from the Old | *135* |
| 15. Invitation to a Bombing | *147* |
| 16. A Night without City Light | *157* |
| 17. Dog Day Afternoon | *165* |
| 18. Jailbreak! | *171* |
| 19. Clueless in Seattle | *182* |
| 20. Diverging Paths to a Common Dream | *200* |
| 21. Ed Mead Gets His Day in Court | *210* |
| 22. Underground in Oregon | *224* |
| 23. Back with a Bang! | *232* |
| 24. Winding Down | *242* |
| 25. Crying a River | *255* |
| Coda | *273* |

| | |
|---|---:|
| *Notes* | *279* |
| *Select Bibliography* | *313* |
| *Index* | *319* |

ILLUSTRATIONS

FIGURES

1. Illustration from Robert Williams's *The Crusader* inciting African Americans to race war   *17*
2. Riot police belatedly protecting the Federal Courthouse in downtown Seattle during The Day After demonstration, February 17, 1970   *27*
3. Defendants in the Seattle Conspiracy trial flip off the Federal Courthouse   *57*
4. Article on Ralph Ford and Bruce Seidel, *Seattle Times*, March 30, 1976   *70*
5. Bruce Seidel   *71*
6. Rita Brown in the early 1970s   *106*
7. Rita Brown   *107*
8. Leftist Lezzies, 1976   *108*
9. The Washington State Penitentiary Chapter of the Black Panther Party around 1968   *113*
10. Anti–grand jury demonstration   *193*

MAPS

1. George Jackson Brigade actions in Seattle   *xiv*
2. Additional George Jackson Brigade actions in Washington and Oregon   *xv*

ACKNOWLEDGMENTS

This book developed out of prisoners' rights work that I did in college. Our organization, Oberlin Action Against Prisons, made a point of collaborating with political prisoners in the United States in our consciousness-raising efforts. These political activists had been targeted by law enforcement because of the perceived threat they posed to the dominant society or, more commonly, were subject to disproportionate sentences due to the political nature of the crime(s) they had committed. I became curious about those who made no claims of innocence or of having been railroaded: what had they done and why?

In meeting former members of the George Jackson Brigade, I discovered a cohort of partisans of the civil war of the 1970s who were positively disposed to answering my questions. It is to these former members Bo, Ed, Janine, John, and Mark that my primary thanks are due. They patiently participated in over a decade of intermittent interviews, meaning that the story that follows is in many ways a collaboration. My deal with them from the start was that they could decline to divulge information that they deemed sensitive, but could not provide misinformation. The information they withheld, as far as I can tell, concerns people whose whereabouts are not currently known and who need not be drawn back into these matters. Throughout the book I have given pseudonyms to individuals who are identified by first name only.

Reports from daily newspapers form the skeleton of this work, oppositional periodicals and other contemporary publications and reports constitute the flesh, and oral history provides the animating breath. As regards the first two categories, I made extensive use of the index to local periodicals in the Seattle Room of the Seattle Public Library, while the periodical room at the University of California at Berkeley was an invaluable resource as well. Throughout this project I delighted in the treasure trove of the ever-dwindling number of East Bay used book stores, particularly Black Oak (RIP), Moe's, and Shakespeare & Co., as well as the new works on display at the AK Press warehouse and Cody's (RIP). Both the Federal Bureau of Investigation and the Bureau of Prisons responded quickly and thoroughly to my Freedom of Information Act requests, though the former censored the documents excessively.

In addition to the interviews I cite in the bibliography, Chris Beahler, Donald Duffy, Patrick Haggerty, Jo Maynes, Faygele bin Miriam, Shan Otty, Frank "Big Black" Smith, and Lois Thetford generously shared their recollections of Seattle in the 1970s and, in all cases but Jo's, their interactions with Brigade members (future, present, or past). Big Black, Don, and Faygele have all passed on, and, though they play little or no role in the following narrative, I intend this work as a testament to the caring community to which they contributed. Of the three, Don was my close friend, and I miss his indignant wit and proud lechery.

I engage throughout in what might be called "assisted dialogic prosopopoeia." Prosopopoeia refers to speeches in which a later writer "supplies the words which someone else, real or fictitious, might in agreement with the laws of necessity and probability have composed and delivered under a given set of circumstances."[1] I recreate conversations interviewees recalled, filling in details that "the laws of necessity and probability" suggest would have been conveyed under these circumstances. In such cases, I went over the reconstructed conversation with all of the involved parties whom I interviewed: for example, I base my account of the first meeting between Brown, Mead, and Seidel on the recollections of Brown and Mead, the only two of the three with whom I was able to speak. In reconstructed conversations between Brigade members and journalists, the content of the conversation is supplied by the published work of the latter.

One of the six living former Brigade members, Therese Coupez, did not wish to participate in this project. In fact, she wished to be written out of the story altogether. I was unable to comply with this request, considering it too great a distortion of the historical record. Members of the George Jackson Brigade made consistent choices over a number of years that made them both public and publicly accountable; not least of these decisions was claiming political prisoner status after arrest.[2] The political nature of the Brigade entails a responsibility for a disclosure now possible inasmuch as all former members have served their time in prison. While I have no wish to resurrect painful memories for anyone, I feel that my primary responsibility is to recount the tale as accurately as possible. That said, Coupez's lack of participation has of necessity diminished her role in the pages that follow.

On the subject of unquiet ghosts, a member of the current incarnation of the

Left Bank Collective asked me to make clear that their current membership is now far removed from the collective described in these pages.

I have benefited from the collegiality of a new generation of anti-capitalist scholars who share my fascination with the social movements of the 1960s and 1970s, including Dan Berger, Trevor Griffey, Vikki Law, Eric Lyle, José Palafox, Dylan Rodríguez, and Scott Winn, as well as Roxanne Dunbar-Ortiz and Ward Churchill, kindred spirits and mentors of the preceding generation. Dan, Dylan, and Ward provided invaluable comments on the entire manuscript, while Roger Lippman came through with very welcome eleventh-hour corrections and prodded me where he felt I had failed adequately to distinguish the perspective of the subjects from my own. Tom Hayden was kind enough to comment on Part I of the book.

Scott Fleming and Paul Rosenthal were my most steadfast comrades throughout the development and completion of this project, aiding morally with their interest and concretely when the situation called for it. Both my father Peter Rose and my mother Julianne Burton-Carvajal thoroughly edited the manuscript at earlier stages despite their ambivalence about the material. Tom Mayer, associate editor at W. W. Norton & Co., gave generously of his time and ideas, improving my proposal until it was accepted by a publisher I desired. For that acceptance I have Niels Hooper to thank. Gratitude as well to his assistant Nick Arrivo, who ensured a smooth production process. In Peter Dreyer I had a perfect copy editor, careful but noninvasive, and both personally and professionally knowledgeable about the material. I am grateful also to Jennifer Gunther for her initial draft of the maps.

Numerous hands have replaced my own on the keyboard, alleviating the inconveniences of a persistent repetitive strain injury. Among those who did so most reliably were Alyssa, Ava, Fran, Jesse (two of them), Natalie, and Sha. George Johnson, Jamie Schweser, and Dan Spalding contributed to transcription expenses, while Jane Segal secured anonymous support.

The King Street Collective provided shelter during the most intensive period of research in Seattle, from July to December 1999. Candace Falk later provided an informal "writer's retreat" in Berkeley. Laura always provided a haven, and Jennie was a steadfast partner during a dispiriting lull in progress on the book. The instructors and my classmates of Suigetsukan dojo provided a space for consensual violence that was a welcome respite from investigation into vituperative conflict. I wrote this book in pursuit of the balance they seek between the protection of one's self and one's own and unwillingness to oppress others.

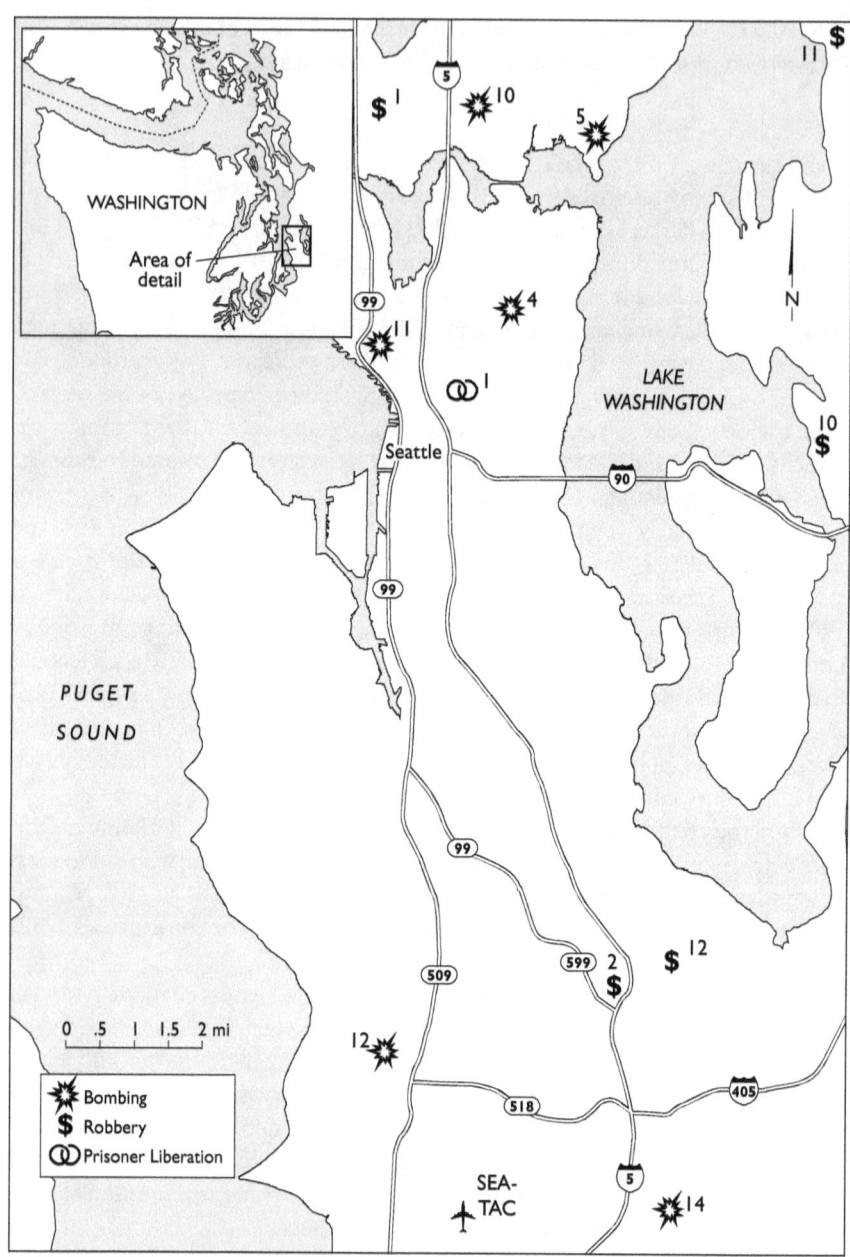

MAP 1. George Jackson Brigade actions in Seattle.

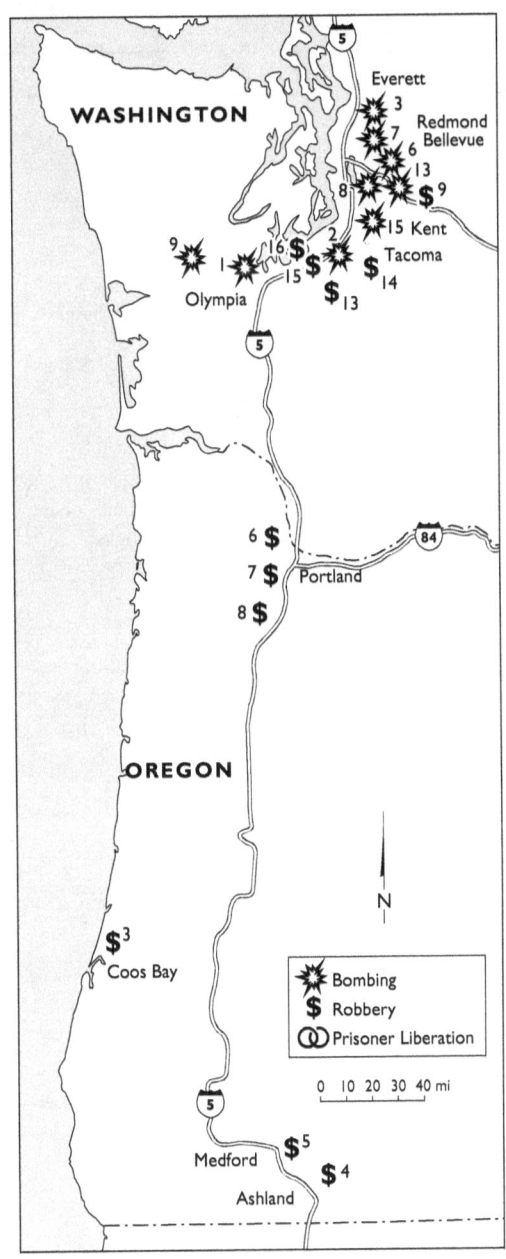

MAP 2. Additional George Jackson Brigade actions in Washington and Oregon.

BRIGADE ACTIVITY

## Bombings

| | | | |
|---|---|---|---|
| 1. | May 31, 1975 | Division of Corrections, Capitol Complex Building | Olympia, WA |
| 2. | June 5, 1975 | FBI Offices | Tacoma, WA |
| 3. | June 6, 1975 | BIA Offices | Everett, WA |
| 4. | September 18, 1975 | Safeway, 1410 E. John (at 14th), Capitol Hill | Seattle, WA |
| 5. | January 1, 1976 | City light transformer, 45th St. and 31st Ave. | Laurelhurst, WA |
| 6. | January 1, 1976 | Safeway regional warehouse and distribution center, NE 12th St. and 125th Ave. NE | Bellevue, WA |
| 7. | May 12, 1977 | Rainier Bank, Overlake Park 2245 NE | Redmond, WA |
| 8. | May 12, 1977 | Rainier Bank, Midlake office, 1815 16th Ave. NE (attempted) | Bellevue, WA |
| 9. | July 3, 1977 | Puget Sound Power and Light Company substation, 16th and Cherry (attempted) | Olympia, WA |
| 10. | October 6, 1977 | Westlund Buick-Opel-GMC dealership, location imprecise for lack of address (attempted) | North Seattle, WA |
| 11. | October 13, 1977 | S.L. Savidge Dodge, location imprecise for lack of address | Seattle, WA |
| 12. | October 15, 1977 | BBC Dodge, 14650 1st Ave. S | Burien, WA |
| 13. | October 31, 1977 | Phil Smart Inc. Mercedes Benz and BMW dealership, 10515 Main St. | Bellevue, WA |
| 14. | December 23, 1977 | Puget Sound Power & Light substation, 180th and West Valley Highway | Tukwila, WA |
| 15. | December 24, 1977 | The Convoy Company, S. 272nd and 72nd Ave. S | Kent, WA |

## Robberies

| | | | |
|---|---|---|---|
| 1. | December 25, 1975 and January 1, 1976 | State Liquor Store (location imprecise for lack of address) | North Seattle suburbs |
| 2. | January 23, 1976 | Pacific National Bank of Washington, 13451 Interurban Avenue (attempted) | Tukwila, WA |
| 3. | June 8, 1976 | Empire branch of the Western Bank | Coos Bay, OR |
| 4. | July 13, 1976 | Crater National Bank | Ashland, OR |
| 5. | August 2, 1976 | Rogue River Valley branch of the Oregon Bank, 1025 Cort Street | Medford, OR |
| 6. | October 28, 1976 | Sunset branch of the First State Bank of Oregon, 805 NW Murray Road | Cedar Mill, OR |
| 7. | January 4, 1977 | U.S. National Bank of Oregon, 4870 SW 76th Ave. | Raleigh Hills, OR |
| 8. | February 7, 1977 | U.S. National Bank of Oregon | Wilsonville, OR |
| 9. | May 21, 1977 | State Liquor Store | Newport Hills, WA |
| 10. | June 20, 1977 | Rainier National Bank | Factoria, WA |
| 11. | September 8, 1977 | Old National Bank, 13233 100th Ave. NE | Juanita, WA |
| 12. | September 19, 1977 | People's National Bank, 12610 76th Ave. S | Skyway Park, WA |

| | | | |
|---|---|---|---|
| 13. | December 8, 1977 | Puget Sound National Bank, Northeast branch | Tacoma, WA |
| 14. | January 10, 1978 | Great Northwestern Federal Savings & Loan Association, Westgate branch | Tacoma, WA |
| 15. | February 28, 1978 | Puget Sound National Bank, University Place branch | Tacoma, WA |
| 16. | March 21, 1978 | United Mutual Savings Bank, 38th and J Street (planned) | Tacoma, WA |

Prisoner Liberation

| | | | |
|---|---|---|---|
| 1. | March 10, 1976 | Harborview Medical Center | Seattle, WA |

# Prelude

The George Jackson Brigade (GJB) placed its first bomb in the early hours of Saturday May 31, 1975. Late Friday evening, Ed Mead and Bruce Seidel drove from Ed's south Seattle home to the state capital in Olympia. In the trunk they carried a 6-in. × 12-in. lead pipe packed with gunpowder, wires, and a flashbulb. A little past midnight they pulled into a parking lot adjacent to the nine-story Capitol Complex Building, where the Division of Corrections had its headquarters. Bruce acted as a lookout from the car while Ed crowbarred open a fire-escape door on ground level. He went up to the second floor, where the Division of Corrections offices were located, and entered through the fire door. Inside, he deposited the explosive under the desk in the nearest office, that of Deputy Director Robert Tropp, flicked off the safety, and exited without leaving a fingerprint. The bomb detonated at 1:22 A.M., demolishing much of the eastern wing of the floor and the floor below.

Back in Seattle, Ed and Bruce each took a quick nap. Bruce woke first, drove to a telephone booth near the intersection of First Avenue and Cherry Street, deposited a communiqué the two men had composed, which announced the existence of the Brigade and railed against "psychofascism" in the guise of mental health treatment in Washington's prisons, and called the media from a different phone to tell them where they could find it.

Two days later, the Seattle *Post-Intelligencer* daily ran what amounted to a positive review of the communiqué: "The drafter of the statement dealt articulately with criminal justice issues, showing more than a casual knowledge of the Walla Walla situation."[1] The journalist also discussed prisoner anxieties about involuntary out-of-state transfers and identified the martyred prison revolutionary George Jackson. The *Seattle Times*, to the right of the liberal *Post-Intelligencer*, focused on the law enforcement aspect, quoting B. K. Uptagraph, assistant special agent in charge of the Seattle office of the Bureau of Alcohol, Tobacco and Firearms, as admitting: "The name of the group is completely unfamiliar to us."[2]

Although the lucidity of the communiqué made the Brigade's attack seem anomalous, this was just another bombing tied to demands. The FBI reported 1,178 bombings in the United States in the first seven months of 1975, resulting in thirty-one deaths and 206 injuries.[3] In Seattle, there had been at least twenty-three bombings since 1971, and even this period had been "a comparative lull," as the *Post-Intelligencer* put it, in contrast to the sixty-six bombings that had occurred from January 1969 to June 1970.[4] The advent of the GJB, as the alternative weekly tabloid *Seattle Sun* would remark in 1976, "shattered the illusion that urban guerrilla actions here are on the decrease."[5]

The Brigade's Olympia bombing caused more than $100,000 in damage.[6] Mead, who was released from prison October 5, 1993, and is today a retired computer programmer once again living in Seattle, remains proud of this figure; indeed, he was a little disappointed when I informed him that he'd placed the pipe bomb under the desk of the *deputy* director of the department, rather than that of the director himself, as he'd been claiming for decades. (Tropp did *soon* become director of the Department of Social and Health Services, under which Corrections was subsumed, Mead points out.) Of the "action," he states: "It fulfilled its purpose, which was bringing public attention to the brutalization of prisoners." In addition, "the prisoners heard, and the guards heard, and the Department of Corrections heard." This latter remark is significant. The Brigade was not narrowly concerned with getting the public to intercede in prison conditions; as commentators immediately remarked at the time, a bombing was unlikely to catalyze sympathy for convicted criminals. Rather, the Brigade sought to pull the chain of the vengeful guardians of the incarcerated, on whose behalf its members acted.

Ed and Bruce—an ex-convict and a graduate school dropout, respectively—were two of the most prominent prisoners' rights advocates in the state. In the spring of 1975, they had received a plea for help from rebellious inmates in the isolation wing of the Washington State Penitentiary in Walla Walla and felt compelled to respond. Ed approached several minority rights and countercultural organizations in Seattle with the idea of putting together a demonstration to draw attention to the situation, but he found no takers. "Wherever I looked for help, there was none to be found," he remembers. Frustrated, he refused to concede impotence. Instead, he and Bruce chose to escalate. By blasting a state office and alarming bureaucrats they would *make* people listen.

The results pleased them, to the point where they used the same methods against other targets. Bruce, however, didn't survive the experiment. On January 23, 1976, he was wounded by police gunfire while robbing a bank with Ed and John Sherman, another ex-convict prison activist, and died in custody the next day. John, too, was shot, and both he and Ed were arrested. Ed spent the next eighteen years in prison. John did a comparable amount of time, though his sentences were punctuated by two lengthy escapes.

Despite the disaster at the bank, the Brigade lived on for another two years, carrying out more than a dozen bombings and as many bank robberies, all the while churning out communiqués denouncing the injustices of life under capitalism.

The modern African American civil rights movement began two decades before the Brigade's first bombing, and "Black Power" militancy peaked in the early 1970s. Direct U.S. involvement in Indochina, which had provoked so much tumult in the 1960s, diminished dramatically after the Paris Peace Accords were signed in January 1973; the South Vietnamese puppet regime collapsed before a communist onslaught on April 30, 1975. In August 1974, President Richard Nixon, who embodied the concept "abuse of power" for the protest generation, resigned rather than face impeachment. In the winter of 1974, at one of the last protests that Ed Mead attended, a confused bystander exclaimed: "I didn't know they still had demonstrations!"[7] What did protesters have left to complain about, let alone complaints that they registered with explosives?

The late date of the George Jackson Brigade's appearance is not its only eye-catching aspect. Those familiar with profiles of the campus bombers who plagued the Reserve Officers Training Corps in the 1960s will recognize only faint likenesses in Brigade members. Certainly, both groups were disaffected with the dominant society and had ceased to believe that it could be substantially altered by peaceful means. But there were marked demographic differences. Brigade members had served more time in prison cells than in college classrooms. Five of the seven were gay or bisexual, a reflection of the loosened limits on gender-orientation in a movement dominated by straight white men up to the close of the 1960s. And by virtue of one black member, Brigade membership spanned the racial divide, in contrast to the separatism prominent among radicals at the end of the 1960s.

The Brigade's ideology also set its members apart from other domestic revolutionaries, especially those "Children of privilege [who] were rediscovering the virtues of command," as Todd Gitlin characterized the "Weatherman" faction of Students for a Democratic Society.[8] In a report dated January 4, 1978, under the heading "Philosophy of the GJB," an unnamed agent in the Seattle offices of the Federal Bureau of Investigation observed: "Unlike other recent student-revolutionary groups, the GJB does not envision itself as an 'elite' faction that will provide a leadership faction for an ultimate revolutionary government, and criticizes those groups who would place themselves in such a role. Rather, the GJB sees itself more as a catalyst to make the masses aware of their oppressed state, and inspire them to create their own general uprising to overthrow their 'oppressors.'"[9]

The Brigade did inspire a few people, but by provoking massive intervention by law enforcement, it also increased the difficulties of those who rallied around the same causes. This bothered Brigade members not at all: they saw polarization as a good thing. In this combative posture vis-à-vis friend and foe alike, the Brigade crystallized one of the most confusing aspects of the late 1960s: the way in which leaders were constantly forced to scramble to keep up with their ostensible followers, while concurrently more-militant-than-thou posturing divorced recognized spokespeople from the capabilities and desires of the ever-growing number of the disaffected. Brigade members came of age politically in a time of mass disillusionment and intensifying revolutionary agitation in militant circles. They were both leaders who sought to follow "the people" and individuals uprooted from a coherent social base.

Who, exactly, did Brigade members claim as their constituency? They took it upon themselves to enforce the well-articulated demands of a broad cross-section of social groups, including women, gays, racial minorities, and workers; all categories to which Brigade members belonged. The early 1970s were a time when a multiplicity of voices echoed the demands for deep democracy first articulated by civil rights organizers, then reproduced within the dominant society by white students. Gender roles were transformed as women broke free from traditional constraints and gays charged out of the closet. Institutions threatened meltdown across the board: the prisons were in upheaval, the U.S. military was close to paralysis owing to G.I. insubordination, and a new generation of workers was boldly disobedient on the shop floor.[10] The Catholic Church produced direct-action-prone militants. Ethnic minorities who had never been included in the American social contract—Chicanos, Puerto Ricans, Americans Indians, and Asian Americans—had run out of patience with being ignored or watching those with power crudely attempt to co-opt their leaders. Like African Americans before them, they plunged into civil rights organizing.

Despite close links to other groups, the Brigade's true constituency—those who could relate not only to its members' anger but to the explosive way in which they expressed it—were those from whose ranks they had emerged and to which they would return: prisoners. In light of the thrust of the 1960s movement for participatory democracy, a consideration of the Brigade raises the question: just how deep can democratic participation go?

In explaining themselves, these veterans of the "war at home" constantly cite the irresistible momentum of "the times." With these words they invoke the pervasive struggles for power on the part of the dispossessed that characterized this era. The widespread success of these struggles—from the decolonization of Africa, which inspired the civil rights movement of the late 1950s and 1960s in the United States, to the revolutions in Cuba and Vietnam, which ignited the imaginations of so many domestic radicals—imparted a sense among all but the most obtuse that change was not only possible, but imminent. The imperative of change demanded active participation in the process of historical creation. Convinced that it was better to act and err than to be paralyzed by complexities, they joined what they discerned to be a collective impulse toward revolution.

Ironically, one of the greatest errors conceded by former Brigade members is, in Mead's words, that "we were out of touch with the times." Well before they began their campaign to inspire revolution, a strong right-wing undertow pulled the country away from the liberalism rejected so vehemently by 1960s radicals, and even further away from the egalitarianism they insisted upon. Brigade members were unwilling to concede that the Movement had already reached its high-water mark. Like the white supremacist bombers who had caused so much agony in the civil rights movement in the previous decade, their attempt to find power in violence revealed as much weakness as it did strength. Also reminiscent of the earlier bombers, to whom they were anathema ideologically, was the way in which their extremism fueled the backlash that destroyed what they sought to defend.

In his autobiography Malcolm X declared: "I *believe* in anger."[11] In 1965, the year of Malcolm X's death, Tom Hayden, one of the seminal figures of white radicalism in the 1960s, reflected: "Perhaps the only form of action appropriate to angry people is violence."[12] This book is a meditation on the tension between self-restraint and anger in the process of social change, and on the conjunction of individual agency and inevitabilities created by world-historical confluences. In it, I document a shadow world commonly ignored in the interests of social peace. I do so in the belief that, counterintuitively, discussing such matters publicly can minimize violence by pointing to the way in which, as one of President John F. Kennedy's speechwriters put it: "Those who make peaceful change impossible make violent revolution inevitable."

In focusing the narrative gaze through the lens of a bombing collective, there is a risk of distorting this commonly oversimplified era. The subject matter also plays to the American fascination with violence, a libidinal current responsible in no small way for the events of the period in question. My intention, however, is to provide the clarity of vision that results from a careful consideration of a perspective vastly different from one's own. Only an awareness of the inequalities that enraged Brigade members can lay a foundation for social peace worthy of the name.

PART I

# Origins

1

# Conceptions of Revolution and Violence, 1961–1967

By the summer of 1961, Monroe, North Carolina, had become a pressure cooker under intense heat. Year by year, conflict between insistent advocates of racial integration and indignant white supremacists had compounded the pressure. Incidents of white-on-black violence occurred almost daily, and Robert Williams, a local African American organizer with an international reputation for militancy, was repeatedly subjected to death threats. The threats were not idle: several attempts had, in fact, been made on his life. As if in retaliation, a string of arsons damaged conservative businesses. When idealistic young "Freedom Riders" came to town and decried racial inequality in front of the courthouse, the city fathers ordered that they be sprayed with insecticide.

The explosion occurred on Sunday August 27, when white rage coalesced into mob violence against the biracial courthouse picket. The demonstrators were beaten bloody, then arrested for "inciting a riot." Such treatment was chillingly common for the Freedom Riders, who had been assaulted in numerous locales in the course of efforts earlier in the summer to desegregate Greyhound bus stations. Civil rights activists in Monroe had declined to join their picket line for just this reason. "We had an agreement with the students that they would do the picketing in a nonviolent way around the courthouse," Mabel Williams, the wife of Robert, later disclosed, "but when they came back to our community, that we would always protect our community with guns."[1] Rather than aspiring to transform their oppressors spiritually, as did the out-of-towner Gandhian Christians, those in the Monroe civil rights contingent contented themselves with a more worldly aim: teaching white supremacists to keep their hands to themselves.

They had had some success doing so. In 1957 the group put an end to the terrifying "nightriding" of the Ku Klux Klan chapter in Union County, in which Monroe was located, by repelling one of its nocturnal motorcades with a barrage of gunfire. Most of the men in the close-knit civil rights circle were veterans who not only knew how to use weapons but felt entitled to do so in defense of their rights as citizens. Female members were no less assertive: they, too, participated in the organization's National Rifle Association–sponsored Rifle Club.

On the afternoon of August 27, 1961, Monroe's black civil rights activists were as prepared as they could be for the impending assault on their community. In response to reports of attacks on isolated African Americans in other parts of town and of the city's jailers torturing detainees, the organizers gathered at the Williamses' home. They erected barricades to seal off the street in front of the house and took up sentry positions with rifles in trees. Williams unpacked two machine guns that had been bought with funds raised by northern colleagues, including Malcolm X, the fiery minister of the Nation of Islam's No. 7 mosque in Harlem. He loaded them and placed them on his front porch under the care of two deputies, then distributed sticks of dynamite with prepared fuses to other reliable cohorts. State troopers set up a perimeter around the neighborhood, not to disarm Williams and company, but to prevent their would-be assailants from getting themselves killed.

As day receded into night, National Guardsmen and vigilantes poured into town. Monroe's chief of police, A. A. Mauney, phoned Williams and declared: "Robert, you have caused a lot of race trouble in this town, now state troopers are coming and in 30 minutes you'll be hanging in the Court House Square."[2] At that point, Williams recalled, "I realized that this thing was not just a local matter, that the U.S. government had entered into the picture. And they were just as determined to destroy me as the Ku Klux Klan."[3] It was clear to Williams that his continued presence in the city would precipitate a bloodbath. "I thought [staying] would get a lot of people killed and I didn't want that to happen," he remembered. His own prospects were dim: even if he survived a confrontation, he would face a "legal lynching" in the courts. So he chose flight. Within two months, he, his wife, and their children surfaced in Cuba under the protection of Williams's personal friend President Fidel Castro.[4]

In principle, the right to armed self-defense was universally acknowledged in the civil rights movement. In a debate with Williams, Dr. Martin Luther King Jr. conceded that "all societies, from the most primitive to the most cultured and civilized, accept as moral and legal. . . . [v]iolence exercised in self-defense." He continued: "The principle of self-defense, even involving weapons and bloodshed, has never been condemned, even by Gandhi."[5]

Roy Wilkins, the staid president of the National Association for the Advancement of Colored People (NAACP), acknowledged in his autobiography, "Like

Williams, I believe in self-defense."⁶ Yet, in 1959, Wilkins orchestrated Williams's ouster from the NAACP after Williams had declared to the press that, in the absence of credible legal protection, blacks must meet white "violence with violence." Before he was run out of the country by law enforcement, Williams was run out of the mainstream civil rights movement by conservatives.

Williams had felt confident taking such a strong public stand because he knew he spoke for the rank-and-file of the Union County chapter of the NAACP, of which he was president. Within the national organization the chapter had a unique constituency—the young and the poor—because Williams's recruitment drive had been atypical: "We got some of the 'worst element' we could find," he explained provocatively. One biographer writes that "Williams painstakingly recruited from the pool halls, beauty parlors, street corners, and tenant farms," a far cry from the well-heeled or socially climbing base of the country's most culturally conservative and tactically restrained civil rights organization.

The NAACP and other prominent civil rights organizations would pay a high price for discouraging the efforts of lowly blacks to organize themselves. Without leaders who spoke directly to poor blacks in their own language, little recourse remained to the urban poor but inchoate outbursts. Once these fires started, they threatened to burn every obstruction in their path.

## SEEDS OF REVOLUTION

Throughout the 1960s, Robert Williams would associate with the world's most successful revolutionary leaders, those of Cuba, Vietnam, and China. His insistence on armed self-defense and commitment to internationalism made him one of the most influential forefathers of the late 1960s Black Power movement. Yet despite some violent manifestos, he was never a revolutionary: he always sought to fulfill the promise of America rather than to destroy the country and create something else. "I had always considered myself an American patriot," he later explained. To him, the Constitution was a document of infinite promise: the problem was the failure of racist, ignorant, and willfully oppressive whites to abide by it.⁷ In his frustrated patriotism, he resembled many white militants. As one remarked in the late 1960s: "I became a radical when I realized I wasn't going to become president."⁸

The concept of revolution percolated into the civil rights and student movements of the early 1960s not by way of practitioners of violence but via pacifists. Members of the Student Nonviolent Coordinating Committee (SNCC), the most innovative and courageous civil rights group of the early 1960s, began using the word "revolutionary" to describe themselves as early as 1961. Students for a Democratic Society (SDS), the primary voice of the youthful upsurge on white campuses, picked up the word from them. The Quaker pacifists associated with *Liberation* magazine reinforced the idea that revolution was the proper goal of activism.⁹

In his contemplative chronicle of the militant young civil rights activists of the SNCC, Clayborne Carson writes of this early period: "For them the word [revolutionary] did not imply a desire to overthrow the federal government, but rather indicated a need to challenge both the segregationist social order and the more moderate civil rights organizations." Likewise, early SDS members understood the "revolution" of their southern counterparts as a challenge not only to southern apartheid but to poverty itself and the morally bankrupt policies that allowed it to fester.[10]

Inspired by southern campaigns to redress racial inequality, a cohort of white students resolved to bring the civil rights struggle into northern ghettoes. This decision set the course of the brewing conflict that was to come between youths and their government. In the South, de jure segregation could be dismissed as an antiquated throwback inimical to the interests of the United States at home and abroad. In the North, however, comparably potent de facto segregation called into question the presumed enlightenment of the society as a whole. The federal government was often an ally—if a reluctant one—in the southern civil rights struggle, but once the campaigns came north, a Democratic administration had little to offer but a cooptive and short-lived "War on Poverty." Radicals' persistence brought them into conflict with the economic inequalities inherent in capitalism. No longer simply do-gooders, they themselves became a threat to "American interests." The intransigence that met the efforts of idealists produced a much more ambitious program of change, one that had little chance of resolution without bloodshed.

On April 15, 1965, Students for a Democratic Society organized the first mass protest against the war in Vietnam in Washington, D.C. Twenty-five thousand people attended, far exceeding the organizers' expectations: it was, at that point, the largest peace demonstration in U.S. history. Though this quintessentially "New Left" organization—like its "Old Left" predecessors—compulsively composed position papers, it also exhibited a propensity simply to plunge into the country's problems and seek solutions while immersed. In response to the demands of an expanded public platform, however, the organization sharpened its political line.

At another massive anti-war rally in D.C. that winter, SDS president Carl Oglesby characterized the underlying system dissidents objected to as "corporate liberalism." He carefully distinguished corporate fealty from the humanism most of his listeners avowed. This distinction, however, did not catch on. From Oglesby's speech forward, radicals denounced liberalism and would define themselves against its adherents, whom they vehemently condemned for their insidious complicity with a system that waged war abroad and denied many of its citizens civil rights at home.

The expanding divide between liberals and radicals often occurred along generational lines. This tension was reproduced in the micro-generations within Students for a Democratic Society. The first SDSers were "junior achievers" with experience in student leadership and publications dating back to high school. They primarily attended elite colleges in the Northeast and Great Lakes regions. Many of their parents were ex-communists, socialists, and liberals, who had influenced their children from an early age by discussing politics at home.

The students' proximity to power was tangible. Tom Hayden, an early SDS recruit, remembers: "Many of us were student leaders who were conditioned to believe that if you spoke out, you would get a hearing from the Kennedy administration." Upon the completion in June 1962 of "The Port Huron Statement," SDS's expansive distillation of its worldview, Hayden and SDS founder Al Haber promptly drove to Washington, D.C., and delivered a copy to White House historian Arthur Schlesinger Jr., who promised he would pass it on to the president.[11] The assassination of President Kennedy the next year drove a sharp wedge between the coalescing youth culture and the country it thought it knew.

By mid-decade a new breed of activists, differing markedly from their predecessors demographically and programmatically, manifested themselves within SDS. In his definitive account of the organization, Kirkpatrick Sale characterizes the newcomers as "middle-American activists . . . raised in the individualistic heritage of the frontier"; they were "anarchists" rather than "politicos." Previously unexposed to left-wing intellectualism, they scornfully contrasted "talk" with "action" and "thinking" with "doing." This emphasis on physical tangibility could be traced to their origin in rawer, less-permissive parts of the country where engaging in oppositional politics—be it hippie dress, long hair, and drug use or clean-cut petition drives—could carry severe consequences.[12] A former SDSer recalled that the new breed, to which he belonged, was "more natively radical. Their radicalism came from almost a nihilism, a root and branch rejection of the society. A profounder kind of alienation than people in the East."[13] This population would do for SDS what the poor of color were doing for the civil rights movement: drive it forward with destructive abandon, constantly thwarting efforts to calm and contain it.

The development of an ornery, rebellious rank and file reflected the success of the civil rights and students movements, which aimed to draw the disenfranchised into meaningful participation in political life. In doing so, they wished to revitalize the country's existing institutions. Yet, as previously dispossessed constituencies awakened to their own potential power, they unloosed pent-up rage caused by the wrongs they continued to suffer. As the alienated came to the fore, many of them declared that society was hopelessly corrupt and that new structures must be created to meet their needs.

Militant politicos turned their eyes to communist revolutions in China, Cuba, and Vietnam, which were making conspicuous progress in addressing economic, gender, and racial inequalities. In February 1967, Greg Calvert, national secretary of SDS, gave a speech in which he explained what people in the organization found inspiring about a Third World guerrilla campaign. Calvert declared:

> [W]hen the Guatemalan guerrillas enter a new village, they do not talk about the "anti-imperialist struggle" nor do they give lessons on dialectical materialism—neither do they distribute copies of the "Communist Manifesto" or of Chairman Mao's "On Contradiction." What they do is gather together the people of the village in the center of the village and then, one by one, the guerrillas rise and talk to the villagers about their own lives: about how they see themselves and how they came to be who they are, about their deepest longings and the things they've striven for and hoped for, about the way in which their deepest longings were frustrated by the society in which they lived.
>
> Then the guerrillas encourage the villagers to talk about their lives. And then a marvelous thing begins to happen. People who thought that their deepest problems and frustrations were their individual problems discover that their problems and longings are all the same—that no one man is any different than the others.... [O]ut of discovery of their common humanity comes the decision that men must unite together in the struggle to destroy the conditions of their common oppression.
>
> That, it seems to me, is what we are about.

The "Guatemalan guerrilla" approach, applied on American campuses, was highly effective. One SDSer raved to another: "You'd be astonished at the reception this gets, when people realize that they aren't alone, that the failures and the problems they ascribe to themselves stem in large part from the society in which they live and the images of themselves they accepted from society." Obviously electrified by martial language, Calvert characterized the upwelling of disenchanted youth precipitated by the campaign as "an indigenous revolt."[14] A first-page story in the *New York Times* titled "The New Left Turns to Mood of Violence in Place of Protest" opened with the line, attributed to Calvert, "We are working to build a guerrilla force in an urban environment."

The article elicited widespread opprobrium both in the country as a whole and in SDS itself. It was symptomatic of a problem that would soon reach crisis proportions: the inability of organizations to constrain their spokespeople, who often took more aggressive stands than those they represented. According to Sale the *Times* article "alarmed most of the constituency, which shied [away] from violence and was by no means ready for guerrilla warfare."[15]

Yet Calvert had not spoken of armed combat. With the exception of some grim locales in the South, organizers in the United States were not compelled to pick up arms in order to stay alive long enough to organize people around collective concerns. But as the Indochinese charnel house burned brighter and the right-wing backlash against the newfound assertiveness of ethnic minorities and the young intensified, many in the movement concluded that, as repression increased, they too would need weapons to protect themselves in their quest for power.

## A CLOSING CIRCLE

As domestic radicals came to identify more closely with revolutionaries abroad, potentially revolutionary developments accelerated at home. Urban riots, in particular, shook the nation. Race riots had occurred cyclically in U.S. history and, up until the 1960s, invariably consisted of whites terrorizing minority ethnic populations: African Americans, Chicanos, or Chinese, depending on the region. The first black riot against white oppression occurred in Birmingham, Alabama, in 1963. No deaths occurred, but the prospect of an uninhibited display of what would soon be called "black rage" was not one that whites relished. Some white politicians came to the negotiating table. Others instructed their police protectors to draw the line.

The Watts riot in South Central Los Angeles commenced on August 14, 1965. Its fires burned for five days, consuming $200 million worth of property. An occupation force of sixteen thousand predominantly white law enforcement officers and National Guardsmen were called in to quell the black uprising. At that point, Gerald Horne writes, "what began as a black revolt against police quickly became a police revolt against blacks."[16] Thirty-four people were killed in the course of the suppression, over a thousand wounded, and thousands more arrested. With its widespread arson, looting, and sniper fire, Watts marked the beginning of what, in the words of Roxanne Dunbar-Ortiz, "in any other country . . . would have been called a permanent state of urban guerrilla warfare."[17] Daryl Gates, a field officer with the Los Angeles Police Department who would rise to the post of police chief by the time of the 1992 LA riot, remembers that in the wake of the 1965 rebellion, he and his colleagues "began reading everything we could get our hands on concerning guerilla warfare."[18]

It was none too soon. A comprehensive list of "every definable instance of left-wing terrorism and sabotage" in the United States drawn up in 1970 showed a sharp increase from 1965 on. Sifting through the daily newspapers of seventeen cities throughout the country, the maverick monthly magazine *Scanlan's* documented sixteen such actions in 1965, 34 in 1966, 56 in 1967, and 236 in 1968. In 1969, the number doubled to 503. By the time the periodical stopped counting in September 1970, there had already been 546 actions, for a grand total of 1,391 in less than a five-year period.[19] The Treasury Department, using much less exclusive criteria for an overlapping period, put the number at over 5,000.

*Life* magazine had no qualms about calling what occurred in Newark, New Jersey, in July 1967 an "insurrection," and a "predictable" one at that. Police brutality provoked the initial outburst. New Jersey's all-white National Guard occupied the black areas of the city to reassert control. The Guardsmen, drawn from New Jersey suburbs, considered blacks vectors of the disorder that was threatening their own modest comforts. Their conduct presented the country with the prospect of an open race war in which whites, armed with tanks and guns, were granted free rein to vent their frustrations on any unfortunate with dark skin. In retaliation for black looting of white stores, soldiers and state troopers smashed or shot up the storefronts of businesses that displayed posters proclaiming "Soul Brother" in their windows.[20]

Such petty vindictiveness paled in comparison to the price community residents paid in blood and tears. The Guardsmen, state troopers, and predominantly white local police killed at least twenty-one black people (their wild "friendly fire" also likely resulted in the demise of a white detective and a white fireman, deaths that were initially blamed on snipers). One thousand people were injured in the disturbance, while 1,400 were arrested. Those enforcing martial law killed at least one young man in cold blood, and were not shy about making remarks to one another such as: "What should happen is they should line up all the niggers and kill them."[21]

As a counterforce to the immediate possibility of suffering a similarly overbearing occupation, African Americans in other New Jersey ghettos hastened to augment their arsenals. This tactic had a certain grim efficacy. On Sunday, July 16, ghetto residents in Plainfield, New Jersey, beat a white police officer to death after he shot and killed a young black man outside a housing project. In preparation against invasion by other policemen and the National Guard, young blacks raided an arms manufacturing plant and distributed carbines among themselves. State and local officials opted for cordoning off the black section of the inner city, rather than penetrating it at a high cost to life and limb.[22]

That same summer in Detroit, it took 10,000 National Guardsmen, plus army paratroopers, to put down what enthusiastic militants quickly dubbed the "Great Rebellion." The official death toll was the highest yet—forty-three—as was the number arrested: 7,200, many of whom suffered acute deprivations while in detention.[23] Though popularly perceived as another "black riot," disquieted police discovered that the majority of snipers they captured in the disturbance were displaced Appalachian whites.[24] This presented another direction in which the country could deteriorate: bitter street wars between the have-nots and the protectors of the haves. The force of the insurgency stimulated some radical brains nourished on tales of the Russian Revolution to imagine the Motor City as an American Petrograd; others pictured it as a starting-off point for a guerrilla campaign against the U.S. government.[25]

Robert Williams was, by this time, relocating from Cuba to China. Throughout his exile, he edited *The Crusader* newsletter, in which, from 1964 on, he called for African Americans to wage guerrilla warfare against their government in order to force it to deliver on its democratic promises.[26] Though periodically blocked by the U.S. Postal Service, the publication was circulated among left-wing revolutionaries around the world. Williams remembers being credited by a high-ranking North Vietnamese official during one of his visits to Vietnam in the late 1960s for providing the inspiration behind their turn to urban warfare. "We read your publication on urban guerrilla warfare and we realized we had to go into the city," Williams

FIGURE 1. Illustration from Robert Williams's *The Crusader* inciting African Americans to race war. *The Crusader* 9, no. 2 (Sept.–Oct. 1967).

recalled being told. "And when we looked at your people in the city of Detroit and what they had done to it, we decided to have the Tet Offensive."²⁷

Regardless of whether or not this conversation ever took place—even if it did, Williams's hosts may have been flattering him—the claim itself reveals the deep interconnection between domestic revolt and Third World revolution. In retaking Detroit, soldiers freshly returned from Vietnam were deployed against U.S. citizens for the first time. For a moment, the urban disenfranchised and the Vietnamese communists had exactly the same enemy.

In 1966, Ernesto "Che" Guevara, the charismatic Argentine doctor who had transformed himself into a guerrilla *comandante* in the victorious Cuban revolution, delivered a bitter rebuke to his fellow revolutionary internationalists. The conflict between the United States and the Vietnamese "patriots" was on his mind. Deeply impressed with the latter and disturbed by the inadequacy of aid from their supporters, Guevara did not mince words: "The solidarity of the progressive world with the Vietnamese people has something of the bitter irony of the plebeians cheering on the gladiators in the Roman Circus. To wish the victim success is not enough; one must share his fate. One must join him in death or in victory."

Guevara appealed to the imagination of those he sought to persuade. "How close and bright would the future appear if two, three, many Vietnams flowered on the face of the globe," he queried, "with their quota of death and their immense tragedies, with their daily heroism, with their repeated blows against imperialism[?]" Such a development would force the United States "to disperse its forces under the lash of the growing hatred of the people of the world!"[28]

Guevara's charge was clear: pick a struggle and claw at the *yanqui* behemoth until it kills you or groans its last. His missive was addressed to the Organization of Solidarity with the Peoples of Asia, Africa, and Latin America, not to those in "the belly of the beast," as the early Cuban nationalist José Martí famously described his time in the United States.[29] But Guevara did cite disruptions in the United States as a promising sign. The letter was published in 1967, the year the Che mystique hit full force in the U.S. protest scene: olive drab military surplus jackets and boots became all the rage, as did imitations of his beard and hairdo. Che posters peppered the walls of collectives and dorm rooms. One of the most popular featured an image of the adopted Cuban sporting his communicable grin under the engagingly vulnerable phrase: "At the risk of seeming ridiculous, let me say that the revolutionary is guided by great feelings of love." In his 1965 essay "Socialism and Man in Cuba," from which the quotation was drawn, Guevara continued: "It is impossible to think of a genuine revolutionary lacking this quality." He reconciled the apparent contradiction between loving and killing with the conciliatory meditation: "Perhaps it is one of the great dramas of the leader that he must combine a passionate spirit with a cold intelligence and make painful decisions without flinching."[30]

"Two, Three, Many Vietnams" turned out to be Guevara's final public address. In October 1967 he was executed in Bolivia while practicing what he preached: guerrilla warfare. In this last communiqué, it was "cold intelligence" on which he placed his emphasis. "Our soldiers must be . . . effective, violent, selective, cold, killing machine[s]." The reason? "[A] people without hate cannot triumph over a brutal enemy."[31]

Régis Debray's *Revolution in the Revolution? Armed Struggle and Political Struggle in Latin America,* which followed on the heels of Guevara's salvo, identified the crucial innovation of the Cuban revolution as the centralization of the political power of the revolutionary forces in the guerrilla band, which Guevara termed the *foco* (focus). While the enforcement of the demand of self-defense for those to whom it had been customarily denied remained a revolutionary goal in the United States, Debray set the bar even higher by scornfully dismissing self-defense with an increasingly common revolutionary put-down: it was reformist.[32] Debray discounted self-defense for the same reason that militants from the United States, such as

Williams, had promoted it earlier in the decade: "self-defense undermined the security of the civilian population."[33] Debray imbued his notion of "total war" with the considerable prestige of the Cuban revolution—his tract was first published by the Castro regime.[34]

U.S. radicals' psychological identification with their Third World counterparts obscured the material differences between them. Domestic radicals were located in the most powerful country the world had ever known, while the guerrillas with whom they identified dogged crumbling regimes and even then suffered enormous casualties. Despite the destabilizing influence of intensifying horrors in Vietnam, many domestic radicals maintained their ability to discern the tactical differences dictated by their physical circumstances. Of these, some vehemently rejected the importation of guerrilla tactics into the United States as wildly inappropriate and dangerously counterproductive. Yet a vocal minority considered such distinctions in tactics—and the inherent risk differential—an unethical acquiescence to an international ranking in which the lives of the affluent were more highly valued than those of the destitute. To announce their noncollaboration, they too proclaimed that "total war" was the way to go.

2

# A Cresting Wave, 1967–1970

The threat of a large-scale white riot prompted by U.S. policies in Indochina cropped up for the first time in the planning of the October 1967 march on Washington. Dave Dellinger, a Quaker pacifist first incarcerated for refusing to serve in World War II and the editor of *Liberation* magazine, was the primary organizer of the affair. He recognized that the anti-war movement was at a grow-or-die juncture, and, committed to enhancing its appeal to the young, invited Jerry Rubin to collaborate in its planning. In 1965, Rubin had participated in the organization of "Vietnam Day" on the campus of the University of California at Berkeley, the first mass protest against the war anywhere in the country.[1] Since that time, he had shown himself to be a creative innovator of protest tactics, able to draw in energetic constituencies and discomfit those who collaborated with the war effort.

As an organizer of the October 1967 protest, Rubin proposed that the marchers target the Pentagon, the staging base for U.S. aggression abroad and control domestically, rather than Congress, a symbol, to many, of democracy. In the negotiations with government agencies over permits for the proposed march, it was clear to both sides that if authorities blocked the demonstrators' path, the protesters would wreak havoc at whatever point the obstruction occurred. This "riot," as it would inevitably be called, might easily turn deadly. It was not that the protesters would be armed and dangerous; it was that the police—civilian and military, as well as federal marshals and U.S. troops—would be. Government negotiators reluctantly conceded to civil disobedience in front of the nerve center of America's armed forces.[2]

During the October march, the anti-war movement bared its teeth. Dissidents were upset by the government's policy of ignoring opposition and seduced into escalation by the media's lack of attention, absent dramatic new developments. Also weighing on radical young minds was the instructive contrast of the massive violence faced by rebels in the ghettoes the previous summer. The new attitude of the protesters was captured in its slogan "From Protest to Resistance"; instead of passive dissent, such as petitions and public dialogues, the anti-war movement would now give priority to active interference with the government's war-making capability.

New segments of the African American community had participated in the riots that had been shaking the country. Black men, in particular, had, up until the emergence of the "civil disturbance," largely boycotted the civil rights movement, because they found that its insistence on nonviolence insufferably constrained a perceived patriarchal duty to protect women and children.[3]

In a similar way, the confrontationalism of the movement in October cut through the dismissiveness with which other segments of American society had previously viewed the "peaceniks." In doing so, it encouraged participation by a wider cross-section of the populace. The ever-optimistic Dellinger contended that

> the protesters' first advance . . . to a higher stage of struggle . . . electrified the country. It stimulated imaginations and won support in crucial new sections of the population, most notably GIs, returning veterans, and high school and junior high school students. It aroused the interest of a few dissident members of the working class, including rank-and-file unionists and some local and second-echelon leaders schooled in the tradition of the strikes, sit-ins, and other direct actions of the thirties. It also appealed to the scattered members of the "lumpen proletariat" (the uprooted and dispossessed), including welfare mothers, prisoners, American Indians, Chicanos, and members of some big-city youth gangs, such as the Blackstone Rangers [black] and Young Lords [Puerto Rican]. Until then, few workers or lumpens had seen any real point in the prevailing forms of protest, which the more vocal had decried as polite, middle-class attempts to inform the oppressor that he was immoral.[4] (brackets in original)

The building occupations by students at Columbia University in April 1968 infused a tangible sense of power into the campus-based movement. Students overcame their ambivalence about their privileged position in society by confronting their own universities' complicity in war-making and slumlordism. Students for a Democratic Society, riffing on Che Guevara, propagated the slogan "Two, Three, Many Columbias." Other "Columbias" irrepressibly sprung into being. There were hundreds of demonstrations on campuses across the country, many involving sit-ins and strikes; some included occupations and hostage-taking. Concessions flowed from three-quarters of the country's institutions of higher learning. Blood flowed as well when administrators called in police to dislodge the students they couldn't placate.[5]

This new combative posture, on the campuses and in the streets, prompted a counteroffensive from the government, which had been deeply alarmed by the sea of protest that had immersed the capital in October. Police brutality quickly became standard at anti-war protests. As a prominent national organizer, Dellinger had a comprehensive view of occurrences throughout the country. He described the developments that winter and spring: "major violence had been launched against hippies and antiwar demonstrators in Los Angeles, New York, Oakland, Boston, Buffalo, Madison, Chicago ... and many other cities." The police attacks were not subtle, but neither were they frontal assaults:

> [T]he police usually did *not* attack the main column of mass marches to rally sites that were acceptable to the authorities. But invariably there was police brutality around the edges—which meant that in large demonstrations any number from a few dozen to a few hundred would be clubbed or roughed up—in feeder marches, while traveling to or from the demonstration or while bringing up the rear. The attacks often (but not always) became massive when protesters tried to get close to a forbidden area [such as the South Vietnamese embassy in Washington, D.C.].[6]

## DECLARATIONS OF WAR

On April 4, 1968, prospects for peaceful change, which had been receding for years, were dispatched altogether by an assassin's bullet in Memphis, Tennessee. Riots broke out in over a hundred cities upon news of the death of Dr. Martin Luther King Jr. Sixty people died and thousands were injured in the ensuing upheaval. Fifty-nine thousand federal troops, in addition to harried local law enforcement, were employed to suppress the disturbances. One pundit observed: "there were machine-gun emplacements in the Capitol and near the White House. Those are not ordinary occurrences which we can point to on many occasions in our past."[7]

A new clarity was born of the consuming rage. Oakland, California, was practically the only city in the country with a substantial African American population that did not erupt in flames upon news of King's death. In 1966, the Black Panther Party for Self-Defense had been founded in the city by Huey Newton and Bobby Seale, two community college students seeking to forge widespread dissatisfaction in the black community into a force powerful enough to overturn the colonial dynamics between blacks and whites. The Panthers sought to organize the black urban poor to fight for their own interests for the first time since the 1961 dissolution of the civil rights contingent led by Robert Williams in Monroe, North Carolina. That the organization put a high premium on the right to self-defense was apparent in its name. The Oakland Police Department systematically violated this right, making a showdown inevitable.

On October 28, 1967, Newton, the Black Panther Party's "minister of defense," was involved in a shoot-out with two police officers. All three men were struck with bullets; one officer died. Newton was charged with murder, potentially a capital offense. The subsequent campaign to "Free Huey" catapulted the young organization to national and international prominence. In addition to innovative community programs, the phrase "Black Panther" would remain synonymous with confrontations with law enforcement.

When Dr. King died, the Panthers called for calm. Their motivation in preempting a riot was not to protect the status quo. Instead of permitting people's anger to climax in a brief outburst, they sought to effectively harness this force into a prolonged campaign to achieve power. But despite initial public cohesion, the Party itself was divided. It was a paramilitary body, and its people had clearly declared war, yet the organization's arsenal remained unused. Impatient cadres demanded: "Is this the promised vanguard?"

The sense that the Party was lagging when it should be leading particularly galled Eldridge Cleaver, author of the best-selling *Soul on Ice,* a prison conversion narrative and polemic following in the path blazed by *The Autobiography of Malcolm X.* Cleaver had become the Party's "minister of information" upon his release from San Quentin State Prison. The incarcerated Newton decried undisciplined spontaneity as destructive, but he could not restrain his ostensible subordinate.

Two days after Dr. King's death, Cleaver penned an essay entitled "Requiem for Nonviolence" in which he wrote hypnotically: "[I]t is all dead now. It's all dead now." The murder of King marked the "final repudiation by white America of any hope of reconciliation" with blacks.[8] That same night, Cleaver led a caravan of armed cadres into West Oakland looking for a police patrol to ambush. The cops found the Panthers first. Cleaver and another Panther were injured by the ensuing police fusillade; seventeen-year-old "Li'l Bobby" Hutton, the Panthers' first recruit, was killed.[9]

Despite—perhaps *because*—of the defeat suffered in West Oakland, the slogans "It's time to pick up the gun!" and "Off the pigs!" electrified Party chapters across the country. As if walking a middle ground between Newton and Cleaver, a Panther leader in Seattle explained to an audience of enraged youth that the Party advocated, not restraint per se, but calculation. "If you're ready to fight," he exhorted, "don't throw rocks in broad daylight; get yourself a gun and go out at night!"[10] Unrestrained by elders capable of tempering their militancy with prudence, the youths charged into a war they had no chance of winning.

## "CZECHOSLOCAGO": A FESTIVAL OF DEATH

An air of foreboding arose around the "counter-convention" against the Democratic National Convention in Chicago in August 1968, the first major anti-war protest since the October March on Washington. On April 15, 1968, Chicago Mayor Richard J. Daley set the tone for the coming showdown with protesters by chastising the city's police officers for not having used enough force against rioters after Dr.

King's death. The next time, he ordered, they were to "shoot to kill arsonists and shoot to maim looters." Thus encouraged, police killed one protester before the "counter-convention" even began.[11]

Hippies and politicos had planned to counter the Democratic Party's deadly intransigence in Vietnam with a "festival of life." Looking after one another with free food, housing, and medical care, they would create the new world they desired, rather than simply complaining about the one they occupied. Unfortunately, as Carl Oglesby, former president of SDS, lamented after a wedge of Chicago police officers chipped into his audience with billy clubs, there were "undertakers in the delivery room" in which the counter-conventionists labored to give birth to a new world. In previous demonstrations, protesters had displayed a celebratory exuberance. In Chicago, only two parties enjoyed themselves with a degree of consistency: the police, who, though overworked, were able to release their resentment against disrespectful youth;[12] and a corps of streetfighters who seized the opportunity to test their mettle against "the pigs." The promised festival of life, stillborn, became a festival of death.

Organizers of the protest had staged martial arts workshops for participants beforehand. Consistent with the efforts of "Yippies" to use the press to broadcast a subversive message, the instruction was more theater than a practical concern. Counter-convention organizers allowed the press to photograph an open-air karate class and a lesson in the "snake dance" that the Japanese student federation Zengakuren used to break police lines. In the confrontations with the police that would follow, these preparations proved practically worthless.

The police assault began on the night of Sunday, August 25, the eve of convention week, when police insisted on clearing Lincoln Park, where many demonstrators planned to sleep, despite being denied a permit to do so by the city of Chicago. The officers pursued the evictees into neighboring Old Town, isolating and beating them without provocation. Throughout convention week, Chicago police, joined by National Guardsmen with fixed bayonets, cracked the heads of those who claimed to carry a new world in their hearts. By Nomination Day, when Oglesby gave his speech, fully 12,000 police, armed with billy clubs and tear gas, 6,000 Army troops with bazookas and flamethrowers, and 5,000 Guardsmen bolstered by military jeeps sporting anti-crowd barbed-wire contraptions, faced off against 10,000 concerned citizens.[13]

Police did not limit their violence to counterculturals: they brutalized the press as well and destroyed reporters' film footage, which revealed the violence suffered by anti-war protesters since the October March on the Pentagon to an international audience.[14] Protesters cast "Chicago" as the domestic equivalent of the suppression of that year's Prague Spring. Lame-duck President Lyndon B. Johnson was likened to the Soviet leader Leonid Brezhnev, who, only days before the Chicago counter-convention began, ordered in troops to crush a democratic flowering in Czechoslovakia.[15]

Others saw in the police assault the stamp of an even more sinister opponent.[16] Journalists, irate that officers of the law had beaten both press *and* protesters, badgered Mayor Daley with questions about his "police state." From center stage inside the convention, Connecticut Senator Abraham Ribicoff denounced the "Gestapo tactics in the streets of Chicago." (Daley blasted back in front of live television cameras: "Fuck you, you Jew son of a bitch. You lousy motherfucker, go home!") Robert J. Donovan, chief of the Washington bureau of the *Los Angeles Times*, called the police vindictiveness on display in Chicago "a prescription for fascism."[17] Renault Robinson, a Chicago policeman and chairman of the Afro-American Patrolmen's League, was present at a police "victory party" where a white police captain stood at attention while his men shouted "Sieg Heil!"[18]

## MILITARIZING THE MOVEMENT

The events of convention week in Chicago convinced many in the anti-war movement that they would have to militarize to survive state repression. Bruce Seidel, a future co-founder of the George Jackson Brigade in Seattle, was, in all likelihood, at the Chicago protests, as was Ralph Ford, who would accidentally obliterate himself planting a pipe bomb behind a Safeway in Seattle several years later.[19] Also shocked by the police violence in the streets of Chicago was Karl Armstrong, a working-class youth from Madison, Wisconsin, who in 1970 initiated "The Vanguard of the Revolution," a small bombing collective also known as "The New Year's Gang." Tom Hayden, one of the primary organizers of the Chicago protests, later said of this time: "It seemed impossible to tell what country we were in."[20] Disoriented, a significant number of activists decided to imitate revolutionary communist movements in the Third World. The most prominent of these was "Weatherman," one of two factions that claimed the mantel of SDS in the wake of the Chicago protests. In the fall of 1969, Weatherman declared war on "honky Amerika"; in January 1970, SDS was closed down, and members went underground a few months later.

The incoming Nixon administration confirmed protesters' worst fears. In one of many grim pronouncements by high officials, Deputy Attorney General Richard Kleindienst declared: "If people demonstrate in a manner to interfere with others, they should be rounded up and put in a detention camp."[21]

The "roundup" seemed to have become a reality with the indictment of eight purported organizers of the Chicago protests. The defendants were accused of violating a rider to the 1968 Civil Rights Act that forbade crossing state lines with the intent of encouraging anyone to participate in a riot. The relevant statute defined "riot" as a congregation of three or more people engaged in actual or threatened violence against property or people (in that order).[22] Organizers of events in which such circumstances occurred did not need to be cognizant of the illegal acts, or even present at their execution, to be held criminally liable.

The cantankerous Judge Julius Hoffman appeared determined to convict—indeed, the defense acquired a tape of Hoffman telling another judge early on of his intent to do so.[23] Hoffman retaliated against the efforts of the defense to counter his prosecutorial favoritism by accumulating contempt charges, which he carefully collected and dumped on the defense at the end of the trial.

The Chicago conspiracy defendants knew that their only hope lay in shifting their trial from Judge Hoffman's courtroom to the court of public opinion. Activists who opposed the war in Vietnam were the defendants' primary constituency, and on three distinct occasions during the trial, the most verbally and physically threatening of these made themselves heard. The first was the "Days of Rage" in October 1969. In this four-day spectacle, several hundred members of the dominant "Weatherman" faction of SDS rampaged through downtown Chicago, smashing windows and anyone who got in their way. Police pummeled many participants, as they had done the year before with less provocation. The Chicago conspiracy defendants were disturbed by the way in which their militant supporters chose to actualize the most paranoid fears of establishment ideologues.

On October 15, in an event known simply as "the Moratorium," over two million people from all walks of life protested the war in their workplaces, their schools, and the streets. A demonstration in Washington, D.C., one month later provided an encore for this unprecedented showing. It was another high-water mark of mass civic involvement: 750,000 people gathered under the Washington Monument. A breakaway from the main event, led by Chicago defendants Abbie Hoffman and Jerry Rubin, charged toward the Justice Department, which protesters pelted with smoke bombs, bricks, and rocks. The building's defenders replied to this barrage with tear gas.[24]

The culminating protests of the conspiracy trial came The Day After (TDA) the contempt sentences were delivered. One estimate put participation in the outpouring at a half-million.[25] Angry protesters participated in highly visible, coordinated demonstrations across the country. In New York City, two thousand people broke through a police barricade, blocked rush-hour traffic, and, at one point, pelted officers with snowballs. In Berkeley, following a mass rally, a thousand people tore through downtown. A pressworthy minority smashed store windows, inflicting more than $100,000 in damage.[26]

The rowdiest "TDA" demonstration in the country occurred in Seattle. Attended by two thousand people, the demonstration whose theme was "Stop the Courts!" began with a small group kicking in the glass doors of the Federal Courthouse downtown, then chucking in canisters of various noxious gases. A second wave hurled rocks at upper-story windows and splattered the building with paint-filled balloons.

In response, a flying wedge of twenty-five tactical squad officers attacked the crowd with clubs swinging. In expectation of police violence, a number of demonstrators had formed affinity groups to protect one another. They wore helmets, gas

FIGURE 2. Riot police belatedly protecting the Federal Courthouse in downtown Seattle during The Day After demonstration, February 17, 1970. Photo courtesy of Alan Lande.

masks, and padded vests, and carried sticks. Those who had innocently come to the demonstration without taking such precautions got battered. After 175 more officers entered into the fray, inflicting injuries indiscriminately, the cry went up in the crowd: "Downtown!" Two and a half hours later, shattered glass littered the sidewalks of the commercial district. Estimates of the damage ranged from $40,000 to $75,000. The crowd suffered over seventy-five arrests and innumerable injuries before dispersing. Protesters weren't the only ones hurt: policemen, and their cars, suffered as well. Acting Police Chief Frank Moore called the occurrence "the worst as far as intent on property destruction and viciousness" ever to occur in the city.[27]

## TWO, THREE, MANY CHICAGOS

From 1965 to 1970, domestic bombings evinced a clear progression from property destruction to violence against people. On February 12, 1970, the Thursday before the protest following the Chicago contempt ruling, two pipe bombs exploded in the parking lot of police headquarters in Berkeley, California. The blasts, which were timed to coincide with heavy foot traffic, destroyed three police cars and damaged thirteen others, injuring six officers. Only an unpredictable delay in a shift change saved dozens of other officers from injury.

Following the bombing, an investigator had difficulty pinpointing any one reason for the attack. It might have been retaliation for the previous week's disclosure that a 22-year-old undercover officer had infiltrated three campus organizations, Lieutenant Henry Sanders speculated.[28] Another possibility is that it was an early, unclaimed attack by the Weather Underground, which detonated bombs in other police stations around the same time in a manner calculated to inflict casualties.

The Berkeley police station bombing was symptomatic of a harsh polarization, which can be traced among young, primarily white residents of the college town to the abuse they had experienced at the hands of the city's finest during the Free Speech Movement. Berkeley police had begun the era of campus unrest as the proverbial "Good Cop" to Oakland's "Bad Cop." One participant in the December 2, 1965, sit-in in Sproul Hall—the first major confrontation of the nascent campaign to permit political expression on campus—praised the Berkeley police as "quite civil, even kind at times, and, as policemen go, understanding." The Berkeley police "dragged us rather nicely," she wrote, referring to the women, although: "The boys got dragged down the stairs." Once on the first floor, however, "the Oakland police dragged us horribly."[29]

All police were pretty well established as "the enemy" by February 1969, when first the Alameda County Sheriff's Department, then, at the behest of Governor Ronald Reagan, the California Highway Patrol (CHP), followed by the National Guard, were called in to break a coalition of students of color demanding that an Ethnic Studies department be established at the university.[30] The crusading anti-communist movie star had glided into office in 1967 on a wave of suburban ire at uppity blacks (the Watts riot, in particular, had deeply disconcerted his Southern California power base) and student misbehavior (especially that which took place on the Berkeley campus). As with President Nixon two years later, Reagan wasted little time putting the disobedient back in their place, beefing up the Highway Patrol (which the press called "Reagan's Raiders") and siccing it on the opposition. Reagan decried the "Third World Strike" at Berkeley as an "insurrection" and characterized the entire University of California system as wracked by "guerrilla warfare." The only way to improve the situation, he maintained, was to "eliminate" the opposition.[31]

If any subtleties lingered in protesters' minds regarding the police, they were vanquished May 14, when Alameda County Sheriff's Deputies used birdshot and buckshot to repel a planned occupation of an unpaved parking lot that a countercultural-politico coalition wished to turn into a "People's Park." One hundred and ten of the thousands of would-be gardeners were shot; one man was blinded, another killed. Governor Reagan again called in the National Guard, which was bolstered by CHP, the Sheriff's Department, and city police. The troops imposed martial law, which remained in force for seventeen days. Pat searches of pedestrians were common; confiscations and beatings were not uncommon. Possession of cameras—the capability of sharing disturbing scenes with a watching world—elicited special wrath. Congregations of more than three people were prohibited. The demonstrations that occurred anyway were dispersed with tear gas and other forms of physical intimidation.[32]

To those already disenchanted with America, this repressive overkill clearly revealed that the dominant society had no reply but violence to those who questioned it. To curtail—and, ideally, abolish—what they regarded as a death culture, idealists too considered killing.

Along with C. Wright Mills, Albert Camus was one of the most popular writers among young white leftists in the United States in the 1960s. In an effort to comprehend the thought patterns that had precipitated World War II, Camus posited that ideologies, regardless of claims to the contrary, were infected with the virus of violence. Hoping to avoid this "plague," he himself sought to be neither an "executioner" nor a "victim"; his ideal was the "true healer."[33] But Camus' cautions could not restrain the late 1960s cohort in America, which felt, above all, the imperative to do *something*. Among those influenced by the People's Park campaign were those who grokked what the reggae phenomenon and Third World liberation icon Bob Marley cried so plaintively five years later in "I Shot the Sheriff": "Every time I plant a seed he say: 'Kill it before it grow.' He say: 'Kill it before it grow.' And so . . ."[34]

# 3

# Delivering on Threats, 1971–1975

In the late 1960s, as anti-war activity reached its crest, a dramatic confrontation between young radicals and the criminal justice system took shape. Penal reform work had been a periodic cause in forward-thinking circles throughout American history—the "penitentiary," as opposed to the prison, was one of its early innovations. In the late 1960s, consistent with the new generation's rejection of existing institutions, dissidents launched an unprecedented attack on carceral institutions and the state's capacity to punish.

Prison reform work in the mid-1960s was, in effect, a continuation of the civil rights movement by other means. Prisons housed a disproportionate number of people of color, and nearly all their denizens were impoverished. In prison work, whites, who, with few exceptions, were expelled from African American civil rights organizations in the movement toward Black Power, could continue to address glaring social inequalities without facing contentious objections regarding their involvement.

Glaring differences between convicted criminals and "free" African Americans promised difficulties for would-be reformers. Just as participants in the anti-war movement discovered the disenchanting reality that American foreign policy is not easily altered through democratic participation, those who criticized the criminal justice system came up against a keystone institution obstinately opposed to change. The routine abuses of the country's penal institutions, such as negligent medical care, capricious regulations, stark isolation cells, and disproportionate sentences, became insufferable to reformers who had formed friendships with prisoners. Just as institutional intractability radicalized anti-war activists, so, too, many prison reformers quickly decided that the criminal justice system must be completely dismantled and replaced with community-based nonpunitive programs.

The Black Panther Party not only worked to improve prison conditions but elevated prisoners to the status of revolutionary actors. Unlike the Nation of Islam, which recruited heavily in prisons, college-educated Panthers did not seek to recreate the criminal element in their own, more respectable, image. Instead, they sought to imbue themselves with the "badness" of their street-level recruits. Huey Newton, in particular, felt that the lack of investment in society that characterized the crime-prone "brothers off the block" made them a potentially powerful force in the risky endeavor of social transformation.[1] The Panthers used the Marxist term "lumpenproletariat" to describe this crime-prone demographic, but they ignored Marx's characterization of it as "the scum, offal, refuse of all classes"—a cesspool of backward ideologies whose members were easily persuaded to collaborate in their own oppression and that of others.[2] On the contrary, the Panthers held up these urban déclassés as the basis for the liberation of the "black colony" within the United States.[3] Others followed the Panthers' lead in this, and soon radicals were casting "the lumpen" as instigators of the anticipated new American revolution.[4]

In the late 1960s and early 1970s, the most popular phrase in prison activism was a line from one of Ho Chi Minh's poems: "When the prison doors are opened, the real dragon will fly out."[5] Malcolm X, a street hustler and convict who developed into a brilliant orator and won international prominence, symbolized this possibility in the United States.

Eldridge Cleaver modeled himself on Malcolm. He learned how to preach as a member of the Nation of Islam in San Quentin State Prison in California, and penned a best-selling collection of essays, *Soul on Ice*, in which he explicated the political factors that had formed the personal choices he had unconsciously made in his life. Upon release, Cleaver joined the Panthers, bringing them not only his prestige but disaster as well. In 1968, he precipitated an internal rift over the issue of "armed struggle," which he vehemently endorsed. The split became full-blown in 1971, and Cleaver became the putative leader, from exile in Algeria, of the Black Liberation Army, which would answer the Panthers' call to "Off the Pigs!"[6]

While Cleaver sounded off from abroad, another fiercely intelligent young black man was considered so dangerous by the California Department of Corrections that guards literally welded him into an isolation cell. At age nineteen, George Jackson had been sentenced to serve one year to life in prison as an accessory in a $70 robbery. Over a decade later, he gained fame when—after three prominent black prisoners were shot down on the yard of Soledad prison in rural California—he and two comrades were accused of having severely beaten, then dumped a white guard off a third-story tier. The killing of the guard was an innovation in prison culture. With it, Jackson expanded the gang principle "If you kill one of ours, we kill one of yours" to include correctional officers, who had previously been considered untouchable by illegal prisoner organizations.[7] The demands of the civil rights movement for equality had penetrated the prisons, though in such a way as to give their original proponents night sweats.

Jackson propagated a conceptualization of communal self-defense that included *offense* against those who injured oppressed communities. He declared: "Any serious organizing of people must carry with it from the start a potential threat of revolutionary violence."[8] Violence, in Jackson's experience, was not a choice but a reality. Embracing these circumstances, he argued that overcoming state violence necessitated overwhelming force on the part of challengers:

> We must accept the eventuality of bringing the U.S.A. to its knees; accept the closing off of critical sections of the city with barbed wire, armored pig carriers crisscrossing the city streets, soldiers everywhere, tommy guns pointed at stomach level, smoke curling black against the daylight sky, the smell of cordite, house-to-house searches, doors being kicked down, the commonness of death. Then we must learn the forms of resistance: the booby trap, the silenced pistol and rifle, the pitting of streets to slow them down, the wrecking of heavy equipment to block their efficient movement, false walls, hidden sub-basements, tunnels (Vietnamese style), destruction of the critical elements of the facilities that support establishment order . . . [9]

A consensus emerged in prisoners' rights circles: Jackson was "the real dragon."

## DEADLY SYMBIOSIS

In the fall of 1970, campus radicals' collaboration with convicts passed a point of no return. A cohort of campus-based anti-war activists and ex-felons launched a robbery spree, the proceeds from which were to go to the Revolution, which was deemed imminent after the chaos that followed Nixon's April 30 announcement of bombing raids into Cambodia. The first bank robbery was successful, as was a break-in at the National Guard Armory in Newburyport, Massachusetts. Rifles, ammunition boxes, and other military equipment were "liberated," as were contingency plans for control of the civilian population should martial law be declared. The latter were promptly released to the public.

Then the crew's luck ran out. On September 23, 1970, they robbed the State Street Bank & Trust Company in Brighton, just outside of Boston. Fleeing the scene, one of the ex-convicts shot and killed a policeman. Sensationalistic media coverage followed. The officer had nine children, was popular on the force, and was remembered as friendly by the citizenry. The public failed to see his death as anything other than a brutal and senseless murder, which it was.[10]

Five people were eventually charged with the crime: William Gilday (who did the shooting), Stanley Bond, Katherine Power, Susan Saxe, and Robert Valeri. The three men, all former prisoners, were apprehended within weeks. Power and Saxe disappeared. The two had been roommates at Brandeis University, where they had been involved in the National Strike Information Center, which coordinated the student strikes that closed fully a third of U.S. institutions of higher learning in May. Boston Police Commissioner Edmond McNamara announced that a radical student movement was behind the robbery and other killings and crimes. On October 17, the two women were placed on the FBI's "Ten Most Wanted" list.[11]

The destructive crest of this combustive combination occurred on the West Coast. On November 6, 1973, a Symbionese Liberation Army (SLA) hit team "executed" Oakland's African American Superintendent of Schools, Marcus Foster, with cyanide-tipped bullets and bloodied his assistant with a shotgun blast. In a "warrant issued by the Court of the People" released the day after the attack, the SLA denounced Foster for attempting to implement a plan to bring police into Oakland city schools and to issue identification cards to the students.

The organization's choice of target—Foster was one of at least eighteen possible candidates they had discussed[12]—was unfortunate in the extreme. Less because of their violence than their strategic imprecision, the SLA discredited a popular struggle instead of augmenting it. The client community had strongly denounced the school policing proposal, and Foster himself had voiced private concerns about it.[13] Progressive forces had seemed poised to win the dispute until the vicious assassination derailed them.

Before the attack, people flirting with the underground had steered clear of those who would form the SLA because they spoke like agents provocateurs, employing crude rhetoric and displaying great enthusiasm for "heavy" actions. After the SLA was in the limelight, the *Berkeley Barb, Black Panther,* and *Los Angeles Free Press* pointed out that its leader, Donald DeFreeze, had been and might well *still be* a police informer.[14]

The next bid for attention by this multiracial band of campus politicos, a Vietnam vet, ex-convicts, and militant feminists was the kidnapping of Patricia Hearst, the nineteen-year-old daughter of the newspaper magnate Randolph A. Hearst, publisher of the *San Francisco Examiner* and a board member of the powerful Hearst Corporation media chain. The SLA used the notoriety it had won to spit invective at the country's corporate leaders. "DEATH TO THE FASCIST INSECT THAT PREYS UPON THE LIFE OF THE PEOPLE," it proclaimed, in what became its signature sign-off.

The "insects," however, got them first. On May 17, 1974, 410 officers of the law, representing the Los Angeles Police Department (LAPD) and its Special Weapons and Tactics (SWAT) Unit, the Los Angeles County Sheriff's Department, the FBI, and the California Highway Patrol, poured over 5,000 rounds of ammunition and 83 tear gas canisters into a Compton bungalow in which six SLA members, including

Donald DeFreeze, were holed up. One of the rounds ignited the flimsy building and, pinned down by continuous fire, those inside died of smoke inhalation, caught bullets, or, in DeFreeze's case, committed suicide.[15]

Before launching the attack, the LAPD marshaled the media into place. The incineration was broadcast live on national television, as though to exorcise the radicalism that had been corroding the conservative core of the country. At least some of the police performed their task with the glee of an Old South lynching. One SWAT member quipped of DeFreeze, who had changed his name to Cinque (which DeFreeze pronounced "Sin-Q") Mtume, after the leader of the 1839 revolt on the slave ship *Amistad*: "He may have been Cinque yesterday, but he's bar-be-que today."[16] The message couldn't have been clearer: anyone ornery enough to challenge the U.S. government—whether a black ex-convict or a white dropout from the University of California—would be annihilated.[17]

## ENTER THE DRAGON

Ed Mead had been out of prison for two years when he read the communiqué, reprinted in his local paper, in which the Symbionese Liberation Army demanded $70 worth of food for every poor person in the state of California as a precondition to releasing Patricia Hearst. Mead—who, as an ex-convict, would have met the SLA's criteria for participation in the food distribution program had he lived in California—was so moved that he wept. His few years of activism in the free world had left him with a sense of frustration and impotence: how could organizing and consciousness-raising alone mount a challenge to the U.S. government sufficient to force it to desist from its omnicidal war in Southeast Asia and its destructive imperial adventures in nearly every other part of the world, and to persuade it to distribute wealth equitably at home? As Mead saw it, the answer had come from the world's impoverished people, from the Chinese, the Cubans, and the Vietnamese. They had "picked up the gun," and their counterparts in the United States were doing the same. So, too, would he.

Mead resolved to join the SLA and hitchhiked down to San Francisco. He didn't find the organization, but he did encounter the "New World Liberation Front" (NWLF), a band of well-organized Marxist-Leninist-Maoist bombers who displayed a particular animosity toward the Pacific Gas & Electric Company. The NWLF schooled Mead in the art of being an "urban guerrilla," even setting him to work running off copies of the late Brazilian theorist-practitioner Carlos Marighella's *Mini-Manual of the Urban Guerrilla* on their own clandestine printing press.[18]

The popularity of this incendiary pamphlet within the underground was an ominous sign in and of itself. Marighella was expelled from the Brazilian Communist Party for pro-Castro stances. "It is the duty of the revolutionary to make revolution," Marighella declared, quoting a popular phrase of Fidel Castro's. Revolution, as depicted in the *Mini-Manual*, was a violent contest for state power. Cities were a key arena of combat, Marighella stressed, a new phenomenon in peasant-majority Latin America. The *Mini-Manual* was both an instructional manual for "urban guerrillas" and an exhortation to become one.

The qualifications were, in Marighella's opinion, more physical than intellectual. For indoctrination, guerrillas required only "a certain minimal political understanding," which could be gleaned from reading Che Guevara's *Guerrilla Warfare* and other available tracts. The *Mini-Manual* is chock-full of lines such as "The urban guerrilla increases his effectiveness as he increases his firepower" and "The urban guerrilla's reason for existence, the basic condition in which he acts and survives, is to shoot." Imported into the United States, this militarism found a handful of dedicated adherents. Mead read it with critical enthusiasm; he felt the *Mini-Manual* overstated its case—armed action, in his mind, needed to complement popular organizing, not supersede it—but he did feel that it pushed the movement in the direction in which it needed to go if it was serious about attaining power.

## THE FIRST WAVE OF BOMBERS AND THE CRISIS OF CONSCIENCE

May 1970 was the nadir in relations between the U.S. government and the youth of the country. Following President Nixon's revelation of U.S. incursions into Cambodia, a nationally coordinated student strike erupted throughout the country. On May 4, National Guardsmen opened fire on a crowd at Kent State University in Ohio, killing four and injuring nine. On May 14, at Jackson State College in Mississippi, highway patrolmen shot into a women's dormitory, killing two more students and injuring another twelve. Over half the colleges and universities in the country were marked by protests of unprecedented vigor; a third of the largest and most prestigious institutions experienced violent demonstrations. Sixty-nine arson attacks and bombings were committed that month against campus, corporate, and military offices.[19] The continued escalation of the war—despite five years of public opposition, despite promises of withdrawal from two successive presidents—created a cocktail of impotence and rage. The student deaths added a shot of terror.

The first wave of domestic bombings, simmering since 1965, burned itself out in the crucible of 1970. Weatherman, which had insisted in 1969 that armed action should be the movement's number one priority, pulled back abruptly after three of its members accidentally blew themselves up in a Manhattan townhouse on March 6, 1970. Weatherman's "New Morning, Changing Weather" communiqué was released December 6, 1970, well after the embers of the May disturbances had died down, leaving little organizational coherence on the Left in their aftermath. In the communiqué, what was now the "Weather Underground" dubbed its earlier "tendency to consider only bombings or picking up the gun as revolutionary, with the glorification of the heavier the better... the military error." Henceforth, it pledged, it would put "politics in command."[20]

The consequences of not doing so had been illustrated by the New Year's Gang in Madison, Wisconsin. After committing a few firebombings of offices that were on the shit list of the student movement, the group detonated a two-ton fertilizer bomb under the building that housed the Army Math Research Center on campus. The attack claimed the life of one graduate student, injured several other people, and did $6 million of damage. Those who had previously cheered the group recoiled; the radical Left, whose belligerent rhetoric was born of a sense of impotence, could not escape a period of introspection.

FBI Director J. Edgar Hoover called Weatherman the "most violent, persistent and pernicious of revolutionary groups,"[21] but after its townhouse turnaround, Weatherman made *defusing* impulses of the like-minded that might result in injury to others one of its primary goals. Not only were police or building security to be given sufficient time, via a telephone, to clear a building, but the targets were to be carefully cased beforehand to log the schedules of anyone who might be there after hours, such as janitors. It was also stressed that, unlike its Latin American guerrilla *compañeros,* Weatherman would not be committing kidnappings or assassinations.[22] Its bombings were purely symbolic. As one Weatherman communiqué put it: "We have obviously not gone in for large scale material damage. Most of our actions have hurt the enemy on about the same military scale as a bee sting."[23]

## THE SECOND WAVE OF BOMBERS

Beginning with the Symbionese Liberation Army in 1973, there emerged a second wave of bombers who hardly noticed the lines the first wave had declined to cross. The SLA ruptured the prohibition on assassinations and kidnappings, and most other second-wave bombers considered employing similar tactics. The New World Liberation Front sent live bombs to the homes of two right-wing members of the San Francisco City Council. The Emiliano Zapata Unit bragged of having firebombed a San Quentin prison guard "chosen because of his especially pig-like attitude and actions."[24] The George Jackson Brigade planned to kidnap the director of the Washington State Department of Rehabilitation and Health Services, which oversaw the Department of Corrections, and force him to answer questions about prisoners' conditions of confinement. In effect, the second wave brought U.S. extremists back onto the path trodden by the post-collegiate radicals of West Germany, Italy, and Japan, who committed casualty-inducing bombings, kidnappings, and murders, and hijacked planes. They did so with less emotionalism than radicals in the late 1960s. This unromantic attitude was typified by the George Jackson Brigade's comment: "While we don't particularly want to shoot police, we don't particularly care either."[25]

Post-college bombers such as the Weather Underground, eager to flee class and race privilege by plunging into dangerous solidarity activities, had been derided even by their allies as "armed and incompetent."[26] The ex-convicts' and veterans' greater experience with firearms and explosives was a disturbing development for those who wished to heal the injuries of the war at home. For the former campus radicals with whom they constituted these bombing collectives, however, this enhanced familiarity with the weapons of war was a boon.

The most violent group of the period was the Black Liberation Army (BLA), which operated on both coasts. Its cadres were driven underground by police repression and the compulsive purges of the reform-oriented Oakland headquarters of the Black Panther Party. The BLA directed its energies against drug dealers and police officers, both of whom it considered agents colonizing the black community. From the BLA's inception in 1971 to 1973, the U.S. government attributed the deaths of twenty police officers to the organization. Police, in turn, claimed responsibility for the deaths of seven BLA suspects and the capture of eighteen others.[27] A body count in the BLA's war on drugs is not available.

The Fuerzas Armadas de Liberación Nacional (FALN), a Puerto Rican independence organization, claimed responsibility for dozens of bombings in the 1970s. In 1975, on one day alone, it detonated ten pipe bombs in three different cities.[28] Earlier in the year, the organization claimed responsibility for one of the bloodiest attacks of the period: the bombing of the Fraunces Tavern in New York City on January 24, 1975, which killed four people and wounded fifty others. This made the FALN a prime suspect in the most lethal act of domestic terrorism that had ever occurred: the explosion at LaGuardia Airport on December 29, 1975, in which eleven people died and seventy-four were injured. The bombing remains unsolved. (Suspects at the time, in addition to the FALN, included the Palestinian Liberation Organization, the Jewish Defense League, and a partisan of Croatian independence.)[29]

The epicenter of the second wave of bombings was the San Francisco Bay Area. In addition to the nationally active Weather Underground and the BLA, local players in mid-to-late-1970s San Francisco, San Jose, Oakland, and Berkeley included the Chicano Liberation Front, New World Liberation Front, Red Guerilla Family, Emiliano Zapata Unit, Iranian Liberation Army, Sam Melville–Jonathan Jackson Unit, and Black Guerilla Family. In 1975, the *San Francisco Chronicle* declared that bombings in the Bay Area—most of which confounded police investigators—were occurring at the rate of two a month.[30] These armed propagandists were so prolific that, by 1976, the countercultural tabloid *Berkeley Barb* had to abandon its policy of printing all the communiqués it could reasonably authenticate. "It is an unfortunate fact that the growth of the *Barb* has not kept pace with the apparent growth of the underground," the editors wrote apologetically.[31]

The domestic groups were aware of one another and their international counterparts. (The George Jackson Brigade, for example, committed a bombing in protest of the prison deaths of four members of the West German Red Army Faction.) This explains the rhetoric of the communiqués: while those who composed them sought to speak clearly to "the people," they employed language that excluded all but radicals. In the absence of a clear constituency, the armed organizations became one another's audience and support network.

This, then, is the fifteen-year picture: the 1960s began with a propulsive global promise of a new democratic era. Those who saw the culmination of this promise as inevitable were chastened by the difficulty of its implementation, and alienated from the powers that resisted such efforts. The Indochinese charnel house mercilessly amplified the desperate imperative to halt the death toll. The end of the decade was like the explosion of a firework, showering light in every direction. Many of these sparks continued to smolder and break out in localized flames. This book charts the course of one such brushfire.

PART IIa

# Consciousness

*Comrade Criminal*

# 4

## A Child Prodigy

*In which Ed Mead discovers his calling: crime*

The four-year-old Edward Allen Mead stared transfixed at a calendar painting on his grandmother's wall that depicted a squadron of B-17s flying toward the horizon, while a boy sat beside an orange-crate airplane—complete with crude wings, propeller, and tail—crying because the men had left him behind when they went off to war. Mead identified—in his imagination, it was *he* who sat there.

Born November 6, 1941, Mead was a child of wartime California. He was transplanted to rural Iowa directly after the Allied victory. Except for a stint in juvenile detention, he subsequently bounced between his mother's homestead outside of Fairbanks, Alaska, and his father's house in Compton. In Alaska at fifteen, he engaged in compensatory combat that was decidedly less patriotic than that in which he had longed to participate a decade earlier. One time, when he and his friend Junior heard the low purr of a B-52 bomber or a cargo plane returning to Eielson Air Force Base near Fairbanks, they grabbed 30-30 rifles, rushed outside, threw themselves on the ground, and took aim. The aircraft was coming in low, and Ed and Junior emptied their rifles at it.

"It's so low we couldn't miss!" Junior exclaimed.

They turned and watched the plane glide down toward the landing strip. It showed no signs of distress.

"Darn!" Ed cried. "We didn't bring it down!"

Ed was not one who inspired confidence with firearms. When he was eleven, living in Compton with his dad and step-mom, his father gave him a coveted Daisy Air Rifle. Ed promptly shot out a window in a restaurant full of customers. Later, he shot his sister in the back after she declined to play with him, leading his father to destroy the BB gun.

By fifteen, Ed was already an ex-convict, having done time at the Utah State Industrial School for boys in Ogden the previous year for shoplifting a carton of cigarettes while on probation for burning down an aircraft hangar. He was released into his mother's custody.

In Alaska, guns were everywhere. His favorite was a .25 caliber nickel-plated pearl-handled automatic pistol that he had bought in a pawn shop. It fit in his pocket. But it was not big enough to bring down the B-52s constantly flying overhead. He and Junior had hoped that their rifles would be. Though they were disappointed, it didn't stop them from trying again.

The Alaska foray was a relatively recent development in the lives of Ed and his mother. The frontier ethos of this most isolated of the United States, however, encouraged Ed's clearly established propensity for dangerous mischief to flourish. Ramona had worked as a welder in the California shipyards during World War II. She was one of the women who, as a matter of wartime necessity, was granted entry into an industrial field that had previously been the exclusive domain of men. She found the work satisfying and earned a dramatically higher salary than ever before. She was thus disappointed when, along with the other sisters of "Rosie the Riveter," she was displaced at the end of the war when male factory workers returned from combat. Ramona was forced to scrounge for poorly paid, dumbed-down versions of her previous employment. Alaska proffered another option. In the early 1950s, one of her girlfriends visited her from the Great North, brimming with enthusiasm for the opportunities that were available there. Ramona decided to give it a try. She left her children—Ed, his older sister Mary Ann, and his younger sister Virginia—in the care of their father, her ex-husband Edward.

Edward had remarried, and his new wife and the son who bore his name clashed. Little Edward was thus delighted when, at age twelve, his mother invited him to live with her again.

Alaska did not provide Ramona with the solid blue-collar work she had hoped for. To support her kids, she worked as a bar girl in one of the numerous establishments on Fairbanks' Cushman Strip, which catered to construction workers and military personnel. California's inner-city public schools had left her son ill-prepared for academic success, and his own inclinations, in contrast to those of his younger sister, were far from bookish. Ed reacted to increased demands by skipping school, and he was once briefly expelled for urging others to do the same.

The family had a hardscrabble existence; as far as the child could see, nearly all other whites were better off. Ed developed an ethical code under which it was permissible to take from those who clearly had an excess. "They couldn't *need* all that," Ed told himself. In an interview with the *Seattle Times* two decades later, he credited his mother with this view, recalling that she "sort of taught us if we didn't have enough and someone had more than what they needed, that in some circumstances, it wasn't wrong to help yourself."[1] His crimes were petty at first—collecting the discarded coins of one of his mother's boyfriends, stealing crates of empty bottles for the deposit money, siphoning gas to fill the car his mother had bought him at age thirteen, decapitating parking meters—but established a pattern that stretched into adulthood. He drank and smoked as a child and was generally feral.

The aircraft hangar arson that sent him to prison before he had ever emptied his rifle at a U.S. Air Force plane was inspired by after-school kvetching. Leaving the school grounds one day, one of Ed's friends vented: "It's too bad our school is made of concrete. Otherwise we could burn it down!" A dilapidated aircraft hangar, constructed of wood, stood in a corner of the schoolyard. "We could burn *it* down," one of the children suggested. A challenge over "guts" resulted in Ed committing to carry out the arson that night. He and a friend crept into the building and, despite the friend's misgivings, ignited the oil-soaked insulation that hung from the walls. Within ten minutes a roaring inferno illuminated the night sky. Ed had previously derived pleasure from being a hellion. Now the possibility of consequences dawned on him suddenly. He later recalled: "I remember . . . feeling some apprehension over the possibility this incident may be more serious than I thought would be the case."[2] This would not be the last time that Ed would overreach himself in a criminal endeavor.

The next day Ed's collaborator fingered him as the culprit. Ed's denials crumbled when the third member of the trio in the initial conspiracy came forward and Ramona disclosed that her son hadn't been home at the time the conflagration began. Ed was put under juvenile court supervision and released into the custody of his mother.

He was not, however, one to be cowed: a fear of consequences did not restrain him. He remained impoverished and could not perceive a way to attain the little things he wanted within the confines of the law: hence the cigarette theft, which landed him in juvenile detention. He was shipped out of state because Alaska did not have a proper facility of its own; a later report by one of Mead's federal probation officers acknowledged: "This commitment was largely due to a lack of suitable placement in the community."[3]

Barely a teenager, Ed was one of the smallest of the boys at the Utah State Industrial School. He was bullied accordingly. He primarily endured verbal intimidation, though he was physically assaulted once. Ed avoided the primary recreations of the inmate population—boxing, tattooing, and sniffing gasoline—and was released nine months later into the custody of his father and stepmother in Compton, California. He described the legacy of the institution succinctly: "At U.S.I.S. I was initiated to cruelty, taught insensitivity . . . inculcated with hatred of authority, and learned the fine art of masturbation."[4]

Ed's father and stepmother had achieved the material success of the middle class. Ed back-burnered prohibited means of self-advancement and embraced the kiddie capitalism of a paper route, quickly winning a citywide subscription drive contest with the *Los Angeles Examiner*. He stayed wild, however, and a car theft episode provoked his father into sending him back to Alaska. The most painful part of leaving California, for the fifteen-year-old, was separating from a younger boy who had become his first lover.

Ramona, Ed, and his two sisters Mary Ann ("Ann" for short) and Virginia, were homesteading a 160-acre plot outside of Fairbanks. Ed entered ninth grade. Living on uncleared land was easier to do in the summer than in the winter. During the cold months, Ed stayed wherever he could in town. In the spring of 1956, he was jailed for vagrancy, placed in a home for wayward children, then reunited with his family on the homestead. They didn't have enough money to eat regularly and scrounged construction materials so as to continue building a dwelling. Tools were often "borrowed" from neighbors without permission, and were only returned when identified by the proper owner. The parole officer observed: "The home was seen as lacking in control and supervision and agencies felt that low moral standards were present."[5]

Ed dropped out of school in tenth grade and got by on odd jobs and petty thefts. At eighteen, irritated when a woman whom he was courting chastised him for being careless with a .22 caliber pistol, he put it to his head and, thinking that the chamber was empty, pulled the trigger. A surgeon closed him back up but was unable to save his left eye.

He ran with a crew who were used to breaking and entering: gas stations, groceries, and liquor stores. It didn't take long for their crimes to catch up with them. When Ed was nineteen, he, Junior—the veteran of the attempt to shoot down the B-52—and another friend were arrested in Anchorage. Breaking the law abruptly became distinctly less fun. During the following six months in jail, Ed was downright unhappy, and convictions resulting in three years in prison only made matters worse.

An older prisoner offered Mead a way to direct his unhappiness against the courts. The man was a white-haired "jailhouse lawyer"—prisoners without law degrees were, unlike outside citizens, permitted to offer legal advice to other inmates—also confined in the Anchorage State Jail. The old-timer rejected the notion that the authorities would "go easy" on defendants who admitted their guilt and cooperated with their prosecution. He instructed Ed and his co-defendants to "never wave anything but the red flag." Persuaded, the three withdrew the guilty pleas they'd already made and demanded a jury trial. They were all convicted, and the process extended their time in jail, but it revealed to Mead that, despite its intimidating cohesion, the criminal justice system did contain internal checks and balances, which, if he made the effort to discover them, could work in his favor.

In the coming years, Mead's involvement with the law would create some of his most shining moments. But this was after a definitive break with the norms and values of the dominant society. Before being arrested for the burglaries, Mead had not considered his own behavior to be particularly abnormal. He contrasted his own wildness to the perceived timidity in others, but bold behavior and drunken revelry were far from uncommon in 1950s Alaska. His juvenile incarceration had been highly unpleasant. Afterward, he felt both ashamed and proud of the intensity of his experience, but he understood imprisonment as an isolated incident, not the beginning of a pattern. After being incarcerated on the burglary charges, however, Mead began to identify as a criminal. This adjustment was something of a psychological survival mechanism, permitting, as it did, a positive framing of his increasingly acute alienation from working-class respectability. The permanent outsider status of "criminal" laid the groundwork for the oppositional identity Mead would embrace in his early thirties: that of a communist revolutionary.

# 5

# Jailhouse Lawyer

*In which Mead learns the art of legal self-defense*

Alaska did not have a prison of its own, so Ed and his co-defendants were turned over to the federal government, which placed Mead in the Federal Correctional Institution (FCI) in Lompoc, California. The institution was governed with military discipline, necessitating unwelcome adjustments from the new inmate, who was accustomed to a high degree of independence. FCI Lompoc urged self-control on its wards, prompting Mead's first interest in psychology. When prisoners' internal disciplinary controls faltered, prison staff were present to enforce external ones.

In the face of oppressive doctrine, prisoner camaraderie formed around their most obvious common denominator: their criminality. It was not that they liked one another or enjoyed being in prison—Mead was terrified of a number of the convicts he encountered, constantly fearing sexual assault, and being caged in the institution made him miserable. It was that, once branded, pride in a criminal identity was the clearest alternative to continual self-reproach. This only encouraged the destructive behavior that had landed them in prison in the first place. Ed recalled: "We talked to each other not only about the crimes we committed, but bragged about those we wished we had committed, and even those we were going to commit once released."[1]

Regardless of his feelings toward crime itself, Ed did not wish to return to prison. A counselor advised that a high school diploma and a trade would enable him to remain free once paroled. Mead put in for a transfer to the federal reformatory in Chillicothe, Ohio, where the airplane mechanic school was reputed to be the best vocational option in the federal system. After a circuitous journey, which included an extended stay at the U.S. Penitentiary in Leavenworth, Kansas, Ed arrived in Chillicothe. There he began reading for the first time on a range of subjects that caught his interest: psychology, Eastern philosophy, and investigations of inexplicable phenomena. Halfway through the vocational program, he was ejected for cheating. He took correspondence classes and started an astronomy club.

Mead was paroled on May 20, 1963, at twenty-one, and returned to Alaska. There, he brooded on the injustice done to him by the criminal justice system. A quick immersion in the federal prison system might have scared him straight, he speculated, "[b]ut instead they went ahead and made me angry, bitter, and frustrated." This psychological state was common among his fellow inmates, nearly all of whom, like Mead, felt that the state had committed a greater crime in punishing them excessively than they had in committing the original act. "Just about everyone," Mead later wrote, "experienced a desire to even things up."[2] In the future, Mead would channel the collective rage of the incarcerated, packing it into lead pipes and detonating it on the property of those he blamed for their plight. At this time, however, he was concerned with personal, not collective, retribution. In both cases, he was unclear as to whom to hold responsible for his pain.

The three burglaries of which Ed had been convicted, combined, had netted no more than a few hundred dollars. In his view, these negligible proceeds were in vast disproportion to the two unpleasant years of his life impounded by the state. Rather than submitting to the logic of punishment—that "crime doesn't pay"—Mead felt even more alienated from the society that condoned such harsh sanctions. *He* was now the injured party.[3] Crime seemed an appropriate way to collect on what was owed to him. It was no longer simply taking what he wanted; rather, crime became a form of retribution he conceptualized as morally correct.

Ed got a job inspecting airplanes, but he could not relate to his co-workers' straight talk and clean-cut aspirations. He felt comfortable with the bar set he had hung out with before being incarcerated, nearly all of whom broke the law on a regular basis. Junior, for one, had quickly violated his parole. Ed helped him steal cars and, occasionally, food and liquor in bulk.

The incident that landed Ed back in prison began with an indulgence in a petty crime he had become accustomed to committing while living on the homestead: stealing a car, when hitchhiking proved unfruitful, then ditching it close to his destination. He was drunk and on foot the night he passed the offices of the U.S. Fish and Game Department. A truck behind the building resisted his efforts to hotwire it, so he kicked open the front door of the offices and plucked the key from the wallboard. He also noticed a small safe, some walkie-talkies, and a rifle, all of which he took. He gave the walkie-talkies and rifle to Junior and his friends Lemon and Benny. These three were arrested for other crimes. Under FBI interrogation, Benny fingered Ed as the source of the government property, as well as the perpetrator of other assorted burglaries. Ed was charged accordingly.

Feeling that there was little likelihood of his being acquitted, Ed skipped bail and flew down to Seattle. His older sister Mary Ann joined him on the run. They made brief stays in Idaho and Colorado, working in available jobs and running check-cashing schemes. After several months of this, Ann decided to settle in California. Ed didn't. He hooked up with one of his sister's friends—a married woman—and, joined by a new male friend, the three drove east. They ran out of money in Arizona. The odd man out soon split. Within a couple of weeks, Ed was rearrested—he couldn't determine whether his hard-up former friend or the husband of his paramour had ratted on him. He was shipped to the federal detention center in Florence, Arizona, the site of a World War II U.S. Army administered detention center for Japanese Americans and German and Italian prisoners of war. He pled guilty to the burglary of the Fish and Game offices, and, on March 6, 1964, was sentenced to three years and shipped back to Lompoc.

While petitioning for a transfer back to Chillicothe to complete the Airframe and Powerplant mechanics program there, Mead began a casual study of the law. The prison didn't have a law library, but he perused four volumes of the United States Code, which inmates were only permitted to read for an hour a day. He looked to challenge his own conviction and fell in with a like-minded fellow prisoner who enjoyed discussing their legal strategies. Mead borrowed a complaint from a fellow Alaskan to copy the relevant material for his own case. A guard spotted him returning the document, confiscated it, and "infracted" (prison lingo for "charged with a violation of institutional rule") both men for "Illegal Procedure in Writing a Writ." Mead was placed in "The Hole," an isolation cell with a wooden bed inches off the concrete floor. A guard confiscated the blanket and the mattress during the day, and Mead, like the other prisoners in disciplinary segregation, was fed reduced rations. This was the first time he was punished for practicing the law. It would not be the last.

Mead experienced his first paper-pushing victory over a year after the old Alaskan jailhouse lawyer had taken him under his wing. His opponent was an administrator who attempted to prevent him from resuming the course from which he'd been expelled in Chillicothe. He received a diploma from Sherman High School in Chillicothe and scored 118 on the IQ test, placing him in the "bright normal range."[4] While completing the program, he filed a post-conviction relief petition contending that his guilty plea had been involuntary. As Ed consumed books on increasingly mature subject matter—geography and history, instead of Atlantis and flying saucers—his inherited anti-communism took its first blow: the portrayal of a communist country in the British-American correspondent Felix Greene's 1961 travelogue *Awakened China: The Country Americans Don't Know* impressed him favorably.

Mead was paroled on November 10, 1965. Before the release, his counselor issued a prognosis of "guarded."

Mead was released in Fairbanks, Alaska, the site of his induction. He soon picked up an Inuit woman named Margo Wicker, who became his girlfriend. Over her objections, Ed resumed committing burglaries for party money. When Ed was fired from his aircraft maintenance job for poor performance, the two tried out the roles of pimp and prostitute. Ed dissolved Margo's initial resistance using lines he'd learned from convicts who claimed to have had stables of women on the street, but they both found the scheme too painful and discontinued it after a weekend's misadventure. In his unpublished autobiography, he observed: "In those days I had no understanding of sexism or of the dynamics by which men exploit women. I did, however, have a fairly good shit detector. It did not take a ton of bricks to fall on me to see that I was damaging Margo with what was now clearly a sick trip."[5]

Ed and Max, a buddy Ed had first met at the Leavenworth penitentiary, robbed a pharmacy together. The two ex-convicts were arrested, armed, inside the drugstore. Ed insisted on a jury trial, a right Max declined. Mead was convicted of burglary, larceny, and possession of a firearm by a convicted felon and sentenced to ten years, while Max, in contrast, pled guilty and was only sentenced to three years. Ed had heard of the "jury tax," in which those defendants who insist on their constitutional right to a jury of their peers are given harsher sentences if found guilty—a means of retaliation for consuming the time of the court. This, however, was his first direct experience with the phenomenon. Rather than leading him to defer to the authorities, this denial of what he had understood to be his rights fueled Ed's determination to obtain personal justice.

On federal parole at the time, Mead was remanded to federal custody to serve the balance of the preceding sentence. In December 1965, shortly after turning twenty-five, Mead arrived at the U.S. Penitentiary (U.S.P.) on McNeil Island, a nineteenth-century structure situated on a bucolic island in Puget Sound, which had long received the hard cases from the federal prison in Lompoc, California. It dawned on Mead that he was inadvertently climbing the prisoner hierarchy of toughness, an ascent that he had had no desire to make.

McNeil Island Penitentiary contained a centrally located law library, which inmates referred to as the "writ room." In it, Mead began to educate himself about the law in earnest. Initially, he paid an experienced prisoner to help him write a writ, but he soon found that the man took as much money as he could get for the least amount of work. More disconcertingly, McNeil Island's in-house legal expert often appeared high on heroin.

Mead began to do his own legal work. He was not lacking for material: a federal case, a state motion for release on bail, and an appeal to the Alaska Supreme Court were all in play. Mead expanded his understanding of the law by reading every criminal case in the weekly advance sheets for the relevant jurisdictions—Federal Second Circuit and the Supreme Court—as well as the *Federal Supplement* and *Pacific Reporter*. He learned to discern patterns in cases and decisions. This provided his first insight into the law: that guilt and innocence were less relevant than precedent. This was a game set up against the poor and ignorant, an observation that paved the way for Mead's development, at the beginning of the 1970s, into something of a champion for what radicals were then calling "the imprisoned class." At this time, Mead was drawn to the challenge of winning against the odds more than he was driven by a desire to achieve class justice. Other prisoners benefited from his personal determination; he began taking on their cases, as well as his own. He charged a sliding-scale fee for his services and invested the proceeds in additional public resources for the writ room.

Mead's first victories were in his own cases. In response to his first writ, he won a transfer to the U.S. Detention Center in Florence, Arizona, for another hearing on his underlying conviction. There he argued that the guilty plea that had resulted in his original federal incarceration had been induced by fear; he was, he asserted falsely, innocent of the crime. Mead's command of applicable facts and statutes obliged the judge to vacate the original sentence and permit him to enter a plea of not guilty. Mead was then returned to Alaska to stand trial on the U.S. Fish and Game burglary charge that had precipitated his reincarceration.

This success was accompanied by another. Mead got the Supreme Court of Alaska to direct the Superior Court to set bail on appeal for the state conviction on the pharmacy robbery, something the trial court had refused to do. His mother put up the homestead as collateral for his bail, and, in August 1967, Ed once more hit the street. Thoroughly chastened by his ordeals in the criminal justice system, he pledged to stay clear of trouble.

This resolve lasted little over a year. Once again, his problematic relationship with firearms played a key part in his difficulties. A gun heist seduced Ed away from his determined go at the straight life. He had worked his way up from a job on the cleaning and construction crew of the Parks Projects of the city's Community Action Agency to assistant youth programs director for the same agency. He was fired, however, on a presumption of guilt, after being arrested on a burglary charge; at this point, he couldn't get his own mother to believe he was innocent. The charge had been filed by the brother of a woman Ed had briefly dated while involved with Margo. The man had taken offense on his sister's behalf when Ed discontinued the relationship. The grand jury that was convened to evaluate the charges against Mead was so offended by their falsity that they attempted to indict the person who had filed them for perjury.

Ed interrupted his subsequent unemployment with occasional bouts as a firefighter in Alaska's wilds. He and Margo needed little: the money she brought in from dancing at a bar met most of their costs. Together they smoked pot, drank wine, and lived without any ambition beyond enjoying the moment. "Looking back, I suppose I was something of a hippie, only with short hair," Mead reflected.[6] His inner placidity gave him the strength to turn away his old cronies whenever they came to him with illegal proposals. In time, though, their persistence paid off. In August

1968, two old friends, Lemon and Junior's little brother Red, came to him with what one of them called "a sweet deal." "We could use your help," the other proposed.

"No, thank you," Ed answered quickly. "I don't want to be involved." A sword of Damocles, in the form of a possible ten-year prison sentence for the federal burglary, was hanging over his head, and he had no desire to fray the rope that suspended it. After the two did the crime on their own, the police questioned Ed, because he was high on their list of usual suspects, but didn't bring any charges against him. Soon afterward, Lemon and Red returned.

"It's easy money," Lemon beguiled. "We just have to come up with some weapons for these guys from the States. They'll pay us in cash."

Ed refused to participate and sent them away, but suggested a sporting goods store that they could hit. Lemon and Red tried to knock off the place, but, lacking lock-picking skills, they couldn't even get inside. When they reported their failure to their patrons—gangsters from the Lower Forty-Eight—they were physically menaced. The pair returned to Ed, desperate. When he finally gave way, it was a matter of pride: "Okay, I'll show these novices how to do a job right," he told himself.

His girlfriend Margo had observed this cycle before. She complained: "You're going to the penitentiary again."

"No I'm not," Ed asserted cockily.

"You want guns, I'll get you guns," Ed told Lemon and Red. He directed Ray, their driver, to the National Guard Armory. Not only would he help his friends, he'd give the government a black eye.

Ray dropped the three off. They gained access to the building through a window and located the arms vault. They exited, stole a government truck and cutting torches, opened a garage door, and drove into the armory. Ed cut a hole big enough to crawl through in the bottom of the vault door. They loaded the truck with five M-60 machine guns, a grenade launcher, numerous .45 caliber pistols, a number of M-14 rifles, cases of ammunition, C rations, smoke bombs, walkie-talkies, and a safe. They then transferred the cache to a remote spot in the woods. Before departing, Ed admonished his fellow criminals, "You need to leave this alone until the heat dies down!"

The next day the papers went crazy. The FBI publicly speculated that the missing guns were destined for the Black Panther Party, which, after charging into the California State Capitol building in Sacramento with shotguns on May 2 of the previous year, had become one of the primary bugaboos in the imagination of white America. They were, however, hardly a credible threat in the blindingly white state of Alaska. Any destination for such a large stash of weapons was nevertheless ominous; additional agents were flown from the continental U.S. to aid in the investigation. Once again, Ed was prompted to wonder, "Did I go too far?"

Lemon and Red immediately took their gun contacts to the stash. They gave the gangsters some M-14s and .45 pistols, then drove the safe to Ed's mom's property, where, after blasting it open, they discarded its burned-out remains. An unmarked black car containing a white man in a suit pulled up in front of Ed and Margo's cabin and became a fixture.

An agent from the Federal Bureau of Investigation approached Ed's attorney. "We don't want to prosecute anyone," the agent declared. "We simply don't want those weapons to fall into the wrong hands. We'll end the surveillance on your client and guarantee not to prosecute if he returns those weapons. That's all we ask."

Ed talked the proposal over with Lemon and Red, and they decided to comply. By mid-September, life was back to normal. Ed worked as a mechanic at Interior Airlines. On September 26, while he was putting oil into the engine of a plane, he heard a voice behind him instruct: "Bring your hands out of there slowly. You're under arrest." It was the FBI. They already had Lemon and Red.

While in Fairbanks's jail, the Northern Regional Correction Institution, Mead aided another inmate in an escape attempt. When the plot was discovered, Mead was the one charged with attempted escape. During the subsequent trial, the inmate testified that he, not Mead, had been the intended escapee, but the jury convicted Mead anyway. He was given five years, the maximum sentence, to be served concurrently with the ten years for the pharmacy burglary, which, since his rearrest, had been "affirmed pending appeal."

As with his previous sentences, Mead felt that a great injustice had been done to him. He had not been sentenced for the armory robbery, of which he was guilty, because there was insufficient evidence to try him. Instead, he had been convicted of a crime he had not committed because there *was* sufficient evidence. "Because of the overwhelming evidence of guilt I did not have the right to a fair trial!" he later complained. "Such luxury no doubt being reserved for the clearly innocent!"[7] Though he himself had no compunction about lying to a court, as he had done in the Arizona hearing, he was outraged over the U.S. legal system being anything less than scrupulous. Though this double standard hardly elicits sympathy, it drove him to secure his grasp on the law so as to access the pockets of judicial fairness that did exist.

6

# Strike!

*In which McNeil Island Penitentiary experiences its first shutdown by prisoners in its century-long history*

Back at McNeil Island, Mead immersed himself in legal pleadings as never before, petitioning the Ninth Circuit Court of Appeals to review the state pharmacy conviction and appealing the federal conviction for attempted escape in Circuit Court. He continued to assist others. This was not philanthropy: he did it for himself, because the law intrigued him. He became fascinated by the possibilities concealed behind the veil of obscure language. Fitting the cases of concern to himself and his fellow inmates into the course of precedents and prevailing decisions had become the first socially sanctioned intellectual challenge of his life, and his identity as a jailhouse lawyer his first positive self-conception.

Mead's competence and prodigious energy quickly established him as the pre-eminent writ writer in McNeil Island. So many inmates asked him to take on their cases that he collaborated with a professional typist. He won the release of a couple of prisoners, which amplified his renown. Gangsters began hiring him simply for the prestige of having him on their payroll. Mead continued to invest the fees he charged for these cases in subscriptions to *Federal Reporter* advance sheets and legal tomes to supplement the law library's meager offerings. As he had done when first orienting himself in the legal realm, Mead read all the criminal cases in relevant federal jurisdictions. He began to be able to predict the decisions of the U.S. Supreme Court with respectable accuracy. In concert with the rhythm of court decisions, he looked for prisoners whose issues were similar and filed on their behalf. Before he completed his sentence, Mead took two of his clients' complaints to the U.S. Supreme Court. Under the influence of Justice William O. Douglas, the Court strongly supported prisoners' rights, including the right of inmates to provide legal advice to one another. In both cases, the Court made rulings favorable to Mead's clients.¹ Mead's only disappointment was that the Court denied his petitions to argue his clients' cases in person in Washington, D.C.; the experience would have certainly been one of the highlights of his life.

Mead's political consciousness developed in the writ room, where the institution's best and brightest congregated, as well as in dialogue with his seven cellmates. They were a spectrum of white Americans, each with his own push-button issues: one was anti-clerical, but indifferent to all else; one was a businessman, in for fraud, whose only allegiance was to the almighty dollar; another was a devout Christian and anti-communist. This latter was Sam Bowers, an imperial wizard of the White Knights of the Ku Klux Klan in Mississippi, who was doing ten years for violating the constitutional rights of Mickey Schwerner, an organizer for the Congress of Racial Equality, by ordering his "elimination" in May 1964. The murder of Schwerner and his fellow activists James Cheney and Andrew Goodman was one of the seminal events of the civil rights movement, prompting widespread outrage and, as a consequence, federal involvement on an unprecedented scale. Bowers had also been implicated in a less publicized case in which another civil rights worker died after his house was firebombed.²

The bigoted southerner was a private person and gave a highly selective account of the events that resulted in his imprisonment. As other prisoners filled in the outrageous details, Ed recoiled from the Klansman, from whom he was already divided by age and local origin. Discussion was always lively, and Mead, who had never put much thought into the civic sphere, listened avidly. Despite vast political chasms, Mead recalled, "On one point we were all agreed: the government was fucked and in need of radical change."³

The Vietnam War became an increasingly hot topic in the cell. Mead's passivity on the subject began dissolving when he noticed that those who were against the war also supported the rights of prisoners. He began to consider the arguments presented by the anti-war camp in the publications that they sent into the prison free of charge. Their views increasingly became his own. One additional prod was that Mead desired to distance himself from any position Bowers took, and Bowers, predictably, was vehemently pro-war.

A new inmate, John Sherman, was assigned to the cell and, initially, accepted by its other denizens. Sherman was serving a three-year sentence, less for the crime for which he had been caught—driving a stolen car across state lines—than because the Los Angeles County sheriff had written to the Multnomah County sheriff telling him of the check and credit card scams that Sherman had been getting away with for years, and the Multnomah County sheriff showed the letter to Sherman's judge before sentencing.

Mead and Sherman became fast friends, but the relationship was cut short when word came via the prison grapevine that Sherman had provided information on others in the credit card ring in order to reduce his own sentence. Whatever their other differences, the cell wouldn't tolerate a snitch.[4] In a vote from which Mead abstained, the cell members decided to eject Sherman's belongings over the guard rail. When Sherman tried to approach Mead after this rejection, Mead turned his back to him. This was his first, wrenching adherence to collective discipline.

A different collective action occurred in response to the death of an Alaskan Amerindian due to medical neglect. About six months into Mead's stay on the island, an ailing prisoner had been repeatedly turned away from the hospital, either with aspirin or nothing at all, despite prolonged and insistent pleadings of severe pain. When, due to pressure by his cellmates, he was finally admitted to the hospital, he was given painkillers and ignored. He died a couple days later of an erupted stomach tumor.

Mead typed up affidavits from the inmates who had witnessed this slow-motion atrocity and mailed copies to the headquarters of the Federal Bureau of Prisons in Washington, D.C., as well as to Alaska's senators and state representative. In order to gather information for a complaint, he took a job in the hospital as the clerk of the chief medical assistant. The outraged circle of inmates who met in the writ room contacted the dead man's family with the idea of pursuing a lawsuit, but found that the family was too poor and isolated to pursue the matter. Without the involvement of the next of kin, the plan was abandoned.

On October 15, 1969, the political ferment occurring outside the institution manifested itself inside when two prisoners observed Moratorium to End the War in Vietnam Day. In addition to campus-based groups this national protest against the Vietnam War involved a wide array of civic, professional, and religious organizations. With more than two million people participating, it demonstrated the breadth of opposition to the war with a force that surprised even its organizers.[5]

The participating prisoners were John Sherman and Donovan Workman. Workman was a communist who had been convicted of attacking U.S. marshals with a chain during an anti-war demonstration; a report by political surveillance officers of the Portland Department of Public Safety and the FBI named him as a Weatherman.[6] Both men wore black armbands and encouraged other inmates to join them. The two were quickly shuffled off to disciplinary segregation. None of the old-timers on the island could recall an act of defiance akin to this one. The first draft resisters had begun entering McNeil Island several years earlier, but they were all placed in the minimum security "camp" separate from the main-line convicts.[7] The October Moratorium was the first visible opposition to the war inside the penitentiary proper. Mead reconsidered his earlier disavowal of Sherman. When Sherman returned from segregation, the two began talking again, and they soon became collaborators in the writ room.

Other newly inducted inmates added fuel to the political fire. Roger Lippman, a veteran of the Days of Rage in Chicago in 1969, was an early member of Weatherman, the "Action! Action! Action!" shard of the shattered Students for a Democratic Society that would soon go on to form the Weather Underground (of which Lippman was not a member). On January 19, 1970, Lippman attended a meeting to plan a demonstration to take place the day after the announcement of the verdict in the Chicago 7 case.[8] Lippman hadn't even attended "The Day After" demonstration in Seattle: he was rioting in Berkeley instead. But he was among the eight people linked to the planning of the demonstration who were indicted for conspiracy to damage the Federal Courthouse, among other charges. One of those indicted fled, resulting in the "Seattle Seven."

The seven—Lippman, fellow Weatherperson Susan Stern, University of Washington philosophy professor Michael Lerner, Michael Abeles, Jeff Dowd, Joseph Kelly, and "Chip" Marshall—were not docile defendants. Tacoma Federal Judge George Boldt sentenced them to a term of six months to a year, depending on how much contempt he felt they displayed.[9] In a departure from established legal procedure, Judge Boldt declared that the contempt sentences would have to be served *before* the completion of the trial. This, he noted with satisfaction, would prevent the unruly behavior by defendants *and* their lawyers that was becoming the norm in politically charged trials. Judge Boldt credited "divine providence" for his juridical innovation.[10]

Mead found Lippman charismatic and quickly fell under his spell. Mead's response was similar to that of Susan Stern, who recalled on first meeting him in 1969 that he struck her as "a theoretical genius, having read everything by Marx and Lenin and the rest of the boys, deciphered it all, and reorganized it in his head, so that at a moment's notice he was able to explain it very simply and clearly to others. Everything he said had a ring of authority and knowledge that made it very credible to me. His ability to make complicated theories understandable to the average person made Roger a very good organizer."[11] Lippman served only three weeks in "The Big House" in December 1970, but it was long enough to form a lasting bond with Mead, whom he remembers as a diminutive figure in the law library.

Charles "Chuck" Armsbury arrived at McNeil in the fall of 1970. Of working-class origin, he was completing graduate work at the University of Oregon when he founded the Eugene chapter of the Patriots Party, inspired by the Young Patriots in Chicago, which had adopted the "Ten Point Program" of the Black Panther Party for lower-class whites. In Eugene, the Patriots acted as a multiracial adjunct to the local Black Panther chapter, collaborating with the Panthers on a breakfast for children program and other community service work. Like the Panthers, the Patriots quickly came into conflict with violent white civilians and the police. And like the Panthers, too, they were armed and prepared for a standoff or a shoot-out. In the spring of 1970, Armsbury was busted for the possession of a sawed-off shotgun and sentenced to ten years in prison.[12]

Armsbury remained an organizer in prison. He fell in with the writ-room crowd, but rather than contesting his own case, as did most of his peers, he pulled together

FIGURE 3. Defendants in the Seattle Conspiracy trial flip off the Federal Courthouse. Photo courtesy of Alan Lande.

a multiracial group of seven prisoners to file a class action. They aimed not for legal success but to raise the consciousness of inmates and their outside supporters.

The suit sought the support of the U.S. District Court to prevent McNeil Warden Jacob J. Parker, as well as the associate warden and another prison administrator, from continuing what the plaintiffs characterized as their "unconstitutional regulations, customs, and usages enforced by means of willful negligence, dehumanization, and terrorism for the purpose of genocide on prisoners at McNeil Island." More than simply violating the prohibition on cruel and unusual punishment in the Eighth Amendment to the Constitution, the suit claimed, these practices "strip[ped] prisoners of the sacred principles of humanity: human integrity, human self-respect, human dignity, and human spirit, which although not specifically enumerated in any Amendment to the Constitution, are, under the Ninth Amendment, rights always retained by the people."

Speaking for themselves as well as the other 1,200 men on McNeil, the seven authors of the document denounced four instances in the previous four years in which inmates known to be dangerously mentally unstable had been released into the general population, there to be stabbed by other prisoners. Three of the victims died of their wounds.

More expansively, the suit contended: "The Defendants scorn teaching the prisoners true experiences of responsibility, self-reliance, and cooperation but deliberately encourage life styles of untrustworthiness, dependence, and competition by twisting and stripping prisoners of every vestige of integrity, self-respect, kindness, love, creativity, and solidarity which prisoners desperately need for their growth and survival."[13]

Before filing the suit, Armsbury presented it to Mead, who looked it over and declared bluntly: "This is void of legal merit. There's not a chance of winning this." Armsbury was undeterred. He and his collaborators filed the suit that winter. The regional press reported on it in detail.[14]

Despite his apparent ignorance of legal matters, Armsbury made a positive impression on Mead. "He was the first person I met who was not primarily motivated by self-interest," Mead later recalled. This was confusing. "He seems smart, why's he stupid?" Mead wondered. "Anything worth doing is worth doing for money!" On consideration, he was forced to concede that Armsbury was motivated not by greed but by principles. Armsbury called himself a Marxist revolutionary. This, too, struck a discordant note for Mead. Lippman and Armsbury constituted his "first contact with the dreaded communists the schools and media had so carefully trained me to hate.... I was somewhat surprised that they were nice people, probably better than most because they cared more."[15]

On the evening of Saturday February 20, 1971, while returning from the writ room for the 9:30 P.M. lockup, Mead observed a member of the institution's officially sanctioned inmate organization, the Men's Advisory Council (MAC), passing out literature from cell to cell. When he walked into his cell, he saw that everyone was eagerly reading the documents. The first called for a peaceful work strike; the second listed thirteen demands, including improved job training, a pay raise in prison industries, a relaxation of the prohibition on beards and long hair, expanded access to visitors, conjugal visitation, an end to mail censorship, and amnesty for strikers.

After the filing of the "genocide complaint," in early January 1971, Armando "Angel" Vargas, one of the plaintiffs, told the *Post-Intelligencer:* "We want to see some good come out of this process. All we ask is the chance to be heard, and hope the public will show some concern. But," he warned, "there are a lot of men in here who don't have much faith in courts."

"Do you think there might be a strike to draw the public's attention to these issues?" the reporter asked.

"I don't know," Vargas replied frankly.[16]

Less than two months later, on the brink of a jailwide strike, the "genocide complaint" instigators spoke against the move toward confrontational collective protest. These were the men who had first articulated the concerns that became demands in the impending strike. Yet they considered the strike to be acceptance of a calculated provocation: the administration's refusal to permit a visit by supporters of the Black

Cultural Association. Armsbury contended that the administration's public image had been tarnished by their lawsuit. They thus needed to reestablish the public's nightmarish conception of prisoners. The public would perceive a prison strike as a lawless act and in response would sanction increased control by the administration.

The island had never had a prisoner strike. On Sunday February 21, the day after the strike call was issued, the recreation yard was buzzing with debate. Inmates with prospects of parole conditional on good behavior argued against those with little to lose. The concerns of the more experienced organizers among the inmates were submerged as a desire for a show of strength reached critical mass.

Mead was designated representative for C tier, where he agitated in favor of the strike in every cell. His most vociferous opponent was Bowers, who argued that such a provocation would only increase repression.

"Right," Mead mocked. "'Direct action can only hurt us.'"

"If you go on strike, this administration can and should use whatever force it takes to get you back in line!" Bowers barked back.

On Monday morning, only about 15 out of 1,000 inmates reported to work. They were told to return to their cells, as the workshops were too understaffed to function. The victory was nearly complete: all that soured it for Mead was that the only person to report to work from his tier had come from his own cell: Bowers. Regardless, he later recalled, "I suddenly felt a new sense of pride at being a prisoner and experienced a delightful warmth toward my peers in struggle."[17]

On Tuesday, guards appeared in full riot gear armed with pickaxe handles. No one obeyed when work call was announced over the loudspeakers. Prisoners' defiance increased. Convicts began shouting abuse at the guards and throwing things down on "the flats," the open area on the first floor of the cell block where the officers congregated. After the prisoners had spent their initial anger, their mood became celebratory. They were subjected to minor hardships, such as cold meals and the denial of showers, but few complained.

One week into the strike, inmate negotiators and other individuals whom the administration considered to be organizers were rounded up and isolated on two tiers that had been emptied of rank-and-file prisoners. Ed's friends John Sherman and George Sing Louie—a first offender serving a six-year term for fraud, and a companion in the writ room—were among those isolated, but he himself escaped attention. He didn't exactly know why: possibly, the presence of the Klansman Bowers in his cell reflected on him positively in the eyes of the administration; possibly, he was just too small a fish.

On February 28, at the same time as the roundup inside, a demonstration in support of the inmates was organized on the dock of the nearby town of Steilacoom, which handled all the island's boat traffic. The actress Jane Fonda and the folk singer Pete Seeger provided celebrity billing for the protest, which was attended by 250 people. Fonda had begun corresponding with McNeil inmates after visiting the

Pacific Northwest in support of indigenous sovereignty the previous year; Seeger had been around long enough that he had taught civil rights activists what would become some of the most common freedom songs. A peppy Fonda told the crowd: "The prisoners have done what we on the outside have difficulty in doing. They have realized what collective strength is."[18]

After the demonstration some fifty people formed a caravan of cars and drove to the house of Judge Boldt, infamous among leftists ever since the Seattle Seven trial, where they were turned away by Pierce County sheriff's deputies, who told them that Boldt was not at home.[19] The demonstration prompted the media to investigate the strike. The *Seattle Times* clearly found the statements of Warden Parker unconvincing. While Parker stated that 50 to 60 percent of the island's 980 maximum-security prisoners were on strike, the *Times* reported that as few as 20 men were actually working.[20] Independent observers were categorically denied access to the institution. Jessica Mitford, the acclaimed author of the 1963 bestseller *The American Way of Death*, was invited in by the strikers, but Parker turned her away.[21] U.S. Congressman Tom Foley (D-Wash.) fared no better.[22]

Word of outside support increased prisoners' determination. They dropped refuse and burning paper onto the flats. Prisoners in the upper tiers, where smoke from growing fires concentrated, smashed out windows for fresh air. To keep up their spirits, prisoners sang songs and beat out crude rhythms on the walls and floors of the cells. Mead and his cellmates poured paint into medicine bottles, which they shattered against the white jailhouse walls, contributing to the atmosphere of turmoil. It was Mead's first taste of intensely polarizing conflict. It was, he enthused, "glorious and righteous."[23]

On the tenth day, Warden Parker made sufficient concessions to provide prisoner representatives with the appearance of victory. On March 4, enough men had returned to work to recommence production in the prison workshops.[24] Two tiers, however, remained full of inmate organizers and the charred paint-splattered walls and floors served as a constant reminder of the contest. The locked-down organizers reminded those in the general population of their continued punishment by dumping water on them as they passed under one of the ideological quarantine cells on the way to the auditorium. Mead and Ed Doherty—one of the inmates whose case he had appealed to the Supreme Court—smuggled candy and cigarettes, along with law books and paper, to their friends, but were unable to organize more militant support among the general population.

The organizers were released within the next few months, and Ed and his fellow troublemakers chose one another as cellmates. They remained rebellious. Mead painted an abstract mural across one of the cell walls. When an officer ordered him to paint over it, one of his cellmates retorted: "Do it yourself!" The mural stayed. While cantankerous in dealing with guards, they were affectionate among themselves, delighting in one another's insights and talents.

In this cell, Mead first became conscious of the rage inside him. He later recalled:

> I was laying on my bunk feeling this anger and saying to myself, "If I could only get my hands around the neck of the person responsible for doing this to me and every other human being in here, I would sure feel good." But whose neck? Not the warden's, as he's only doing what the courts have told him to do. Not the courts, as they are merely carrying out the applicable statutes. And on and on went my thinking, until finally there was no one left to be responsible for this crime against my person but the American people.[25]

His reading came to concentrate on political matters. Much of it can be understood as an effort to narrow the focus of his inquiry: "Who is responsible for my pain?" The answer became, not the American people as a whole, but the small clique who wielded power over national and international policy. Mead considered many voters complicit with these policies, but those most responsible, he reasoned, were the politicians and business leaders who used the criminal justice system to protect their property interests.

Mead's political study began with receipt of anarchist newsletters, which contained reading lists on the back page. He meticulously ordered and read through the suggested texts: Mikhail Bakunin, Pyotr Kropotkin, Pierre-Joseph Proudhon, and even the Spanish Civil War martyr Buenaventura Durruti. Had he read their biographies as well, he might have found it thought-provoking that Bakunin and Durruti had, like himself, both served time in prison and were often denounced as "only criminals," despite the political motivations of their acts. But at this time, he concentrated on political theory and, in reading about the Spanish Civil War, oppositional military strategies.

Mead ceased to identify himself as a criminal; with a little ideology under his belt to corroborate his deep-seated rebelliousness, he now considered himself a revolutionary. The development surprised him. As he put it later: "In the process of struggle, one day I looked at myself and I saw that I wasn't a criminal anymore."[26]

Mead followed Armsbury's example and launched a class action. With twenty-six others, and himself as the lead plaintiff, Mead challenged the inadequacy of legal materials available to inmates at McNeil. Soon after the suit was filed, Mead was called in to the office of the chief of classification. "You're a smart boy, and you could get out of here soon if you used your head," the administrator advised. "You've got a choice: you can drop the law library suit and go to the farm," as minimum security was called, "or you can push it and get on the bus to Leavenworth. . . . You think it over." The Legal Defense Fund of the National Association for the Advancement of Colored People and the Center for Constitutional Rights had both endorsed *Mead v. Parker*. These endorsements, coupled with precedence and the case's own merit, made it clear that the prisoners were going to win. Mead chose his course reflexively: he went to the law library and told all of his companions what had happened.

Louie, one of the most consistent members of the McNeil's informal prisoner legal collective, immediately took matters out of Mead's hands by pounding out protest letters to the lawyers in the case. Additionally, Mead took part in a hunger strike with a handful of other prisoners.[27]

In retaliation, Mead and three other prisoners were shipped to other federal institutions. An anonymous prison official later acknowledged that they had transferred Mead because of "rumors of unrest in the prison."[28] On the way to the U.S. Penitentiary in Leavenworth, Kansas, Mead was held over in the King County Jail in downtown Seattle. While in King County Jail, Mead learned that anti-war radicals had upped their opposition to incarceration to the point of freeing a prisoner. On September 12, 1970, the Weather Underground orchestrated the escape of Dr. Timothy Leary from a California prison to which he had been sentenced for ten years after being found in possession of a couple of marijuana cigarette butts. In 1969, Mead had begun using Leary's pet drug, LSD, as a method of self-exploration, and he thoroughly approved of the freeing of its primary proponent.

Mead also came to realize that the consciousness-expanding process he had undergone on McNeil Island was being replicated in prisons throughout the country. There had been a "civil rights movement," an "anti-war movement," and now there was a "prisoners' rights movement." Its pinnacle came not long after Mead recognized its existence. George Jackson, a young hoodlum turned black liberation philosopher while in the California prison system, was gunned down in an escape attempt August 21, 1971. A month later, the largest prison revolt in U.S. history occurred at Attica Correctional Facility in upstate New York. When negotiations stalled, Governor Nelson Rockefeller ordered an assault on the institution, which left thirty-nine dead: twenty-nine inmates and ten hostages.[29] This brutality reminded prisoners and their outside supporters that participatory democracy—the quintessential idealistic demand of the civil rights and anti-war movements—would be even more difficult to enact in society's most blatantly oppressive institution than it had been in the ostensibly democratic society as a whole.

The Weather Underground retaliated against both of these traumatic occurrences with bombings of the headquarters of the California Department of Corrections after Jackson's death and the offices of the New York commissioner of corrections after the Attica massacre. As visible manifestations of anger, Ed considered these attacks to be appropriate complements to the bicoastal demonstrations. As with the bomb the Weather Underground detonated in the U.S. Capitol Building in opposition to the escalation of the Indochina War into Laos, the damage appeared to Mead just a foretaste of what the U.S. government had coming for its crimes. Retaliation posed no ethical or strategic difficulty for him. He had never subscribed to the pacifism of portions of the civil rights and anti-war movements, and he was unaware of the devastating effect Weatherman—which by then had become the Weather Underground—had had on mass organizing at the end of the previous decade.

At King County Jail, Mead worked his way into a position as the jail librarian. From this centralized location, he circulated politically oriented literature and organized inmates throughout the institution to participate in a strike. He collated a newsletter, *King County Jail Times,* to augment the organizing campaign and passed it on to the administration to print. The jail superintendent threw it in the trash, declaring, "I refuse to print this filth!" Mead called in the local chapters of the American Civil Liberties Union and the National Lawyers Guild, which promptly lodged letters of protest.

The strike began with the institution's eighty or so trustees. Their demands included the right to publish the *Jail Times.* Guards laughed off the protest and went to look for other inmate workers, but they were surprised to discover that none of the 600-plus inmates would cross the invisible picket line at the threshold of their cells. Two days later the administration conceded to a number of inmate demands, including the publication of the prisoner-run newsletter. Initially ebullient, prisoner enthusiasm declined when it became clear that the prison administration was not honoring its promises. Mead began organizing for a second strike, but U.S. marshals picked him up and shipped him to U.S.P. Leavenworth before he could implement his plans. In his brief stay at King County Jail, Roger Lippman visited him once, which lifted his spirits.

Mead's stay at Leavenworth was not a quiet one. On his initial arrival, he physically protested the routine digital rectal probe, which he called "anal rape." He was subdued by the prison's riot squad and issued an infraction for resisting a lawful search. A few months later an officer found a copy of *Quotations from Chairman Mao* in Mead's locker. The "Little Red Book" was all the rage in China and among many in the French Left and a portion of that of the United States, but it was not a sanctioned possession in prison. Mead was summarily convicted of possessing inflammatory written material and sent to "the hole."

Mead certainly did find the reading inflammatory. He was working through ideologies at a rapid pace; Maoism was his creed of the moment. At first he had been drawn to anarchism, but quickly cast it aside when he discovered it had little means to enforce whatever gains its adherents achieved. Mead then embraced Leon Trotsky, immensely enjoying Isaac Deutscher's three-volume biography. Trotsky, however, he soon dismissed as "Left in form but Right in essence," a phrase Chairman Mao coined at the opening of the Cultural Revolution.

Other rights Mead had become accustomed to at McNeil were routinely violated at Leavenworth—guards, for example, often perused his incoming and outgoing legal mail. He fought back to the best of his ability, writing to prisoners' rights attorneys in organizations on the outside, but relief was not forthcoming.

What he had not anticipated was a tangible gain resulting from Armsbury et al.'s "genocide complaint." The suit had been immediately dismissed by the court, as Mead had predicted, but it had served as a mobilizing device for prisoners' rights advocates. In response to the inmates' plea for greater community involvement in their lives, local prison activists established the Steilacoom Prisoner Support House in a modest two-and-a-half-story Victorian, surrounded by a white picket fence, only a block and a half from the docks that handled traffic to McNeil Island. The relatives and friends of prisoners who traveled long distances to visit them could stay at the Support House, making their trips less onerous. The way in which the house had come about gave Mead pause: *Mead v. Parker*, his well-designed class action, promised victory, but victory would only mean a few more books for the library.[30] The "genocide complaint" was a dismal failure in the legal realm, but as an organizing strategy, it was remarkably fruitful.

Mead constantly read enthusiastic accounts of promising events in the outside world in the publications he received in prison. He was eager to shed the constraints of his cage and add his energies to those fomenting in the streets. John Sherman, Mead's fellow inmate organizer at McNeil, had been released and had moved into the Steilacoom support house with his wife Joanne and her two daughters. The two men had corresponded throughout their separation and, now that Mead's release was imminent, made plans to meet at the new prisoners' rights collective. From there, they pledged to pursue "The Revolution," a concept both mystical and concrete, which they envisioned as an overturning of earthly injustice and a cleansing of the troubles of the spirit.

Once a petty thief compelled by base desires, Mead now perceived himself as a communist revolutionary dedicated to the highest aspirations of "the people." This was an immense leap and an infinitesimal one. Rather than acting only for himself, he now considered himself to be serving the cause of all humanity. Yet his opponents remained the same: those who, unlike himself, had significant possessions. His interest in the law would last throughout his life, but, after his period of initial fascination, he used it instrumentally, as a tool to be wielded when efficacious and cast aside when ineffective. The tool that felt most tangible—the one that he would pick up in promoting his new ideology—was the gun. Since revolution was illegal, and the means he chose to help bring it about were particularly offensive to defenders of the established order, this politicized prisoner was destined to be reincarcerated as a political one. Such a distinction, however, only made sense to himself and his "comrades." To the authorities Mead would attack, he was the same criminal he had been since age fourteen.

Personally, knowledge of the law continued to aid Mead. In the summer of 1972, he won a hearing on the federal escape case in Fairbanks, and the judge granted the pending writ of habeas corpus in exchange for a plea of guilty to cover time served. Mead pled no contest and was released with five years of federal probation.

Ed looked for his old girlfriend Margo. Although the two, as usual, had not exchanged letters during his incarceration, he had thought of her fondly and felt compelled to inform her of his plans. Margo was not difficult to find; she remained immersed in the bar scene. Ed explained to her the change he had undergone during his last incarceration. "I'm a revolutionary now. I'll give my life, if necessary, to combat the injustice of capitalism," he declared earnestly.

"I'll be a revolutionary too," she promised.

"If I said I was a Catholic, you'd become that as well," Ed snapped. "I'm going to Seattle," he told her bluntly.

"I'll come with you."

"No, it wouldn't work. It's a completely different life."

It was difficult for him to leave, but Alaska offered nothing he didn't know. He was drawn irresistibly to the Lower Forty-Eight, where "the movement" was flourishing and "the Revolution" appeared imminent.

# 7

# A Rebel and a Cause

*In which Ed Mead becomes impatient
with reform and recommits to revolution*

> *Please understand that though I would miss you and all the others, though
> I love you dearly, I do not want to live in this world as it is. I do not think of
> myself as one small person among so many. I know what I can do, I know I
> can build and can cause things to happen . . .*
>
> —GEORGE JACKSON, SOLEDAD BROTHER

Ed Mead had read more about the radical community in Seattle than that of any other city while in prison. In the 1960s, Seattle's University District, or "U District," was one of the first blossomings of the hippie scene outside New York City's Lower East Side and San Francisco's Haight-Ashbury District. Toward the close of the decade, the campus boasted one of the nation's strongest chapters of Students for a Democratic Society; Mead still has a clipping from the *University of Washington Daily* describing a march and rally in the spring of 1969 that drew thousands of people demanding an "immediate end to ROTC."[1] On May 5, 1970, the day after the Kent State killings by the Ohio National Guard, 7,000 protesters shut down Interstate 5 downtown in Seattle. The next day they repeated the performance.[2] By then bombings were already a common occurrence in the city. In the fall of 1968, the most dramatic ROTC firebombing in the country occurred on the "U Dub" campus; students danced around the flames that were inflicting $85,000 of damage, chanting:

> This is number one
> And the fun has just begun,
> Burn it down, burn it down, burn it down[3]

As promised, the "fun" continued: on October 9, 1970, the third anniversary of the death of Che Guevara, a group calling itself the "Quarter Moon Tribe of the Woodstock Nation" bombed Clark Hall, the center of the campus Naval and Air Force ROTC.

Nor was armed militancy the sole province of the Left; indeed, campus radicals in moving into bombings and bank robberies poached on territory that had until recently been the private preserve of the Right. The most prominent local example occurred in 1968 when a group of seven men headed by Duane I. Carlson, a local leader of the Minutemen, were arrested for conspiring to rob four Seattle banks and bomb the Redmond police station and a local power plant. This, their defense attorney divulged, was to prepare for the inevitable guerrilla warfare that would occur after "communists had seized control of the United States from within."[4]

Ed touched down in Seattle only briefly after his release from prison, then moved to the Prisoner Support House in Steilacoom. There he enjoyed a quiet reunion with John Sherman, who was living with his wife Joanne and her children. Talking politics into the wee hours, Ed and John got into a disagreement about when the Revolution would come. "Five years," Ed insisted, while John countered vehemently that it would be ten. "He was more in touch with reality than me," Ed granted with a chuckle in a 2005 interview.

John and Joanne wanted a place of their own. Shortly after Ed's arrival, they moved to Kent, a bland stretch of suburban sprawl between Tacoma and Seattle. This left Ed as the only male in the house, an uncomfortable position in light of the fact that most of the visitors were the girlfriends or wives of the sexually inaccessible convicts across Carr Inlet. After an inappropriate late-night liaison, Ed called Roger Lippman, his closest contact in Seattle, and asked: "Can I come live with you?" "Let me think about it," Lippman replied. Ed took offense: "Well if you have to think about it, then probably not." "That wasn't what I had meant," Lippman remembers. "I just liked to think about things. Ed did come to live with me and I was quite pleased with the arrangement."[5]

Roger occupied a spacious two-story house on Capitol Hill. Except for the occasional visitor, the two had the place to themselves. Roger and some colleagues had begun an auto repair business on the curb in front of the house and in the one-car garage in the back; a year or so later, when they got a proper garage, they christened the enterprise "Black Duck Motors." Ed, knowledgeable about engines from his days as an airplane mechanic, offered to help out. He also did occasional work for Seattle's bustling "Cooperating Community," the network of collectives that sought to provide necessary services while subverting capitalist organizational structures and the ethically corrosive profit motive.

John, for all Ed could tell, wasn't doing anything in Kent other than smoking dope. "You have an incredible ability to inspire prisoners," Ed encouraged him. "I've seen you. You should move up to Seattle. We'll get a place together and work on behalf of prisoners."

John did move to Seattle, where he, Joanne, and Ed got a place on the city's eastern slope. Roger had warned Ed, "The closer you get to Lake Washington, the more bourgeois people become," but Ed wasn't particularly concerned about this. Ed and John discussed organizing a "prisoners' labor union," a concept that had originated in the San Francisco Bay Area in the late 1960s and had spread across the country. In 1968, a glimpse of the potential of concerted prisoner action became visible in two "Unity Strikes" at San Quentin State Prison. The intention of the protest— backed by unprecedented outside support from counterculturals—was to transcend the racial divisions that kept prisoners at one another's throats and distracted them from the injustices perpetrated against them by the administration. The sociologist and prisoners' union organizer John Irwin observed:

> The San Quentin unity strikes mark a turning point in the developments inside U.S. prisons. After these events, more and more prisoners throughout the country began redefining their legal and social status, adopting political ideologies, and becoming involved in various forms of political activities. New outside organizations formed, and existing ones refocused to work on reform or to eliminate the prison. The general public raised the prison issue to the top of its list of concerns. Political activists and radical political organizations shifted their attention to the prison and generated the prison movement.[6]

Over the next few years, a wave of prison strikes swept from coast to coast, crashing in such out-of-the-way places as Florence, Arizona, Michigan City, Indiana, and Deer Island, Massachusetts. On December 22, 1970, over 1,400 prisoners at the Washington State Penitentiary outside Walla Walla, another nineteenth-century maximum security prison, went on strike to protest Warden Bobby J. Rhay's prohibition of beards and mustaches. Other grievances included the poor state of the medical facilities and the treatment received there, restrictive visiting regulations, and conditions in isolation.[7]

Efforts to establish a collective bargaining body often followed the strikes. The very idea of prisoner participation in the institution that governed their lives was antithetical to the 1950s "Big House" total institutions that had produced most of the administrators and guards in control in the late 1960s. More innovative criminologists, however, reflecting the new spirit of direct democracy, advocated as much prisoner involvement as possible as a way to combat the institutionalization process itself, which they often blamed for high recidivism rates.

The prisoners' union campaign was influenced by the "lumpen" ideology of the Black Panthers and other intellectual efforts of the time, which used Marxist terminology to advocate ideas distinct from those of Marx himself. Unionists espoused the logic that those who became criminals and were thus incarcerated often did so due to unemployment. Unemployment was a necessary condition of capitalism— without the threat of job loss, how could employers keep their workers in line? Prisoners, then, were just those pushed out in the economic game of musical chairs.

Once in prison, they were forced to work for pennies to buy the amenities denied them by the state. To improve these conditions, they, like other workers, needed to join together *as* workers. This new consciousness of collective power would enable prisoners to gain control over other aspects of their lives as well. By the early 1970s, prisoners' unions existed in the federal system, California, Michigan, New England (Maine, Massachusetts, New Hampshire, Rhode Island, and Vermont), New York, North Carolina, Ohio, and—because of Ed and John's dual enthusiasm—Washington State.[8]

Quickly after they went public with the Washington Prisoners Labor Union (WPLU), Ed and John heard a knock at the door of the house that they'd moved into together. Ed answered it. Outside was a young, short, smiling white man. "Hi! Let me introduce myself. I'm Bruce Seidel. I do prison work. I hear you guys do prison work too."

"Come on in!" Ed said.

Bruce had heard about Ed and John through the Seattle chapter of the National Lawyers Guild, for which Ed, still interested in the law, had volunteered. Bruce lived in a collective kitty-corner from Roger's house. Inspired by a line from one of Ho Chi Minh's poems—"When the prison doors are opened, the real dragon will fly out"—they named it "Dragon House." The three men drank wine and smoked dope and waxed poetic about the possibilities of prisoner control of the criminal justice system. Bruce had recently gotten busted smuggling weed in to one of the prisoners he visited at the Washington State Reformatory (WSR) in Monroe and was no longer allowed to enter the institution, but he still wanted to help organize it.

The WPLU started up the *Sunfighter,* an erratic newsletter packed with information on prison struggle from across the country. They named the periodical after the Jefferson Airplane album dedicated to those who had died in Weatherman's townhouse explosion. The organization printed up membership cards emblazoned with their icon—chains arcing over the acronym "WPLU"—and commenced a membership drive. They also printed up stickers, distributed them to inmates, and plastered the inside of the reformatory with them every time they visited. Initially, they were allowed in under the auspices of "Inside Out," a reform-minded organization that had participated in the demonstration supporting the work strike at McNeil Island Penitentiary. The WPLU also worked with the National Lawyers Guild, in particular around the legacy of the Attica rebellion.

While Ed was focusing his anger into organized opposition, an event on May 14, 1973 reminded him of the possible cost of failing to do so. A young man had taken a rifle to a hilltop overlooking highway 405, which connects I-5 to Seattle's upscale eastern suburbs, and began shooting drivers. He killed one and injured another, then attacked two young female hikers, tied them to a tree, and raped them.

Carl Harp was quickly captured. He was dubbed the "Bellevue Sniper." The press expressed incomprehension at his crimes. Ed, however, understood the anger,

## Of life and death in radical circles

By LEE MORIWAKI and JOHN ARTHUR WILSON

They were self-styled revolutionaries from middle-class families, young men who traveled in the same political circles, were inclined toward literary pursuits — and in the end died the most violent of deaths.

Ralph Patrick Ford, 23, was killed September 15 as he apparently tried to plant a pipe bomb at a Capitol Hill Safeway store.

Bruce R. Seidel, 21, was killed in a shootout with police during an attempted robbery of a Tuckwila bank January 23.

BOTH WERE embraced as "comrades" by the George Jackson Brigade, a band of radicals which has claimed responsibility for a series of bombings in the Seattle area as well as the thwarted Tuckwila bank robbery and the subsequent escape of one of the men arrested at the bank.

"Years of struggle for progressive change taught him [Seidel] that poor and working people will not listen to Communists who are unwilling and unprepared to back their demands with revolutionary violence," the brigade said in its latest communique.

The brigade, in an earlier communique, said Ford "died because his oppression . . . was so real that he found it necessary to risk death in order to free himself."

THE VIOLENT deaths of Ford

Ralph P. Ford

Bruce R. Seidel

and Seidel left their families in shock.

Mr. and Mrs. Fred Seidel, of Skokie, Ill., a middle-class suburb of Chicago, have declined to talk about their son with reporters.

Lawrence J. Ford, a state employe in Sacramento, C lif., portrayed his son as always concerned about the safety of others. The young Ford was active in protests while in high school, according to the father, but kept an eye out "to see that no people were injured."

INTERVIEWS with friends of Ford and Seidel showed that both men wrote for various leftist publications here.

Dale Van Pelt, director of the United Farm Worker's Seattle Boycott, said Ford had once called him up for some information to be used in a newsletter Ford was putting out. The newsletter was called Red Moon Rising.

Van Pelt described Ford as "gentle, quiet and polite." Another person who knew Ford said he was "very intense."

Seidel also has been described as "intense," especially in the area of prison reform.

SEIDEL, like Ford, came to Seattle in the early 1970s. In 1973, Seidel met John Sherman and Edward Allen Mead, both Tuckwila robbery suspects, and worked in the Washington State Prisoners Union at the state reformatory at Monroe, according to one source in the radical community.

Seidel and Mead worked together on a publication called Sunfighter, a prisoner-oriented newspaper.

Seidel, while attending Seattle Central Community College, met Mark Edwin Cook, also a suspect in the bank robbery, according to another source. Seidel and Cook were involved at S. C. C. C. in the Prisoners Coalition, a group of ex-convicts and students.

An acquaintance of Seidel said that while Seidel appeared calm and controlled, he was "seething underneath."

The George Jackson Brigade's latest communique has sent tremors of concern through Seattle's radical community, especially among those who knew either Ford or Seidel.

BY CLAIMING responsibility for the bank robbery and the violent escape of Sherman (Cook and Mead are still being held in King County jail), the brigade has for the first time identified possible members of the unit.

Today the brigade authenticated its latest communique by sending a dental appliance supposedly from Sherman's mouth to Bellevue radio station KZAM. The station said the appliance, which arrived in the morning mail with a Seattle postmark, was turned over to the F.B.I.

Members of the leftist community interviewed by The Times voiced concern that friends of the bank-robbery suspects could be swept up in an intensified Federal Bureau of Investigation probe.

One source said Ford and Seidel knew each other, but the source doubted they ever acted in concert.

When asked if the naming of brigade "comrades" would be useful in identifying other members of the George Jackson Brigade, John M. Reed, special agent in charge of the F.B.I. office here, said: "That would be a logical assumption. A lot of this, of course, will be brought to the attention of the United States attorney and they may issue warrants or subpoenas . . . That's up to them."

SAID ONE activist who knew both Ford and Seidel: "I don't want to get involved in that (bank-robbery investigation). We don't know nothing about it, and we don't want to get into any trouble (by talking)."

He said of the George Jackson Brigade, "I think they're crazy." Another activist said the brigade was "a small, romantic sect (who) in no way represent or advance the movement for radical social change in this city."

FIGURE 4. Article on Ralph Ford and Bruce Seidel, *Seattle Times*, March 30, 1976. Copyright *Seattle Times*.

though he had been able to channel his own more constructively. Harp claimed to be a "political prisoner." Ed decided to visit him at the jail and listen to what he had to say.

Harp vehemently denied his guilt, insisting that his wife and a friend had framed him. Ed quickly decided Harp was not a political prisoner, but a fuckup. The rapes disturbed him more than the shooting. Harp, Mead recalls, exhibited no awareness of his misogynistic violence, prompting Ed to leave disgusted. Harp was convicted of assault with a deadly weapon, first-degree murder, rape, and sodomy, among other charges, and sentenced to fifty-five years in prison.

In speaking to the press about the work of the nascent union, John didn't play up the prevention of "atrocities" like physical abuse or arbitrary long-term confinement, though he did say that eliminating such practices would certainly be among the goals of the prisoners' union. Instead, he pointed to the recidivism rate at Monroe, which he put at 80 percent, as an illustration of the administration's incompetence. He attributed such a high degree of failure to "lack of prisoner control and a lack of prisoner participation." His solution: to give prisoners control of every aspect of the institution aside from guarding it. "Prisoners could hardly do worse than the people who are now in charge of 'rehabilitation,' " John told a reporter from the

FIGURE 5. Photograph of Bruce Seidel taken by a friend shortly before his death.

*Post-Intelligencer*. If the public wanted protection from crime, it should support the genuine efforts of prisoners to create an institution in which personal change could take place. The WPLU sought to cross the line of permissible reforms, to "affect the absolute control" the administration held over prisoners.

October 19, 1973, Reformatory Superintendent Roger Maxwell and some of his deputies met with John for an hour and a half. Maxwell was not pleased. He later told the press that the WPLU "wanted to run the place."[9] After the meeting, he declared that he would not even consider recognizing the organization.[10] John called a work strike. Some prisoners responded, but it didn't have nearly the same duration or intensity as the one John and Ed had participated in on McNeil Island that spring.

Undeterred, John set his sights even higher, trying to organize the guards as well.

He appealed to Ed: "They're workers too. They need to know that their interests are those of the prisoners, who are simply *unemployed* workers!"

"We're not gonna get anywhere with that," Ed countered. "They're reactionary and narrow-minded. They don't care what their own interests are."

"We have to try anyway." So John called the office of the guards' union and asked to address them at their next meeting as the prisoners' outside representative. The union functionary grudgingly granted a time slot. John addressed them, flanked by Ed: "We're with the Washington Prisoners Labor Union. We're both ex-convicts who went to prison because we were unemployed. Prisoners are just working people—simply ones denied work. You and prisoners share the same enemy, the administration. It is not in your interest to be antagonistic to prisoners organizing a union. Prisoners are just working people, and, like any working people, should be allowed to represent ourselves in a union."

The speech was not received warmly. The two consoled each other on the way out. Ed commented: "At least this put a face on the prisoners' union for them. Now they know that at least we're people they can speak to."

The organization seemed to be doing better inside. An informal poll conducted by a prisoner member put union membership at WSR at 97 percent of the prison population. The prison administration conceded that some 450 prisoners had signed a petition circulated by the WPLU. Though the numbers appeared encouraging, Ed felt that the organization was failing to transform the consciousness of the prisoners. "This is a mile wide and an inch deep," he brooded.

From August 12 to August 17, 1973, the American Correctional Association (ACA) held its annual "Correctional Congress" in Seattle. The ACA was ostensibly a nationwide regulatory body comprised of prison administrators, but its rare sanctions carried little weight and its conferences had of late developed into trade fairs facilitating the marketing of goods and services. Jessica Mitford, describing the 101st Congress of the ACA at the Americana Hotel in Miami Beach, Florida, in 1970, wrote: "A man from Mars dropping into the Americana might be forgiven for concluding that all is serene in the world of Corrections; he would have no way of knowing that an unprecedented, bloodstained upheaval is rocking the prisons from coast to coast."[11] The serenity of the conferences was ruptured in Seattle. The theme of the year was "Criminal Justice: Everyone's Responsibility," and the WPLU members took their responsibility seriously.

The conference was held at Seattle Center, where, luckily for the rabble-rousers, the friend of a WPLU member worked. The insider provided Bruce, Ed, John, and other collaborators with the identification badges of conference no-shows. Ed went as "Captain Jenkins from the Arkansas Correctional System." They all dressed conservatively so as to blend in.

The year's keynote address, to be delivered by three former American POWs in Vietnam, was on the psychological effects of long-term incarceration. When the

POWs moved to the stage, the Prisoners Union infiltrators stood and started shouting: "How about talking about American prisoners and the effects of long-term isolation!?" Others from the audience echoed their cry. They pushed to the stage and seized the microphone from the bewildered veterans. A third of the audience walked out immediately. Another third listened skeptically to the denunciation of conditions in U.S. prisons, then drifted off. The final third stayed for the complete "browbeating," as Mead characterized it. The infiltrators congratulated themselves on having thoroughly disrupted the convention.

While involved in the WPLU, Ed began dating Jill Kray, who was ten years his junior and pregnant with another man's child. She gave birth soon after she and Ed met, naming her daughter Odessa.

Several years earlier, Ed's mother Ramona had bought property in Addy, a small town in northeastern Washington. In the winter of 1973, she asked Ed and Jill to take care of her horses for a few months while she attended to affairs in Fairbanks. On earlier visits to the farm, Ed had driven his old white Volkswagen plastered with bumper stickers blaring Movement slogans. Now, for the first time, he began practicing the art of what the Brazilian guerrilla theorist Carlos Marighella, whose work Mead first read in prison, called "dissembling": blending in; deflecting notice. He drove a hulking green Ford pickup, which he kept clean of propaganda.

Jill settled in, but Ed remained restless. Beyond basic maintenance, his only commitment to the land was the planting of fifty pot plants. February 13, 1974, Ed opened the paper and found a clarion call. It was a communiqué from the Symbionese Liberation Army, which had kidnapped the newspaper heiress Patricia Hearst in Berkeley the previous week. This communiqué described the organization's proposed "People in Need" program: Patricia's father Randolph A. Hearst was called upon to provide $70 worth of food to every poor person in the state. Poverty was defined by possession of "welfare cards, social security pension cards, food stamp cards, disabled veterans cards, medical cards, parole or probation papers and jail or bail release slips," meaning that, had he lived in California, Mead would have qualified.[12]

Ed was so moved that he cried. He decided on the spot to join the SLA.

It took Mead approximately a month and a half to get down to San Francisco. Jill remained on the farm until Ramona returned. Ed pulled up the scrawny cannabis stalks and baked and ingested a portion (to little effect). He hitchhiked back to Seattle and printed up a ream of posters featuring the SLA's seven-headed cobra icon against a blue background.[13] Superimposed over the graphic, in dark blue lettering, was the injunction: "Give Them Shelter." The posters were designed to fit over the advertising space in bus stops, one of the places the SLA instructed "the people" to use in order to communicate with them.

Mead then traveled to San Francisco, where he stayed with George Sing Louie, one of his law library comrades from McNeil Island. Louie was struggling to get his conditions of parole liberalized. He had been consistently penalized in the federal system for his legal challenges to conditions of confinement, suffering long stretches in "the hole" and the consequent denial of "good time," as well as punitive transfers and discriminatory treatment by the Parole Board. When he finally succeeded in getting a court to order the Parole Board to reconsider one of its decisions, it released him with the stipulation that he be placed under "maximum supervision."

Instead of the standard monthly report to his parole officer, Louie was required to report in person each week and was subjected to continual monitoring at his home and workplace. In challenging these practices, Louie told the presiding judge, Alfonso Zirpoli, that, consistent with his right to the counsel of his choice, he wanted a fellow jailhouse lawyer to represent him: Ed Mead. The judge unexpectedly consented.

This was a victory in and of itself. Mead wrote an article on the case for *Contempt*, the newsletter of the Seattle chapter of the National Lawyers Guild. He stated that it had been their intention "to make an assault on the legal profession's privileged status as the 'priests' of the law, and the pervasive 'closed shop' policy that excludes qualified laymen from practicing." Ed had been skeptical that, once in court, the judge would let him speak. Yet Zirpoli permitted him to make a case on behalf of his fellow ex-convict.[14] In the end, the judge did, however, deny the petition.

The Hearst kidnapping was the news story of the decade. On April 18, the script changed when the 19-year-old debutante was captured on a surveillance camera participating in the robbery of the Hibernia Bank in San Francisco's Sunset District. SLA members shot two people in the course of the robbery, which netted $10,660. The image of Patricia sporting a black beret and wielding a carbine quickly became iconic. That same day the SLA released an audiotape in which young Hearst announced that she had joined the revolutionaries and changed her name to "Tania," after a *compañera* who had died with Che in the Bolivian jungle. Ed's pro-SLA posters were by no means the only visible support for the group.[15]

Illicit pleasures punctuated Mead's trip to the Bay Area. The gay liberation movement was in full swing: the Stonewall riots in New York City that are conventionally used to designate the beginning of this period had occurred a full five years earlier, on June 28, 1969. Although Mead did not consider himself a homosexual—his primary identity was as a revolutionary, and the political scene was still dominated by a conventional heterosexual outlook—he did like to have sex with men. While postering in the rollicking gay mecca of San Francisco's Castro District, Ed picked up and was picked up by several different men.

Mead's initial forays into the radical political scene of the Bay Area were less successful. He didn't make contact with the SLA, which at the time was holed up either in a flat in the Fillmore District or a Daly City bungalow.[16] One of his first visits was to Wilbur "Popeye" Jackson, chairman of the United Prisoners Union (UPU), but it proved a disappointment.

Popeye had known George Jackson in San Quentin, and this connection earned him instant respect among outside organizers upon his release from prison. Like Jackson, he was a rough character, reputed to have murdered several other inmates. He was not as politically developed as "Comrade George," but he was a charismatic organizer. In February 1971, he attended a meeting of California prison activists in the state capital. The two hundred and fifty attendees took as their constitution the demands made by striking prisoners at Folsom the previous year.[17] They called themselves the California Prisoners Union.

In 1973, Popeye was ejected from the Prisoners Union for having stolen money; after getting the news, he returned to the union's offices with a gun and chased members around, threatening to kill them, then publicly denounced the primarily white organization as racist. He founded the United Prisoners Union, which drew away most of the parent organization's radical convict members.[18] In February 1974, the UPU was one of the groups designated by the SLA to coordinate its "People in Need" program. (Reverend Cecil Williams's Glide Memorial Church, in San Francisco's Tenderloin, which provided office space to the UPU, was another of the groups named.)

In April, concurrent with Mead's visit, the UPU published the first issue of *The Anvil*, in which it put forward the concept of a "Convicted Class." It defined this group as those "subjected to a continuous cycle of poverty, prison, parole, and more poverty." Theirs was "a social condition of inequality and degradation that denies us the opportunity to rise up and pursue a dignified way of life. . . . Once convicted, forever doomed."[19] The purpose of the union was not simply to expand civil rights for prisoners but to overturn a social order in which anyone who had been caught in the criminal justice system was consigned to the bottom.

As ex-convict revolutionaries and organizers of prisoners' unions, one might expect Ed and Popeye to have much in common. Ed had certainly hoped so; he was eager to coordinate his activities, and even receive guidance, from this colleague of George Jackson's. But Popeye expressed little interest in Ed or the Washington Prisoners Labor Union, which disappointed Ed immensely. He had been looking for a leader, but left with the impression "I'm *way* ahead of this guy!"

Ed's prison activist credentials gained him entry into other quarters. He put the word out that he was looking to be involved in "heavy action," and he was soon contacted by an active guerrilla cell preparing to launch an offensive.

The New World Liberation Front was composed of Maoists, committed, like the Chinese People's Liberation Army, they said, to "the process of criticism/self-criticism and firepower backed by principled theory."[20] They adhered to Chairman Mao's doctrine of self-reliance, refusing to count on the aboveground Left for support. They had their own printing press, which Ed worked, running off an edition of

Marighella's *Mini-Manual of the Urban Guerrilla*. When Ed had first encountered this seminal text on guerrilla warfare in prison his reaction had been a spectator's "Cool!" This time, he read it with an eye toward immediate practical applications.

The NWLF cell was prepared for a police assault. One safe house had sliding plates of armor that could be placed over windows in case of a siege. Members no longer lived in San Francisco: they commuted to carry out their bombings.

NWLF members worked with deliberation and care. They taught Ed how to make pipe bombs, providing a hands-on tutorial without gunpowder. They stressed that the threads at each end of the pipe must be wiped down thoroughly so that no gunpowder remained—if this was not done, Mead's tutor warned, the overlooked grains could combust from the friction of screwing on the nipple, detonating the device in the maker's hands.

Ed and one of the female members of the organization became lovers. He did not confess his bisexuality, and the group would have likely been surprised to learn they had a gay man in their midst. Less than two years later, the NWLF collectively published an article in their aboveground organ *The Urban Guerrilla*, or *TUG*, in which they characterized homosexuality as a "bourgeois deviancy" that would have to be corrected after the revolution. A no-longer-closeted Mead was one of many who wrote in protest; by that time, he was already in jail in Seattle on account of his own guerrilla activities.[21]

After leaving Addy, Jill rented an apartment on Capitol Hill, near Roger Lippman's home. When Ed returned to Seattle, he moved in with Jill and Odessa. He picked up a job as an aircraft and power-plant mechanic working in a propeller-overhaul station at Boeing Field. He ruminated constantly about the best way to put his newly acquired skills to use. The May 16 televised incineration of six SLA members in a safe house in Compton, Los Angeles, added to his sense of urgency.

In 1972 or 1973, Roger had invited Mead to participate in the discussion groups of an aboveground Weather Underground support group which later developed into a branch of the Prairie Fire Organizing Committee. The conversations were regularly attended by from twenty to thirty people interested in dismantling U.S. imperialism's home base by mounting a domestic revolutionary movement. One of the more vocal participants was Paul Zilsel, a middle-aged former nuclear physicist in his fifties, who, in conjunction with six others half his age, had co-founded Left Bank Books, an anarchist collective with a storefront in Pike Place Market. Zilsel differed from many radicals in the United States in that he'd had direct experience with European fascism, a version of which he and his contemporaries were certain had cropped up in the United States. He had been born in Austria in 1923. When he was fourteen, he and his family had fled the Nazi regime. According to Zilsel, they were among the last Jews to do so legally.[22]

July 24, 1974 saw the appearance of *Prairie Fire: The Politics of Revolutionary Anti-Imperialism: Political Statement of the Weather Underground*. It sold out quickly, and

Ed was involved in producing the second print run. The tract was intended to be a practical revolutionary prescription like Lenin's *What Is to Be Done?* The original printing of *Prairie Fire* caused a small sensation when it appeared at the doors of community bookstores across the country. More than 20,000 copies of the red-bound book, printed by the "Red Dragon Print Collective" of the Weather Underground (a subsequent edition was published by the Prairie Fire Distribution Committee) were soon in circulation.[23]

The book was, as Weatherpeople Bernadine Dohrn, Billy Ayers, Jeff Jones, and the pseudonymous "Celia Sojourn" introduced it, "a strategy for anti-imperialism and revolution inside the imperial US." The product of twelve months of collective, cross-country consideration, "squeezed between on-going work and practice and action,"[24] it argued that a revolutionary push in the United States was just as important after the Vietnam War as it had been during it. The Weather Underground called for single-minded dedication to the Revolution, a path that promised want and hardship, as well as "inevitable victory."

The collective spoke of a contagious commitment to revolution. Their statement read: "PRAIRIE FIRE is based on a belief that the duty of a revolutionary is to make revolution. This is not an abstraction. It means that revolutionaries must make a profound commitment to the future of humanity, apply our limited knowledge and experience to understand an ever-changing situation, organize the masses of people and build the fight. It means that struggle and risk and hard work and adversity will become our way of life, that the only certainty will be constant change, that the only possibilities are victory or death." This last assertion is an example of the willful muddling of the differing consequences for revolutionary activism faced by First and Third World peoples. The erasure of such distinction was, in fact, a goal of Weather Underground and its fellow travelers.

Underground for the previous five years, the Weather collective needed a new wave of revolutionaries to pick up the torch. "We have come some distance in evaluating the political situation, the priorities for revolutionary work since we began this writing. Now many more revolutionaries will need to shape and change the paper. The politics cannot be realized unless and until the content of the program is activated in thousands of situations, among thousands of people in the coming period. PRAIRIE FIRE will be a growing thing."

The Weather collective invited people to join in, intellectually and in praxis. "We hope the paper opens a dialectic among those in the mass and clandestine movement; we hope people will take PRAIRIE FIRE as seriously as we do, study the content and write and publish their views of the paper as well as their analysis of their own practice. We will respond as best we can." In making this appeal, *Prairie Fire* was addressed to a wide array of social groups in open rebellion, groups already engaged in a potentially revolutionary dialogue: "PRAIRIE FIRE is written to communist-minded revolutionaries, independent organizers and anti-imperialists;

those who carry the traditions and lessons of the struggles of the last decade, those who join in the struggles of today, PRAIRIE FIRE is written to all sisters and brothers who are engaged in armed struggle against the enemy. It is written to prisoners, women's groups, collectives, study groups, workers' organizing committees, communes, GI organizers, consciousness-raising groups, veterans, community groups, and revolutionaries of all kinds; to all who will read, criticize, and bring its content to life in practice." The gist of the book was "an argument against those who oppose action and hold back the struggle."[25]

Much of the tract addressed the changes in U.S. imperialism after the "Vietnam victory." The Weatherpeople saw a void in strategy and, with *Prairie Fire,* moved to fill it. "Our movement urgently needs a concrete analysis of the particular conditions of our time and place. We need strategy," the introduction continued. The goal was the creation of a revolutionary communist party, then the establishment of a revolutionary communist state. "We need to battle for a correct ideology and win people over. In this way we create the conditions for development of a successful revolutionary movement and party. We need a revolutionary communist party in order to lead the struggle, give coherence and direction to the fight, seize power and build the new society." The plan was one Mead obviously approved of: "Getting from here to there is a process of coming together in a disciplined way around ideology and strategy, developing an analysis of our real conditions, mobilizing a base among the US people, building principled relationships to Third World Struggle, and accumulating practice in struggle against US imperialism."[26]

In a 1976 interview with a movement tabloid, Mead recalled this period: "I felt this restlessness, I felt this need to do something more than just talk, I didn't feel good about the level of my political work—my efficiency or productivity. I felt that this [armed struggle] was the direction to go."[27]

In September 1974, Ed had an opportunity to aid a fellow revolutionary when a member of the American Indian Movement (AIM) came to Ed for assistance. A decade earlier, Leonard Peltier had been part owner of a Seattle auto shop; the same building had served as a halfway house for recovering indigenous alcoholics and ex-convicts attempting to improve their place in the community. When Peltier came to Seattle in 1974, he was a veteran of the AIM occupation of the offices of the Bureau of Indian Affairs in Washington, D.C., the culmination of the "Trail of Broken Treaties" that had commenced in San Francisco in October 1972, and a number of other native protests and occupations. In July 1973, a bench warrant for his arrest had been issued after he failed to appear for a trial in Milwaukee in which, he felt, he had been set up on a charge of attempting to murder a police officer.

Peltier asked Ed for false ID and parts for his truck. He was likely referred to Ed because Ed had engaged in illegal activities with people in the Seattle AIM chapter, such as a fruitless attempt to raid Forestry Service sheds further north for dynamite. Ed didn't have the capability to produce fake ID, but he knew people who did. Peltier would soon become one of the most famous political prisoners in the world, but at the time he was a foot soldier little known outside American Indian activist circles. Ignorant of Peltier's identity, Ed's contact denied the request with a dismissive remark about it being intended for only criminal, as opposed to political, purposes.[28] Peltier was arrested September 20 on Mercer Island, just east of Seattle, and charged with possession of illegal weapons. He had been on his way to join the Kootenai, a small band in Idaho who had declared war on the U.S. government.[29]

Ed worked with the Seattle chapter of the National Lawyers Guild (NLG) raising money for the Attica Brothers Legal Defense (ABLD) committee. In September 1974, the Seattle chapter of the NLG sent Ed to Buffalo to help organize the first national "Attica Day" demonstration. (In Seattle, at the First National Bank Building, protesters burned Nelson Rockefeller in effigy and displayed a coffin representing the dead for whom they held him responsible. They then joined with a group at the U.S. Courthouse protesting Nixon's pardon by President Gerald Ford.)[30]

In Buffalo, Mead stayed at a crash pad with more than a dozen other activists from around the country. He quickly came into conflict with the organization, balking when volunteers were asked to canvass door-to-door in support of a liberal assemblyman who supported the work of ABLD.[31]

"He's a bourgeois politician!" Ed exploded. "What are we doing? The prisoners are telling us what they want us to do, but we're ignoring them." He had read letters from prisoners saying they wanted to see more militancy, but ABLD, which existed, obviously enough, to coordinate the legal campaign, felt that excessive obnoxiousness would alienate both the court and the jury pool. Ed ignored their concerns. When he went out wheat-pasting up "Attica Is All of Us!" posters with other volunteers, he made a point of covering the courthouse and police station. The next day someone from the court called ABLD and demanded: "What's going on?"

Ed dealt poorly with the inevitable rebuke. A Buffalo-based organizer called him a "Stalinist," meaning he had a strong personality and ignored the concerns of others. "Liberals!" Ed countered. He found a different place to stay.

After the Attica Day demonstration, Ed hitch-hiked back to the Bay Area one more time. He met some interesting people there, but they didn't talk much about politics. Mead was no longer looking for leaders.

Upon returning to Seattle, Ed wrote up a criticism of Attica Brothers Legal Defense, which he distributed to the Left Bank Collective and Prairie Fire Organizing Committee, as well as to members of the local NLG chapter. He contended that lawyers were in control of the organization and weren't listening to prisoners.

The paper was poorly received. "No one wants to hear any criticism!" Ed complained to himself bitterly. "They just want to hear that everything is rosy and the Revolution is proceeding on schedule!" His own plans were firming up. "I can't keep waiting for these people," he told himself. "The Revolution's always gonna be in the future with them. It's time to make it *now!*"

On October 31, Ed made a public display of his disdain for what he deemed to be Seattle's less-than-radical Left. At a Halloween party at El Centro de la Raza, in the abandoned Beacon Hill School, which Chicano activists had seized in October 1972 and turned into a cultural center, he set up a booth in the basement with a large bowl of unshelled peanuts on his table. Above it, he hung a banner bearing a pronouncement he attributed to George Jackson: "Leaders who don't back up the demands of the people with the threat of revolutionary violence, end up serving the people only peanuts."[32]

8

# The Destroyer's Creation

*In which the Brigade comes into existence*

*In some countries, I said to myself, the only life you can properly desire is that of a destroyer.*
—OWEN BROWN IN RUSSELL BANKS'S NOVEL *CLOUDSPLITTER*

*In the opening stages of conflict, before a unified left can be established, before people have accepted the inevitability of war, before we are militarily able to organize massive violence, we must depend on limited, selective violence tied to exact political purposes.*
—GEORGE JACKSON, *BLOOD IN MY EYE*

In December 1974, Seattle Police Chief Robert Hanson decided to arm his force with hollow-point bullets, highly lethal projectiles designed to explode inside their target. Local organizers immediately called a demonstration to decry the policy. Ed Mead walked with the crowd, which was supervised by officers on horseback, but he declined to participate in the chants: "Power! Power to the People! It's the People's Power and It's Gettin' Stronger by the Hour!" and "There Ain't Enough Pigs! In the whole world! To Stop the People's Power!"[1]

"Idle threats," Mead disparaged silently. "If we really intend to stop police violence, *we* should be getting hollow-point bullets!" It was one of the last rallies he attended before his next incarceration. "The hollow-nose bullet was the end for me," he told a *Seattle Times* reporter less than a year and a half later while confined in the King County Jail. "I decided that the way you stop them from using hollow-nose bullets is to use hollow-nose bullets in your own gun."[2]

On New Year's Day 1975, the Menominee Warrior Society occupied the unused Alexian Brothers Novitiate property in Gresham, Wisconsin, intending to turn it into a health center. The occupiers were immediately besieged by several hundred law enforcement officers, backed by armed white vigilantes. After an exchange of gunfire, the National Guard was dispatched under strict orders from the governor to enforce a cease-fire.³ Ed supplied a "soldier" by sending Eddie, a friend who had been on the periphery of the Prisoners Union and had participated in the crashing of the American Correctional Association convention, in a van that the Seattle chapter of the American Indian Movement sent to defend the Gresham clinic. By early February, however, when the Seattle contingent arrived, the occupation had been discontinued. (Peltier, who had declined to appear in court in Washington, as he had regarding earlier charges in Wisconsin, *had* arrived in time to participate.)⁴

The most militant protests in Seattle occurred in the primarily black Central District. Tyree Scott, the charismatic leader of the United Construction Workers Association (UCWA), denounced local contractors who received federal money to hire blacks but persistently refused to do so. UCWA offices were only a block from the Dragon House, and Bruce Seidel and his close friend and housemate Michael Steinlauf hung out there often, talking politics and smoking unfiltered cigarettes.

Major black construction worker demonstrations occurred on February 12 and 13. Protesters marched along the old I-90, targeting a work site on Rainier Avenue South and Empire Way South. Seventeen protesters were arrested on the first day, sixty-two the next. The second of these to be brought to trial was Bruce's housemate Michael.⁵

Ed and Bruce didn't get caught, but they certainly broke the law. Like a dozen others, they carried one-by-ones for use either in battling police or, after wrapping them in rags and diesel fuel, as torches. They and a handful of others damaged property belonging to the Redmond-based J. J. Welcome Company, costing the contractor an estimated $200–$300. This was not an isolated case. At roughly the same time as the march, an expensive backhoe was set on fire at a Welcome Company work site on Rainier Avenue. That October, more equipment was severely damaged in Issaquah, Washington, by putting gravel, dirt, and sand in its motor.⁶ On a different UCWA march on a span of I-90 crossing Lake Washington, protesters detached a portion of the floating bridge so that police could not follow.

The UCWA was strong enough to scare the courts. On March 24, thirty-five demonstrators marched into a hearing of some twenty arrestees chanting things like "Fascism in action!" (A reference to the court's behavior, not their own). The irate municipal court judge, T. Patrick Corbett, ordered the protesters "to come forward and be committed to jail." "The intimidation of this court has gone to its limit," he stormed, and he threatened to denounce the conduct of one of the defendant's lawyers, Michael Withey, to the local Bar chapter.⁷ The UCWA was such an intimidating force that one crucial witness—Leroy "Bud" Welcome, owner of the J. J. Welcome Company—declined to testify against those who had damaged his equipment for fear that others would retaliate, costing him even more. In response, UCWA Director Scott complained angrily to the press that Welcome was "making us look like terrorists now."[8]

Both Ed and Bruce considered this an ideal struggle to augment with a little armed force. After one of the breakaway marches, Bruce exclaimed enthusiastically: "These people are ready to take it to the next level!" One contractor had already caved after one of his sites was trashed, refusing to testify against the perpetrators in court on the grounds that he had already suffered enough. Ed thought that escalation was a good idea. He wanted to see it happen, but he was reluctant to participate himself. Still on parole, he ruminated querulously: "Is this one act worth risking everything?"

If Bruce and another unaffiliated radical mind named Eddie were beset by similar doubts, they didn't show it. The two decided to firebomb the headquarters of one of the targeted contractors. Ed, torn, declined to participate. He was at the house of Eddie's girlfriend when Bruce and Eddie departed, and he was there when they came back, grinning and reeking of kerosene.

In the following days, the three men listened to the response to the deed at the social centers of the political community and found it to be overwhelmingly positive: "Right on!" "Cool!"

This swayed Ed, who concluded: "We might be able to go somewhere with this!" He already knew the next issue he wished to support. Tensions between inmates and the administration had long been brewing at the Washington State Penitentiary. On Monday December 30, 1974, the inmate governing body, the Resident Governmental Council (RGC), called a meeting that was attended by nearly 1,100 inmates. The topic of discussion was a list of demands, some of which dated back to 1967, ranging from disciplinary rules to medical care. The inmates were tired of waiting; a sense of urgency was tangible. A prisoner read the list of demands to the inmate body; each was approved unanimously. This culminated in a fiery proclamation: "The administration accepts our demands or we *burn this institution to the ground!* Yea or nay?!" Uproarious applause.[9]

The RGC met with Superintendent B. J. Rhay and two of his assistant superintendents directly after the meeting. "We want a yes on every item on this agenda," RGC President Phil Owens told the superintendent.

"I want your suggestions, but *I* run this institution," Rhay replied.

Concurrent with the negotiations, a handful of inmates delivered on the collective threat. Danny Atteberry, a heroin addict who had been caught robbing supermarkets to support his habit, was one of the organizers. Like a number of young people in the institution, the 27-year-old was a hellion. He and his partner had fled at the prospect of arrest. The police killed his partner, while Atteberry wounded two of the officers with shotgun pellets and took a family of seven hostage before being persuaded to surrender.[10] Carl Harp, the "Bellevue Sniper," who had made such a poor impression on Ed the previous year, was also present. The plan was to divide into two groups of "stand-up cons," who would seize and secure crucial areas to be used as a base for the complete takeover of the institution.

As the RGC members were being rebuffed by Superintendent Rhay, Atteberry and an inmate named Harry Edwards seized the hospital. Simultaneously, Harp and others took five guards hostage in 8-Wing. Prisoners outside the two areas of contention broke into a canteen and stole candy and cigarettes.

The plan went awry as soon as the inmates seized the hostages in the hospital. The disaster was self-inflicted. Another conspirator, Mark LaRue, had vouched for Edwards: "Harry's a stand-up guy who will do right in the hospital." But once the hostages were taken, instead of securing the area against police assault, Edwards rushed to the dispensary and tossed bottles of drugs out the hospital window to prisoners below—approximately 6,755 narcotic pills, a later inventory discovered, in addition to morphine, cocaine, and other hard drugs.[11]

This was a popular move, but taking the drugs incapacitated numerous prisoners and ensured that the planned inmate takeover failed miserably. The druggie potlatch also thoroughly muddled the purity of the inmates' demands. The next day, the *Seattle Times* opportunistically reported: "drugs were the apparent motivation for the take-over." Only further on did the article acknowledge that the takeover had been a coordinated action and was a protest against the unmet grievances of prisoners.

Atteberry held one prison nurse close with a blade to her throat as protection against a police assault. Upon seeing an assembly of some twenty-five members of the institution's riot squad gather outside the hospital windows, the hostages frantically yelled at them to back off. Instead, the officers shattered the glass and jumped in on the hostages. Atteberry began slashing, cutting the nurse, Wanda Goins, and Annie Sporleder, a dental assistant. Two other hostages, Dolores Day, an office worker, and Gene Miller, an x-ray technician, were injured by broken glass. Atteberry and Edwards were quickly disarmed and shuffled off to the Intensive Management Unit (IMU), one of the institution's segregation wings.

The conflict was resolved more peacefully in 8-Wing: the Resident Governmental Council and a legal aid lawyer negotiated the return of the five hostages. The entire institution was placed on "deadlock." A shakedown for drugs was conducted and inmates were watched for signs of overdose. In a move toward normalcy, prisoners were served a hot dinner in their cells on New Year's Day, and many were allowed out to watch a movie.[12]

Initially, Atteberry and Edwards were the only inmates charged in the disturbance. At a news conference on New Year's Eve, the day after the takeover attempt, Superintendent Rhay asserted that "the only identifiable ones causing the trouble were the ones with the hostages." Yet he also attributed blame to the RGC, stating that its agenda had "created a psychological climate for the disturbance."[13] On January 10, Joseph Franklin Green, a member of the RGC, was charged with conspiracy to commit riot in the hospital and placed in segregation.[14]

From the IMU, the takeover organizers sent out a plea for outside support. The typewritten letter was intended for the Portland Trailblazers rookie center Bill Walton, a radical celebrity. Instead, it ended up in Ed's hands. He canvassed the Seattle political community for support: El Centro de la Raza, the Black Panthers, the Left Bank Collective . . . "These people have fought, struggled, sacrificed—*can't we come to their aid?*" he pleaded. All were either too preoccupied or uninterested in helping to organize a demonstration.

Ed decided that a little property destruction might compensate for a lack of public concern. A pipe bomb in the offices of the Division of Corrections would let them know that the demands of prisoners could not be ignored. By attracting some publicity, the bombing would serve as a shortcut to the public-awareness-raising campaign Mead would have liked to have seen take place.

Ed told Jill of his intentions. "This needs to be done, and I'm the person with the skills and inclination to do it. . . . So I'm gonna do it." Jill cared for Ed, but was not a particularly political person. Having a toddler on her hands added another obstacle to continuing the relationship. Ed moved out. The two continued to see each other, but the intervals between their meetings increased.

In the spring of 1975, Ed rented a house for $100 a month in the heart of Georgetown, a working-class industrial area in south Seattle. The house—one of only a few on the slim wedge created by Denver Avenue South and South Lucile Street—was only a block away from the rail yards. There was nothing about it to indicate the politics of the new tenant other than the "Uppity Woman" sticker on the white Volkswagen of a movement woman who occasionally visited Ed for sex and companionship.

Ed discontinued his attendance at the Prairie Fire discussion group and otherwise left off frequenting political meeting places. The WPLU, by that time, had already been disbanded; the prisoners had liked it, but they hadn't made it their own and the union's outside organizers were ready for something else. Roger didn't know his old friend's new address, but he and Ed sometimes saw each other at Jill's.

Ed informed Bruce of his plans. Bruce declared: "I can't let you do this alone. Somebody's gotta look after you!" He dropped out of aboveground work as well, offering little in the way of explanation to other organizers. Rather than cut his ties completely, as Ed had done, he stayed on in the Capitol Hill collective "Dragon House."

Ed's neighbors were an Amerindian man and a white woman named Bonnie. One night the man came home drunk and began beating the woman. Ed charged over, threw him down the back steps, and shouted: "Never come back!" His subsequent friendship with Bonnie helped earn him and Bruce what Ed would later characterize as support from "the people"—those who were not conventionally defined activists or intellectuals—as opposed to "the Left." Soon afterward, Bonnie entered Ed's house without knocking, only to discover him constructing a pipe bomb. "Don't come in here, it's not safe," he warned her sternly. Later he explained his goals to her. "I'd like to help," she offered.

Ed and Bruce decided that the headquarters of the Division of Corrections in Olympia would be an excellent target for their first action. Ed wrote the communiqué, with Bruce piping up sporadically. As they were putting the finishing touches on it, Ed said to Bruce: "Let's give this thing a name."

"Like what?" Bruce inquired.

"George Jackson taught that a serious movement for revolutionary change must contain within it, from the very beginning, the potential for revolutionary violence. He had also promised to 'dog his tormentors from the grave.' I don't think people have been doing enough of that."

"I like it," Bruce nodded, pleased. They signed the document "The George Jackson Brigade."

Ed bought the component parts for the pipe bomb from different stores—lead pipe from a plumbing store, nipples from another—and bought other items as well in order to disguise his intentions. For gunpowder, he drove to the countryside, where people often bought significant quantities in order to blow out old tree stumps.

As instructed by his Bay Area mentors, he was scrupulously careful in the bomb-making process. He used two tables, each covered with a clean white sheet of cloth, and wore rubber gloves, which he carefully disposed of afterward (if a police investigator had gotten hold of them, they would have likely obtained his prints). He arrayed all the component parts before him—a section of six-inch lead pipe, two nipples, three flash bulbs, epoxy cement, electrical wire, a sheet metal screw, an AA battery, the container of gunpowder, a Westclox Travelalarm, and a soldering iron—and wiped each down with alcohol to destroy any prints. He then transferred the pieces to the second table, where the assembly process began. Bruce observed, assuming the role of apprentice.

Ed drilled an eighth-of-an-inch hole through each cap and inserted a wire through each hole. He clipped the minute hand off the clock and set the hour hand to nine. "I'm giving us three hours," he informed Bruce. He then heated the sheet metal screw and inserted it through the face of the clock, soldering one wire to the sheet metal screw, the other to the back metal face of the clock. When the clock hand hit the screw the circuit would be closed, lighting the filament in the bulbs and igniting the gunpowder. After this was complete, he pulled all the connections to test their strength: at best, a loose wire could cause a dud; at worst, a deadly premature detonation. Next, he sealed the holes in the nipples with epoxy cement and tested the electrical circuit with an ohmmeter. In the last step, he filled the pipe three-quarters full with gunpowder: with any less space for expansion, detonation would likely be stifled.

On the night of May 30, 1975, Ed put the pipe bomb in a satchel, deposited it in the trunk of his car, activated the timer, and set off with Bruce for Olympia.

PART IIb

# Consciousness

*Sister Subverter*

# 9

# Woman over the Edge of Crime

*In which Rita Brown's criminal past is related and she is introduced to the political thought of George Jackson in time to understand the significance of his death*

This is how Rita D. Brown once described her origins: "I grew up in Klamath Falls, a redneck Weyerhaeuser town in rural Oregon; my parents fled the poverty of the South a couple of years before I was born. I have one sibling.... My mom was a passive, nagging, battered wife and my dad an uneducated, insecure alcoholic most of my life."[1] As a child she found sanctuary from the violence of her home in the bookmobile that visited her school. One of the first books that made an impression on her was a biography of Captain Jack, or Kintapuasch, the Modoc leader who catalyzed his people in a heroic defense against white immigrants and the Union Army. The Modocs had made their final stand in volcanic craters only twenty miles from her home. Her father once took her there. It was one of his many contradictions: though a racist, he had a deep respect for Native American peoples and their way of life, at least before they became disenfranchised, discouraged, and desperate "drunk Indians."

Captain Jack defined Brown's conception of dignity and became her first role model. She intuitively understood the principle that he embodied: "You can push us only this far, and no further."

In 1964, when Rita was seventeen and in her last year at Klamath Union High School, she and a sixteen-year-old named Janice became lovers. "As far as I knew we were the only queers in the world and I had never heard of a clitoris," she later wrote. The couple had a major run-in with the law after they decided to take Janice's dad's car out on a joyride. The car had been protected with a dummy wire from the alternator to the distributor, but Janice knew where he kept the real one. The pair cruised around all day, burning up nearly a tank of gas.

When Janice's dad got home early and saw that his car wasn't in the garage, he panicked and called the police. Janice and Rita were just returning when sirens intercepted them. At the police station, Janice's dad, embarrassed, dropped the charges. This may have been Brown's first encounter with the police, though a résumé she composed in 1974 contained the line "Prior [to] 1964—Juvenile Arrests" under the header "Arrest & Conviction Record."[2]

The idea that his "little girl" was a "dyke" made Janice's father squirm. That his daughter's apparent girlfriend had criminal proclivities made him angry. The year following the joyride incident, he attempted to entrap the young couple in a compromising position so that he could have Rita, a newly minted adult at eighteen, prosecuted for "statutory licentiousness."

This was 1965 in Klamath Falls, a conservative, primarily white, company town just north of the California border, where Rita and her younger brother Kenny were born. Their dad Frank worked in the Weyerhaeuser lumber mill, processing the Douglas firs, sugar pines, and other assorted evergreens that came in from the dense forests of southern Oregon. Their mother Ina stayed at home. By age five, Rita knew she didn't want to be a housewife like her mother, and after a decade of watching her father drink and rage, she knew it would destroy her to be like him.

The idea of escape presented itself with increasing urgency when Rita entered her late teens. Small-town prejudices—of which the incidents with Janice's father were only the beginning—contributed to the mounting pressure for her to depart. There was also the simple issue of boredom: her after-school job during her senior year of high school was working as a "tray girl" at the Klamath County Nursing Home.

Other than Janice, there was nothing to hold her in Klamath Falls. She won a partial scholarship to the University of Oregon, but, being ignorant of work-study programs and loan options, she believed she still couldn't afford it. Her parents took out a small loan and sent her to a local business college. "They did this because I was good in school and it was all they could do," Brown wrote. She continued: "I transferred to the Salem branch where I graduated with accounting and IBM skills. Almost got kicked out of the dorm for a hot romance with a wonderful womyn; we never made it to bed and she had to stay there so I called them all a bunch of liars and squeaked by." After Rita completed the summer program at the Merritt Davis School of Business, her dad tried to get her a position at the mill, but he was politely declined.

Two enticing coastal cities were conceivable destinations from the hills of southern Oregon: San Francisco and Seattle. Rita didn't know what in particular to expect from either of them: simply *life,* something different, the freedom that would come with anonymity. Her friend Lloyd had moved to Seattle, which made the choice for her. Some eight months later, Janice graduated from high school and joined her girlfriend in the big city.

Rita's first job in Seattle was as an accounting clerk at a bank. She detested the requisite skirts and blouses. After six months, she was offered an opportunity to transfer to the computer department. She would have been the first woman to do so. But, because she was only nineteen, her boss—also a woman—would not give her permission. Impatient with her circumscribed options at the bank, Rita began to apply for other jobs.

Janice, for her part, was chronically unemployed. To ease the constraints of a limited income, the two occasionally shoplifted items at downtown department stores. Janice stashed desirable clothing items under her own clothes while Rita acted as lookout. On December 18, 1967, they were caught. Each was sentenced to a year's probation and some community work. Their drama-prone relationship ended shortly thereafter.

The Post Office hired Rita as a clerk. When she completed the probationary period and was granted a permanent position, she threw away her dresses. One day her co-worker Claude—a white Korean War vet, thirty-five years old to Brown's twenty, confided: "I know what you are. I'm one too."

Claude took her to 614 First Avenue, a gay bar in Pioneer Square, a dilapidated part of town near the docks. This six-square-block area bordering Chinatown contained cheap hotels, black and Indian bars, and half a dozen gay bars—including one just for lesbians. Rita was still under age, but the vet got her in. In the bars, for the first time, she found a community of women who loved women. "I became a working class bar butch dyke," she recollected. "I drank a lot, got even tougher and went to work every day for over a year." Brown came out on the job, a move made easier by the fact that "[t]here were other queers there and we were pretty strong and took care of one another even though we never organized as such."

Rita had first discovered alcohol at age nine and first blacked out at fifteen. After definitively breaking up with Janice, she briefly moved into a single-occupancy apartment and once again became a black-out drunk. In the bars, she met Pinky and Sandy. Sandy was pregnant and Pinky, who later changed her sex and married a man who had become a female, played daddy. Rita moved in with the couple. They introduced her to DJ, a flamboyant femme who was the only biological woman performing in the drag shows at 614. Brown fancied that DJ, with her red hair, freckles, and vibrant countenance, resembled a shapelier version of Janis Joplin.

DJ was an insider who'd known the people she partied with since childhood. She enticed Rita, who was pleasantly surprised by her attention. "She chased me till I caught her," is how Brown described their courtship.[3] Dating DJ catapulted Rita from being a "dumbfounded hick," as her later convict self considered her uninitiated self to have been, into the in crowd at the bar. As DJ's partner, Rita always had her own table close to the stage when her girlfriend was performing. As the resident butch, she watched over any of the drag queens' valuables that they cared to deposit. Any one of the queens who wanted to take a break and be admired by the crowd would sit with Rita.

Rita turned this newfound popularity into a business opportunity. She began to sell weed, acid, and occasionally mescaline. Her supplier was an outrageous queen. The profit margin was good: she paid $200 a kilo for the marijuana and sold it for $10 an ounce, making a profit of over $100, while keeping plenty for herself. Mescaline, which she cut 50/50 with Nestle's Quik, she provided cheaply: $5 for a "double ought" pill two people could share comfortably.

Rita and DJ moved in together, initiating a consciousness-expanding period for both of them. DJ guided her caringly through her first acid trip—on pure Orange Sunshine—and many subsequent ones. When DJ didn't want Rita to go to work, she spiked her coffee with it. They also engaged in threesomes. Rita became acquainted with the countercultural lifestyle.

The two even made a foray into making a queer family when they brought three young gay boys into their home. Driving home one night after the bars closed at 2 A.M., Rita and DJ, no more than twenty-one themselves, spotted the young men, who appeared to be sixteen or seventeen, hustling carelessly on a corner. Rita called them over to her car. "You're crazy. Who are you? What are you doing out here?" DJ invited the kids into the car and they went to ToeMain Tommy's, a late-night joint whose name was a play on ptomaine poisoning, and she and Rita listened to the boys' stories. All three were runaways from the Minneapolis–St. Paul area. Two had escaped from a psych ward in which they'd been confined for being effeminate—one for a period of two years. The other, who came from a more privileged background, quit school to move in with an older male hairdresser. He was later picked up on the street by the police for hanging out with his two escapee friends. While institutionalized, the boys had been subjected to all the negative conditioning techniques in use at the time, including shock treatments and electric probes to their genitals. The basic cognitive function of one had been disrupted by repeated electroshock treatment. He could write his name. He could count to ten, sometimes.

The effeminate trio lived on and off with Rita and DJ for a few years, crashing with other people when it was a desirable option, but always returning to Rita and DJ's place. Rita and DJ's hospitality gave the young newcomers a chance to orient in the scene safely. Two enrolled in cosmetology school and soon received their licenses.

Two years into the relationship with Rita, DJ became uncertain if it was what she wanted. She didn't *not* want Rita, but she wanted other things as well. DJ was a dope fiend who wanted to clean herself up, but when her previous girlfriend, San, with whom she had used to shoot heroin, got out of jail, DJ's resolve wavered. Rita put DJ up in a Pioneer Square hotel and instructed: "Figure out what you want. If it's me, call." DJ called a month later and Rita picked her up.

Rita stayed at the Post Office for three and a half years, enjoying the physicality of the work: unloading railroad cars, unpacking bags, sorting mail onto belts. Later she was transferred to the distribution center, a hub for the Pacific Northwest located down in the old industrial district on Alaskan Way South. This position presented Rita with opportunities for illicit self-advancement. Cold cash passed through her hands in envelopes. She decided that pocketing some wasn't a bad idea. Although she considered it unethical to take tenants' rent money—her mill town upbringing imbued her with a strong *us* and *them* class consciousness—she did occasionally grab dough landlords mailed to the bank.

The Post Office noticed a discrepancy. On February 17, 1971, Postal Inspector Merlin L. DeVere prepared a test for Brown: three envelopes containing cash were sent through her station. They entered and didn't come out. The same day, she was stopped leaving the Post Office. The marked bills were discovered in her pocket.

DJ freaked out when Rita was arrested for the Post Office theft. Rita had been in court several times for failing to pay the moving-violation fines that her ratty car magnetically attracted, but this was obviously different. DJ was concerned for her partner; as an emotional and financial dependent, she was also scared for herself.

On March 9, a federal grand jury charged Brown with three counts of possession of stolen mail, one for each of the letters stolen. The letter addressed to Wayside Chapel contained $9.50; the one to Pan Pacific Collection Agency $8.35. The amount contained in the one to the Commercial Bank of Seattle wasn't disclosed.[4]

On March 15, in front of U.S. District Court Judge William T. Beeks, Brown plead guilty to one count of mail theft. A public defender represented her; Assistant U.S. Attorney Jerald E. Olson prosecuted. Brown signed a document stating in part: "being a postal service employee, to wit, a regular clerk, [I] did unlawfully detain, delay, open, secrete and destroy a letter and mail entrusted to [me] which had come into [my] possession which was intended to be conveyed by mail."

Judge Beeks looked critically at Brown and her girlfriend DJ who was sitting in the stands behind her, and pronounced the sentence: "a year and a day."[5] Sentences of a year or less could be served locally: the extra day meant that Brown was going to the federal penitentiary. The nearest federal correctional institute for women was Terminal Island in San Pedro, California. Contending that she could parole out of prison sooner than she could be released from jail, the judge later claimed: "By giving her that extra day I make it possible for her to serve a much shorter sentence than she would if it had been a year."[6]

Brown didn't buy it. In the federal jail she would have been able to earn money in a work release program and apply for weekend leaves, early release, and placement in a halfway house. None of these options existed in the penitentiary; she would be lucky to see the parole board once.

Brown, increasingly out regarding her gender orientation and standoffish when confronted with what she conceived to be prejudice, interpreted the sentence as retaliation for being lesbian.

"You old prick," she fumed quietly. "Anyone who goes to the penitentiary does more time, and anyone would rather stay in their own city than get sent to another state!"

## TERMINAL ISLAND

*The very first time, it was like dying. . . . Capture, imprisonment, is the closest to being dead that one is likely to experience in this life.*

—GEORGE JACKSON, *SOLEDAD BROTHER*

A U.S. marshal and his wife escorted Brown down to Terminal Island on a commercial flight. It was Rita's first time on an airplane.

The complex of old barracks that constituted the women's prison was on a peninsula past a military base and the men's portion of the prison. While being bussed in, Rita caught a pleasant glimpse of the sea. It was the San Pedro Channel, coursing between the California coast and Catalina Island. She then entered the small Admission and Orientation (A&O) building in which new inmates were confined for a thirty-day period.

In A&O, Brown was placed in a cell—clean, innocuous, small but not cramped—with another inmate named Brown. The woman was an African American dope fiend with close-cropped, bleached hair who was in for boosting to support her heroin habit. She bragged: "I can fit a TV between my legs and walk outta a store with it!" and used a rolled-up blanket to demonstrate her technique for stealing fur coats. Rita made sure her pallid cellmate ate properly while the junkie, in return, hipped Rita to penitentiary survival skills. The two passed their interminable period in bureaucratic limbo playing cards, something Rita's father had taught her.

In the general population, Rita was assigned to a housing unit on the second floor of the administrative building. The thirty-odd inmates she shared the floor with were a mix of short-termers, long-termers, and people on work release. Each was assigned a cot in a cubicle with a door, toilet, sink, and dresser-desk. "This feels like a toilet stall," Rita observed sourly when she first stepped into her private compartment. "Two toilet stalls put together," she decided in a second, more generous, appraisal. A clipboard on one of the walls was the designated area for personalization.

Prisoners were allowed one phone call a month. After three or four months, DJ started missing their phone dates. Rita began calling Ellen, a Filipina dyke friend from the Post Office, with whom she also corresponded. Although not a lover, Ellen proved to be the better friend than DJ.

Brown was assigned to the landscape maintenance crew. The Southern California climate was completely alien. "It's hot as fuck down here!" she thought, having never previously been this far south. She cut the legs off her pants and the sleeves off her shirt. While her own comfort was her primary concern, the tough individualization of her clothing flagged her as a butch, a desirable minority in the institution of sexually deprived females.

After a few weeks, the supervising officer stopped showing up. For two and a half months, the inmates continued to do their work so that they could be outdoors without being harassed by "correctional officers" (C.O.s), as the Bureau of Prisons

(BoP) dictated that their guards be called. Brown worked with an older white woman who read people's fortunes in playing cards in exchange for cigarettes. The woman mowed; Rita watered.

Together they ranged across "the campus" (another deceptively innocuous term imposed by the BoP) from the administration building to the drug offenders' dormitory. One day they paused in front of a fence that barred the view of the ocean. The psychic mower introduced Brown to meditation. "Stare at the fence until it disappears," she instructed, a cigarette dangling from her mouth, "until all you can see is the sea.... That's meditation." Rita practiced diligently. Before she left the penitentiary she was able to do it.

In the fall, the prison hired several new guards. Three of the women were ex-military and, though closeted, were obviously dykes.

One of these women, Officer B., was assigned to order around the landscape crew. She was astounded to discover that the inmates had continued to do their jobs without supervision. She wrote them letters of commendation, and requested that they be given back pay—$5 for each of the months they had worked.

The administration paid everyone but Brown. They sent Officer B. to tell her that they would not pay her because they didn't like the way she dressed.

Brown was irritated by the order: by the administration, which, perversely, employed a dyke to tell her not to be a dyke, and by the person in front of her, whose allegiances were sufficiently confused for her to carry out the directive. Brown huffed: "Tell them I'll dress the way I wanna dress. Not even my momma tells me how to dress anymore... and I know why they sent *you* to tell me!" All inmates were officially sexless. Butch dress not only forced the existence of inmate sexuality into public view but highlighted its ostensibly perverted, homosexual form. Brown, though she did not engage in any sexual activity in the institution, refused to change her ways for the comfort of heterosexist prison bureaucrats.

There were ten men to every woman in prison at Terminal Island. Half of the women were in on drug charges—many were "mules" caught importing drugs into Los Angeles International Airport. The male drug offenders were channeled into a program established by the Narcotic Addict Rehabilitation Act (NARA) of 1966, which was part of the rehabilitation ideal cresting around the country. The program included a "therapeutic community" with its own dorm, which was known as the "NARA unit." Psychology students and their professors from colleges throughout the LA area facilitated "Group." On paper, the program wasn't mandatory, but prisoners knew that if they didn't go, they would be docked points on the invisible ledgers maintained by the C.O.s.

The administration considered the male drug offenders' counseling group successful enough to begin a similar program once a week for all the female inmates.

Though the organizers of the sessions assured the prisoners that everything they said in Group was confidential, the prisoners knew the professionals and students immediately divulged any information they had gleaned to the C.O.s and prison administrators. Rita and a black inmate named Pearl both checked out the counselors cautiously. They each threw out questions and observed people's responses. When the results proved unsatisfactory, they declined to participate. In contrast to other prisoners, who liked to jabber, Rita and Pearl kept quiet. They did decide, however, to speak to each other.

Pearl was in an underground black women's reading group and began bringing Rita books. One of these was *Soledad Brother*, a collection of prison letters from George Jackson, a black communist accused of killing a white guard. Jackson, now an inmate at San Quentin State Prison, was facing the death penalty. His words to his mother, little brother, defenders, and supporters, vacillating between poignancy and rage, depict his development from a child who "loved people" and "understood from the beginning that the end purpose of life was simply to live, experience, contribute, connect, to gratify the body and the mind" into a damaged adult, who detailed his own advanced state of spirit death with clinical detachment.[7] Of his time in prison, Jackson wrote: "It has destroyed me as a person, a human being that is, but it was sudden, it was a sudden death, it seems like ten days rather than ten years."[8]

Brown had only encountered the defiance in Jackson's prose in one other man: Captain Jack. There was an added quality about Jackson's writing that moved her: his capacity for love while trapped in a "concrete grave."

Jackson's discussion of the psychological impact of American racism prompted Brown to recall the few experiences she had had with black people. In high school, she had become friends with the daughter of an Air Force pilot stationed nearby; theirs was the only black family in the neighborhood and, being military, soon moved. Family visits to Arkansas were more disturbing. One time she was walking with her boy cousins when a black woman, hands full of groceries, approached with her children. Rita stepped off the sidewalk to let the woman pass. Her cousins razzed Rita incessantly about this show of deference. The civil rights movement was only a spectacle on the TV news, which produced bigoted jeers from her father. On her visits to the South, Rita could not comprehend "colored only" drinking fountains and other manifestations of de jure segregation.

In the penitentiary, Rita played cards with a group of black women. She was respectful but not a fool. When one of the players encouraged her to smuggle drugs in through the visiting room, she replied bluntly: "That would be stupid." Being caught would subject her, a short-termer, to an increased sentence, while succeeding would open her up to the machinations of the institution's illicit drug trade. As a compromise, she snuck in candy, which she shared.

One evening, Rita passed the cafeteria and heard jazz. "That sounds really good!" she thought. She followed the arpeggiated shouts of the soloist into a room off the main dining hall and stepped in. She immediately realized that she was the only white person. "Am I even supposed to fuckin' be here?" she wondered.

An old black butch probed calmly: "You like this music?"

"Yeah!"

"Then sit down and be quiet."

She did, and she came back. Each night of the week, the administration turned this cafeteria adjunct over to prisoners of different ethnicities for them to listen to the music of their culture. The jazz aficionados were primarily heroin addicts from LA. Once a week they got high and chilled out. Brown had known that jazz existed, but she had had no idea of just how far out Coltrane could go. Records by the Ramsey Lewis Trio, Dexter Gordon, and Miles and Satchmo were supplemented by live performers considerate enough to enliven the inmates' existence. The extraordinary jazz vocalist Abbey Lincoln performed at Terminal Island during Brown's term, as did the funky rock band Hot Tuna, who were accompanied by Papa John Creech on an electric violin.

In recognition of Brown's expanding consciousness, one of the women in the bridge-playing group invited her into the dayroom to watch a PBS program on black male prisoners. Soon after, devastating news about George Jackson arrived. On August 21, 1971, he and a small band of comrades carried out an escape attempt. Jackson was shot down by a tower guard before he reached the institution's outer gate. The placement of bullets made it apparent that after being wounded, he had been executed at close range.[9]

In observance of the death of "Comrade George"—as prisoners and outside politicos alike warmly called this symbol of black male revolutionary potency—the women prisoners at Terminal Island stopped work for a day. They learned that the female inmates at the federal correctional institute across the country in Alderson, West Virginia, did the same, observing a day of silence upon receiving news of Jackson's death. The women were in the midst of a protest against a dictatorial parole board when the news of the Attica uprising hit. The inmates immediately declared a total strike, refusing to return to their dormitories and "cottages." When their demands on the issues of parole, better wages, and access to mail, and treatment facilities for drug addicts were rejected out of hand, they rioted until they were tear-gassed and forced back to their cottages. Three women escaped from one of the enclosed housing units and contacted the press. In retaliation for the rebellion, the Alderson administration transferred sixty-six women to the male youth reformatory in Ashland, Kentucky. Additional guards were brought in to maintain order.[10]

Ahead of parole, Brown was enrolled in a work release program at a Salvation Army store in San Pedro. The prison drove the inmates to the edge of the federal property and permitted them to take a bus into town, provided that they report back by a certain hour. Brown worked with a couple of old ladies, who were friendly despite her convict status. The women at the store culled donated clothes, while the men sorted and carried furniture. Because she was fast and strong, Brown was quickly placed at the front of the clothes line. She was only there for six weeks. During that time the older women put together a trunk for her, filled with clothes and bedding, and told her, "Come by and get this on your way out."

Before leaving the pen, Brown found satisfaction in exposing one of the prison administration's misdeeds. The incident centered on a woman Rita had gone out on work release with. She was in a counseling group that met in the men's dormitory. Like many other primarily heterosexual prisoners, she outsmarted C.O.s in order to be intimate with a male prisoner. The C.O.s responded to the inmates' duplicity by harassing women for petty infractions like not wearing bras. When a proclamation came down from the administration—"Those without bras are not permitted to leave the dormitory to go to Group"—inmates returned to the checkpoint with their bras on over their shirts. This particular woman became pregnant and, before she began showing, attempted an abortion with a knitting needle. Brown had never given the woman much thought until she learned that she had bled to death in her cell.

An FBI investigation team invaded the institution after the discovery of the corpse. Agents came on strong, coercing prisoners into identifying the inseminator and any female inmates who might have helped with the illicit operation.

Brown refused to cooperate with the investigation. When she was called in for interrogation and asked if she knew the deceased woman, she replied combatively: "Yeah, I knew her. We rode the bus together out of the pen every morning. So the fuck what?"

The day after the FBI invasion, Rita and a young white dyke named Carolyn on a similar work schedule breakfasted together. Carolyn's girlfriend, Mace, lived in the NARA unit, where the death had occurred. Mace was a biker—one of the prison's most visible subgroups, with their confrontational machismo and leather fetishism. Since bikers, all white, commonly derided blacks, Brown had kept her distance from both Mace and Carolyn in the past. In this situation, however, Mace provided interesting information about the ongoing crackdown.

Work-release prisoners were the only ones who could get out of the institution. Brown and her co-conspirator, noting they hadn't seen anything in the press about the death, made a plan to leak the news. They drafted a paragraph to read to the press. At the first opportunity, each would go to a public telephone. Rita would call one paper and Carolyn another. They did this the following day, and the prisoner's death and the subsequent investigation were on the front page of local newspapers the day after. Before reporting back to the penitentiary, Rita and Carolyn stopped by a bar to celebrate.

# 10

# Women's Work

*In which Brown is released from prison
and becomes a prison activist*

> *I do not feel that in any way I am a menace to society, and will never again see fit to commit any criminal acts.*
> —RITA D. BROWN IN A LETTER TO U. S. DISTRICT COURT JUDGE W. T. BEEKS, JULY 27, 1971

As her time at Terminal Island ran down, Brown's mind turned from the daily grind of the institution to her life after release. The most obvious question mark was DJ, who had been her girlfriend for three years at the time of her incarceration. Though they had never broken up, DJ was a less-than-avid correspondent.

Brown had known it would be difficult for the relationship to survive a period of forced separation but, she consoled herself when she was sent to prison, "I'm not gone that long."

Brown's question about the status of the relationship was answered ten days before she was released from Terminal Island, when she received a "Dear Jane" letter from DJ. "Goddammit!" Brown cursed. She left the prison in April 1972, with five months of parole still ahead of her.

DJ was first and foremost in her mind. "I'm gonna clear this up!" Brown resolved. She called DJ en route to Seattle and declared: "I want to see you. If you have something to tell me, tell me to my face. If you don't come to see me, I'm gonna kick in your damn door." DJ ambivalently acquiesced.

Never one to be alone, DJ was living with San, whom she'd been with on and off since San got out of jail. They shot heroin together. San supported the two of them by hustling, turning tricks for people with peculiar interests, such as being shat on, which she liked because it paid well and she wasn't compelled to have intercourse with her clients.

Rita and DJ took San's old Cadillac to Rainier Valley, where they stayed in a hotel for a weekend. They had sex, but DJ didn't let Rita harbor any illusions about being a couple again. "I'm strung out but I'm doing what I wanna be doing ... I can't do it with you but I can do it with San."

Lacking direction, Rita rented an inexpensive studio apartment on Capitol Hill, close to DJ and San's modest apartment (which, Rita observed cattily, was smaller than the one Rita and DJ had shared). The couple's place was furnished with some of Rita's furniture and her stereo.

In the first few months of this proximity, DJ came to stay with Rita after one of her periodic fights with San. A few days later, with the first pangs of dope sickness, heroin called and DJ returned. The cycle continued, more distressing to Brown each time. At one point, desperate, Rita told DJ, referring to heroin, "If you like that shit so much, shoot me up."

"I can't," DJ refused. "I love you too much."

"My Scorpio evil was rising," Brown recollects. Dark fantasies crystallized into a double homicide plot. It would be easy enough to do: she could overdose them both and no one would know. Rita alarmed herself because she believed she could actually execute such a plan. Lurching to her senses, she quit Capitol Hill and got an apartment in West Seattle, a fifteen-minute drive away.

Each weekend she stayed in the bars until she collapsed. Two queer men befriended her and got into the routine of taking her home after closing time. They would drag Rita to her car, with one driving her home while the other followed behind.

After a few months, Rita tired of this depressing routine. When someone would say the wrong thing to her while she was under the influence, she would smash something or take a swing at them. The immediate prospect of becoming like her father—not only a drunk, but a violent one—chastened her. Rita hadn't smoked a joint until she was twenty-one, but after coming to the city, she consistently fell in with drug addicts. She realized she would have become one herself had she grown up in a city.

Sobered by this epiphany, Brown proceeded to get her life in order. She went to the Department of Vocational Rehabilitation (DVR), where she was certified as a "social deviant" eligible for rehabilitation money. She took the aptitude tests demanded of her and her scores were high enough to make a positive impression on one of the staffers.

"You could be a doctor or a lawyer," he commented.

"You need money for that, don't you?" she responded pointedly. He didn't deny it.

Her first job was in a kennel. The owner treated her terribly, and she soon quit, but not before picking up Gi Gi, a cute German co-worker on methadone. The two dated for a year. She also acquired a Doberman named Kazam. Her second job was at a center for the blind on Beacon Hill. The DVR then paid her tuition at a private printing school in downtown Seattle.

Rita didn't have a car, so she moved to the Central District, which had direct public transportation to downtown. At the printing school, Rita met Jean, who lived in a lesbian feminist collective. One day Jean invited Rita over. A brightly colored poster of a frizzy yellow newly hatched chicken caught Rita's eye. The image was framed by the declaration: "Women Aren't Chicks." Rita, like most others in her circle, commonly called women "chicks." At that moment, however, she realized: "Chicks are just little fluffballs that get stepped on and die or become hens that lay eggs that people eat." She resolved not to use the word any longer.

Rita completed the printing program but quickly hit the glass ceiling at local copy shops, which remained completely closed to women. She returned to DVR and complained, "I can't get a job." The man who had been impressed with her test scores informed her, "There's a new program starting up at Seattle Central Community College. It's a two-year printing course. I can sign you up, if you like." Rita readily consented.

In addition to tuition, DVR provided her with a $200 monthly living stipend, cash for books, and an annual supplement for clothing. Combining this with food stamps, cheap rent, and a quiet return to drug dealing, Rita was able to live comfortably.

In sharp contrast to the demographics of the city as a whole, Seattle Central Community College (SCCC) was remarkably diverse. The majority of the student population was white, a quarter African American, while Asians, Pacific Islanders, and Native Americans were visibly present as well. Rita was exposed to perspectives she had not previously encountered. In her psychology class, the white professor had his students take Robert Lewis Williams III's "Black Intelligence Test of Cultural Homogeneity," popularly known as the "black IQ test," which was as culturally loaded in favor of African Americans as the standard IQ test was toward whites. Predictably, all the black students did well, and the white ones performed poorly. Of the whites Rita did best, because she could catch pop culture references like those to Chubby Checker, Martha and the Vandellas, Little Richard, and Diana Ross. She had been exposed to soul, as well as blues and jazz, in the bars and the penitentiary.

Rita wore a denim jacket around campus that had DYKE spelled out on the back in pink rhinestones. When one of her fellow students, a young black man, demanded, "Why you put that on your jacket?" Rita exclaimed: "In case you didn't know!" They laughed and exchanged experiences of prejudice.

Rita was pleased to discover that the college had a "Prisoners' Coalition" that offered services similar to those provided to other disadvantaged members of the student population, such as women and people of color.

Prison activism in Seattle found its best institutional support at the University of Washington campus, known as UW, or "the Dub." Rita first visited the Dub campus with some of Jean's housemates for a 1973 International Women's Day celebration. One workshop was on women in prison. The presenter was a Quaker social worker who expounded on the plight of poor women. Rita's irritation with the patronizing tone of the presenter swelled until it popped. She interjected: "You don't know what it's like in jail 'cause you've never been in jail!"

"It sounds like you should be running this workshop," the presenter retorted.

"Okay!" Rita agreed. She completed the workshop by recounting her impressions of the women she'd encountered at Terminal Island and the problems they faced. Then she opened the workshop up for discussion.

The UW campus had a program that received men on parole from the Washington State Penitentiary at Walla Walla. The men lived in a dormitory on campus and attended classes. Rita investigated the program and found the participants well-informed and politically conscious.

A female political science student who worked with the prisoners invited Rita to one of the convicts' meetings. The men made paid presentations in colleges in the Seattle area. Since they didn't have anyone to present the perspectives of women prisoners, they asked Rita to join them. She began speaking about women prisoners at schools in the Seattle area and got paid for the presentations.

A number of the parolees were colorful characters. One, "Nick the Greek," ran a prison activist organization at SCCC connected to the Prisoners Coalition. He was a swanky man in a gray pin-striped sharkskin suit. In his presentations he would proclaim: "I've been in prison. I'm doing a 40-year parole." He'd warm to the subject, then jam a wrist into the air dramatically, revealing a handcuff with the chain clipped off. "I keep this here to remind myself that I am not free. I wear this handcuff always to remind myself how much time I have to do, and how close I always am to prison."

Nick worked in the Drama Department at SCCC and organized a group there that took college students to the Washington State Reformatory in Monroe to visit prisoners. Rita participated, but became wary of Nick when she noticed his special interest in displaying cute young women to prisoners. A nagging thought asserted itself: "How come we're only visiting male prisoners? Why isn't there a group for women? This dick is showing off his ability to get women to these brothers inside!" she concluded.

Rita acted on the impulse to create an organization for female prisoners with an intellectually oriented, committed politico named Therese Coupez. Therese worked as a secretary in the Drama Department at SCCC while majoring in political science at the Dub. Her class background was mixed. Her father, Victor, had worked his way up from a clerk to vice president of a bank, siring three children along the way with Therese's mother, Nancy. When Therese, the oldest child, was about twelve, her father deserted them. Her mother held the family together.

A strikingly bright child, Therese skipped two grades and entered college on a UW scholarship. A traumatic experience as a teenager impacted her consciousness.

In high school, she babysat for Edwin Pratt, the executive director of the Seattle Urban League. Pratt played a major role in the desegregation of Seattle neighborhoods and schools, and, in the process, developed powerful enemies. On the night of January 25, 1969, in response to a snowball hitting his house, Pratt opened the front door and caught a shotgun blast to the face at close range. He died instantly. This disturbing end to the city's most visible civil rights leader came only nine months after the assassination of Martin Luther King Jr. Therese had looked after Miriam, the five-year-old daughter of Edwin and his wife Bettye, the previous night, and had been slated to work for the Pratts the night of the murder.[1] The crime was never solved.[2]

At UW, Therese was influenced by an anti-war political science professor, Phil Meranto, an avowed Marxist whom the university had hired in June 1971, then threatened to fire after discovering he had been arrested at protests at the University of Illinois. The dispute made the professor a campus cause célèbre.[3] At one time Therese rented a room in the house Meranto shared with his wife, Barb Seeley, proprietor of the socialist feminist bookstore Red & Black.

Rita and Therese began talking and dating. They shared an interest in prison issues and a desire to work with women prisoners. This sisterhood impulse coincided with the opening of the state's first correctional institution exclusively for women, which was located in Purdy, only an hour by car from Seattle. Throughout the entire preceding history of the state, female prisoners had been housed in an afterthought annex at the Washington State Penitentiary in Walla Walla.

Purdy, in contrast, was a national innovation. It displayed a "campus" layout and had pretensions to penological enlightenment. Apartments were set aside from the primary dormitories for well-behaved women nearing their time of parole. These women were also eligible to pursue off-campus educational opportunities. Rita, Therese, and a couple of their companions discovered that several of these women prisoners were attending the community college in Tacoma. They drove down to meet them and discovered that they were lesbians. They all became friends. From that point on, Rita and Therese drove down to Tacoma once a week and, through these new contacts, contacted a lesbian couple at Purdy, Mickey and Kathy, whom they proceeded to visit.

In the summer of 1973, Brown and Coupez formed a group to support women prisoners. They called it Women Out Now (WON). Learning from Rita's disaffection with social-worker types, rather than providing what they thought the women needed, the organization asked the women themselves what they wanted. Echoing the most famous phrase from Martin Luther King Jr.'s "Letter from a Birmingham Jail," WON's "Constitution," written in February 1974 to satisfy a legal obligation in attaining nonprofit status, declared: "We recognize that convicts must define their own needs and the pace at which they move." The document continued: "Our function in relation to convicts is to provide advice at times and support always, though

FIGURE 6. Rita Brown in the early 1970s. Photo courtesy of Rita "Bo" Brown.

not uncritical support; and to help prisoners recognize their power to demand change as a united body."[4]

According to a funding proposal dated November 30, 1974, the group sought to "assist women in prison in Washington State in their fight for control of their own lives." This was only a first step in a revolutionary process. "The ultimate goal is the abolishment of prisons and the full restoration of all human and civil rights."

The document explained: "Prisoners historically have been among the most oppressed and forgotten segments of this society. In America, to be a convict and a woman is double oppression. Women in prison are treated as children and force-fed dependency and regression. They suffer mistreatment and powerlessness."

Homophobia compounded this "double oppression," "[b]ecause lesbians are considered 'criminals' or at least 'sick' by most of society simply on the basis of their sexuality." For this reason, "a large part of our services, especially those requiring financial assistance and legal help, have been provided to lesbians at Purdy." This focus made them unique: "WON is the ONLY group relating to the prison which includes recognition of and a commitment to struggle around womens' [sic] oppression as lesbians," the prospectus asserted.[5]

Mickey and Kathy filed a petition with the Purdy administration to form a Gay Activists Alliance. The headquarters of the Department of Corrections in Olympia refused to process it. On Rita and Therese's next visit to the women's prison, the gay inmates informed their outside sisters that they had been stonewalled.

"Give it to us!" Rita exclaimed. "We can help sue the state on your behalf." She

FIGURE 7. Rita Brown. Photo courtesy of Rita "Bo" Brown.

FIGURE 8. Illustration accompanying an article on the Leftist Lezzies coalition of gay women activists, *Northwest Passage*, August 30–September 19, 1976, 19.

stored the papers in the Prisoners Coalition office, reasoning that it would be more secure than the collective in which she and Therese then lived. The "10th Street Collective"—a two-story Victorian so named for its location on Tenth and Mercer, just a block off Broadway, Capitol Hill's main drag—often hosted political meetings and, as a consequence, was likely monitored by law enforcement. Brown and Therese informed the women's community about the campaign to form a lesbian prisoners' organization. In the spring of 1974, they organized a fund-raising party at the Coffee Coven that brought in $30 and another at the gay bar Shelly's Leg that netted $150.[6]

As a result of the organization's new visibility, the women students who had been visiting male prisoners at Monroe with Nick approached Rita and Therese: "We're sick of going to the men's prison, all they want to do is cop a feel. Nobody wants to talk to us at all. They're a bunch of dicks. We'd like to go to the women's prison and see what that's like." The students met Mickey and Kathy and, through them, other female prisoners. To his chagrin, Nick couldn't persuade the young women to return with him to the men's institution in Monroe.

Nick distributed the paychecks for the Drama Department staff. One Thursday, in retaliation for what he perceived as poaching on his private preserve, he withheld Therese's paycheck. He didn't show up at the college on Friday, and didn't answer phone calls. "Fuck him," Rita declared to Therese after a fruitless wait. "We're going to his house."

Nick invited Rita into his house, where their conversation quickly escalated into a screaming match. Nick's ego-driven pettiness was subverting the politics he espoused, Rita contended. Her temper, short before incarceration, was now combustible.

"I'm the boss!" Nick insisted. "People come get their checks from *me!*"

"We've never done it before, but now we do something for ourselves and you wanna be the man!" Rita shouted back.

"I don't *have* your damn check, and I wouldn't give it to you if I did!"

"Gimme the check or you and I are goin' out into the street!" Rita bellowed.

"C'mon," Nick invited. "Let's go outside."

The challenges and counterchallenges continued. Rita interrupted: "Gimme the fucking check or, fuck the street, I'll take you right here in your house." With a little more complaining, Nick handed over the check.

As she left the house, Nick screamed at her, *"Don't come back!"*

"I don't wanna come back! And nobody else wants to come back! Fuck you, you little worm motherfucker!"

The following Monday, Rita and Therese went to Myra, a secretary for the professor who managed Therese, to inform her, "We want to start a women's prison group on this campus." Myra got the keys to the office of the Prisoners Coalition so that they could retrieve their files. They discovered that Nick had disappeared them. Without documentation, they were unable to pursue the complaint of discrimination against the administration of Purdy. They realized that the time had come to get an office of their own.

## 11

# Inside Out

## *On the Activities of the Women Out Now Prison Project*

> *Into the prison we smuggled uncensored knowledge resources, revolutionary ideals, and unqualified support for women trying to define themselves in a confusing, hurtful situation.*
>
> —KARLENE FAITH, UNRULY WOMEN

Rita, Therese, and a handful of like-minded people in the women's community publicized the first meeting of the Women Out Now Prison Project primarily by word of mouth. They announced it at the Seattle Liberation Coalition, an umbrella organization of the Seattle Left, and posted flyers in local schools. Some thirty women showed up. They heard a rap about the conditions of women prisoners—psychological as well as physical—and were encouraged to explore conditions for themselves by making direct contact with inmates.

In order to secure access to Purdy, the organization played on the rehabilitational pretensions of the Washington Department of Corrections. "These women are going to be released to the community," a WON representative contended. "They need to know what resources will be available to them." The administration conceded. Organization members made their first sanctioned visit in November 1973.

WON held regularly scheduled meetings with the administration of Purdy to facilitate the program. After the first meeting, Rita decided she couldn't attend any others: her temper was a time bomb, and if she popped, the prison might investigate her, discover her criminal record, and use it as an excuse to close the program. As it was, the prison was in its first year and wasn't particularly wary of outsiders. Still, WON organizers quickly got the idea that the administration's dislike of them was in direct proportion to their popularity with the inmates.

WON set out to organize an event for the women each month, but there was so much enthusiasm on the part of presenters and prisoners that they staged more than twice as many events as originally planned. The speakers were diverse but all shared an oppositional perspective. A self-defense instructor with the Feminist

Karate Union elicited wall-shaking "Hee*yahs!*" from her students as they practiced striking, alarming the supervising guard and the administration; Arlene Eisen Bergman, an anti-war organizer who had relocated to Seattle from the East Coast, lectured on women's issues as they related to Vietnam;[1] and Janine Bertram, coordinator of the local chapter of Call Off Your Old Tired Ethics (COYOTE), a prostitutes' organization, facilitated a discussion of the sex industry and the need for decriminalization. Radical therapists, members of the Seattle Lesbian Resource Center, and the radical feminist puppeteers Puppet Power, came as well.[2] By the fall of 1974 representatives from over thirty organizations had visited the institution, most of them doing presentations. The programs were popular with the inmates, who discussed them enthusiastically with one another. Participation increased steadily, while a politically conscious core of potential organizers developed. To keep the connections made in person alive, WON found outside correspondents for inmates.

Seeking to awaken and channel prisoners' agency, WON organizers asked their inside counterparts, "What can we do to help?" The most common reply was, "Bring us visitors. I want to see my kids." To counteract the isolation of incarceration, WON began organizing car trips from Seattle. Visitors came primarily from the Central District and Rainier Valley, though WON made occasional pickups in Tacoma. At least twenty families participated, ten regularly. Most of them were black, though white ones were involved as well. The pickups took place at the residences of grandmothers and other women, mostly single, who, as next of kin to the incarcerated single mothers, had fallen into the role of primary caretakers for their children.

Rita did most of the driving. She and Therese shared a Dodge the same forest green color as some of the state's police cars. Others in the women's community lent their vehicles: Shan Otty, her white Chevy Impala "Ester"; Molly, an old Dodge truck called "Gertrude." The 1974 prospectus stated that group members visited the institution eight times a month.

Most of the kids on the visiting trips to Purdy were six years old or younger. Rita and Therese sang with them and told them stories during the drive. If Rita was making a particularly good connection with a child, she indulged in a guaranteed method of eliciting cries of terror or delight by pulling out her dentures, which she had acquired courtesy of the federal Bureau of Prisons.

WON created a Survival Fund "designed to meet the immediate needs of women needing to change their names, to get on their feet after being paroled or deported to other countries, to fight custody battles for their children, to survive." They also established a Legal Defense Fund in order to provide "[c]ontinuing legal assistance for women inmates who maintain their dignity and pride by refusing to bow down to 'the man.'" In the first year of the organization, "Free legal services . . . have been provided almost entirely by women lawyers." But, the proposal stressed, "these dedicated people must be reimbursed if they are to survive themselves and continue their work for the dispossessed."

Despite the harrowing episode with Nick the Greek, Rita and Therese understood that there were several male prison activists with integrity in Seattle. The one they respected most was Mark Cook, a diminutive black man in his late thirties. Mark had already served a decade-plus in Washington's juvenile institutions and maximum security joints, the latter for armed robbery.[3] As a young man in the Washington State Penitentiary (WSP) in Walla Walla, he was taken under the collective wing of a group of powerful black inmates known as "The Super Crew." Mark collaborated on an underground prisoner-produced newsletter, *The Bomb*, which agitated for expanding prisoners' civil rights. With others, he pushed for and won an innovative self-governing body for prisoners, while clandestinely organizing for prisoner control of the institution. In addition, he co-founded a chapter of the Black Panther Party, one of only a handful of in-prison chapters in the entire country. In 1971, toward the end of his stay at WSP, Mark also co-founded Pivot, a furniture and upholstery factory designed to develop skills valuable to prisoners upon release.

Although Mark, like Rita, was a student at SCCC, he first noticed her at a prison event at the University of Washington. In addition to continuing work with Pivot, he was in the midst of organizing CONvention, a conference of people doing prison work in Seattle, which was to be held in the fall of 1973 at Centro de la Raza. In addition to his other projects, Mark became involved with WON. He caravanned with Rita, Therese, and others, taking family members of his contacts inside to visit.

Mark was a private person who was very selective about who he let into his life. In the course of doing political work together, he began to hang out with Rita and Therese. Years later, Rita asked him, "Were Therese and I the best friends you had in Seattle?" He considered for a moment before replying, "Yes, I think you were."

The keynote speaker at the first CONvention was Frank "Big Black" Smith, the "Chief of Security" for the rebellious inmates in the Attica uprising. A 6'1", 230-pound African American, "Big Black" was aptly named. Originally incarcerated for robbing a craps game, Black's affability and physical prowess placed him in the position of the prisoners' football coach. In this role he became acquainted with a broad cross-section of the prison population, a familiarity that proved invaluable when it came time to choose a team to order the chaos of the initial flood onto Attica's D-yard. This team maintained order on the yard and ensured the safety of the negotiators who entered the prison.

When the institution was retaken by prison guards and state troopers, special torments were reserved for Black. Guards had been informed, falsely, that he had castrated a hostage. As with other inmate leaders, an X was chalked on his back.

FIGURE 9. The Washington State Penitentiary Chapter of the Black Panther Party around 1968. Mark Cook is fourth on the right. Photo courtesy Mark Cook.

Guards and troopers made him lie naked on a table with a football under his chin, at which point he was informed sternly: "If it falls you'll be killed or castrated." They then beat him around the head and testicles and dropped lighted cigarettes and hot shell casings on his belly for hours. Prodding him with batons, they later forced him to walk barefoot across broken glass toward a corridor from which he could hear the rhythmic clack of clubs against a wall and voices chanting, "We're waiting for you, Frank!" That night he was dumped, naked and bleeding, both wrists broken, into an isolation cell. A guard aimed a gun at him and played Russian roulette.[4]

Big Black was released in 1971 after activists, lawyers, and popular outrage forced the prosecutor to drop the charges that had initially been brought against him. He then worked with Attica Brothers Legal Defense in Buffalo, which was pursuing a suit against the parties responsible for the massacre.

Figuring it would make him feel more comfortable, the organizers of Black's visit to Seattle had asked a prominent black community leader to host him. But early on the morning of the day after his arrival, Black called Rita and Therese and ordered: "Come get me out of here!" Rita and Therese picked him up and took him out to breakfast. He had been completely ignored by his putative host—he hadn't been offered food or given any other attention. "You gotta get me out of there," he stated plaintively, making eye contact. "Can I stay at your house?"

"That might be a bit complicated," Therese said diplomatically. The 10th Street Collective had been established by Rita, Therese, and their friend Martha, who was also a lesbian—thus the collective's casual moniker "The Dyke House." No adult male had ever stayed there overnight.

"You could stay at Mark's," Rita suggested. "His place doesn't have any windows. Mark likes it, but not everyone who's done time would." Rita looked to Therese for confirmation.

"Mark could stay with his girlfriend," Therese offered, and, addressing Black, continued: "You could have it all to yourself."

Black decided promptly: "Let me see that place. Take me there!"

Mark's place was 910 Mercer, on the western slope of the city, overlooking Puget Sound. Mark invited the party into his basement apartment and showed Black around. Black was pleased. "I can have all this?" he inquired, making an encompassing gesture.

"Of course."

Mark and Black became fast friends.

On his last morning in town, Black called the 10th Street Collective early. "We want to make you breakfast," he announced. "Can two black men come over to your dyke house and cook for you?" He obtained a groggy consent.

In 1975, WON brought Smith back to the city to present *Attica*, Cinda Firestone's new documentary on the rebellion. In addition to a public event in Seattle, WON organized screenings with Smith at both Purdy and the Washington State Reformatory in Monroe.[5]

Rita made a new friend in Janine, the COYOTE organizer who had done a presentation at Purdy. With personal lives and politics inextricably intertwined, Rita heard Janine's activist autobiography as an integral part of her life story.

The Tacoma-born Janine had come to COYOTE in the same way in which she had initially become involved in organizing and politics: by following her heart and her sense of what was right. She had become something of an outsider by high school, and gravitated to an underground paper in her school called *The Iconoclast*. "I was intuitively against the status quo," she told Rita. In her junior year, she became involved in civil rights work, volunteering at the Hilltop Community Center (Hilltop being what passed for a ghetto in Tacoma). The civil rights struggle in the Pacific Northwest was less about voting rights and overt segregation than about institutionalized discrimination such as racist hiring policies. Janine participated in programs discussing racism with black youth and teaching black history. Life experience had taught her something about the sexual psychoses complicating black-white relationships. She had become close to a member of the black community, but its leadership put a stop to this friendship, fearing the alarmist publicity that would inevitably result if a fifteen-year-old white girl had or was rumored to be having sexual relations with a black man.

Riotous images of the civil rights struggle entered the Bertram household via the evening news. On April 4, 1968, rioting broke out in Hilltop on the news of Martin Luther King Jr.'s death. Janine headed for the door. Her father blocked it.

After high school, Janine attended Fairhaven College in Bellingham, but she left after a few years because she wasn't down with "The System." In high school her first lover had been another girl, but she didn't think of herself as gay until she dropped out of college. At that time she began to consider herself bisexual, though most of her intimate relations were with men.

"My political beliefs were what just seemed right," Janine stated. She was a hippie, a "free spirit"; she was environmentally aware, into natural foods, and rejected monogamy as a patriarchal construct. She opposed the war in Vietnam, but didn't follow the conflict closely.

Janine felt particularly strongly about feminism. She devoured the core curriculum of the women's liberation movement: Simone de Beauvoir's *The Second Sex*, Betty Friedan's *The Feminine Mystique*, and Shulamith Firestone's *The Dialectic of Sex*. Firestone's solution to gender inequality was to advocate that women seize the means of *re*production, which for the first time in history (or *her*-story, as some feminists began to call it) was scientifically possible. It wasn't Firestone's sci-fi techophilia that captured Janine's imagination; rather, it was the discussion of men's "virgin-whore complex" and the way in which it injured women that resonated with her. Though her father was a good man, Janine had been abused by men. In feminism she found an explanation for and a solution to hurtful acts of the past.

After college Janine lived on a commune on Whidby Island. She liked the collective lifestyle: shared food and shelter, the occasional odd jobs for cash, the constant company. Following an impulse to explore the world, she made plans to hitchhike across Europe. Then she received a letter from a friend in Tarang'anya, Kenya. Tom Grief was teaching in a *harambee*—a community-based school named after the word for "together" in Swahili—and encouraged Janine to join him. She readily agreed. Tarang'anya was only a few miles from the border of Julius Nyerere's Tanzania, which was then instituting an ambitious anarcho-communal restructuring of villages and communities. This proximity raised the political consciousness of the other teachers at the *harambee*, all of whom, except for Janine and Tom, were from Kenya or other African countries. Schools were government-run but staffed by independent-minded people. They accepted students varying in ages from childhood on into their thirties; classes were organized by students' knowledge rather than age.

Many of the teachers jokingly took communist names: "Chairman Mao" or "Ho Chi Minh." "As I got to know them, I realized all the other teachers were well-intentioned misfits, like myself," Janine recalls.

The intense racism of the residual British colonists in Kenya shocked Janine deeply. Expats made disdainful comments to her about "the natives," such as "Independence was a big mistake. These people obviously can't govern themselves."

Back on the *harambee,* all the teachers engaged in passionate discussions about how best to use the egalitarian principles of Marxism in combination with distinctly African—and Kenyan—culture for the benefit of its inhabitants. The contrast between this idealistic intellectual ferment and the dismissive contempt of the colonials forced Janine to pay attention to economics for the first time.

Janine spent six months in the bush, and planned to stay longer, but the headmaster hadn't gotten around to renewing her work permit so she could no longer work legally. "I also felt that I didn't have much to offer the students that an African couldn't," she admitted frankly. "It was time to leave." Her return to the United States was hastened by the death of her father and her mother's threats of suicide.

Back in Tacoma, Janine got a job as an aide to a high school teacher. She lived with her mom at first, but when her old friend Chris Beahler invited her to move into a local activist collective called Sheridan House, she gladly accepted. Janine was introduced and became close to many local organizers.

She became involved in the Tacoma Rap Center, a people's mental health collective established by Dan Kelleher, another friend. Run out of the Martin Luther King, Jr. Center, a larger community-based place of learning, the Rap Center existed as a way for people—especially poor people—to connect with peers with similar psychological problems. At the center, people dealt with addictions, the problems of parenthood, sexual confusions, and clear-cut mental illness. One client might be suicidal, another looking for help finding housing. Some involved in the center had formal backgrounds in therapy; others, like Janine, just enjoyed lending an ear and getting to know a broader swath of the community.

Janine also became involved in Shelter Half, one of the many "G.I. coffeehouses" that were cropping up across the nation. Opened in the fall of 1968 at 5437 South Tacoma Way, Shelter Half provided a venue where young inductees or damaged veterans stationed at nearby Fort Lewis could come for counseling on their options for either avoiding a tour in Vietnam or getting out of the service altogether. They could also just chill out, socialize and, however briefly, forget they were in the Army. Shelter Half was a venue for political performers such as the San Francisco Mime Troupe and the Red Star Singers. It was sufficiently effective that the military attempted to make it "off-limits" to servicemen, a designation that was only withdrawn on threat of lawsuit.[6]

Janine became occasional lovers with her friend Lois Thetford, one of the East Coast transplants. Together they initiated a gay women's rap group. Janine and others also organized a conference on gay liberation aimed at helping social service professionals and volunteers understand gay issues.

A record put out by Lavender Country, a gay country group fronted by her Seattle friend Patrick Haggerty, posed a challenge to Janine's instinctive nonviolence. The album included a song called "Waltzin' Will Trilogy" which told the story of three victims of homophobic attack. The chorus cried:

> Let's not just talk 'bout revolution
> Don't avenge me pound for pound
> There ain't no hope for a solution
> Rise up and rip this goddamned system down
> Cause there ain't no hope till it tumbles to the ground

Upon pondering the words, Janine decided she was of the same opinion.

In mid-1970s Janine moved to Seattle with Chris and Dan. It was her first time in the big city. They called their collective house "Flako Drift," because, as Janine put it, "We were a little flaky and a little drifty." Janine became the collective's mama hen, cooking, cleaning, and listening to people's woes. The others worked outside the house. Chris served as a cook at a nursing home; Dan, a psychiatrist, was the primary breadwinner.

Janine first heard about Call Off Your Old Tired Ethics, or COYOTE, when a woman she was dating came back from San Francisco and excitedly told her about the new prostitutes' union. The idea captured Janine's imagination. "We should have one of those in Seattle!" she exclaimed.

To get started, Janine sought out Jennifer James, a professor at the University of Washington who specialized in sex work. She intercepted James while the latter was doing a presentation at the Center for Addiction Services, where Janine volunteered. Janine presented the proposal to James, who exclaimed: "Oh! Come with me *now!* Let's go and talk about this!" James provided Janine with a host of contacts, both among working women and social service agencies. Together they established a board of directors. U Dub students and community members collaborated with working women to publicly challenge discriminatory treatment of prostitutes.

COYOTE's founder Margo St. James challenged the discrimination inherent in prosecuting prostitutes but not johns. In Seattle, Janine quickly found the prostitutes immediately refuted this position because they didn't want their johns jeopardized, considering that it would interfere with their business. Instead, COYOTE advocated decriminalization of prostitution, as opposed to legalization, which, Janine protested, "would have made the state the pimp."

Janine, like Rita and Therese in the Women Out Now Prison Project, asked the women she sought to aid "What do you want?" "Jobs," they replied. "Other options for work." At the time the federal Comprehensive Employment and Training Act, enacted in 1973, was pumping money for job training into community programs.

The Seattle chapter of COYOTE renamed itself the Association of Washington Prostitutes to make itself a more palatable grantee. It won funding and set up an office and job-training program, for which Janine became a paid administrator. Consistent with the cultural shift toward integrating women into conventionally male trades, the most popular new careers for the women were bartending and welding.

COYOTE maintained a public presence using its original name, speaking out in public forums against discrimination and hypocrisy. They helped working women survive everyday hassles, finding lawyers to defend them after busts and occasionally providing shelter from abusive pimps. More broadly, they worked with the public defender to file suits challenging public ordinances against solicitation and initiated an ACLU suit charging the improper use of tax dollars to pay civilians to entrap prostitutes.[7]

Janine was intelligent and committed, but inexperienced as the coordinator of an organization. At one of their early sit-downs, Rita coaxed Janine's vision of COYOTE from her and mapped it out on paper. Janine was struck by her companion's clarity of thought. She also became aware of the first inkling of a crush that would have dramatic consequences.

The two women were quite compatible. Janine shared Rita's interest in prisons. She had attended the first CONvention and was particularly impressed by a speech Mark made demanding voting rights for ex-convicts, who are routinely disenfranchised. Rita, conversely, considered a prostitutes' union a powerful and timely idea. Her concern with the conditions of Seattle's sex industry had been piqued by her conversations with Bridget, one of her immediate post-prison girlfriends who worked in a massage parlor and medicated herself with heroin to deal with related psychological strains.

Another thing the two women had in common is that they partied hard. Both Rita and Janine were Movement drug dealers. By this time Rita rarely visited the bars anymore, opting instead for private parties or community dances in the basement of the Metropolitan Community Church, the gay congregation based in Los Angeles. She made this choice because the scene that had raised her into an independent adult was changing. "The women were becoming more politicized; the men ... weren't," Brown recalls. Not only were people changing, but the construction of the Kingdome stadium was destroying Pioneer Square.

Rita would bring a couple of joints to the parties; Janine would provide lines of coke. Rita liked to pour herself a large glass of whatever liquor was on offer and dance the night away. Even though the locale changed, the pervasive use of drugs and alcohol remained.

While Rita and Therese were a couple, Janine and Rita's relationship was platonic. But when that relationship came to a close, the two were quickly in each other's arms.

12

# Days and Nights of Love and War

*In which the massacre of the Symbionese Liberation Army in Compton indirectly prompts Rita and Therese to take a vacation*

On May 17, 1974, the Symbionese Liberation Army was incinerated in Compton, Los Angeles. Four hundred and ten officers of the law—the combined forces of the Los Angeles Police Department (LAPD), Los Angeles County Deputy Sheriff, the FBI, Special Weapons and Tactics (SWAT), and the California Highway Patrol—poured over five thousand rounds of ammunition and eighty-three tear gas canisters into the East LA bungalow in which the would-be urban guerrillas were holed up.[1]

The band of Berkeley radicals, led by the escaped convict Donald "Cinque" DeFreeze, had grabbed international media attention on February 4 when they kidnapped Patricia Hearst, daughter of press magnate Randolph A. Hearst. The kidnapping dovetailed with Rita's budding affinity for class warfare and she cheered the conversion of the granddaughter of "Citizen Kane" into "Tania," a bank robber for the revolution renamed for Che Guevara's companion Tania Burke, who followed him to the death on his ill-fated Bolivian campaign.[2]

Hearst's media empire owned the *Post-Intelligencer*. In it, as in the other publications in the chain, Randolph Hearst enforced a highly conservative editorial stance, constantly running op-eds defending the war in Vietnam, among other things. When his own family drama unfolded in the most public way imaginable, Rita commented to herself wryly: "Couldn't happen to a nicer guy!"

Rita liked the SLA in part because it included one openly lesbian member, Camilla Hall, as well as her bisexual former partner Patricia Soltysik. The two women had begun living together in Berkeley in 1971 at a time when neither dreamed she would ever "pick up the gun." They separated the next year, much to Camilla's disappointment. Camilla traveled to western Europe, contemplating possible life paths and writing pining poetry to her ex-girlfriend. She returned to Berkeley in February 1973. By March, Patricia had a prominent new lover: "Cinque Mtume," or Donald DeFreeze, a recent escapee from Soledad Prison whom she was sheltering. Instead of drawing away from Patricia, Camilla remained as close as possible. Both women were among the SLA "soldiers" burned to death in Compton when their safe house was ignited by one of many tear gas canisters launched by SWAT units. Of the six killed that day, they were the only two who didn't have any charges pending against them.

By way of obituary, John Bryan, editor of the countercultural *San Francisco Phoenix*, wrote: "It was not the politics of the prison movement that brought Camilla Hall, 'Gabi,' to her death in Los Angeles at the age of twenty-nine. It was her love for Miz Moon [Patricia]."[3] Some of the poetry Camilla wrote to "Miz Moon," as she dubbed her beloved astrologer, was collected and printed by a women's press after the 1974 incineration and shared by the political women's community in Seattle.[4]

The massacre was disturbing to all but the most bloodthirsty TV viewers. The entire Compton affair was constructed as a modern day witch-burning, conducted on television instead of in a public square. After the SLA hideout had been pointed out to them, the LAPD notified the press that there was *going to be* a deadly gun battle. Bryan commented: "They obviously wanted a worldwide audience for what they had in mind." The press was directed to a parking lot a block and a half from the stucco bungalow in which the SLA was holed up: "Far enough away to miss the opening shots of the police assaults, but close enough to drop right over once it had started and record the extermination of SLA as a grim object lesson for any other 'crazies' out there who might be seriously considering fucking with 'law 'n' order.' "[5]

The SLA, in death as in life, was one of the most extreme manifestations of the militant anti-war call to "Bring the War Home." A number of the officers who dispatched these "crazies" were freshly returned from Vietnam. The episode appeared calculated to communicate to domestic radicals that they would be the object of the same bloodlust with which the U.S. armed forces had pursued the Viet Cong. A slogan employed by Nancy Ling Perry, another of the Compton dead, reveals the mind-set of the would-be "Ameri Cong": "There are two things to remember about revolution: we are going to get our asses kicked, and we are going to win."[6]

From childhood, Rita had identified with rebels and cherished the image of a completely different order. The first and most prominent struggle to develop her consciousness was that of Captain Jack and the Modocs, but the experience of growing up in a company town had made her combative. Despite periodic strikes against Weyerhaeuser, the mill never stopped production. The company always brought in strike breakers, who were met with violence at the picket line.

On a visit back to Klamath Falls during her first year in Seattle, Rita met with a woman with whom she had grown up and the woman's new husband. He worked at the mill, and proudly told Rita of his participation in a sabotage operation during a labor dispute. Proclaiming, "If no trees come into the mill there'll be no work for the scabs," a band of men followed the lumber train tracks up the hill and, at a suitable distance, tore them up.

Rita inherited contradictory attitudes from her parents. Frank and Ina lived through the Great Depression in dire poverty. They were very conscious of a wealthy "them" and a deprived "us." Their perspective, though oppositional, was also defeatist. One of Ina's refrains when Rita was growing up was "You can't fight City Hall." The couple obviously wanted to believe in the "American Dream." Rita's mother once told her, "This is America. You can be whatever you want." Ina's own life, however, had not borne out this assertion.

In his posthumously published *Blood in My Eye*, which Rita read, George Jackson quotes his younger brother Jonathan's condemnation of "You can't fight City Hall," and similar assertions commonly heard in black communities, as "pig-shit." Jonathan put the words in the mouths of blacks conditioned to believe in the lethal efficiency with which the white man protected "this system . . . his product and property." The logical extension of these expressions, the younger Jackson wrote, was that "all we can ever hope for is a reforming or expanding of the system to include the few of us who can make ourselves acceptable."[7]

By the time George composed what became *Blood in My Eye*, his younger brother Jonathan was dead, killed in a hostage crisis he provoked at the Marin County Courthouse. Jonathan's intent had been to negotiate the release of his older brother by, among other things, taking a judge, a district attorney, and three jurors hostage at the trial of a politicized black San Quentin inmate accused of stabbing to death a guard. Jonathan's dream: to broker safe passage by plane for himself and his brother to Algeria, like Eldridge Cleaver before them, or to Cuba, as other black revolutionaries had succeeded in doing.[8]

Rita, like a vocal minority of her generation, was unwilling to collaborate with an unjust social order. Her inclination for direct confrontation combined with a heated intellectual climate, in which prominent figures from Latin America to Africa to the former leadership of Students for a Democratic Society in the United States had been advocating armed action to achieve revolutionary change. In 1974, the most high-profile of these groups in America, the Weather Underground, produced a manifesto called *Prairie Fire*. In Seattle, a box of these tracts was anonymously dropped on the doorstep of the 10th Street Collective, which was known in the community as being receptive to the doctrine of the "heavy revies," as proponents of domestic armed struggle were called in the movement.

Within the Weather Underground, a complementary insurgency was being waged: one against male chauvinism and entitlement. Mary F. Beal, a West Coast writer and teacher, describes this process imaginatively in the novel *Amazon One*.

Published in 1975, the book was awarded the prestigious Atlantic Grant award. Beal's publisher, Little, Brown, then asked her to do a piece on the Symbionese Liberation Army. She turned one in and it was quickly rejected: Beal had crossed over from sympathy with the proponents of armed protest to an attitude that could easily be construed as an endorsement. Published by a feminist collective in 1976, *Safe House: A Casebook Study of Revolutionary Feminism in the 1970's* brought to the fore the question of women's relationship to violence. It framed the question thus: How can women, the bearers of new life, protect themselves and their children from the increasingly uncontrollable death urge that possesses powerful men? It took as a starting point the observation of Phyllis Chesler in *Women and Madness:* "Women, like men, must be capable of violence or self-defense before their refusal to use violence constitutes a free and moral choice, rather than 'making the best of a bad bargain.'"[9]

"[W]omen may soon be forced to make choices," Beal wrote urgently. "To continue to submit or ignore growing violence against their sex is both masochistic and anachronistic. . . . The near-universal use of physical violence to control women's behavior has focused feminist analysis of violence through the eyes of the victim." This focus, however, ignored the pervasive cultural rationalization of male violence. It was time for women to learn what "every man knows": that "he can be beaten up until he learns how or gets big enough to fight back. Only at the point he is able to defend himself will others leave him alone."

The more independent women become, the more men fear their loss and act with increasingly irrational violence, Beal observed. "The conjecture now is that without women to tyrannize, to fight over and seek succor from, without a female support-system, could this country's 24 percent white-male minority sustain its brutish reign here and abroad?" The question would be answered, because the divide between the sexes was growing: "most men are unaware of the women quietly retreating to the mountains, to the backstreet communes of the cities and to the middle-class groups in their very neighborhoods to redefine literature, work, economics, sexuality and power."

This "new female-defined culture" was already having to face the question of which weapons to use to secure their independence. The options were limited. "The feminists who espouse political non-violence have not shown any organizational lifesigns to date. With no effective pacifist leadership, will women closest to the frontlines be able to develop measures short of violence in the time remaining?" Adopting national liberation struggles as a model for women's independence, Beal observed: "Playing the victim has never won a war of self-determination for nations or oppressed groups."[10]

Rita had been introduced to the idea of female autonomy by reading utopian feminist works of fiction. One was *Les Guérillères,* a poetic depiction of a society without men, one that had developed organically instead of in direct reaction to patriarchal oppression. The book presented itself as a "feminary," dense with allegory, which could be consulted by those seeking insight and wisdom. It invoked the names of women of the world, connecting them to one another and sisters past and future, and promulgated a correlation between the infinite embodied in the circle of the vaginal opening and the myriad cyclical profundities of the natural world. In a pat summary of the women's movement's propensity for making myth when concrete *herstory* had been obscured, one character, evoking a common memory predating patriarchal oppression, exhorted: "Make an effort to remember, or, failing that, invent."[11]

The vision was communalistic, anarchic: the revolution itself was violent. The woman warriors took no prisoners. At one point they swear to one another: "The time approaches when you shall crush the serpent under your heel, the time approaches when you can cry, erect, filled with ardor and courage, Paradise exists in the shadow of the sword."[12]

The women had overturned the industrial machinery of male society, confiscating factories and communications centers and turning them into art installations. The change envisioned was primal, scouring every aspect of culture of the germs of domination: "[I]n the first place the vocabulary of every language is to be examined, modified, turned upsidedown, . . . every word must be screened."[13] This war of independence was intended to avoid the cyclical disappointments of revolutions by dispersing power rather than clutching on to it. Unlike male-dominated revolutions, which rushed to replicate the oppressions they had initially rallied against, this one would serve the interests of all creation, including men. One guerrilla assured a young man as the war came to a close: "We have been fighting as much for you as for ourselves."[14] Originally published by Editions de Minuit in 1969, a highly politicized press founded clandestinely during the German occupation of France, the novel was reprinted in the United States by Avon Books, a division of the Hearst Corporation.

In Seattle, it was paranoia, not utopia, that was on the rise. Information was distributed in radical circles that police could listen in on a wiretap even when the telephone was not in use. 10th Street residents began putting the phone in the refrigerator during the host of formal and informal convocations that took place in the collective. They destroyed three phones this way. AT&T, which leased the phones free of charge, delivered an ultimatum: "If you break another one, you will have to pay for the replacement." The conscientious conspirators then purchased a long extension cord and moved the phone through three doors to the bathroom, where they placed it on the rim of the bathtub, while a dripping tap provided sonic interference.

Rita was influenced by *Blood in My Eye* and *Prairie Fire*, but her girlfriend Therese, who consumed political tracts with the compulsive hunger characteristic of Marxist intellectuals, was the real reader. The discussions generated by *Blood in My Eye* in particular caused both Rita and Therese to critically evaluate the way in which they were applying their activist energies. In Jackson's view, "reform is the essence of fascism." People who aimed to improve the conditions of day-to-day life were in fact providing capitalism with the feedback it needed to improve its efficacy and deepen its hold on the planet, thus strengthening the system they were ostensibly against.

The couple took this challenge seriously: What was Women Out Now doing to confront capitalism? It was easing the conditions of the system's victims and expanding the latter's consciousness of the system that was oppressing them, as well as of ways of resisting it. But wouldn't it be a better allocation of their limited personal resources if they themselves, aware of the workings of the system, attacked it where it was vulnerable? The only chance for victory, Comrade George contended, was if do-gooders dropped reform efforts and joined in confronting the system itself. The issue of collaboration versus confrontation became more pressing as WON's initial rate of progress slowed and the initial thrill of contact with like-minded incarcerated women gave way to the obligatory drudgery of providing services to them.


By a fluke Patricia Hearst and her comrade captors Bill and Emily Harris were not at the Compton safe house when the police assault began. Examination of the charred corpses failed to identify Patricia Hearst, so she retained her place as the Most Wanted Woman in America. Rumor had it that the SLA remnants had headed north.[15] The police were looking for the fugitives in a blue van with California plates. A van matching this description happened to be parked in the driveway of the 10th Street Collective.

One day when Rita left the house to walk Bandit, her bull mastiff, she noticed undercover officers sitting in the car across the street. "Therese, come 'ere!" she hollered. Rita pointed to the cops: "Will you watch 'em and see if they follow me?"

The police didn't follow Rita but they did continue to watch the house. Rita and Therese decided that it was a good time to travel.

An opportunity presented itself for Rita first: that summer there was a women printers' conference in Eugene, Oregon. Though she hadn't been able to find work in the male-dominated field of printing, Rita was involved in an underground press (both secret and in a basement) owned by the women's community. Called "Workin' On It," the press was used by different lesbian organizations: one night "The Gorgons," a separatist formation; another night, Women Out Now. Interesting conversations arose in the course of sharing the press. Sometimes Rita and others challenged one of the positions of the separatists, such as their rejection of boy children. At other times the Gorgons had questions for them, like "Why are you workin' with men? Why are you workin' with the enemy?" Rita drove down to the West Coast Women's Printing Conference with a couple other women from Workin' On It. More than 150 women attended the conference.

A chance for a real vacation came for Rita and Therese with an invitation to drive down to the Amazon Women's Music Festival in the Santa Cruz mountains that August. "I had never been with so many women at one time, and half of them were bare-breasted!" Brown remembers. She found it exhilarating. Rita and Therese, doing their propagandistic duty, distributed the copies of *Prairie Fire* that had been left on their doorstep the previous Christmas.

The only cloud came as a consequence of the venue. The organizers of the music festival had rented a biker bar for the weekend. One biker arrived and, after being informed that the bar was closed, refused to leave. He wandered among the crowd, ogling topless women and ignoring repeated injunctions to leave. The situation soon came to blows. The biker bloodied the face of a black woman and proceeded to get pummeled by a crowd of women of all races. Acting pragmatically, the women refrained from destroying his bike and left him in decent enough shape to ride off on it.

In Santa Cruz, Rita and Therese stayed in a collective with Nancy Stoller, a student at UC Santa Cruz involved with the Santa Cruz Women's Prison Project. The prison project organized activist educators—primarily feminists, socialists, and prison abolitionists—to go to the California Institution for Women, located five hundred miles to the southeast, every weekend, where they offered college credit for courses in Women's and Third World Studies, as well as critical discussions of capitalism and other elements of a class-based society.[16]

Rita and Therese continued down the coast. It was the first real vacation of Rita's life (the working definition of "real" being that she didn't have to visit any family members).


The couple stopped at Pismo Beach, south of Hearst Castle. The sand dunes seemed to stretch into infinity.

They stayed in a campground above the beach for one night, then decided to stay on the beach itself. They were almost alone in the park. The wind calmed down after the sun set, augmenting the aura of peace. The next morning they left their tent up and set off to play. When they returned that evening they had difficulty finding their car; it had been swallowed by a sea of weekend warriors.

Rita demanded of the closest person: "What's going on?"

"It's Labor Day. Didn't you know about the dune buggy races?"

"Oh, fuck!"

A Winnebago driver had parked on top of their campsite. He asked them to move so he and his friends could camp together.

The couple refused. "It's getting dark. We were here first. We'll leave in the morning."

The man and his friends got drunk by the camper. They eyed the couple as they put up their tent.

Rita and Therese ate dinner and crawled into their tent to sleep, planning on getting out early the next day. But the men built their campfire practically on top of the couple's tent. They circled it, getting drunker and making obnoxious remarks.

At one point Rita got out of the tent, went to the car and got her hunting knife. She decided, "If they catch this tent on fire, or if they try to come in, I'm gonna stab a couple of 'em."

In the early hours of the morning, the couple finally fell asleep. They woke up at 6 A.M. "Come on. Let's get out of here." They got everything into the car, then Rita pulled out her knife. She wanted to slash the Winnebago's tires, but as she approached the camper she saw its owner was awake. She kept the knife concealed and departed.

The couple went to the park ranger's office to file a complaint. "We didn't like resorting to the police, but we decided we didn't have a choice," Brown states. They could have saved themselves the moral strain: the rangers wouldn't accept their complaint. "They just shrugged," Brown recalls. Rita and Therese left the park.

Their furthest stop south was in Venice, California, to see one of the gay boys whom Rita and DJ had cared for before Rita's incarceration. He had become a girl. She had her own place, and was turning tricks and using the money for operations and hormones. Her cognitive function, severely impaired by the electroshock therapy that had been inflicted on her when she was institutionalized as a child, had been somewhat restored. She could write her name and do basic math. But there was much that would never return.

The woman told Rita that she had visited her parents' home after the death of her father and was accepted by her mother in her new identity. Rita commented to Therese after they left, "I'm glad to see that she has some happiness in her life." Rita and the woman exchanged phone numbers, but they never called each other.

# 13

## New York, New York

*In which Brown and Coupez cross the country in order to attend the Attica Day Protest in Buffalo and visit fellow female prison activists in Brooklyn*

As the summer came to a close, Rita and Therese decided to solidify their ties with their colleagues in Attica Brothers Legal Defense by attending the annual Attica Day demonstration in Buffalo, New York, on September 21, 1975. After the protest, they would drive to Brooklyn and meet others who provided support to incarcerated women.

Two of the Attica Brothers they had brought out to Seattle, Frank "Big Black" Smith and Akil al-Jundi, lived in the collective houses of prison activists in Buffalo. Possibly because of parole restrictions, the two men stayed at different ones.

Rita and Therese were hosted by the collective where Akil stayed, as were a pair of black lesbians—perhaps students at the University of North Carolina in Durham—who represented a women prisoners' group similar to Women Out Now. The group had developed out of the case of Joanne (or Joan) Little, an African American inmate at the Beaufort County Jail who, on August 27, 1974, had killed a white guard, Clarence Alligood, with an ice pick when he tried to rape her. After the Joan Little Defense Committee formed and became quite successful at publicizing Little's plight, the Durham activists expanded their attention in order to confront the atrocious conditions in the Correctional Center for Women (CCW) in Raleigh.

The previous summer the prison activist group to which the two women from North Carolina belonged had provided support for an impressive protest by women. On June 15, 1975, CCW inmates staged a peaceful demonstration protesting dangerous sweatshop-like working conditions in the prison laundry, inadequate and inept medical care, and excessive drugging, as well as the poor quality of prison counseling and rehabilitation programs. Action for Forgotten Women, a Durham-based group to which the women attending the Attica Day protest may or may not have belonged, described the protest as an "all-American, any-time-we-want-to ass kicking."[1]

Some 450 male guards in riot gear from the men's prison in Raleigh, equipped with billy clubs, tear gas, pepper spray, and attack dogs, were brought in to control the prisoners. Backed by 150 highway patrolmen and 50 city police, with the National Guard standing by outside, they occupied the CCW for five days. One prisoner participant described the protest as a "small-sized Attica." Women were physically subdued. Thirty-four of them were cuffed together in a chain and shipped to the men's prison in Morgantown. They were held there for forty-nine days, where some of them were confined in the isolation unit.[2]

Rita and Therese hung out with the North Carolinians on the long day of the Attica protest itself. Before parting, each couple promised to keep the other apprised of their activities, contributing to the expanding national network of female prison activists.

Rita and Therese pushed on to New York City. Through Shelley Miller, a politicized dyke who'd passed through Seattle several years earlier, they met Judy Clark, Sylvia Baraldini, and other women who did prison work. Clark had been in Weatherman in 1969–70, and was indicted and arrested for her participation in the Days of Rage. Years later, on October 20, 1981, she would participate in the attempted robbery of a Brinks truck in Nyack, New York, which left two policemen dead and resulted in the long-term incarceration of many of the Weather Underground and the Black Liberation Army remnants who had carried out the attack. The Italian-born Baraldini was a former SDS leader. She had attended the University of Wisconsin at Madison in the headiest days of the late 1960s ferment but had, like so many others, fled the scene in anticipation of the crackdown that would follow the Army Math bombing of August 21, 1970. As the 1970s progressed, Baraldini too would choose the guerrilla path. Though federal prosecutors couldn't marshal sufficient evidence to convict her for participation in the Brinks robbery, she, along with five others, was convicted of broad conspiracy charges and sentenced to forty years in prison.

Rita and Therese didn't know these women's stories, but they could tell that they were serious and committed individuals. Both Clark and Baraldini were among the activist women who focused their energies on aiding female prisoners struggling against abuses at the Bedford Hills prison for women in Westchester, New York, where another "mini-Attica" had occurred the previous year.

On or around August 29, 1974, over 300 male officers in riot gear and equipped with clubs and tear gas invaded the institution in response to the popular refusal on the previous day of twenty-eight prisoners to stand by passively as a fellow inmate, Carol Crooks, was beaten and abused. A participant gave the following account:

> On August 28, 1974, myself and many of your sisters and mine, witnessed the inhuman treatment of a fellow comrade, Sister Jermilia (slave name carol crooks)[.] She

was dragged, beaten bloody, bruised, and almost crippled by male pigs, one sister with no fighting chance against 20 male watch dogs. This became a cruticial [crucial] era in the lives of many sisters and comrades at the "camp[.]" We could no longer allow all this, so we choose to unite and prevent the pigs from taking these severe actions. ... We too then were beaten, cut, punched, bones were broken, stomachs, arms faces and hands were lacerated. Noses were broken[,] heads were clubbed, blood was severely shed, yes, comrades this was done to twenty-eight women by three hundred men. ... We were then put in cages, within cages with wounds that needed immediate medical attention. ... Many casualties of this war are still not able to return to their mental or physical health. We were kidnapped and totally isolated, letters of pleas were never mailed, food was deliberately left to be contaminated and indigestible, no water was given, no beds, no heat. Sisters and Brothers this was done for ninety days. ... They are not finished with us ... [3]

Twenty-two of the women were quickly shipped to a psychiatric correctional facility without hearings. Called "slow learners" by the guards, they were subjected to further physical abuse and forced medication. The former Panther Afeni Shakur spoke out against this treatment, as did several survivors of the Attica massacre. A collective statement by the Attica Brothers reads in part:

> We the Attica Brothers have suffered much of the same kinds of oppression as our Sista Crooksie and despite the vicious assaults, 43 deaths and hundreds of criminal acts leveled against us by the US government, we will remain ever resolute.
>
> Our support of Carol, our Sista's in Bedford Hills as well as all political prisoners enslaved in the many flesh pits throughout the US[,] is unconditional and unequivocal.
>
>     FIGHT ONWARD TO VICTORY!
>     ALL OUR FREEDOM OR DEATH!

The central place the Attica rebellion occupied in the consciousness of prison activists perhaps prompted the anonymous Bedford Hills inmate quoted earlier to declare: "It's quite evident that 'Attica' was not enough."[4]

As with their West Coast counterparts, the political women in Brooklyn lived in collective houses. Yet their community boasted one institution Seattle lacked: a Women's Liberation School with a karate class. Although Rita and Therese didn't do any punching drills, they did accompany their new comrades to one of the trials of Assata Shakur, captured maven of the Black Liberation Army, in Brooklyn. More than 100 women were in attendance, the largest gathering of political women either of them had seen to date. Although Rita had no inkling of it at the time, within the decade she would be one of Shakur's neighbors in the highest security penal unit for women in the United States, the Federal Reformatory for Women in Alderson, West Virginia.

Rita and Therese also attended the trial of Pat Swinton, a recently arrested fugitive who had gone underground to avoid the same conspiracy bombing charges as Jane Alpert, ex-girlfriend of Sam Melville, an anti-war bomber caught and sent to Attica, where he was shot down during the seizure of the institution.[5]

On the day they attended Pat's trial, a hitchhiker—subsequently identified in Alpert's autobiography as "Lonnie"—whom Jane and Pat had picked up in California while they were fugitives, was on the stand. He had previously testified to the FBI that the women had showed off a gun to him, so he appeared as a prosecution witness. To the delight of the defense, however, as Rita recalls it, on this particular day, he declared under oath: "They [the FBI] intimidated me, they forced me to sign whatever it was that I signed and in all reality I never saw anything. We never talked about nothing."[6]

The demonstration outside the courthouse was quite different than that outside Shakur's trial. Rather than being united in denouncing an unjust prosecution, the women were divided into two hostile camps battling out a division that Alpert had brought to a head within the women's movement. While underground, the easily influenced Alpert had been dazzled by the feminist poet and writer Robin Morgan, a celebrity in the women's movement since the publication of her seminal 1970 anthology *Sisterhood Is Powerful*. Morgan was deeply critical of the male-dominated Left and felt that a true space for women's liberation could only be created outside of "politics" as traditionally conceived. In early 1974, with Morgan's encouragement, Alpert penned a denunciation of the gratuitous sexism of her former partner Melville, as well as of several men in the Weather Underground—Bill Ayers, Jeff Jones, and Mark Rudd—whom she had encountered as a fugitive.

Ostensibly addressed to her "Dear Sisters in the Weather Underground," the open letter was circulated to the women's movement at large. The letter urged Weatherwomen to "leave the dying left in which you are floundering and begin to put your immense courage and unique skills for women—for yourselves." She exhorted them to "let your own self-interest be your highest priority." Alpert decried the women's "resistance to discussing your personal experience, your trivializing of your own pain and suffering, your insistence that the oppression of others is more important than your own." As for herself, in reference to the Attica massacre, in order to "ensure I would never again be addressed as [Melville's] grief-stricken widow,"[7] Alpert declared: "I will mourn the loss of 42 [sic] male supremacists no longer."[8]

Already underground for more than three years, Alpert was tired of the fugitive life. On November 14, 1974, she turned herself in.[9] In a plea for a leniency, she provided information to the FBI on her life underground, including contacts she had had with other fugitives such as "male supremacist" and Weatherman co-founder Mark Rudd.

Besides Morgan, Pat Swinton was the woman Alpert was closest to while underground. Alpert claimed she had notified Swinton before she turned herself in, and that in the interrogations, she falsified parts of her life involving Pat.[10] Yet information she provided on the time period when she was living underground with Pat inevitably helped the FBI track down Swinton. When Swinton—who was going by the name "Shoshana" and working at a health food store in Brattleboro, Vermont—was nabbed quickly thereafter, politicos denounced Alpert as the culpable party. Thus, the women who stood outside the courtroom constituted two distinct factions: the politicos, who supported Swinton and denounced Alpert; and "anti-left" feminists who defended the author of "Mother Right," Alpert's treatise, in which she proclaimed that the root of feminine consciousness and the basis of a feminist transformation of society lay in women's capacity to give birth.

Stimulated by their new experiences and exposure to new ideas, Rita and Therese brought new perspectives with them back to Seattle.

# PART III
# Underground

## 14

# Liberating the New World from the Old

*In which a furtive effort to launch a guerrilla cell*
*out of an anarchist bookshop ends in disaster and*
*the Brigade turns itself into Public Enemy*
*Number One with its poorly thought out response*

> The early stages of armed struggle seem to be as destructive and alienating as an urban riot.
> —SNAPDRAGON, LETTER TO THE GEORGE JACKSON BRIGADE

Ed and Bruce both found their May 31, 1975, bombing of the Division of Corrections headquarters in Olympia empowering. The most unresponsive branch of the state government could not ignore a detonation in its own central offices, nor could the capitalist-owned press. Neither of the two men bragged to friends about the event, but they did print their communiqué in the newsletter they themselves edited, *The Sunfighter*.[1]

Absent immediate repercussions, they continued on their course. The next "mass struggle" that they perceived to be in need of armed support was that of the American Indian Movement on the Sioux reservations of Pine Ridge and Rosebud in South Dakota. There a violent and uneven battle was being waged between traditionalists and compradors on land drenched in the blood of over a century of conflict. This was part of the area in which the Oglala Lakota leader Red Cloud successfully fought off the U.S. Army between 1866 and 1868, in what was, in effect, the first war lost by the United States—and the only one until the Vietnam War.[2] It was also the site of the 1890 Army massacre of approximately 300 surrendering Minneconjou and Hunkpapas, one of many slaughters carried out after the resumption of hostilities in 1876.

In the late 1960s, after a century of forced cultural assimilation and grinding poverty, a new spirit of resistance erupted among Amerindians. It was part and parcel of the youth rebellion shaking the country. To an extent not seen since the civil rights movement of the early 1960s, urban activists joined forces with disenfranchised rural elements. The primary vehicle for channeling this surge was the American Indian Movement (AIM), which was founded in 1968 in St. Paul, Minnesota.

This rising consciousness was evident in the Pacific Northwest. Young Amerindian activists played an important part in the fishing rights struggle that began in the late 1960s, while established social justice organizations such as the American Friends Service Committee contributed their support. In November 1969, an ad hoc group calling itself Indians of All Tribes occupied Alcatraz Island in San Francisco Bay, demanding that, in accordance with treaty provisions, the unused federal land (hosting the abandoned maximum-security prison there) be returned to the descendents of the land's first inhabitants. The following March, in order to increase pressure on federal negotiators, activists seized an unused portion of Fort Lawton, near Seattle. Ejected by military police, they took the site twice more in short order.[3]

In response to a growing realization of the commonality of Amerindian grievances, people on the Rosebud reservation, contiguous to Pine Ridge, put forward the idea of a "Trail of Broken Treaties." A cross-country caravan, initially to start in Seattle (in actuality, it began in San Francisco) would take collective complaints to the Bureau of Indian Affairs (BIA) headquarters in Washington, D.C.[4]

Russell Means, an Oglala Sioux and AIM member, soon became one of the most dynamic spokespeople of the indigenous insurgency. His ties to Pine Ridge, where he was an enrolled member and owned land held in trust by the BIA, accelerated polarization there until it reached the point of civil war.

Means's opponent was Dick Wilson, a corrupt comprador backed by the BIA and obliging to regional white financial interests. After winning the tribal presidency in 1972, Wilson quickly formed "Guardians of the Oglala Nation" (GOONs), a paramilitary force that he used to intimidate AIM members and their local allies, the traditionalists of the Independent Oglala Nation. At stake were billions of dollars in mineral deposits on disputed lands and the integrity of over one hundred years of land claims, as well as the immediate question of cultural survival.

By 1973, Wilson was attempting to enforce a "total ban" on "AIM-related" activities. Traditionalists initiated impeachment proceedings in February, at which point some seventy members of the U.S. Marshals' Special Operations Group "set up a command post at the BIA building in the town of Pine Ridge, installed machine guns on the roof, and began training the BIA police in riot formation and in various weapons and tear-gas techniques." FBI agents arrived to give aid as well. "The town of Pine Ridge, Wilson's stronghold on the southern border of the reservation, became an armed camp; Wilson a besieged despot," Rex Wayler writes.[5]

Wilson oversaw his own impeachment proceedings and, in a session boycotted by most members of the decision-making Tribal Council, exonerated himself of all charges. He then expanded his campaign against political participation by prohibiting "all public meetings and demonstrations" on the reservation.[6] AIM retreated to Rapid City, whence they demanded congressional hearings on treaty abuses.

On February 27, a 54-car caravan carrying approximately 200 people and bolstered by the presence of several Oglala Sioux chiefs drove to the site of the 1890 massacre. A press conference planned for the next day was preempted when GOONs, BIA agents, and federal marshals set up roadblocks. On the orders of Alexander Haig, vice chief of staff at the Pentagon, one Air Force and one Army colonel were dispatched (in civilian garb) to evaluate the scene. Soon F-4 Phantom jets were doing daily flyovers, while seventeen armored personnel carriers secured the perimeter around the "occupiers" of Wounded Knee. Supporters drove in food, medicine, weapons, and ammunition when possible. When the perimeter was too tight, they backpacked in supplies at night. Some of these people stayed on as reinforcements. This route, however, came at a great cost to personal safety: in the two and a half months of the siege, eight or more people may have been summarily executed and buried in unmarked graves after being intercepted by the paramilitary forces.[7]

On March 11th, after two weeks of lopsided gunplay, the Wounded Knee community declared itself the sovereign Independent Oglala Nation. By that time it had more than 300 citizens. The siege lasted until May 5. Two defenders had been killed, and federal law enforcement agents were orchestrating the arrests of supporters of the occupation throughout the country: one legal defense worker put the total number of Wounded Knee–related arrests at over 1,200.[8] The indigenous activists were unable to wrest any concessions from the federal government, which continued to support Dick Wilson and his private army. According to the most thorough study available, in the next three years—from mid-1973 to late 1976—"at least sixty-nine AIM members and supporters were to die violently on and around Pine Ridge, while more than 300 were physically assaulted and, in many cases, shot." The murder rate on the reservation thus approached that in Chile following General Pinochet's coup against President Allende.[9]

Under constant threat of deadly violence, AIM members and traditionalists clumped together in armed enclaves that GOONs were unable to disperse.[10] The federal government moved in to do the job. Indigenous activists and their allies decried this as an "invasion" that effectively resumed the Indian Wars of the previous century. On June 25, 1975, two FBI agents, Ronald Williams and Jack Coller, entered a AIM-protected compound in the company of two GOON-affiliated BIA officers. They claimed to be looking for a teenager accused of stealing a pair of used cowboy boots, but neither agent was in possession of the warrant they said they were serving. The agents left, rounding up three AIM supporters for interrogation on their way back to headquarters. Ward Churchill and Jim Vander Wall comment:

"[I]t is widely believed on Pine Ridge that the whole 'cowboy boot caper' was contrived by the Bureau as an expedient to gathering tactical intelligence and establishing a prior justification for an already decided-upon confrontation."[11]

The next day, the two agents returned to the compound, stopped their car in an exposed field, and began shooting at a group of residents. The defenders of the encampment returned fire. The FBI agents had picked a disadvantageous position from which to initiate hostilities, but their cockiness was well-founded: state troopers, U.S. marshals, a SWAT team, BIA police, and GOONs had already gathered less than a mile away. Yet, as it became clear that their colleagues were in desperate trouble, these forces made no serious effort to rescue them. Coller and Williams were both killed in a forty-minute exchange of gunfire. Later that afternoon the combined forces of local, state, and federal police as well as vigilantes seized the compound. In doing so, it is quite likely that they murdered a defender, Joe Stuntz Killsright, whose previous wounding had necessitated that he be left behind when others fled.[12]

The next day a federal invasion of Pine Ridge began in earnest. Approximately two hundred FBI agents were bolstered by U.S. marshals, BIA police, white vigilantes, and GOONs. They used at least nine armored personnel vehicles and several of the same Bell "Huey" helicopters used in Vietnam to search for their colleagues' killers and disperse the traditionalist forces, which had proven too strong to dislodge with a lesser force.

In the Pacific Northwest, the Native American community and supporters of indigenous rights organized a march from Seattle to Portland to draw attention to the invasion. Continuing to fill the niche they'd selected for themselves—an armed, retributive complement to the mass movement—Ed and Bruce broke into the FBI offices in Tacoma and the BIA offices in Everett on August 5 and 6 respectively. They took turns planting pipe bombs; both devices detonated as planned. In neither case were warnings given. The two men did not release a communiqué because, as others in the Brigade later explained, "we didn't want to draw attention away from the pressing issue of FBI terrorism against Native Americans."[13] Someone associated with the Brigade did, however, telephone the *Post-Intelligencer* and stated: "We exploded two bombs at Everett and Tacoma in protest of FBI activities at Pine Ridge and Rosebud reservations."

The press took little notice of the Seattle-Portland march or the FBI and BIA bombings, but members of the radical political community already favorably disposed to direct action certainly took note of the Brigade's Division of Corrections bombing. No less notable was the fact that whoever had done it seemed to have gotten away with it. After the Brigade's one claimed bombing, Paul Zilsel—a refugee from Nazi-controlled Austria, one-time nuclear physicist, and anarchist radical—and his young comrades of the Left Bank Collective were apparently inspired—and emboldened—to pursue the same path. Unfortunately, like those of the Weather Underground (whom many Collective members resembled demographically), the early efforts of the guerrilla group that overlapped with the Left Bank Collective met with disaster.[14] Unlike the Weather Underground, however, their early setbacks were sufficiently disastrous to convince them to desist. (As we shall see below, the cell around the Left Bank Collective *did* maintain their arsenal and would become one of the George Jackson Brigade's few public defenders.)

Ed knew that Left Bank Collective members Paul Zilsel and Ralph "Po" Ford were interested in domestic armed struggle and seriously considered engaging in it themselves: *everyone was* in the Prairie Fire discussion group in which all three of them had participated. Ed was acquainted with several others in the Left Bank cell, but he had no advance knowledge that they too would choose the path of the urban guerrilla. Indeed, these were precisely the city's publicly identified activists with whom Ed had sought to cut ties by going underground.

Paul and Po did not know of Ed's period of understudy with the Bay Area's most prolific band of bombers, the New World Liberation Front. But Left Bank members would have read portions of the NWLF's prodigious commentary on their many bombings in the Bay Area Radical Collective's *Dragon,* which served as a clearinghouse of communiqués of underground groups across the country, and the NWLF's own *TUG: The Urban Guerilla.* In addition, they would likely have heard of the group's exploits from the frequent passers-through who brought up-to-date information from the Bay Area, as well as from the countercultural periodicals the *Berkeley Barb* and its inadvertent progeny the *Berkeley Tribe.*

In their early writings, the NWLF invited others to join in similar actions under their banner. Their rationale was as follows: the public appearance of various new NWLF "combat units" would bridge internal problems of communication in the underground by allowing people in different cells to know of one another's activities, because they probably would not know one another personally. The public identification of different units would also serve the complementary purpose of confusing the police. Encouraged by the "success"—defined as the ability to inflict damage without getting caught—of the NWLF and the George Jackson Brigade, and exhorted to join in, the new members, who overlapped with the membership of the Left Bank Collective, chose to call themselves the "New World Liberation Front, People's Forces Unit IX."[15]

At 2:45 P.M. on Friday September 12, a call came into a government office announcing, "A bomb is going to go off in the new Federal Building." At 3:20 P.M. the local branch of the Associated Press wire service received a call directing it to a phone booth in which the callers had placed a communiqué proclaiming: "Today we bombed the Federal Building in Seattle. We attacked in the spirit of our slaughtered brothers in Attica and our comrades in Chile." It was signed, "People's Forces Unit IX New World Liberation Front."

The bomb did not go off as planned. At 1:15 p.m. on Saturday—nearly twenty-four hours after the initial call—a search team discovered a 2-inch × 12-inch galvanized steel pipe, chock-full of gunpowder, in a canvas disposal container on the 13th floor. An attached timer—the detonating device—was set for 3:00 P.M., fifteen minutes after the first phone call the previous afternoon. Police recovered a fingerprint from the explosive, but never made a match.

In response to the discovery of the pipe bomb, a security net was thrown up around major federal buildings in the Seattle area. Ten new guards, hired from private security agencies, were in the new Federal Building on Monday morning, manning desks facing building entrances, only one of which remained open on each side of the building. They conducted searches of the purses and briefcases of all those who entered. The government's protection agency placed guards on special duty to patrol the federal building and other government facilities. Every entrance to the U.S. Courthouse and the old Federal Office Building was locked to the public except for the front doors.[16]

On September 15, the Seattle-based NWLF cell tried again. They constructed a pipe bomb and planted it behind the Capitol Hill Safeway at 1401 East John Street, at the intersection of Fourteenth Street. The device detonated prematurely, killing the perpetrator instantly and sending pieces of his body as far as 150 feet away. Four Safeway employees doing restocking inside were not injured. Damage to the building was estimated at between $3,000–$5,000.

Police quickly announced that the deceased was Ralph Patrick Ford, a 23-year-old from Sacramento, California; that Ford had had his wallet on him at the time of his death aided in his identification.[17] Though no communiqué accompanied the action, police had little trouble deducing that the bombing was political: within a few days, Seattle's daily papers disclosed that Ford had joined with the local chapter of the United Farm Workers in the fall of 1973 in support of its long campaign against poor pay and conditions in the fields that stocked Safeway with produce.

The death electrified the city's political community. Ford was "Po," a popular member of the Left Bank Collective; the same "gentle man" who had stood out to Ed in the Prairie Fire discussion group for his welcome absence of abrasive machismo. Ed and Bruce, like everyone they knew, were caught by surprise.[18] Bruce was even close to the action itself: the "Dragon House," in which he resided, was only a block away from the targeted Safeway.

For Ed Po's death confirmed a suspicion: that the Left Bank Collective overlapped with "Unit IX" of "the People's Forces." Later he heard why the Collective's Safeway bombing was such a disaster. Unlike the New World Liberation Front Ed had known, the Seattle affiliate didn't know much about using explosives. Nor did the Seattle cell practice their namesake's policy of "you build it, you plant it," as the Brigade did.

Ed and Bruce's personal sadness at the loss of a kindred spirit was infused with a sense of pride that their own resolve had moved others to commit similar acts of anti-capitalist aggression. These two emotions combined into a sense of compelling responsibility. Like so many soldiers who are driven by the death of a comrade to go on fighting, the Brigade members resolved to finish what Po had started. Ed later explained: "Safeway isn't the target we would have picked. Po picked the target and we were determined to show the ruling class that if one of us falls, another will immediately take his place."

Ed constructed a pipe bomb for use against the same Safeway Po had died attacking. As he was assembling the components, the news came that Bill and Emily Harris and Patricia Hearst, the last three members of the Symbionese Liberation Army, had been captured in San Francisco, along with Wendy Yoshimura, an antiwar fugitive who had been living with Hearst. This additional defeat reinforced Ed and Bruce's sense of urgency.

On the afternoon of September 18, 1975, Ed purchased a fifty-pound bag of dog food from the Capitol Hill Safeway. He took it home, unstitched it, placed a bomb with an activated timing device in it and sewed it shut. He then loaded the bag back into his car and returned it. "I bought the wrong brand of dog food," Ed told a clerk, presenting his receipt. "My wife says our dog won't eat this. Can I go get the right kind?" He placed the bag below several others on a front window display near the checkout aisle.[19]

As Ed tells it, he then called the Safeway from a nearby public payphone. A young woman picked up: "Bakery department?"

"This is the George Jackson Brigade. We've just planted a bomb inside your store. Evacuate *immediately!*"

Click. The woman hung up.

Ed was disconcerted. "Did she think I was a prank caller?" he wondered, then put the thought out of his mind. Just before 9:30 P.M., Ed's Georgetown neighbor Bonnie placed a call to KING TV. She announced: "This is the George Jackson Brigade. A bomb has been planted at the Safeway Store at Fifteenth and John. It is retaliation for the arrests of the Symbionese Liberation Army brothers and sisters."

The blast occurred seconds later, with twenty-five to thirty people still inside the store. The impact blew out several large windows. Capitol Hill resident William Mitchell exclaimed to reporters: "It was like a cannon."

Shane Nation was one of the injured. "I'd already paid for what I got, started to pick it up, when everything just blew up in front of me," he told the *Post-Intelligencer*. "I was between the cash register and the door. It was like somebody hit me with a big firecracker." Nation had small cuts all over his face and glass embedded in his arms. Laurie Cummings, a store checker, commented: "The whole front of the store just seemed to blow apart."

Both Kay E. Robinson, a checker at the store who had been standing twelve feet from the bomb when it detonated, and Jerva Harris, a bus driver with Metro Transit, were treated at the Group Health Hospital across the street from the grocery store. Robinson had welts from flying debris; Harris, knocked unconscious by the blast, had a head injury and suffered from shock. Nicky L. Anderson was treated for chest cuts at Providence Hospital. Marguerite Richard and her mother, Frances Simmons, were also knocked to the floor. They had been in the baked goods section a good distance from the blast. Richard, unlike her mother, was injured not by the force of the detonation, but by complying when a security guard yelled, "Hit the floor!" They went to Harborview Medical Center complaining of abdominal pains; a year later Simmons still suffered from hearing loss.[20] Helen M. Mathers and Danny E. Yaplee both complained of ear problems and saw private physicians.

Police kept people out of the store while they checked for the presence of a second device. They feared that the first detonation had been intended to draw a crowd so that a second one could inflict more casualties.[21] Roy Skagen, acting police chief while Robert Hanson was out of town, declared that the bombing was intended to kill or seriously injure people. "We're dealing with a pretty fanatical group here," he concluded.[22]

In a communiqué written later that night, the GJB stated: "At 9:15 this evening we placed a call to the Safeway store at 15th and E. John and clearly told the employee who answered that 'high explosives were planted in the store and would go off in 15 minutes—Evacuate the store!'. . . . There had been no effort to heed our warning and no evacuation even in process. . . . We clearly realize that our attacks must be discriminate and both serve and educate the everyday person." Yet they were unrepentant about the injuries: "as the contradictions heighten, it becomes harder and harder to become a passive and innocent bystander in a war zone."

The Brigade proclaimed two motives for its act: "First and foremost, it was an act of love and solidarity towards the courageous comrade who risked his life in the furtherance of his political convictions. Second, the bombing was in retaliation for the capture of four members of the Symbionese Liberation Army."[23] As for the choice of Safeway as a target, the writers impatiently recounted what they considered to be self-evident: "We will not belabor the ways in which Safeway criminally exploits farmworkers and its clerks, rips off the public through price fixing, and sells food poisoned by preservatives. Safeway is not only an agribusiness, but its tentacles reach out through the entire world and suck the spirit and blood of poor and oppressed peoples. These crimes are all well documented and have been the subject of numerous educationals, marches, demonstrations, boycotts, strikes, and even anti-trust suits."[24]

Predictably, the Safeway attack was roundly denounced. In an editorial, the *Post-*

*Intelligencer* called the Capitol Hill Safeway bombing "a bizarre act of terrorism," "[a]n irrational act."[25] In a collective statement, sixteen Asian, black, Chicano, and white progressive community members stated their case even more forcefully:

> As members of the left community and progressive working people we condemn this act as politically and socially irresponsible, even though the George Jackson Brigade claims to have given Safeway a 15-minute warning.
> A store where poor and working people shop is a not correct target for those who would stand for a humane society.... We believe in a society where wealth does not control, where people can hold productive and meaningful jobs, and where racism and sexism are eliminated ... [but] the struggle is not aided by such acts of lunacy as the attack by the George Jackson brigade on the Safeway store. We as progressive working people disassociate ourselves from this act."[26]

The most biting public rebuke came from those who knew Po best: the Left Bank Collective. Their statement read, in part:

> We know, from our friendship with Po, that his first concern at all times was the safety and security of people with whom and for whom he struggled. The action last Sunday (Sept. 14) [in fact in the early hours of Monday 15] most certainly was in outrage against the giant Safeway corporation which exploits and rips off the people, particularly poor people.
> If the Sept. 18 action by the George Jackson Brigade, in its choice of location, was intended to be an act of solidarity with Po, as well as with the SLA, then its gross disregard for the safety of the people was in total contradiction of everything Po stood for.
> Po's bomb was placed so that only mechanical equipment could be damaged. It was done at night, so that the safety of passersby would be assured. The Sept. 18 action failed to take even minimal precautions, and injured seven people. As Po's friends, we know he would have strongly disagreed with such lack of responsible concern. There can be no connection between the hasty actions of people whose callousness injures others, and Po, whose concern for others was so great that concern for himself became secondary.
> "The true revolutionary is guided by great feelings of love."—Che Guevara[27]

A wave of bomb threats, continuing throughout the week, forced the evacuation of a number of public buildings. On Friday 19, the new Federal Building in downtown Seattle, the Snohomish County Courthouse complex in Everett, a Ferris wheel at the Western Washington Fair in Puyallup, the Tacoma County-City Building, and Everett Community College, were all emptied and searched in response to phoned-in bomb threats. The George Jackson Brigade and the Seattle branch of the New World Liberation Front were not responsible for any of these. Although the Seattle police usually refrained from discussing bomb threats and bombings so as to discourage copycats such as these, on September 19 Acting Police Chief Ray Skagen held a press conference in which he revealed that bomb threats had increased some

50 percent in the months preceding, and that he feared that there were more bombings to come. He elaborated: "not only here in Seattle, but I think that fears perhaps exist across the nation now that Patty Hearst is incarcerated and her trial will be coming up. Sympathizers to her cause and those types of movements might find it an opportune time to increase their activity." In response, he announced that police would investigate "political groups" that had participated in bombings in the past.[28]

This wave of bombing and bomb threats was significant, but it was not unprecedented. In 1968, $1.2 million in damage was attributed to firebombings. In the eighteen-month period from January 1969 to June 1970, sixty-six bombings occurred in Seattle, causing an estimated $400,000 of damage. Most of these occurred in the Central Area, an impoverished African American neighborhood. Mayor Wes Uhlman opined that many of these destructive acts stemmed from the District's "well of hopelessness."

Between June 30, 1970 and September 19, 1975, twenty-five more bombings were reported in Seattle; citizens discovered five unexploded bombs as well. On top of this, seven major firebombings occurred, and police registered scores of bomb threats. Of the above, overtly political attacks included a blast that ripped through the ROTC building at Seattle University on May 6, 1972; the bombing of the Pacific Northwest Ball Building on Capitol Hill on February 17, 1971; the discovery of a bomb, which was disarmed, at the Remington Rand Corporation Building in downtown Seattle on February 5, 1971; the blasting of Clark Hall, the ROTC building on the University of Washington campus on October 9, 1970; and a detonation that damaged the doorway of a University District bank on July 2, 1970.[29]

These actions quickly attracted the most cynical elements of law enforcement, which sought to use informants not only to discover bomb plots but to *create them* as well. David Sannes resigned from the FBI's undercover informant corps after being asked to take part in a bombing in which the FBI would supply a booby-trapped explosive designed to detonate prematurely and kill one of the bombers.[30] A variation on this theme occurred when Larry Ward, a 22-year-old African American recently discharged from the military, was shot dead by police while planting a bomb in the inner-city Central District in a plot that had been organized by a police informant.[31]

Like that of the nation, Seattle's bombing problem was concentrated in the late 1960s and early 1970s. By 1975, a lull had convinced some that the phenomenon of the homegrown radical bomber had played itself out. In April that year, the *Seattle Times* ran a six-part series entitled "The Revolution That Flopped." Staff reporter John Wilson profiled Lynn B. Meyer who, over the course of a three-year period, 1970–73, committed arsons, planned bombings, and shot at police officers in service of what Wilson termed "the New Left revolution."[32] Then, that summer, flying in the face of the *Times* editors' wishful thinking, came the George Jackson Brigade and, in short order, "People's Combat Unit IX" of the New World Liberation Front.

In the wake of the Brigade's attack on September 18, 1975, security was beefed up at Safeway and "other potential targets," as Acting Police Chief Skagen put it, such as post offices, federal office buildings, and other government offices, in order to avoid further "terrorist activity." At the Capitol Hill Safeway, two female guards cheerfully but firmly checked women's handbags and all packages before they were allowed inside the store. Guard Denise Pritchard, sent up from Yakima by the Safeway Corporation, informed the *Post-Intelligencer* that most customers were delighted to have their bags inspected. "They say they feel a lot safer," she continued, although, she confided, "a few got mad and left." One customer, a tiny, white-haired lady, giggled while opening her bag. "This is the first time this has happened to me in my whole life!" she exclaimed giddily.[33]

Despite possessing the remains of a dead bomber and several communiqués, law enforcement was at a loss as to the identity of the other perpetrators. When a member of the press asked Philip T. Basher, the special agent in charge of the Seattle office of the FBI: "Is this the same NWLF which claimed a series of bombings in San Francisco last spring?" Basher replied frankly, "I have no idea."

"Are they related to the August bombings of federal buildings in Everett and Tacoma?"

"We have no known people tied to the [NWLF] in this city. It's a new surfacing of this group here."[34]

City police hardly appeared more competent. A *Post-Intelligencer* reporter painted a plodding picture of the Seattle bomb squad based on interviews with two of its members. "It's going to be a normal, thorough, lengthy investigation," one squad member said of the second Safeway bombing.

"You'd better not say 'lengthy'," the other advised. "What if we make an arrest tonight?" The apologetic colleague then told the reporter: "We have a lot of little bits and pieces."[35]

A Seattle Police Department spokesperson didn't even recognize the name of the George Jackson Brigade until a reporter pointed out to him this was the same group that had claimed responsibility for bombing correctional offices in Olympia the previous summer.[36] Despite a consensus on the part of Po's friends and family that he was not involved with the Brigade—"We feel morally certain that he had nothing to do with these people," Paul Zilsel stated forcefully on behalf of the Left Bank Collective[37]—police continued to search for "a potential tie-in."

Skagen advised the public to expect more violence coming from dissidents. "Now that Patty Hearst has been incarcerated, with a trial coming up, sympathizers to her cause, and those type of movements, might find it an opportune time to increase their activity in the bombing area." The day after the Brigade's attack on the Capitol Hill Safeway, a person arrested for making bomb threats in Tacoma said it was in retaliation for Ms. Hearst's arrest.

Citing the "political" implications of the acts being committed by the George Jackson Brigade, the FBI joined the search for the perpetrators of the two Safeway bombings.[38]

## 15

# Invitation to a Bombing

*In which Brown is invited to join the Brigade and decides to do so on the condition that the organization make a public apology for its carelessness in its first Safeway bombing; and in which Mead's old friend Sherman signs on as well*

> That awful life of having to choose between being a criminal or going straight was over. We were going to legitimize ourselves as criminals!
>
> —JILL JOHNSTON, LESBIAN NATION

In the midst of the storm of criticism, Rita Brown received an intriguing invitation from Bruce Seidel, a fellow prison organizer with whom her girlfriend Therese had first became acquainted on the University of Washington campus.[1] "Would you like to meet with the George Jackson Brigade?" Bruce asked. Like Therese, Bruce was a prodigious reader with a quick mind. He had been a student in the Economics Department at the University of Illinois at Urbana-Champaign until the faculty refused to accept his thesis on how to correct capitalism so that it would benefit the people. When Therese introduced Bruce to Rita, the two liked one another immediately, but they never spent any time together outside of prison work.

The couple first heard of the Brigade that summer after the Olympia Division of Corrections bombing. Rita and Therese had read the accompanying communiqué in *The Sunfighter*. It indicted capitalism as the culprit in creating crime: "Crime is the natural response for those caught between poverty and the Amerikan culture of greed, aggression, sexism, and racism." Conditions wouldn't improve, the authors contended, until "people get together and drive our criminal ruling class and its fascist government up against the wall."[2] "Well put," Brown thought at the time.

Yet Rita and Therese, like everyone else in the Seattle's left activist community, were distressed by the carelessness of the Safeway bombing, feeling that it made radicals look like callous crazies. Brown, for one, however, wished to "put words into action," as the Brigade was intent on doing. Flattered and wary, she accepted Bruce's invitation.

The meeting took place at the new safe house Bruce and Ed had established on Beacon Hill. As they entered the house, it became immediately apparent to Rita that the Brigade consisted only of Bruce and his former Prisoners Union colleague Ed.

Rita knew Ed from occasional work they had done with the Prisoners Union, *Sunfighter*, and CONvention. As they sat down to talk, Ed laid out a flash bulb in a sprinkling of gunpowder on a pan and connected a timer to the wires that protruded from the bulb. He set the timer, placed the pan at a far end of the room, and came back to discuss business. With his characteristic penchant for drama and oratory, Ed initiated the discussion with the proclamation: "It's time to join with our brothers and sisters around the world to fight imperialism in its heart."

"Why are you so sure the time has arrived?" Rita demanded skeptically.

"We know the time will arrive. When it does, are the skills to fight a guerrilla war going to drop out of the sky? . . . We need to prepare ourselves so that when the time does arrive, we'll be ready."

The gunpowder exploded with a flash, causing the visitor to jump. Mead laughed conspiratorially. Rita calmed down and joined in the laughter.

"You've read Comrade George's *Soledad Brother*, I imagine?" Ed asked her.

"I was reading it in prison when he died," Rita stated with pride.

Ed nodded enthusiastically. Rita noticed his glass eye.

"Then you'll recognize this quote," he continued, and recited forcefully: "'the monster they've engendered in me will return to torment its maker, from the grave, the pit, the profoundest pit. Hurl me into the next existence, the descent into hell won't turn me. I'll crawl back to dog his trail forever.'"

"It's been four years since Comrade George's death and conditions have only gotten worse. A rising tide of oppression is sweeping the country and U.S. imperialism is still killing our brothers and sisters around the world. In the event of his death, George wanted 'something to remain, to torment his ass,' to dog the imperialists and their lackeys. We've formed the George Jackson Brigade because we think it's high time to deliver on this promise."

"So you did the Olympia bombing?" Rita inquired.

"Olympia isn't the first action we did," Bruce volunteered.

"You followed the struggle of the black construction workers against discrimination?" Ed asked; the words were midway between question and statement.

Rita nodded.

"We participated in their demonstrations. They quickly became increasingly militant," Bruce interjected.

Ed continued: "In one, we, with our fellow oppressed workers, broke away from a march and stormed through a construction site, tearing up equipment, kicking things over. Some of us wore hoods. People were obviously open to more than picketing or appealing to the city to protect their civil rights. We decided to push our advantage."

Bruce picked up the thread: "We made Molotovs and threw them through the windows of one of the racist contractors. Then we asked people in the community if they'd heard of the action and what they thought of it.... We didn't tell 'em we were the ones who had done it, of course."

"The response was positive," Ed boasted, smiling broadly.

"So we developed our capabilities," Bruce continued. "We didn't claim these actions because we didn't want to draw attention away from the jobs issue."

A lull ensued, which Bruce interrupted: "We've invited you here to ask if you would like to join the Brigade. We know you do good work and are committed to the overthrow of capitalism."

"Are there any other women in the Brigade?" Rita asked.

"No," Ed answered. "But we're committed to anti-sexism, we're committed to creating an organization as diverse as the people oppressed by the system."

Rita paused for a moment, processing. She came back with: "I liked the Olympia action, but the Safeway one was *stupid*. If we're against the company, hit the company, don't blow up the customers!"

"I called the store," Ed responded defensively. "I said very clearly: 'This is the George Jackson Brigade. We have planted a bomb in your store. Evacuate *immediately!*' The clerk decided to blow it off as a prank call!"

"The papers said you called the wrong store," Rita retorted.[3]

"Yeah, well, everything the bourgeois press says is true!" Ed countered irritably. Another pause.

"I'll think it over ... "

Rita mulled over joining the Brigade for a few days. The men had read her correctly. She too believed that it was an appropriate time to join in armed struggle in the United States, but she did not want to throw in her lot with inflexible dogmatists. She decided to join on one condition: that the group "apologize for the fucked-up Safeway action," as Brown put it. The men consented without protest.

Ed and Rita liked each other but had never spent any time alone. They decided to drive down to Eugene on an errand for the growing collective as a way of getting to know one another. The errand was acquiring false IDs. Oregon was the ideal place to do so because it was updating its system: within a limited window of time, all the state Department of Motor Vehicles required to issue a driver's license was a birth certificate. Ed acquired birth certificates in the same manner left-wing guerrillas had been using since the late 1960s: by finding the names of dead infants who would have been roughly his own age. He filed for copies of the birth certificates through the mail, then he and others in the collective passed them off as their own.

The two made the drive at night, smoked pot, and rapped about feminism and gay politics. Because Ed had up until recently been living with his girlfriend and her child Rita thought of him as straight; she didn't know that he and Bruce had been exploring the possibility of being lovers.

Ed proffered Rita an idea that had been circling in his head. "The only way for men to provide women the space to heal from thousands of years of patriarchy is for men to take care of each other's needs, including sexual ones." Rita had heard this idea voiced in the women's community[4]—it was a logical extension of men being left to their own devices—but she had never heard a man say it.

This prompted Rita to pop a nagging question. "I heard there's fucked up sexual shit in some of the other underground groups, like the women have to service the men. The men say 'I can't function without getting my dick sucked and I'm a revolutionary, so to be revolutionary, you have to *suck my dick!*' "

Ed listened intently. He'd heard the same criticism of the Weather Underground in its early days, and likely was aware that the same dynamic had prevailed in the Symbionese Liberation Army. "No, that's not a problem in the Brigade," he stated emphatically.

"Good. It better not be. I don't care what you boys do with each other, but don't bring that shit over here."

Ed continued to mull over the conversation. Rita, who didn't accept men easily, decided she could trust him.


In building the Brigade, Ed had another idea for a recruit: his old friend John Sherman, whom he'd first met in McNeil Island Penitentiary and with whom, after both of them had been released from prison, he had founded the Washington Prisoners Labor Union. In late 1972 or early 1973, as the Prisoners Union dissolved after the failure of the prisoners' strike at the Washington State Reformatory in Monroe, Ed and John took separate paths. While Ed became an independent actor dissatisfied with existing organizations, John joined the Revolutionary Union (RU).

Founded as the Bay Area Revolutionary Union in 1968, the group initially considered itself the white counterpart to the Black Panther Party. It focused on interesting white New Lefties in Labor and succeeded in creating one of the first worker-student alliances since the 1930s. A shard of the vibrant student movement of the 1960s, the Revolutionary Union, like so many sectarian organizations, proved itself to be prone to acrimonious splits throughout its long existence (it endures today as the Revolutionary Communist Party). Several early members had been in Progressive Labor, which, like Weatherman, had claimed the mantle of Students for a Democratic Society after the spectacularly combustive conference in Chicago in the summer of 1969. One of them, Liebel Bergman, spent time in China and his experience there was partly responsible for the RU's strong Maoist bent. Cofounder Bob Avakian was a Bay Area SDS organizer while an undergraduate at UC Berkeley and was close, for a time, to Eldridge Cleaver.[5]

Roxanne Dunbar (later Dunbar-Ortiz), an anti-war activist and militant feminist, briefly joined the Revolutionary Union in 1971. She did so in order "to be a part of something larger," as a way to have an organizational anchor when everyone else seemed to be drifting out to sea. Her primary contacts were the collective in Palo Alto, in which the central figures were the Stanford English professor Bruce Franklin and his wife Jane. Their group, Venceremos, had merged with other collectives in San Francisco, Richmond, and Berkeley-Oakland to form the Revolutionary Union several years earlier. In her autobiography *Outlaw Woman*, Dunbar-Ortiz describes how the group appeared to her roughly a year before John joined a chapter in a different city:

> I visited collective meetings and a community health center and preschool in the Chicano barrio of Redwood City. I met dozens of "cadre," as RU members were called. Many of them were undergraduate and graduate students at Stanford, but there were also students at working-class colleges—San Jose City College, De Anza College, and San Jose State University. Other cadre were high school students organizing in their schools, Vietnam vets organizing at Fort Ord, a happy couple who worked with runaway street kids, even a biker who was trying to organize a revolutionary motorcycle club. All were dedicated and motivated. I detected no signs of dogmatism or factionalism. Everyone was friendly and enthusiastic, even fun. These were people I liked.[6]

The first indication of the organization's problems came with her introduction to two Protestant missionaries—one an ordained pastor—who now professed a belief in revolutionary communism. Lawrence Goff serviced the organization's guns, which all RU households were required to possess, while his wife Betty Sue tended to their children. The two were treated with special deference by the primarily middle-class intellectuals of the organization because they were "authentic working-class people," as one member described them at the time. Federal law enforcement was aware of this fawning attitude toward plebeians and had utilized it to their advantage. That October, the Goffs testified before a congressional committee on the RU's subversive activities.[7] They had been paid FBI informants all along.

That wasn't the worst of it. Dunbar was summoned before Avakian and some of his posturing strongmen and interrogated about her writings denouncing "male-chauvinism." She relates: "I was terrified of those men, not personally but for the first time since I'd considered myself a leftist, the thought crossed my mind that fascism was not limited to the right wing. Juan Perón in Argentina, Huey P. Long of Louisiana, and Mussolini were all authoritarian proworker radicals. A poster of Stalin loomed over Avakian's kitchen table."[8]

Dunbar dropped out of the organization before her membership was officially accepted. She was distraught. In her effort to stay connected with the struggle of the times, she joined the national underground providing shelter to revolutionary fugitives. Within a year, she and some close comrades formed a cell, which planned to knock out some of the oil infrastructure on Louisiana's Gulf Coast, but the collective pulled away from the guerrilla path before they committed an irrevocable act.[9]

For those who resisted despair and sought to further radical social change in the United States, these were the two prevalent options in the early 1970s: joining a party-building organization or one that concentrated on armed attacks against the government and corporations. The RU itself divided along these lines: the Franklin group accused Avakian and company of abandoning the Black Panthers, especially the so-called "Cleaver faction," which was agitating for and carrying out armed attacks on police.[10]

It appears that Sherman hadn't followed the events surrounding Venceremos closely. He was more attracted to the workerism of the Avakian faction. He remembers: "I was very much drawn to the RU and the Marxist-Leninists because of their discipline and clarity."[11] The critical role attributed to workers also appealed to him. He himself had been trained as a machinist on the East Coast before he became a petty criminal in California. At the time he joined the organization, he was making use of these skills at Pacific Car & Foundry in Seattle.

John's enthusiasm for the Revolutionary Union drove Ed away. "RU people were like Jehovah's Witnesses," Mead recalls today. "They only interacted with other true believers, unless their purpose was to proselytize."

Sherman's job at the Foundry ended when a senior co-worker was dismissed and the management offered John his former colleague's position. "I refused. They fired me for that."

His next job was extraordinary, given that he was an ex-convict and an organizer for a communist group with the stated goal of establishing a "dictatorship of the proletariat" by the armed overthrow of the U.S. government. John recounts:

> I drove by that big, huge Boeing plant on East Marginal Way many times looking for work. It never occurred to me that there was any point in even applying there, given my criminal record. Then one day, just because I hadn't had any luck doing anything else, I was driving past Boeing and thought, "Aw, what the fuck!"
>
> I was still with the RU. I was still leafleting and doing flyers. I was also working on the local edition of the newspaper, *Revolution*. I went into the personnel office, filled out an application, lied where it was appropriate—knowing that nothing was going to come of it anyway—and then by some stroke of incompetence on their part, they hired me. And they hired me for their Research and Development facility, which requires clearance, which I was granted. I thought, "I'll just play this as long as it'll play."

Sherman explains that he worked on "cruise missiles, Minutemen, that stuff." Knowing that the products he perfected would be used against the opponents of U.S. imperialism caused him no psychological strain. "The contradictions are easily resolved," Sherman states with heavy irony. "Everything we do supports [the capitalist system] anyway. The purpose is revolution, not these little considerations." He continues: "It was the best job I ever had. A lot of money. I worked graveyard shift, which was only six hours, and got paid for eight. Most of that time we played Ping-Pong." Sherman adds: "The RU was of course *extremely* happy to have me there."

John's prison record was never discovered, but within six months he was laid off, a casualty of the postwar economic slump. This was not his only problem. As he explains self-deprecatingly: "My whole life was falling apart, to whatever extent it had ever been together." Joanne left him, taking their infant son with her. He was also entering what he describes as "a period of disillusionment" with the Revolutionary Union.

Sherman's dispute with the RU recapitulated that between the Avakian and Franklin factions in 1971. All members of the Revolutionary Union were required to own guns; the implication was that weapons would be necessary in the imminent revolution.[12] This revolution, however, hovered indefinitely in the future. On the occasions when Ed and John did actually see one another, Ed delighted in pointing out to John that the RU leadership would never allow the cadres to let loose with their firepower.

John became increasingly frustrated at the organization's "hesitance to even consider the possibility of illegal work." The organization periodically encouraged its members to voice criticisms, but the "Central Committee" had the final say. "I got into quite a dispute with the hierarchy in the Party," Sherman recalls. He quit soon after.

In the latter half of October 1974, Ed went to visit John in Rainier Valley. The two saw one another only once a month since Ed had moved to Georgetown. John had read about the disastrous Safeway bombing; he remembers thinking: "The whole thing had 'Ed' written all over it." When Ed brought up the subject—without disclosing his own involvement—John lit off on a tirade similar to Rita's: "That bombing was really stupid! The whole idea of putting a bomb where ordinary working people could be injured is stupid! It's not doing anything for anybody!"

Ed didn't interrupt. As John calmed down it became clear to Ed that a constructive proposal lay behind his criticism. On October 17, workers at Seattle's public utility City Light had gone on strike. "This is a group of working people, fighting alone, with few resources. I don't see how they can win," John told his old friend. "It's just possible that a small amount of destruction in the right place might swing things in their favor." The light that had dimmed in Ed's eyes during John's harangue returned brighter than before. Ed didn't need to cajole: John was in the Brigade.

Rita, however, had reason to be less than enthusiastic about John's participation, not because of any personal experience she had had with him, but because he had recently been a member of the Revolutionary Union, which had a disparaging position on homosexuals. Rita recalls that one of her most disturbing experiences in Seattle's political community occurred when a female RU member invited herself over to the 10th St. Collective to have tea with activist women, then launched into a confessional: "I used to be a lesbian until I understood that it was a capitalist deviation. I righted my ways after joining the RU."

To recover from their disgust, Rita and Therese organized a community forum discussing the position on homosexuality put forth by the various communist and socialist sects operating in the city, part of a series that included information on the Trident nuclear submarine base in Puget Sound and indigenous struggle for fishing rights. All the local socialist organizations were invited. The International Socialists, one of the first predominantly white, working-class-oriented organizations to accept gays, sent a representative, as did the Socialist Workers' Party. The RU was the only group that was invited but didn't participate. The organizers of the event, however, obtained and distributed a copy of the RU's position on homosexuality. The document contained passages like "As for homosexuality, this too, is perpetuated and fostered by the decay of capitalism, especially as it sinks into deeper crisis," and "In brief, the heart of our disagreement with lesbianism is that in the final analysis lesbianism, and even radical lesbianism, represents and promotes a dead-end 'alternative' to the dominant oppressive relations and an incorrect understanding of the source of women's oppression."[13] In the impossible event that the Revolutionary Union should come to power, gays were, as in communist China, destined for reeducation camps.[14] Rita figured John must have a flawed character to ever have been involved in such an organization.

Not all of Ed's recruiting efforts went so well. "We need people like you, people with your organizational ability," he entreated his old friend Roger Lippman.

"There isn't a movement to support this kind of underground activity. It's not going to get us anywhere," Roger retorted. As far as this veteran of the student movement was concerned, "The Revolution" had died years earlier. What's more, although he respected Bruce and John, Roger had been put off by Eddie, whom he considered a loose cannon. "I could see to stay away from it," Lippman remembers. "Obviously, I was right." He concedes: "The Brigade did some good actions as armed propaganda, but they weren't strategic."[15]

The men decided they needed two things to be effective revolutionaries, neither of which they had: guns and money. Eddie announced that he had a contact in Denver who could provide them with "some heavy artillery." Bruce asked Mark Cook to provide the funds. Cook, whom Bruce knew through the Prisoners Coalition at Seattle Central Community College, had organized a Black Panther Party chapter in the Washington State Penitentiary in Walla Walla in the late 1960s and was the founder of CONvention, an annual Seattle prisoner activist conference. A steady worker and saver, he had money on reserve. He was delighted to assist the nascent urban guerrilla organization. Indeed, he had been tasked by several of his African American comrades who were still incarcerated in the Washington State Penitentiary in Walla Walla to find out who was invoking the name of "Comrade George." Mark was pleased to find out that it was people he already knew and respected. He pledged to help them out any way he could. On his next visit to Walla Walla, Mark's friends asked "Did you find out who the George Jackson Brigade is?" He enjoyed the looks on their faces when he replied: "It's white folks!" Another, less important factor, was that Cook, long accustomed to using overt and clandestine means complementarily to achieve his ends, had been piqued by Ed's public denunciation of him as "a liberal" at the 1974 CONvention. Ed was deriding Mark's efforts to restore the vote to convicts.

Ed and Eddie drove to Colorado. When they got there, all that the contact had on offer was a beat-up pistol and a shotgun. They purchased them, but Ed, who had knocked off an entire National Guard armory in his youth, considered the mission a complete bust. The only saving grace was that the weapons had been stolen and were thus untraceable.

Donations from Cook were not a permanent solution to the collective's money problems. Opting to seize what they needed rather than begging or trying to hold down day jobs in addition to the mounting task of preparing for a bombing campaign, the men of the cell decided without consulting Rita to rob a state liquor store. They reasoned that, as it was a state-owned enterprise, they wouldn't be harming a small business owner. They planned to carry out the robbery between Christmas and the New Year, when they figured that there would be a lot of cash on hand. They settled upon a store in the North Seattle suburbs. They cased it, identified which alarm service it subscribed to, and, just before the hold-up, called a bomb threat in to the company as a diversion.

Ed was an experienced burglar and John had run many a scam, but none of them had ever committed an armed robbery. Before entering the store, they were all terrified. They hesitated outside the store for a moment—Ed with his pistol, John with a shotgun under a raincoat, Bruce armed as well—hoping that the customers would thin out. They then donned their ski masks and charged in, shouting, "This is a robbery! Everyone get on the floor!"

As planned, John stayed at the front door, where he could see the parking lot and the entire store. Bruce and Ed took the manager to the safe in the back. When they emerged a few minutes later, Ed and Bruce were dragging the pillowcases they'd brought to carry the loot. The sacks appeared quite heavy, which John took as a good sign. Ed and Bruce emptied the cash registers, then all three charged off.

In the car John's comrades informed him that his initial impression had been mistaken. The store had just made a bank deposit: all they'd netted was three to four hundred dollars that had been on hand as change. When they got back home, they decided to climb one step higher on the ladder of illicit profit. As Sherman puts it: "It was really obvious we had to rob banks."

## 16

# A Night without City Light

*In which the Brigade deprive an affluent suburb of power on New Year's Eve and bomb Safeway—again—to show that they can be precise in the damage that they inflict*

> *I say bomb the suburbs because the suburbs have been bombing us for at least the last forty years. They have waged an economic, political, and cultural war on life in the city. The city has responded by declaring war on itself.*
> —BILLY WIMSATT, BOMB THE SUBURBS

One evening in October 1975, Rita Brown and a companion were sitting in a Pioneer Square bar across from the train station on Jackson Street. Suddenly everything went dark. She and her companion grabbed their glasses of beer and walked outside. Looking down Jackson to the waterfront, they could see that power to the whole area was out. They investigated further and found that a fuel truck had crashed on the Alaskan Way Viaduct, the coastal rim of downtown, and was pouring flaming oil onto a terminal of City Light, the public utility, below. City Light workers, who had been on strike since October 17 demanding a retroactive pay raise and the negotiation of a new contract, refused to repair the damage. Their obstinacy prolonged the power outage.[1]

The next week different members of the George Jackson Brigade walked the picket line with the rank and file of International Brotherhood of Electrical Workers Local 77, a common way of demonstrating solidarity. In the bantering conversation that accompanied the purposeful pacing, the topic of the blackout came up. "It was great!" one electrical worker enthused. "It showed the city our power!"

During their next meeting, the collective decided what their next targets would be. The City Light worker strike was so prominent on the minds of individual Brigade members that an attack on the public utility was practically a given. City Light was an ideal target; not only was it on the wrong side of the city's most prominent labor dispute, but it had been accused of overcharging as well. Thus, it was disliked by both workers and consumers. In addition, on September 24, eight of the company's ten female employees had been terminated. Their initial training program, which sexually integrated the reluctant utility, had only begun in the summer of 1974. The eight women were dismissed for having been impertinent enough to complain to the city's Office of Women's Rights that they were underpaid and had not been trained as promised.[2] The problem of sex discrimination made City Light a particularly appropriate target for the Brigade's first action as a sexually integrated organization.

The collective meeting continued. The New Year was coming up. It was the country's bicentennial, and members of the group viewed the patriotic outpouring as a provocation.

"How 'bout an action on New Year's Eve?" Bruce tossed out.

"Let's take out a transformer in a rich neighborhood," suggested Ed, whose internship with the New World Liberation Front, a constant adversary of Pacific Gas & Electric in the San Francisco Bay Area, had given him a taste for disrupting critical infrastructure. "Let 'em bring in the New Year in the dark so they can feel how the poor do when City Light cuts off their electricity!"

Once this was agreed upon, collective members realized that there were enough of them to carry out more than one action simultaneously.

"Is there a way we could criticize ourselves on the Safeway action and show that Safeway still deserves what it has comin'?" Rita inquired.

"How about we bomb Safeway again, so it's clear we still consider them a class enemy, but we'll criticize ourselves for recklessly endangering working people in the previous action," suggested Bruce.

Rita supported the choice of Safeway; she considered it an obnoxious chain that profited from communities while ignoring their concerns. The company's dispute with the United Farm Workers (UFW) had made it notorious among progressives, nearly all of whom respected the UFW's plea for a boycott. The company had also imposed a new store on Capitol Hill recently, despite vociferous objections from neighborhood residents, including those whose homes were demolished so as to accommodate the massive grocery store. This latter issue was inflamed at the time when Rita and Therese moved to Capitol Hill: the Broadway branch of the store opened a block away just as the women were creating the 10th Street Collective.[3] Once in the neighborhood, the couple learned of another corporate practice that completed, in their eyes, the company's anti-life profile: not only did Safeway routinely discard large quantities of perfectly edible though cosmetically challenged produce, but it locked its dumpsters so that no one could eat it. This particularly infuriated Rita and Therese's new friends Patrick Haggerty and Faygele bin Miriam, two of the most enthusiastic dumpster-divers in the gay community.

In contrast to the impatience of the communiqué accompanying the first Safeway bombing, the one the Brigade composed in preparation for their New Year's Eve actions clearly spelled out their objections to the company:

Safeway ... is the world's largest food chain and a powerful agribusiness and imperialist. Safeway has effectively monopolized all facets of the food processing, distribution, and retailing industry on the west coast. As a large international landowner, it is the recipient of large federal subsidies and [has] actively forced the small farmer from his land and liv[e]lihood. As a large grower, Safeway has consistently and violently oppressed the farmworkers and fought their struggle for a union. Safeway makes its superprofits by charging poor and working people outrageously inflated prices for nutritionally deficient and chemically poisoned food.[4]

Brigade members—particularly Bruce—had also not forgotten the killing by what they called a plainclothes "mercenary" of a suspected shoplifter the previous summer at the Safeway on East John Street. The Brigade's previous attack on the corporation, however, "was wrong because we brought violence and terror into a poor neighborhood." Though modest, this one line was the only public apology by a paramilitary organization throughout the United States in the entire 1960s and 1970s.

In the face of all these corporate crimes, "it is not surprising," the communiqué continued, "that Safeway has been the target of massive resistance by the people including pickets, boycotts, educationals, demonstrations and anti-trust suits. And it is not surprising that Safeway has been the target of bombings and armed actions up and down the west coast throughout 1975." One of these other attacks occurred on Sunday December 28, 1975, as the Brigade were composing their communiqué, at a Safeway in Belmont, California. Other bombs had been found or set off at Safeway stores in Oakland, San Francisco, and San Jose.

The Brigade quoted Assata Shakur, a jailed ex-Panther being tried on numerous charges stemming from involvement in the Black Liberation Army, to illuminate the invisible mechanisms of coercion in life under capitalism. "They call us bandits, yet every time most Black people pick up our paychecks we are being robbed. Every time we walk into a store in our neighborhood we are being held up. And every time we pay our rent, the landlord sticks a gun in our ribs."[5] After Assata's word "Black" in the first sentence of the above quotation, the collective inserted "and poor and working"; otherwise, as a predominantly white organization, there was little place for them in the struggle Shakur described.

As for City Light, the communiqué stated explicitly: "We of the George Jackson Brigade are *not* City Light workers, but we do live and work in Seattle and City Light is our enemy too." They explained that they had been inspired by the "courageous" efforts of City Light workers to resist "a massive campaign by the ruling class to force poor and working people to shoulder the burden of this economic crisis."

Appeals followed to both City Light employees and the Seattle public. City Light workers were urged "to rely on the people" both to win their strike and "to further the complex process of revolution and liberation for all oppressed people." "[A]ll workers, poor, oppressed and progressive people in Seattle," in turn, were asked to "demonstrate their support for City Light workers."

In sum, "We have tried to make this New Year's attack a reflection of the lessons we learned this past year." "We are not terrorists," they insisted. Their plans to place a pipe bomb in a park in a residential neighborhood did not contradict their self-criticism of the fall Safeway bombing because: "We have no qualms about bringing discriminate violence to the rich." "Safeway and City Lights are our own class enemies and the class enemies of all who have felt hunger in their bellies or who have been cold in the winter because they couldn't pay their electric bill," the communiqué continued. Thus, they were legitimate targets.[6]

As for where to hit City Light, Brigade members went to the public library to research income patterns around the city. They narrowed down the wealthiest areas to Broadmoor, Innis Arden, and Laurelhurst. They chose Laurelhurst because it looked as though the transformer could be knocked out without affecting a poor neighborhood.[7]

Authorities anticipated just the sort of attack the Brigade was planning. As early as the first week of October 1974, California Attorney General Evelle Younger told the Senate Internal Security Subcommittee that terrorists within the United States were planning to mark the Bicentennial with an "era of superviolence."[8] On December 29, Lieutenant Jerry Andersen, head of the Seattle Police Department (SPD) Intelligence Section, said he expected bombings in the city in the New Year, and that the Weather Underground would likely be the culprit. "We are coming into an election year in a Bicentennial year.... We know there are groups who advocate a 'Second Revolution' ... in this area." Andersen predicted that the number of "terrorist" incidents would increase in the New Year. Continuing to ignore the Brigade's two claimed actions, Andersen asserted that the Weather Underground would "provide the fireworks" in 1976, just as they had in 1975. Advertising the sort of ignorance that would only help the Brigade, Andersen told the press: "The typical terrorist is from an upper middle class home and has a college education. He or she is usually a veteran of the anti-war movement of the 1960s."[9]

Police Chief Robert Hanson also provided a pessimistic forecast: "There are people in the U.S. that are planning acts of terrorism to interfere with this year's Bicentennial activities."[10] "These people have told us that they are going to blow out the candles on our birthday cake," Major W. F. Moore, head of the SPD Criminal Investigations Division, stated dryly.

At 6:00 P.M. on December 31, the state Highway Patrol received a warning that there was a threat of a hundred bombings of public buildings at midnight. The source of the information was unclear, but it likely originated with the Bureau of Alcohol, Tobacco and Firearms (ATF), which was investigating a massive blast several days earlier at New York City's LaGuardia Airport.[11] The December 29 attack was the most lethal act of domestic terrorism that had ever occurred, taking eleven lives and injuring seventy-four people.

Despite forewarning, law enforcement had no idea how to defend against the amorphous threat of the "urban guerrilla." Thus no police officers saw Ed Mead and Mark Cook carrying a heavy box between them into a park on a knoll overlooking the University of Washington in the affluent Laurelhurst district in northeastern Seattle. Nor did they see them cut through a wire fence surrounding the City Light substation at NE Forty-fifth Street and Thirty-first Avenue, on the park's west end, and carefully set down their package. Police similarly failed to intercept John Sherman and his partner as they made two similar deposits—one under an unoccupied wing of Safeway's new Administrative Headquarters, the other between a small pumping station and an adjacent water tank—at Safeway's Regional Warehouse and Distribution Center, a barbed wire enclosed complex at NE Twelfth Street and One Hundred Twenty-fifth Street NE in Bellevue.

The tip-off to law enforcement came from the people who had made these deliveries. At 11:20 P.M., the Seattle police received a call from a man who claimed to be with the George Jackson Brigade warning that bombs had been placed in the Laurelhurst park and the Bellevue Safeway.[12] The SPD immediately sent officers to evacuate homes near the City Light substation, and called the Bellevue police with the Safeway information. Seattle police were already in the area when a column of fire spouted from the park and the first frantic calls came in reporting power outages. Bellevue police were on their way to the Safeway Center when they heard the first explosion at 11:40 P.M. The second blast came ten minutes later.

At about 12:30 A.M. on the morning of January 1, a man called into the Bellevue radio station KZAM, which was about a mile from the blasts, and told program manager Tom Corddry: "We've detonated three bombs this evening." The caller—described, by the sound of his voice, as being in his twenties or thirties—said a communiqué, with details, was taped to a wooden sign in front of the building that housed the radio studios.[13]

After delivering the communiqué, those who'd carried out the actions returned to the safe house on Beacon Hill where Ed lived. There they joined Rita, who'd been monitoring the police scanner. Together, they listened to the radio in high anticipation. The New Year came and went without any information regarding their contributions. Anxiety mixed with impatience until the news flash came: a spectacular flame was illuminating the sky above the City Light substation in Laurelhurst. The explosion that caused this plume had knocked out power to much of the neighborhood.

Collective members cheered, laughed, put on music, danced, and dropped acid. In an hour or so, the mood quieted. Bruce, Ed, and John went to bed. Rita and Mark began to converse. Despite having been friends for well over a year, this was the most intimate talk they had had. As they watched a lamp morph, Mark began to share his childhood experiences in the Washington State juvenile justice system: the electroshock and cold water therapy; the continual gurneys carrying shrouded corpses; his escape attempt and subsequent chaining and beating. One particularly chilling image was his recollection of being forced to scoop up blood with a dustpan and dump it into a bucket when he worked as an orderly in a unit in which another prisoner had punctured several of his fellow inmates with a shank. Rita listened quietly. Mark's incarceration had been worse than even she, with her expansive ability to believe the worst of institutions, had imagined.

Mark rose as daylight broke. "I'm going home now."

"You should stay here," Rita stated.

"No, I should get home."

"Are you sure you can drive?" Rita queried.

"I think so. I've never taken this stuff before."

"Call me when you get home," she instructed with consternation.

It took over an hour for firefighters to quell the inferno in Laurelhurst, because tanks of oil in the transformers fed the blaze.[14] Fragments from the blast were found as far as a block away. The sonic impact broke eleven windows out of the nearest house and sent a stream of burning oil into its driveway, torching a Ford van parked there.

Agents from the Bureau of Alcohol, Tobacco and Firearms and the FBI assisted Seattle and Bellevue police, combing through blast remains for evidence and shipping bomb fragments to a forensics laboratory in Washington, D.C., for analysis. Of the hundreds of bombings prophesied to take place throughout the country on New Year's Eve, the Brigade's three pipe bombs were the only ones to materialize. Despite the declaration of responsibility from the Brigade, Lieutenant Andersen of the SPD's Intelligence Section continued to insist that the Weather Underground was responsible for the blasts. Contradictorily, he didn't disclaim the responsibility of the George Jackson Brigade, and declined to publicly discuss possible connections between the two groups.

The damage at Safeway's Regional Warehouse and Distribution Center was relatively small. Police didn't immediately release a dollar estimate of the damage inflicted by the first explosion; the second they placed at $50.

The destruction of the City Light substation, on the other hand, cost the city an estimated $250,000, making it the costliest bombing to occur in Seattle since 1969, when an explosion at the University of Washington Administrative Building did nearly $350,000 worth of damage. The Laurelhurst blast was not only dramatically expensive, it inconvenienced many people as well. Nearly a thousand homes lost electricity, which wasn't restored until noon on the next day, and traffic lights went out. There was a five-second power outage as the Children's Orthopedic Hospital switched to its backup generator, a particularly unwelcome interruption for those on respirators.[15]

Power was restored to the area by 8:30 A.M., with electricity being relayed to the damaged neighborhood from some of the city's other hundred-plus substations;[16] a new transformer, City Light officials explained, couldn't be put in place for at least thirty days (in actuality, it wasn't completed until late March).[17] In the meantime, City Light Superintendent Gordon Vickery asked Laurelhurst residents in the affected district to cut down on their electricity use at prime times. For several days afterward, reporters solicitously checked in on neighborhood housewives. One woman shared: "We can't use our color TV, but we can use our black-and-white." "Our coffee pot is not heating as fast," another said. Though the source of the outage was novel, outages themselves had been commonplace over the preceding few years due to faulty underground wiring.[18]

When asked about the Brigade's reference to striking City Light workers in their communiqué, Vickery stated: "We see no connection with this bombing and our labor problems."[19] The International Brotherhood of Electrical Workers immediately disavowed the attack, but on January 2, City Light workers announced their refusal to provide emergency assistance to repair the bombed out substations. This delighted Brigade members and caused consternation among the local political elite and opinion makers. Immediately after the attack, Charles Silvernale, Local 77 business representative, declared "We are abhorred by this act and certainly didn't want support from any group like that . . . we don't consider such senseless action as support."[20] On January 2, he reiterated that the union "deplores any such action." There would be no return to work, however, without management approval of a wage increase, as well as an entrance into a marathon bargaining session to work out a contract for 1976. At the outset of the strike, the union had said that it would have a standby crew of linemen available in case of emergencies. But it did not consider the Laurelhurst detonation a real emergency, because there was no threat to life. The union's precedent for this claim was its refusal to repair the damage brought about by the tanker truck explosion on the Alaskan Way Viaduct.

The union local announced that it would not picket the bomb site as long as outside contractors were not brought in to do the work. Supervisors were thus forced to repair the damage themselves. A "safety surveillance" team of striking union members observed their supervisors to make sure that they didn't injure themselves or others. In response to the local's position, Superintendent Vickery complained that the union's conditions for assisting in repair of the substation "amounted to settling the strike on the union's terms," and that such a decision would require a city council ordinance.[21]

An angry editorial by the *Post-Intelligencer* denounced the anti-democratic ideas inherent in the Brigade's attempt to influence local politics by force. "Bombs substitute for ballots among ideologues afraid to stand up in public to submit their ideas for discussion and vote," the paper steamed. "[S]uch bombings are the acts, not of the brave, but of those who fear that their ideas, if submitted to the rough-and-tumble public debate, would be rejected." "The real crime," the editors continued, "is not just intellectual. It's that they are willing to risk the lives of other humans to get attention for ideas that in their own minds they apparently feel too feeble to stand the sunlight of free and open debate."

City Light workers, furthermore, didn't need any such assistance: "The electrical workers know they can take care of themselves, on or off picket lines," the paper asserted.[22] This, however, was not the case. The beleaguered strikers settled with the company shortly after New Year's Day on terms inferior to those they had gone on strike demanding. Though the *Post-Intelligencer* claimed that "The striking unionists ... deplored the bombing," the official disavowal didn't mean that none of the strikers derived satisfaction from the act. One of City Light's first "linewomen," though fired and not yet reinstated at the time of the blast, discussed the matter with her co-workers once she returned to work. "Let's just say there were a lot of happy people!" she remembers.[23] Another former City Light worker recalls that, in the years immediately following the attack, a cohort of her colleagues toasted the Brigade every New Year's Eve.

The *Post-Intelligencer*'s editors also asserted: "The last place any ideological bomber would dare stand and equate a bomb with progress is at a union meeting."[24] Inasmuch as the behavior described would certainly bring well-deserved charges of being an agent provocateur in the employ of the company and/or police, this statement is certainly true. But it ignored the strong "stick it to 'em!" class warfare impulsiveness of American labor, especially before "the Great Compromise" between labor and capital that followed World War II. This earlier period was very much a living memory for the city's unionists in the 1970s.[25]

"Let the bourgeois press howl!" Ed proclaimed with glee, reading the press coverage. The *Post-Intelligencer*'s rant simply confirmed what to him had become irrefutable: there was an undeniable power in domestic armed struggle. Yet it was also clear to labor activists that such actions, even if they stopped short of being counterproductive, were not a path forward. Del Castle, secretary-treasurer of Longshoreman's Local 52 and a longtime socialist, commented to a reporter for the *Northwest Passage*: "Of course everyone gets a certain feeling of pleasure when they see their enemy dealt a blow. But these more immediate surface reactions are not the kind of thing you want to base a serious political strategy on."[26]

17
---

# Dog Day Afternoon

*In which an overambitious bank robbery ends in disaster*

After the New Year celebration, cash became a pressing issue. With each of the three bombings costing approximately $250 in preparatory materials, the New Year's Eve attacks had drained the collective's limited resources. Additionally, an afternoon of target practice ran about $50 in ammo.[1] Neither Ed nor John had held on to their jobs at Boeing Field, and Bruce was similarly unemployed. Mark Cook, the donor of the funds used to buy the guns in Denver, had a day job as supervisor of Pivot, the convict-operated upholstery shop he had co-founded while incarcerated at the Washington State Penitentiary in Walla Walla, and was offered a position doing prisoners' rights organizing with the American Friends Service Committee. He was always generous with his income, but his contributions weren't enough to support the organization's full-time members. Another consideration was that Bruce, Ed, and John, three white men, were too proud to rely on Mark, an African American, for donations.

The collective's last hundred dollars disappeared in a wallet John claimed to have lost. Everyone went to search the area where he had been in the fruitless hope of recovering it. 'Is John lying?' Ed wondered. 'Did he take the money?' The thought came as an epiphany: he hadn't doubted his friend since the painful incident at McNeil Island Penitentiary when John had been ejected from their cell after the other inmates had denounced him as a snitch. In a decision that would haunt the collective, Ed opted against sharing this concern about John's honesty with the others.

The Brigade had become a full-time job. The question was: Who was their employer when they acted in the interests of "the people"? "Let the rich pay for their own destruction," Ed resolved.

"What we need is a big take from a bank," he told the others. "I'm not gonna be doin' this every week. We need more than drawers: we need a vault."

In a quick-entry bank robbery, the stickup person demanded that one or more of the tellers empty their cash drawers. These drawers often contained less than $1,000, just enough to complete the petty tasks performed on a shift, like cashing checks, disbursing small withdrawals, and making change. In busy periods, such as on paydays, banks employed a cash cart, pushed around by another employee, to refill or empty the tellers' cash drawers. Besides this, most currency was kept in the vault, which was difficult to raid: it required more time than the drawers and invited an undesirable hostage situation.

Flush with the success of the New Year's Eve actions, robbing a bank vault didn't strike anyone in the organization as overambitious. Collective members decided to start scouting for a bank with the appropriate qualities: close access to the freeway, light security, and, ideally, a location a safe distance from the nearest police station. They found one with two out of three of these characteristics. The Pacific National Bank of Washington at 13451 Interurban Avenue was located on a straightaway beside an I-5 onramp. It wasn't even in a solid building: pending the completion of a permanent structure the branch was housed in a mobile home. The one downside of the location was that a police station was only a few blocks away.

"We'll place diversions far away from the station to draw out the pigs," Ed, the most experienced criminal in the collective with the exception of Mark, decided. "No one'll even be in the cop shop if the alarm is sounded at the bank."

The collective members dreamt about what they would do with all this cash. The men would take a small amount of money and use it to travel around the country to establish contact with like-minded individuals in other cities. This would allow them to plug into the national underground and coordinate strategy personally, instead of being isolated in the Pacific Northwest and acting based on reports in publications like the Bay Area's "urban guerrilla" bulletin *Dragon*. Most of the money would be turned over to the women, who would bury it for safekeeping until the path of the revolution became clearer.

The organization picked Friday January 23, 1976, to commit the robbery. Collective members would be able to pull together everything they needed by then and, they figured, there would be more cash on a payday.

That Thursday the collective went to the woods north of the city for target practice. Ed stayed behind to rent the getaway car using fake ID. He entrusted his Browning 9 mm pistol to John with the proviso: "Don't shoot up all my ammo!"

"Okay," John promised.

When the group returned that night Ed discovered that John had shot up all his ammo. The sporting goods supply stores were closed, but he found an Army surplus store open where he was able to buy bullets.

The collective fashioned fake bombs by placing bricks in shoe boxes, wrapping them with electrical tape and attaching timers. The next day they divided into groups and, as the time for the robbery approached, planted decoys in the south of the county, as far away from the police station as possible. One was planted in the Double Tree Inn near the airport—which, the collective had agreed, deserved harassment as a bourgeois operation—another in a Tukwila restaurant, the third in a Renton motel. Ed drove to an I-5 overpass, lit a package of smoke flares he had bought from a boating supply store, and tossed it onto the freeway. They then called in false bomb reports, drawing King County, Renton, and Tukwila police; the smoke bomb distracted the Washington Highway Patrol.[2]

Mark dropped Bruce, Ed, and John off in front of the bank and parked across the street, listening to a police scanner with a pistol close at hand. Rita waited several minutes away in a clean, conventional station wagon, ready to cart the boys away when Mark brought them back from the heist.

At 4:45 P.M. Bruce, Ed, and John rushed into the bank together and quickly began shouting, "No alarms! Hurry!" Ed was wearing faded gray coveralls, a dark blue hat pulled down past his ears, glasses, and black nylon gloves. He carried a white cloth sack in his left hand and a 9 mm semi-automatic pistol in his right. Bruce sported an orange poncho, blue Levis, sunglasses, and a tan ski mask with a red top. John was cloaked in a field jacket, dark knit hat, and gray wool ski mask, and clutched a 12 gauge sawed-off shotgun at his side.

Bruce rushed to the manager's desk and thrust his cocked .38 caliber long-barreled revolver in the manager's face. Mark Wallbom, who then had been speaking on the phone with the bank's vice president, laid the receiver down on the desk. Bruce gestured for him to get on his feet and pushed him toward the teller cages.

Ed forced a bank teller named Mary Ann Scott to the floor. He then grabbed the manager and directed him to the vault in the back of the trailer. When a second teller came out of the restroom, Ed ordered her to the floor as well. The telephone began ringing continuously.

"Open the vault!" Ed ordered.

"I can't, I don't have the key!" the manager protested.

"Who does?" Ed demanded.

"She does," the manager responded, indicating a prone teller, who ventured a glance up.

"Get it!" Ed ordered. The woman scurried to her cash box, unlocked it, retrieved the key, then lay down again.

The manager opened the outer door, then informed Ed: "I'll need to do the inner vault combination as well."

"Hurry up!" Bruce yelled at him.

"I'm trying! I'll give you the combination if you want to open it!" the manager snapped back. Bruce went to help John empty the teller cages.

The manager fumbled the combination. Ed felt that the white collar was being intentionally uncooperative. He cocked his pistol, placed the barrel against the manager's head and informed him: "One last chance."

John, by the door, yelled: "Somebody's coming!"

"Is it the pigs?!" Bruce shouted back.

"It's customers!" came the reply. John forced a man onto the floor then ran to the back to check on Ed and Bruce's progress.

"C'mon! Let's go!" Bruce urged Ed.

"No, it's alright." Ed was calm, close to the goal. The manager swung open the inner door of the safe. Ed shoved money into the sack while Bruce and John hovered at the door urging "Come on!" Ed passed the bag to Bruce and the three men ran to the front door with Bruce in the lead.

At the door, through the premature winter darkness, Bruce discerned a police officer. The Brigade had lost its gamble.[3]

"Pigs!" Bruce cried, and turned to run back into the bank. As he did so, Detective Joseph L. Mathews raised his sidearm and fired. A Tukwila Police Department hollow point bullet entered Bruce's lower back. "I'm hit!" he yelled. Bruce turned to face his assailant, firing.

Detective Mathews crouched behind his car, only to feel bullets whizzing over him from behind as Mark began firing at him from across Interurban Avenue. One of these projectiles—a .38 slug—blasted through the flimsy siding of the bank trailer and impacted John's face, splattering blood and bone.[4]

Detective Mathews instinctively scurried toward the opposite side of the car, until Bruce's fire reminded him why he had deserted that position in the first place. The policeman, uninjured but caught in a crossfire, fired at Mark, who continued shooting until he ran out of ammo, then drove off. As he disappeared, other police cars pulled into the bank parking lot and joined in the shoot-out.

Inside the bank, Ed shouted "Tell the pigs we've got the manager!" at his damaged collaborators. He broke out a window facing the parking lot and began firing. To his consternation, every second shot failed and he had to manually eject the shells: he learned later that the spring on the firing pins of military issue is stronger than that of civilian pieces—the Army surplus goods accounted for his cumbersome dud rate. Ed's potshots shattered the siren on the closest police car and pocked its steel doors.

Bruce, fully exposed, got off five shots before taking a hit in the chest from a different police officer, Robert W. Abbott. He collapsed. John crawled over Mary Ann and the manager, to the back where Ed helped him toward what they hoped was an exit. It was a toilet. Mary Ann and her boss shimmied through the now unguarded front door out into the parking lot, miraculously dodging police bullets.

Ed and John yelled over and over: "We surrender!" When no reply was forthcoming, Ed fired some more. A policeman with a bullhorn boomed: "We will guarantee your safety if you throw your guns down!"

John threw his unfired shotgun out a broken window. Ed's automatic pistol soon followed; police later said a shot went off as it landed. The two ex-convicts carefully stepped into the open, then outside. Bruce remained inside. His comrades could hear his labored breathing reduced to a chilling gurgle. Bruce was drowning in his own blood.[5]

Mark dropped the getaway car at the designated location and was rapidly shuffled into the back of the station wagon and covered with blankets. Rita, having decided against installing one of the group's illegal police scanners in the "clean" car, couldn't follow the events at the bank. When she saw Mark alone, however, she didn't need to be told that things had gone badly. Back at base, Mark filled her in on what he had seen; they got the rest of the information they needed by listening to the police scanner, which was humming with excited cross-talk. It was clear that Ed and John were in custody and that Bruce was critically injured.

They delivered word of the disaster to Bruce's closest housemate, Michael Steinlauf. Steinlauf called Michael Withey, an attorney with the Seattle chapter of the National Lawyers Guild who had recently defended a Weather Underground fugitive caught in Seattle. "I need you to call the Tukwila police and ask if they have a 'Peter Wilson' in custody," Bruce's housemate told the young attorney.

"Who is 'Peter Wilson'?" Withey demanded.

"I can't tell you. He's white, 5'3", with a stocky build and black hair. He's injured."

Withey called early the next day. He discovered that "Wilson" had been admitted into Valley General Hospital, where he was declared dead early that morning. Bruce's housemate, fearing that he knew too much, disappeared. He was aided in his flight by a monetary contribution from what was left of the Brigade. Bruce's parents, living in Skokie, Illinois, were devastated, and refused to speak to reporters.[6]

The next day police came knocking on the door of the Dragon House, Bruce's former collective. They were disappointed that the remaining housemates could tell them little, but simply discovering the identity of a member of the Brigade for the first time was invaluable.[7]

Bruce's death caused shock and fear in the political activist community. Michael Woo, then a staff organizer with the United Construction Workers Association who knew both Bruce and Michael well, states that up until that point his organization hadn't realized what its radical white supporters had been up to. "When it happened we were sad to lose a friend. But we were shocked to find out that that was going on in our midst. It raised the hairs on our backs and got us more conscious of who was involved with the organization." He adds that at least two undercover agents had regularly appeared around the organization by that time, a result not only of the Brigade's early activities, but of militancy around the issue of job discrimination and the Seattle chapter of the Black Panther Party going back to the late 1960s.

Woo, now co-director of Legacy of Equality, Leadership and Organizing, a successor to UCWA, continues revealingly: "The core people involved in the UCWA didn't see the goals of the Brigade as conflicting with their own. When those isolated incidents of bombings and bank robberies occurred we considered them part of the work we were doing. Were they good or bad? It was different strokes for different folks.

"Though militant, the UCWA's regimen of day-to-day organizing did not induce the millenarianism evident in a couple Brigade members," Woo elaborates. The radical white left, represented by Seidel and Steinlauf among others, was simply one component of a coalition that included other community and faith-based organizations. Of Seidel and Steinlauf, he states: "Those folks were a fringe to what we were doing. After Bruce's death, we just kept moving on."[8]

18

# Jailbreak!

*In which the remaining Brigade members free Sherman, shooting a police officer in the process*

> Is Seattle in for a Northern Ireland episode? To have something like this is a real cancer in our midst. I feel sorry for Seattle.
> —TUKWILA POLICE CHIEF JOHN SHEETS, UPON BEING READ THE BRIGADE'S "INTERNATIONAL WOMEN'S DAY" COMMUNIQUÉ

Bruce's death came as a shock. Brigade members had made a personal commitment to die for their cause, but they had not foreseen one of their own being killed so quickly.

In the wake of Bruce's death, the popular singer-songwriter Holly Near came to Seattle. Despite feeling guilty about enjoying themselves so soon after the death of a close friend, Rita and Therese attended the concert, where they recognized many others in the audience who were also in mourning. The most powerful moment came when Near performed "It Could Have Been Me," her moving tribute to a fallen comrade. A portion of the song declared:

> It could have been me, but instead it was you.
> So I'll keep doing the work you were doing as if I were two.
> I'll be a student of life, a singer of songs,
> A farmer of food and a righter of wrongs.
>
> It could have been me, but instead it was you.
> And it may be, my dear sisters and brothers, before we are through.
> But if you can fight for freedom, freedom, freedom, freedom,
> If you can fight for freedom, I can too.

Ed and John, captured at the bank robbery where Bruce was killed, were initially charged with his death, but the charge was soon dropped. Dual counts of "assault with intent to kill" against two police officers remained.

At 9:30 A.M. on Thursday, February 19, 1976, an inquest into the legality of

Bruce's death opened before King County Judge William Lewis. The inquest jury were instructed that they could declare the death "justifiable homicide" if Detective Joseph L. Mathews and Officer Robert W. Abbott, the Tukwila police officers who shot Seidel, were either in reasonable fear of serious bodily harm or death, or acting in the lawful course of their duties to prevent a felony in progress.

Bruce's family had the right to represent his interests in the inquest, but declined to do so. In an unprecedented decision, the court granted Ed and John's request to speak on behalf of their deceased friend. The two men raised clenched fists as they entered the courtroom.

Once they were seated, Judge Lewis asked: "Do you understand anything you say could be used against you in state and federal trials?"

"I do, but I feel obliged to bring out the facts about Seidel's death," Ed responded. John echoed his statement.

The detainees contended that Bruce attempted to surrender, leapt into a doorway when ignored, and was hit in the left buttock by Mathews's first shot. John said Bruce fell to the floor and was immediately hit again. A ballistics expert testified that this bullet was a .38 caliber short, quite different from the hollow-point bullets used by the Tukwila Police Department: the implication was that it had been fired by the robbers' accomplice, who had been shooting at Detective Mathews from across the street.

Mathews testified that he saw a man in an orange poncho, later identified as Seidel, come out of the bank with a gun. The officer yelled: "Hold it, police!" Seidel turned and fired once or twice. Mathews yelled again, and Seidel turned and pointed his gun at him again. It was only at this point, Mathews asserted, that he fired once. Officer Abbott, who arrived on the crime scene after Mathews, apparently fired the shot that fatally penetrated Bruce's right breast.

Ed and John conceded that they had fired at police after the police began firing at them. If they hadn't done so after Bruce had been hit the second time, John stated plainly, "we'd be dead."

Statements by two witnesses, the bank manager, Mark Wallbom, and seventeen-year-old Donald J. Gorman Jr., supported Ed and John's claim that the first shots were fired from outside the bank. Wallbom claimed that he heard two shots fired at a 3- to-5-second interval outside the bank. Gorman, who was sitting outside the bank in a parked car, "heard one shot from outside and saw the man in the orange coat turn and grab his lower left buttock." Other witnesses supported the police's account of the shooting. Gorman's father, for one, was sure that the shooting started at the south end of the bank, as was a female bank employee in the bank's southernmost room.

Gorman's testimony was not in complete accord with that of the two detainees. The window of his car was blasted out by two shots from the bank within seconds of the first shot, indicating that, despite their claims, at least one of the robbers had fired before Bruce was hit the second time.

The jury of four men and two women had the right to ask questions, but, for the most part, chose not to. They did not ask Ed or John, for example, about their assertion that Bruce was left-handed and could not have fired with his right hand, as Mathews testified. After forty minutes' deliberation, the jury found that Abbott had had reasonable grounds to fire when he shot and killed Bruce Seidel.[1]

In response to the inquest ruling, Ed and John issued a statement proclaiming: "If the rich want to see the existing order maintained through the use of police terrorism, they can expect revolution and class war as their reward."[2] They composed an angry document entitled "On the Death of Bruce," in which they cast Bruce in a heroic light and the police in a menacing one. "Our comrade Bruce" had been "murdered by police hoodlums as he was trying to surrender," it began, continuing:

> Bruce, always conscious of the need to safe-guard the well-being of innocent people, gave the signal to surrender.... As soon as he was exposed the police opened fire. They did so without warning or provocation and in complete disregard for the safety of workers inside the bank.
>
> Police chief John Sheets subsequently told the media that police "arrived at the bank to a fusillade of gun shots from the men in the bank." Police reports claim they killed Bruce in self-defense. This is an outright lie!

"None of us were prepared," they concluded, "for the sudden transition from the orderly and controlled violence of the expropriation to the savage attack by police."

In a preview of their defense strategy, Ed and John cited recent police assaults on civilians—the massacres of prisoners in Attica prison in New York and of Symbionese Liberation Army members in Compton, as well as the Seattle Police Department's recent killing of an unarmed young black man named Joe Herbert—as the source of their own fear of the officers. It was thus to protect themselves that "We opened fire on police." As for the inquest: "Police lawlessness receives another pat on the back!" Provocatively, the two felons included the home addresses of the guilty officers, in case any of their readers felt inclined to mete out some "people's justice."[3]

Immediately after arrest a wounded John Sherman was taken to Harborview Hospital and rushed into surgery. Police hovered about until orderlies banished them to the waiting area outside. After the operation, John requested the identity of his doctor. Staff provided him with the name, and the man came for a visit. Sherman was soon transferred to King County Jail, where the authorities were less accommodating. His jaw was wired shut, making it impossible to eat solid food, but his requests for a special diet were declined. "If it was something I could force through my teeth, maybe mashed potatoes or milk, then I was okay," John remembers. His court-appointed attorney succeeded in forcing the jail to provide him with daily nutritional drinks. But, by that time, Sherman relates, "I was on my way out anyway. It had become irrelevant."

While in the jail infirmary John obtained access to an unmonitored telephone. He contacted his outside comrades and let them know that he was being taken regularly to Harborview Hospital for reconstructive surgery on his damaged jaw. A conspiratorial understanding was implicit in this exchange.

Several uncaptured Brigade members checked the hospital—a modern-day castle on a promontory overlooking downtown—to see if it was a workable location from which to deliver John from police custody. They found no major impediments. An inmate had previously escaped from the hospital, prompting law enforcement to admonish staff not to tell inmates the date and time of their next appointment. However, one health care provider, unaccustomed to security precautions with patients, disclosed this information to John, who conveyed the particulars of his fourth and final visit to his comrades.[4]

On March 10, Rita carried a florist's box into the hospital lobby. Instead of long-stemmed roses to lift the spirits of a patient, it held a shotgun to lift those of a captured comrade. She waited patiently for John to appear. He did so immediately, with the opening of the elevator door. Cuffed in front of his body, he was chatting amiably with a white, baby-faced police officer named Virgil Johnson. John and Rita did not acknowledge one another.

Outside, it was raining heavily. Johnson, John's police escort, had parked the van at the far end of the lot. "Do you wanna run for it?" he offered his charge companionably, as neither had an umbrella.

"No!" John replied emphatically, aware that this would complicate the planned interception.

As they exited the building, Rita trailed the pair while Mark, dressed in a doctor's smock, waited closer to the police van. Another person affiliated with the Brigade circled in a white and green van, pretending to look for parking. Upon reaching the police van, Johnson left John at the passenger-side door. As he went to open the driver's side, he felt a gun in his back. Mark calmly informed him: "I'm taking your prisoner."

Confused, Johnson attempted to comply. "What?" he asked, as he reached for his keys and turned to proffer them to his assailant. The keys were next to his gun, however, and Mark misread his intentions. He fired into Johnson's stomach; the officer fell to the ground. John rushed around to the opposite side of the van, screaming, "Don't shoot! Don't shoot!" as Johnson rolled under a parked car to protect himself.

Rita grabbed John and pushed him into the car. "Get his gun!" she shouted at

Mark, referring to the fallen officer. Mark obliged; Johnson, fearing that he would be killed, played dead while he was disarmed.[5] Rita hopped in the car with John and they sped off. Mark climbed into a dark blue Chevrolet Vega. He and his driver split in the opposite direction.

With an immense wire cutter, Rita clipped off John's handcuffs. She then put a trench coat and hat on him. She separated from John and the driver at the car drop. John, with surgical wire still in his mouth, was set to assume the identity of an injured worker; he was driven off to a new safe house in the suburbs. Rita, in the fifth car of the day, went her own way. In just ten minutes, the jailbreak was complete. In an hour, John was completely "free"—a deeply misleading word to describe someone who had just become one of the most wanted men in the country.

The escape created an immediate news splash. "'Radical' Wounds Officer to Help Inmate Escape" was the top story on the front page of the next day's *Post-Intelligencer*. A portrait of the cherubic Johnson was prominently featured next to a shot of a shackled Sherman smiling diabolically under correctional escort. Press accounts revealed that, after he had pulled himself from under the van, Johnson had struggled to his feet and walked toward the hospital emergency room. He flagged down a Seattle Fire Department paramedic and said, "I've been shot in the stomach." The paramedic helped Johnson, who was bleeding heavily from the exit wound in his back, into the emergency room. The bullet had passed through Johnson's stomach and small intestine, damaging his pancreas and liver. Johnson remained in serious condition after surgery and having received eight units of blood. Police flashed him photos of suspects that night, but he was in no condition to make a positive identification. A doctor told the press that the young man was expected to recover.

Johnson's assailant was described as "a black man, about thirty, with a moustache and an 'afro' haircut." Illustrating the peculiar propensity of black men to multiply in the paranoid white imagination, the *Post-Intelligencer* story continued: "The other suspect, at first described possibly as a woman, later was also described as a black man." "The other suspect" was Brown. Investigators speculated correctly that the man who shot Johnson might be the "mysterious fourth participant in the Tukwila robbery attempt, the one who shot at police and accidentally wounded Sherman in the jaw in a wild gun battle before fleeing in a getaway car."

The *Post-Intelligencer* continued: "the complex planning apparent in both yesterday's escape and the robbery attempt indicate both may be the work of an 'urban guerrilla' force like those who have claimed responsibility for a number of unsolved bombings in Washington. . . . Police said the escape raid was believed to be the work of armed and dangerous political radicals." King County Police Lieutenant Kraske said the persons responsible were "definitely a revolutionary group."[6]

The police were furious that one of their own had been injured. Press reports pointing out the inadequate security around Sherman rubbed salt in their wounds. As a final insult to their competency, the FBI, citing federal charges relating to the bank robbery, claimed jurisdiction over the case and began to order their local counterparts about.

The police knew they were looking for a black man. The SPD Intelligence Unit maintained what was informally called a "crazy nigger" list, and Mark Cook, along with every other former Black Panther the police had ever had the opportunity to log, was on it. Around 7 P.M. on the evening of the escape, Mark was arrested while coming out of a Laundromat. It was a general sweep with about ten men taken in. Cook was held incommunicado and photographed. Police questioned him about Harborview and released him after a few hours.[7]

Rita called him shortly thereafter. "Can you meet me at Third and Jackson?" she inquired. Concern was evident in her voice.

"I'll be there in an hour," he replied.

Rita wove them through the alleys of Pioneer Square as they talked, streets she knew intimately from her days in the bar scene.

"Disappear," she urged, painfully apprehensive. "We'll send you over to where John is. If worst comes to worst, we'll just send you guys out of the state, we'll just smuggle you out." The group planned to leave the city or the state. Traveling with a black man in the lily-white Pacific Northwest would limit their possible destinations to cities, where they would be less conspicuous. But this was a minor concern: Mark's continued liberty was the primary one.

Cook politely declined the offer. "I'm spending time with my son, which I was never able to do when he was a child," because Cook himself had been incarcerated. There was also his girlfriend to think of: "I have Sandra. I have a life. I've only been out a couple years. I'm not willing to give this up."

Seeing the consternation in his comrade's face, he tried to reassure her with teasing levity. "It's okay, they let me go. *They don't know anything!*"

What Mark didn't know was that the police had picked up Autrey Sturgis, an ex-convict he had mentored while in the Washington State Penitentiary, in the same sweep that had pulled him in. He also didn't know that Sturgis, with whom he was not in close contact, was once again a heroin addict. As "Scat," the name by which he had been known in the joint, began exhibiting signs of withdrawal in custody, police began their interrogation. Like any old convict, Sturgis could read the cues police gave him to let him know what they wanted to hear. In this case, it was that Cook was the shooter at Tukwila and Harborview. Cook was a prime suspect because of his record of armed robbery and recent prison activism. Sturgis told the officers that Cook had confessed to him. This is the origin of the central irony in Cook's case: even though he was guilty of the charges against him, he was essentially framed and railroaded due to improper police conduct.[8]

After a couple of days, the police picked Cook up again at his Capitol Hill apartment.[9] They didn't let him go for twenty-three years.

The heat from law enforcement was so intense, Sherman remembers, that "I was afraid to show my head in the window." He let his hair grow, sprouted a beard, and kept entirely out of sight. His mouth was still sealed with wires, which wrapped each tooth and connected to a brace. Yet despite the Brigade's impressive precision, there had been a complication. The Brigade had planned the jailbreak to occur after John's last visit to the hospital because they wanted his medical matters resolved before he returned to the underground. During his last visit, however, his doctor had decided to leave the brace on a little longer. As a result, once freed, Sherman couldn't eat solid food. The best Rita could do for him was to prepare gruel. John self-medicated with whiskey, a foreshadowing of his propensity to addiction. Rita began clipping the wires and pulling them out with pliers, but it was slow going and she broke the noses of several pairs of wire cutters on the tough surgical-grade tungsten steel. This crude improvisation contrasted sharply with the image police were painting of the organization. When asked by a reporter why dentists were not being told to be on the lookout for the fugitive, one police spokesperson asserted: "If these people really are members of a revolutionary group, they'll have access to their own medical care."[10] In a similar vein, an anonymous investigator observed that groups such as the Brigade "have numerous safehouses up and down the coast,"[11] a circumstance Brigade members could only dream of.

The extraction process was excruciatingly painful for John. "It was terrible," he later testified in court. "I was drinking whiskey and stuff to maintain my cool."[12] The "stuff" was acquired by Rita, to whom the thought occurred: "Janine would have some pills."

Bertram picked up the phone around noon on Tuesday March 23. She was babysitting Robin, the child of her housemates Lois and Patrick, who was being raised by a parenting collective.

The caller declared: "You have to meet me right away."

Janine, recognizing Rita's voice immediately, was flustered. "I can't, I'm babysitting Robin."

"How soon can you come?"

"A couple hours."

Rita dictated a complicated set of directions, including bus lines and transfer points that zigzagged throughout the south of the city. Janine wasn't in a security mind-set: "I can just drive there, if you like," she offered.

"No, you can't," Rita corrected.

The circuitous route ended at the Safeway on Rainier Avenue. Rita picked Janine up and drove her in a disorienting manner through the curving, one-block streets of Renton and Skyway. Even if compelled, Janine would not have been able to find her way back to the house.

They pulled up to a bland single-family structure perched on a bluff overlooking the sea. Once inside, Janine was stunned to be greeted by John Sherman. She had known that he'd been "liberated" by the Brigade—Rita had briefed her on the situation in the car—but the information hadn't quite clicked until he was sitting in front of her. Therese was also there. For the sake of a plausible cover, Rita's now ex-girlfriend had agreed to act as John's "wife," and inevitably, she soon became a member of the Brigade. Janine was delighted to see Therese, whom she had admired since their first meeting regarding Janine's presentation on sex-worker organizing at the women's prison in Purdy.

Janine indeed had painkillers to offer John. The Brigade asked her about other business as well: "Can you clean out this house once we go? . . . We'd also like to see what the movement papers are saying about us."

"I might be able to clean the place up for you. And I can certainly pick up some papers," Bertram agreed.

Janine stayed the night. The trio had just finished writing the "International Women's Day" communiqué. Janine and Rita composed a poem, which Rita persuaded the others to tack on to it. The poem contrasted the media's presentation of the Brigade with the way in which group members conceived of themselves:

> We're not all white and we're not all men
> said a white male member
> of our collective
> to a liberal masked media man

Turning their criticism to the aboveground white Left, the pair wrote:

> why struggle with
> arms, tools, commie Q's [communiqués]
> dykes niggers cons
> when you could slip away with
> left support action
> of vague mass movement construction

They rebuffed the oft-stated assertion in both the mainstream and the countercultural press that the Brigade was a self-appointed vanguardist formation:

> Not the vague vanguard
> We are a collection
> of oppressed people turning
> inside out with action

> this united few breaks
> barriers of
> race class sex
> workers and lumpen
> all going together
> combating dull sameness
> corporations, government
> and the established rule of
> straight white cocks

"[A]in't no turning back now," they continued. "[N]o more mass meetings stalemating action." They conflated their path with that of contemporary revolutionary icons—"joining you sistah brother / in freedom, Sue [Saxe], Assata [Shakur] / George [Jackson], Jill [Raymond], Martin [Sostre]."[13] "[N]ew family being sane / small, not like charlie's / leader ship"; the last was a retort to the popular assertion that any efforts to radically reconceptualize "family" inevitably resulted in the psychopathology of the Charles Manson cult.

They closed with a playful mix of a popular lyric by the local gay balladeers Lavender Country and Rita's own incorrigibly dirty mouth:

> We are cozy cuddly
> armed and dangerous
> and we will
> raze the fucking prisons
> to the ground

The trio gave Janine the communiqué and asked her to stash it somewhere and then notify Walter Wright, who had been covering the Brigade for the *Post-Intelligencer*, of its whereabouts. She placed it behind a dumpster on Capitol Hill and called from the airport as she prepared to depart on a family bonding foray to Hawaii with her mother and aunt.

Recovered Saturday 27, the communiqué claimed credit for the attempted robbery at Tukwila and the liberation of Sherman. It was unrepentantly martial:

> We have so far identified the following tactical criticisms of the Tukwila action: 1) We were unprepared for the level of violence that the pigs were willing to bring down on us and the innocent people in the bank. We should have had better combat training. 2) We waited too long to open fire on the pigs. We should have fired without hesitation on the first pig to arrive. Failure to do this allowed the police to murder our comrade while he was trying to surrender, and endangered everyone in the bank.

Third, the Brigade members inside the bank "should have split immediately with whatever they had in their hands" as soon as the phone started to ring to authenticate the silent alarm. "4) Our comrades[14] across the street should have had more firepower than they did. We had an enormous tactical advantage which we were unable to exploit because it took so long to bring [the] superior firepower that we did have into action."

Finally, the Brigade complimented itself on its escape plans: "5) Our getaway route was excellent. Comrades were able to remain in the area, firing on the pigs until the three comrades inside the bank were taken into custody, and still get away clean." The missive ended with a vow to up the stakes: "Over all, this action failed because we were not prepared to meet police terrorism with a sufficient level of revolutionary violence."

The Brigade then turned to the freeing of Sherman, in which the mistake of too little revolutionary violence had not been repeated. The organization was careful to spell out, however, that they did not intend to initiate a game of a blood revenge with the police: "In the course of the escape raid it became necessary to shoot the police officer guarding Sherman. We did not shoot officer Johnson in retaliation for Bruce's murder. In fact, it was our intention to avoid shooting him. He was shot because he failed to cooperate as fully as possible with the comrade who was assigned to him."

According to the communiqué, the shooting of Virgil Johnson was a direct result of the hard lessons of Tukwila: "One of the many lessons we learned from Tukwila is that we cannot afford to give the police any slack when confronting them. *While we don't particularly want to shoot police, we don't particularly care either. We will shoot without hesitation any police officer who endangers us* [emphasis added]."

The Brigade proceeded to vow personal revenge: "[W]e fully intend to get justice for Bruce's murder, but we prefer to retaliate against the murderers themselves: officers Abbot and Matthews [sic]."[15]

Enclosed with the communiqué was a .38 caliber slug fired from the same gun that was used to pin down the police during the robbery of the Pacific National Bank. On March 30, the jaw brace (technically termed a "torsion arch bar") that Brown had extracted from Sherman's face arrived at KZAM radio station in Bellevue; it, too, was sent for the purpose of authentication.[16] "At the request of readers," the *Post-Intelligencer* printed the communiqué in full.[17]

The Brigade sent a copy of the communiqué to the Left Bank Collective, the anarchist bookstore in Pike Place Market, as well. After reading it, the collective revised its opinion of the Brigade upward. Paul Zilsel, the collective's éminence grise, told press that the Brigade was a group of "serious revolutionaries who have the right to be respected as such." Theirs were not simply crimes, but revolutionary acts against the ruling class.[18] *Dragon* opined: "The freeing of a comrade is a truly exemplary act, one to inspire sisters and brothers engaged in all struggle everywhere.... We believe the ability of the Brigade to liberate Sherman so soon after three comrades were put out of commission demonstrates both the dedication of the Brigade and a depth of organization and support."[19]

The FBI, however, was less than charmed. To them, the audacity of the communiqué was insufferable. John Reed, special agent in charge in Seattle, declared that the Brigade had thrown down "a gauntlet" and vowed that lawmen "are not going to back away from it but will pick it up and ram it down their throats." The Brigade had become one of only a handful of radical groups in the country to which FBI Director Clarence Kelley had assigned a high investigative priority.[20]

In the mid-1970s the Justice Department formulated new guidelines for the FBI in the wake of revelations of its counterintelligence program against Martin Luther King Jr. Director Kelley, in a February 1976 hearing on the proposed guidelines before a House Judiciary subcommittee, testified that the Brigade was one of eight groups that might carry out new acts of violence unchecked if the Bureau was hampered by excessive restrictions. Indicating just how Machiavellian the Bureau was, the proposed guidelines were to prohibit the FBI from: committing or instigating criminal acts; disseminating information for the purpose of holding an individual or group up to scorn, ridicule, or disgrace; disseminating information anonymously or under a false identity; and inciting violence.[21] On June 8, the Brigade would again be invoked in the nation's capital when Representative Larry McDonald of Georgia read a long, well-informed statement titled "Terrorism in Seattle: The George Jackson Brigade" on the floor of the House. It began: "Mr. Speaker, like most American cities, Seattle has had its share of problems with revolutionary violence, street militancy, and terrorism."

Police Chief Robert Hanson, freshly returned from a conference of other major metropolitan police chiefs, was convinced that urban guerrilla groups were one of the hardest targets law enforcement had ever faced and applauded the tough talk of SAC Reed. "We can't infiltrate them, they don't respond to financial rewards, and their dedication reminds me of Kamikaze pilots," Hanson complained. He predicted that an unprecedented fear of crime and concomitant support of police by the American people would prove the undoing of such groups. "These hard-core crazies are like ten thousand ants on a log floating down the river. They all form their little cells, and their little groups, and each cell thinks it controls wherever the log goes. But these crazies are not the people, and they are not going to have any impact on where the log goes. The log will follow the river, no matter what the ants do."[22]

The silver lining in the communiqué, from the perspective of law enforcement, was that it revealed conclusively that the Brigade was not the white, middle class, post-college student organization that portions of the Seattle Police Department and the media had insisted that it was. Several voices in the political community complained about this. The Bay Area Radical Collective wrote in its organ *Dragon:* "We think that it was a mistake to give the cops information that they may well not have had."[23]

It was now clear that the Brigade included one or more blacks, lesbians, and ex-convicts. Despite this insight, Seattle's prosecutors, and the FBI, chose to focus their investigative energies on a more familiar target: the city's aboveground Left community.

# 19

## Clueless in Seattle

*In which the U.S. Attorney uses the Brigade as an opportunity to investigate the city's Left, provoking popular ire*

On January 28, 1976, a month and a half before Sherman's spectacular liberation, Jill Kray attended the arraignment of her ex-boyfriend, Ed Mead, with her two-year-old daughter Odessa. On sight of Mead, Odessa cried out: "Daddy!" One federal marshal, on hand to maintain order in court, rushed out of the room; minutes later, he returned with a subpoena for Kray from the grand jury that had been convened to investigate the Tukwila robbery.

In the intervening moments, Mead's collaborator John Sherman, also in the dock, had leaned over from the defendant's table to ask Kray: "Is everyone alright?"

"Everything's alright," Kray had nodded, a gesture the prosecutor couldn't help but notice.

Peter Lippman, one of the younger brothers of Mead's mentor, the former Weatherman Roger Lippman, accompanied Kray to her first grand jury appearance. While sitting in the hallway, he, too, was subpoenaed. Irate, the pair denounced the grand jury investigation as a "fishing expedition"; with a paucity of leads, they contended, investigators were simply casting out line to see what they could catch.[1]

Jill refused to answer any questions, claiming that the probe violated her rights to due process, free association, and to speak with others without government "harassment." On Wednesday, March 3, 1976, in a hallway confrontation with opposing council, U.S. Attorney Stan Pitkin told Jill and her attorneys that she *did* have "relevant information. And I hope you'll testify to get yourself out of this mess!" The next day Lippman provided his fingerprints, a handwriting sample, and a photograph, halting the proceedings temporarily. The government explained that it was looking for a match with the fingerprint samples left on the three fake bombs used to divert police during the attempted robbery at the Pacific National Bank and the handwriting on a Brigade communiqué.[2]

Jill returned to U.S. District Court March 12, adamant in her refusal to testify. Noting that two days earlier a defendant in the case—Sherman—had escaped over the body of a police officer, Presiding Judge Donald Voorhees dismissed her claim of grand jury abuse as "almost frivolous" and asserted that the U.S. attorney and the grand jury would be derelict "if they didn't follow every lead" available to them. He ordered her to tell the grand jury all she knew about the Tukwila episode—its planning, the planting of diversionary devices, and so on—or face contempt proceedings and jail.[3]

On March 23, Jill defied a court order to answer the grand jury's questions. She obviously feared the consequences: she wept openly as Odessa looked on. Voorhees reiterated his position—"It is abundantly clear that what the grand jury is doing here is entirely proper"—and ordered her to reappear the next day and show cause as to why she should not be held in contempt and jailed. Jill asked Assistant U.S. Attorney Peter Mair to leave the grand jury room for a few minutes so that she could "just talk" with the "nice folks" on the jury. He did. The "nice folks" persistently asked her: "If you have no knowledge, why not answer the questions?" After the ordeal, Jill recalled: "I just keep saying, 'I'm fighting for my rights, and if I don't have any rights, the people don't have any rights.'"[4]

The next day the contempt hearing that could have sent the 22-year-old welfare mother to jail was suddenly cancelled. It was a cagey move by the U.S. Attorney's Office, strongly suggesting that Jill had caved the previous day, while also leaving open the possibility that they themselves had balked at the prospect of appearing the bully in the highly publicized case. Pitkin refused to comment on the matter; Jill and her attorney John Ziegler followed suit.[5] It was later disclosed that Kray had, indeed, testified.[6]

Jill Kray and Peter Lippman were not the first people to be subpoenaed to the grand jury investigating the Brigade. That distinction belonged to Michael Withey, the attorney who had called the Tukwila Police Department the day after the attempted robbery of the Pacific National Bank asking for "Peter Wilson." Withey was a well-known leftist lawyer in town; he had recently been the president of the local chapter of the National Lawyers Guild. Investigators wondered how Withey could have known Seidel's alias without having had direct contact with other participants in the robbery.

Withey's status as a lawyer in progressive circles made him a difficult target for law enforcement. When subpoenaed, he claimed "attorney-client privilege," a tactic that had worked for a lawyer who had been subpoenaed to give testimony against her client in a grand jury convened in Des Moines, Iowa, in the wake of the 1975 Oglala firefight between American Indian Movement members and the FBI on Pine Ridge Reservation.[7] Withey's case, however, differed crucially from that of his colleague in that he had no documented professional relationship with Seidel and disclosing the names of other "clients" would be tantamount to opening them up to indictment. Withey chose simply to tell the grand jury that he was contacted after January 23 by one or more clients and conducted an investigation for them.

U.S. District Judge William J. Lindberg offered Withey the opportunity to appear without a government attorney present to explain any circumstances surrounding this privileged relationship. Withey refused, and when he appeared before the federal grand jury before March 23, he gave ambiguous answers. When pressed, he refused to clarify.

Withey protested the subpoena publicly. In response, Assistant U.S. Attorney Jack Meyerson stated that he didn't want Withey "to testify . . . to turn him against any client he may have, but rather to ascertain whether Withey had any independent knowledge of the robbery." Pointing to the shared telephone numbers between the Committee to End Grand Jury Abuse and the National Lawyers Guild, another affidavit accused Withey of mounting a public relations campaign to seek support for his defiance of the court order demanding his testimony. Progressives and a significant portion of the legal community backed Withey. The Board of Trustees of the Seattle–King County Bar Association was among the organizations that supported a motion demanding that the subpoena for the young lawyer be quashed.[8]

Often portrayed as a populist safeguard against government powers, the stated intention of convening a grand jury was to have a group of citizens assess a prosecutor's evidence to see if it merited a trial, thus protecting fellow citizens from unwarranted incursions by the criminal justice system. It could be a check against overzealous prosecutors and a means of investigating government corruption but had been employed by the U.S. government throughout the first half of the twentieth century to bludgeon its opponents. At the end of the 1960s, the government again deployed the federal grand jury as a political instrument. The Organized Crime Control Act of 1970 critically undermined the Fifth Amendment right of those called to testify before the grand jury to refrain from self-incrimination, and, in so doing, marked the death of the grand jury's independence from the central government. The act permitted the convening of special grand juries authorized to provide "use" immunity to those that were subpoenaed. Use immunity, which had been held unconstitutional since 1892, allowed the government to compel a witness to testify by prohibiting their statements from being used as evidence. The witness could, however, be prosecuted for acts disclosed in the forced testimony.

Between 1970 and 1973, grand juries in eighty cities were used to question more than 2,000 people about their connections to the anti-war movement.[9] Recognizing that embroiling activists in legal battles was an effective means of thwarting their efforts, the grand jury was also used simply to bog people down. In one much-publicized case, a grand jury in Gainesville, Florida, subpoenaed a number of Vietnam Veterans against the War, the most prominent and effective anti-war group at the time, during the week of the 1972 Republican Convention in Miami, against which the vets were organizing.

In 1970, one of the most infamous federal grand juries of the anti-war years occurred in Seattle. A young activist named Leslie Bacon was subpoenaed to testify in connection with the Weather Underground's bombing of the U.S. Capitol building in Washington, D.C, on March 1, 1971. She initially testified, then, disturbed by the government's wide-ranging inquiries, discontinued her cooperation and accused the government of "fishing." In 1975, a FBI agent with direct knowledge of the case told the *Washington Post*: "[W]e didn't know a damn thing. Leslie Bacon was the only thing we had and that was just a fishing expedition." Seattle was chosen "because we thought we were more likely to get an indictment out there." Pitkin had been one of the inquisitors.[10]

Pitkin's collaborator was Guy F. Goodwin, the chief of the Special Litigation Section of the Justice Department's Internal Security Division (ISD), a unit created by the Nixon administration in 1971 to prosecute crimes by "revolutionary terrorists." By 1973, the ISD maintained a full-time staff of fourteen lawyers. Goodwin traveled up to three weeks out of every month directing investigations against the diverse domestic opponents of the U.S. government.[11]

A temporary lull in the political deployment of grand juries occurred in 1973 when, in Frankensteinian fashion, the instrument turned on its master and was used to bring key members of the Nixon administration to justice. John Ehrlichman and Spiro Agnew became vocal opponents of the system: Agnew proclaimed that if reform of immunity resulted from the high profile of the process provoked by the Watergate scandal, "the suffering and sacrifice that I have had to undergo in the course of all this will be worthwhile."[12]

By the time the George Jackson Brigade grand jury investigation hit Seattle, it was clear that a new national initiative was under way to disrupt the activities of left-wing activists. Instead of the Justice Department's ISD, the FBI was the propulsive force. Grand jury proceedings hounded a full range of activists in the United States—trade unionists, Native Americans, Chicanos, and gays[13]—deluging these communities with paranoia. So many grand juries followed domestic bombings by urban guerrilla cells that they became a predictable consequence of such activity. Grand juries focused on the Black Liberation Army; in New York City, one sought out Puerto Rican *independentistas* of the Fuerzas Armadas de Liberación Nacional; in San Francisco, one was empanelled to home in on the Chicano Liberation Front, the New World Liberation Front, and the Red Guerilla Family, as well as on the Symbionese Liberation Army; a second grand jury was also convened in Harrisburg, Pennsylvania, to investigate the SLA. In 1976, when the filmmakers Haskell Wexler, Mary Lampson, and Emile DeAntonio clandestinely interviewed members of the

Weather Underground Organization and released their footage as the documentary *Underground*, they were subpoenaed as well.[14]

Lawyers were fair game in the new initiative. In the mid-1970s, a memo was circulated in the Justice Department stating that the defense efforts of the National Lawyers Guild bore partial responsibility for the department's high rate of losses in cases involving radicals. Soon after, several NLG lawyers—Withey among them—were subpoenaed to appear before various grand juries.

Though the NLG defended subpoenees, it did not necessarily defend the captured guerrillas themselves. The San Francisco chapter of the NLG considered the Symbionese Liberation Army so far beyond the pale that in 1975 it resolved that no one charged with SLA crimes should be defended by any of its members.[15] Despite, or perhaps *because*, of Ed Mead's history with the local NLG chapter, after his arrest, the organization issued a statement attacking his politics and refusing to provide assistance.[16]

By the time the grand jury was convened in Seattle to investigate the George Jackson Brigade, numerous educationals had occurred in Seattle, and the movement press had been consistently reporting on the issue for years. One of the chants at a demonstration protesting Jill Kray's subpoena was: "Lexington, New Haven, Seattle, Sioux Falls: We Won't Talk When the Grand Jury Calls."[17] The left-wing community was consciously defending itself against this particular form of government intimidation.

On the night of Tuesday April 13, 1976, a call came in to the 911 switchboard.

"I can tell you where the George Jackson Brigade is," the caller declared, providing a street address and apartment number on Capitol Hill. "They've got guns and ammo there too. Be careful!" As police mobilized to cover the call, another came in. "There are two badly injured people in the apartment!" the caller exclaimed. "Hurry!"

According to the account that 25-year-old Laddie Wright gave the Seattle press, three officers then forced their way into the apartment he shared with his wife, Sherry, knocked him to the floor with a blow to the head, nearly rendering him unconscious, and leveled a shotgun at him. With his wife at work, the only other person in the apartment was the Wrights' four-year-old son Jacob, who looked on as police struck his dad in the face and cursed him. When an officer spotted the kid, the policeman picked him up by his neck.

The police ransacked the apartment, found nothing incriminating, and left the building. In the meantime, a third call had come in, offering detailed information as to the location of the weapons. The police didn't reenter, but continued to watch from outside. Laddie, Sherry, who had subsequently returned from work, and their friend James Stephenson, who had dropped by, stepped outside to see if the police were still hanging around. An officer accosted James, accusing him of throwing rocks at a police car, and moved to arrest him. A fight broke out. Once under control, Wright and Stephenson were taken to the police station in handcuffs. Laddie, after being punched in the abdomen several times, was charged with "disorderly conduct" and "obstructing an officer." James was charged with "reckless endangerment."

Seattle Police Department spokesperson Tim Burgess initially confirmed that officers forced entry and conducted a search without a warrant, stating that this was not a violation of the law because of the immediate danger. After press coverage of the incident elicited indignant condemnations of police behavior, Burgess revised his account. Once the initial informational phone call had been received, he related:

> [W]e felt that it was necessary to move rapidly to protect lives. The chief dispatcher first attempted to obtain Mr. Wright's phone number, but it was unlisted. We went to the apartment building. Four uniformed officers were stationed outside the building and three others, including a sergeant, knocked on Mr. Wright's door. He [Wright] opened the door about a foot. He hesitated and then began to slam the door. The officers at this time pushed open the door and entered. One of the officers was carrying a shotgun, but it was never aimed at Mr. Wright.
>
> The only purpose of our entry was to find the injured people. The search lasted about 30 seconds and no force was used at any time.

At one point, Burgess inserted, the Wrights' child came into the room and proclaimed: "My daddy and his friends hide their guns. And they are going to shoot policemen." He continued:

> Three uniformed officers had remained outside the building in a marked patrol car for surveillance purposes. At about 11:20, an individual [identified by the police as James Scott Stephenson] came out of the building and hid behind a tree.
>
> The individual then hurled a half-pound piece of concrete at the car, barely missing one of the officers. The man then ran back into the building.

Police did not pursue the man into the building because, they judged, such a move could result in gunplay. Wright and Stephenson were arrested about ten minutes later when they came out of the apartment building. A scuffle broke out when police asked them to show identification, and police had to "physically restrain" both suspects.

In sum: "[I]t is clear to us that the calls were made to entrap the police in an overreaction that would lead to violence. That, however, did not happen. Our officers acted professionally from beginning to end." Burgess then insinuated that the Wrights themselves were involved in this plot, charging that the Aquarian Foundation, a church to which they belonged, was "anti-police." This charge was difficult to sustain in light of the fact that the American Brotherhood Alliance, which was affiliated with the foundation, had sponsored a rally several months earlier demanding higher pay and bulletproof vests for Seattle police officers.[18] Wright, for his part, told reporters that he understood the need of the police to investigate urgent calls. "I just don't think I should get beat up and called obscene names while they're checking it out."[19]

The next George Jackson Brigade–related police raid targeted the Capitol Hill political community more precisely. On the morning of Saturday May 1, 1976, a quick rap on the front door of an activist collective located at 905 Fifteenth Avenue East was followed by a terse ultimatum: "Open this door before we kick it down!" The surprised occupants—including Brenda Carter, the girlfriend of deceased Safeway bomber Ralph "Po" Ford and an active member of the Committee to End Grand Jury Abuse—acquiesced and were immediately patted down. A dozen ATF agents, accompanied by Assistant U.S. Attorney Jack Meyerson and an FBI agent, began to search the premises. The raid lasted three hours. Though not under arrest, the five occupants present were not permitted to leave or call their lawyers. According to the *Post-Intelligencer*, the agents never drew their weapons and did not arrest anyone. Across the street, several people gathered and chanted "People, United, Will Never Be Defeated," and "Imm*unity* in the Comm*unity*!"

The agents were armed with a search warrant that permitted them to seize "any and all writings pertaining to the life and works of George Jackson [and] the existence of the activities of the George Jackson Brigade" as well as "any and all documents pertaining to the construction of explosive devices"; pipe bomb components (speaker wire, toggle or safety switches, analog clocks or watches, low-voltage batteries, flashlight bulbs, and smokeless powder); and typewriters. Three typewriters were seized, as well as tape, tools, and personal papers. Among the latter were copies of a collection of Po's illustrations and musings, which Carter had published to memorialize her deceased lover. "It's heavy to me that mourning Po's death brings police repression," she later commented.[20]

An affidavit by ATF Special Agent Dick Smith, one of the investigators of the Capitol Hill bombings, had persuaded the judge to issue the warrant. Smith was among the federal agents who had been pawing through the collective's garbage since before the International Women's Day communiqué was even written—a common form of cooperation with the collection agency, United Waste Control Corporation President Warren Razore stated publicly.

The agents' refuse finds were paltry. On March 17, they discovered a document entitled "V. Brigade Criticism," but it dealt with the wrong brigade: the Venceremos Brigade. Agent Smith made the most of it, imaginatively calling the other brigade a "quasi-political organization that sends people to Cuba to aid the economy there and to be trained in terrorist techniques." (Venceremos Brigaders received no more strenuous weapons training in Cuba than wielding machetes to cut cane on sugar plantations and hammers on construction sites.)[21] On April 7, agents found a note addressed to an inmate at Walla Walla that mentioned Po and the grand jury. On April 14, they found a list referring to the "Agribusiness Accountability Project," which implied that poor people had a right to affordable, healthy food—a suspicious belief in light of the destructive campaign against Safeway.[22]

The findings were shared with an in-house handwriting expert, who contended that it was "highly probable that the April 7 note was written by the same person who signed 'Love and Struggle, GJB' at the end of the poem attached to the International Women's Day Communiqué."[23] In his affidavit, Smith developed this "highly probable" into a statement of fact. The proof went: Carter was "a friend of Ford's" (true); "the Brigade claimed [Po's] bombing attempt as its own" (false); therefore the International Women's Day Communiqué had been written at the Capitol Hill home (also false). The government soon stated its case more clearly: they wanted to speak with Po's friends to find out who might have been grieved and angered enough to plant the bomb in the Capitol Hill Safeway on September 18 of the previous year.

Carter and her housemate Katie Mitchell were subpoenaed to appear before the grand jury. A few days later, the feds caught up with Kathy Hubenet who, unbeknown to them, had moved out of the house, and served a subpoena on her as well. Mitchell, though in the Left Bank Collective, had known Po only casually, as had Hubenet. Like Kray, they were both single mothers.[24]

The new recipients of the subpoenas called a press conference in which they, too, denounced the search as an illegal "fishing expedition." Though irate, they realized that such tactics had become the norm. "It does not surprise us," they commented, "that the government uses grand jury subpoenas and illegal seizures to fish for information and intimidate politically progressive people, but it is not the kind of treatment that we . . . accept as a fact of everyday life." Mitchell drew attention to the preponderance of single mothers in the information-gathering campaign; their overrepresentation left little doubt in her mind that the coercion was intentional. She observed that the government recognized that "women with children are more vulnerable, and expects them to knuckle under to the fear and pressure." Carter and Hubenet pledged to resist the grand jury. "I will not talk," each declared. The residents filed a motion for the return of seized property, asserting that the government had taken items of an "intimate nature" that did not "pertain to explosives or to the George Jackson Brigade." Police had, however, seized the financial records of the Committee to End Grand Jury Abuse, which included a list of contributors.[25]

Government attorneys defended the search of the Capitol Hill home as a lawful and "highly professional part of a federal government investigation into a number of unsolved bombings in the Seattle area." Assistant U.S. Attorney Meyerson acknowledged that officers and agents exercised their right and duty to keep anyone in the house from interfering with the search, and anyone outside from entering and contaminating the search site, but insisted that "Every effort was made to minimize personal inconvenience" of persons in the house. Assistant U.S. Attorney Peter Mair went one step further, contending that, because the grand jury had the right to see all the evidence seized, the objection to the search was a premature attempt to suppress evidence.

U.S. District Judge Morell Sharp heard the dispute. He expressed concern that the agents had seized the list of financial contributors to the Committee to End Grand Jury Abuse. Mair argued that the agents were justified in finding and seizing materials indicating that the occupants were trying to frustrate the grand jury investigation of the bombings. Judge Sharp corrected him: "That type of relationship in the minds of law enforcement people [would have] a chilling effect on people who move against governmental interference." Promising that government agencies had not kept a copy, Mair returned the committee's records, along with a number of other items. One resident complained that they wanted *everything* back; later in the month, a federal magistrate recommended the return of several more items. Dan Wershow, an attorney for the Capitol Hill residents, asked Judge Sharp to issue an order preventing the government from using disputed evidence to prosecute any of his clients at a later date.[26]

On Thursday May 6, another member of the Left Bank Collective was subpoenaed. Like her friend Po, Nancy "Michelle" Whitnack, aged twenty-one, came from Sacramento. Her ex-husband, Jeff, had been friends with Po there. Po had briefly stayed with the couple the previous year, and Whitnack later acknowledged he could have been constructing a bomb at that time: "It's pretty obvious that he was building a bomb somewhere," she conceded. "I wasn't into going into Po's room and poking around."[27]

In Whitnack's case, the government had concrete evidence pointing to involvement in a bombing scheme. In April 1975, she and two others were arrested after police found stolen food in a vehicle parked in the yard of their house. Police searched their property and found a shotgun, blasting caps, and a typewriter, which they promptly seized. The three were quickly released, without bail, by Superior Court Judge Donald Horowitz. They were never charged, suggesting that the Seattle Police Department Intelligence Unit and/or FBI wished to observe them to see if they would implicate themselves or others more deeply in illegal activities. In October, in response to the previous month's bombing wave, Police Chief Robert Hanson criticized the swift release of the three young radicals. It was then revealed that the trio were under investigation regarding a possible connection to bombings.

By the time of Hanson's comments, Whitnack had certainly realized that she was under surveillance. In September, she had found a handwritten note taped to the back of her post office box reading: "Do not put any mail in this box. Give it to M. Smith in the morning." Whitnack removed the note, photocopied it, and replaced it. A few days later, it disappeared. Looking through an adjacent bank of empty mailboxes, she saw two signs in red felt-tip pen proclaiming "DANGER" taped to the back of her P.O. box. Additionally, federal agents were constantly hovering in front of Left Bank Bookstore, taking pictures of collective members and customers.[28]

On Monday May 10, at 7:30 P.M., *Post-Intelligencer* reporter Walt Wright received a phone call.

"Walt, do you know who this is?" Wright immediately identified the voice as that of John Sherman.

"Yes."

"I'm calling on behalf of the Brigade to ask some questions. I also want to make a statement to further authenticate the last communiqué we left you."

"Okay, what are the questions?" Wright asked.

"Who's been subpoenaed by the grand jury?"

"Brenda Carter, Katie—"

John cut in: "You can just use first names."

"Kathy and Michelle."

"Those women know nothing," Sherman declared immediately. "My fingerprints are all over everything regarding the International Women's Day communiqué. We authenticated it with one of my fingerprints. A snide remark a cop made in the paper gave us the idea. It was obviously me. They shouldn't be bothering those women."

"The *Intelligencer* received a photocopy of the communiqué," Wright explained, "so your fingerprints definitely weren't on what we got. They couldn't verify the arch bar as the one that had been put in your mouth either. And they said the slug you sent in was too damaged for conclusive identification."[29]

"That bullet was in good shape!" John protested.

There was a lull in the conversation.

"Is there anything you have to say to people in the community?" Wright asked.

"I love them, and I'm well and I'm safe. The outlook is good, and nothing has changed. My politics are the same as they have been."[30]

John's telephone call was welcomed by several of the Capitol Hill women under subpoena. Carter told Wright: "I'm real glad he did make [the call]. It makes clear that it makes a lot more sense for him to have signed it than for any of us to have signed it."

The authorities' handling of this obvious point—that Sherman was the person most likely to have signed the communiqué—bolstered activists' contention that the accusation about the composition of the International Women's Day communiqué was made in bad faith. Authorities had samples of Sherman's writing from when he was in custody. When prompted, a spokesperson for the FBI stated that Sherman could indeed have been responsible for the signature, but that their comparisons, so far, had been inconclusive. Subpoenee Katie Mitchell opined: "I don't think the [government] believed we signed the communiqué, but I do think they are real interested in who we know."[31]

On June 13, after Sherman called Wright again, the feds urged the fugitive, through Wright, to send them an additional handwriting sample. An agent told Wright, "We really don't have enough of Sherman's handwriting to make a good comparison. If he could send an extensive sample of his handwriting, or if someone else could supply something else that could be authenticated as his handwriting, then we can compare it. He could avoid a tell-tale postmark by sending the writing to someone else for remailing, but I don't have to tell these people how to use 'drops.' They know all about it!"[32] The following week the government, without a new handwriting sample, quietly conceded Sherman's own claim about the signature on the communiqué.[33]

Regarding Sherman's first call, the women expressed concern that he appeared to have recognized them by their first names. "None of us have met him," one of them stressed.[34] Carter suggested: "His recognition of our names might mean that he recognized none of us are associated with the Brigade. Or," she postulated, "someone else might have told him about the subpoenas."

In a jailhouse interview, Wright told Mead of Sherman's call. Mead sent a message to Sherman through Wright: "You are my brother, and I love you." Adding to earlier speculation about the role of women in the Brigade, Ed continued: "Give my deepest feeling for our comrade sisters."[35] He also weighed in on the grand jury's selection of subpoenees. When interviewers with a movement paper asked him to clarify an implication that prosecutors were "getting the wrong people" he laughed, stating simply: "That's what I'm saying."[36]

On May 18, as 100-plus people marched, sang, and performed guerrilla theater in protest against grand jury abuse outside of the Federal Courthouse, Carter was called to testify. She declared herself a political radical denied her rights due to grand jury powers: "I have the choice . . . of being an informer—or going to prison." But, as with Peter Lippman, the government stopped short of making her choose between the two, demanding only a handwriting sample and a fingerprint. She yielded to the court order and was not asked to testify.[37]

The next day Whitnack filed suit against the federal government, demanding $25,000 on the grounds that it illegally intercepted her mail, searched her home, followed her and used electronic eavesdropping devices against her. The government

FIGURE 10. Anti-grand jury demonstration, *Northwest Passage,* March 15–19, 1976, cover.

conceded that it had conducted one search, informing her attorney that agents had poked through her home and belongings the previous September and that she had been subpoenaed as a result of their discoveries.

The same day Kathy Hubenet yielded to a court order to provide handwriting and fingerprints. Though three months of its term remained, the grand jury was then dismissed. Mitchell and Whitnack were excused, at least until the grand jury reconvened.[38]

On the evening of Sunday June 20, police hammered on the door of one of the basement units at the Taft apartment complex at 1213 East Spring Street.

"Open up!" the commanding officer demanded.

"Who's there?" a man's voice responded.

"It's the Seattle Police Department! *Open this door now!*"

"Do you have a warrant?"

"We don't need a warrant, we're in hot pursuit. Open this door now or we'll kick it down!"

The door opened to reveal to police Paul Zilsel, the putative leader of the Left Bank Collective, and two younger collective members, Helene Ellenbogen and Wayne Parker, standing before a table covered with guns and cleaning supplies.

"What's going on in here?" an officer demanded as his men filed into the room.

"We went target practicing today. We're cleaning our guns. They're all legal," Zilsel replied.

Police officers summoned their superior officer Sgt. Chuck Pillon to the scene. Pillon was familiar with intelligence reports on Zilsel and aware of a warning that the George Jackson Brigade might be planning a bombing for the 4th of July.[39] Agents from the Bureau of Alcohol, Tobacco and Firearms were called in and, together with police, inventoried seven guns, sixteen ounces of gunpowder, a funnel, glue, prophylactics, scotch tape, six pens, flyers, some litmus paper, roll fuses, twenty boxes of ammunition, a soldering iron, solder, wire cutters, flash bulbs, electrical supplies, two wigs, and lists police claimed contained the names of corporate officers, banks, and government agencies. Also confiscated were several political books and pamphlets, including a number of books describing techniques for urban guerrilla warfare, some of which provided information on the construction of bombs, and a copy of the Brigade's New Year's communiqué.[40] The three collective members were arrested. Their address books, personal letters, and purses and wallets were taken. They were held for four hours and denied access to their attorneys. Before letting them go, an SPD lieutenant acknowledged that all their belongings were legal and promised to return them the following day, yet by the fall, police still had most of them and, what's more, in September displayed them to the grand jury investigating bombings.[41]

On Monday the Left Bank Collective released a statement in which Zilsel et al. explained that the apartment had been rented (under the pseudonym "Cheryl Swift," a detail they omitted) a few weeks earlier to provide a location for the storage of their weapons, which, though legal, might have been subject to confiscation if discovered in a search of their own homes. They, like the other members of the collective, feared having their homes searched as part of the grand jury's bombing investigation: "Members of our collective have had their houses searched in recent months and have been generally harassed by the police and the federal grand jury and though all the weapons are legal and registered to us, we felt that they might be subject to confiscation in the event of a search."

They denounced the search as illegal, maintaining that it was meant to set them up. While indignant, collective members maintained perspective; they recognized their white privilege, surmising that they would be dead by now if they were Black or Native American. They were determined not to be intimidated by the government. On July 9, they filed a suit demanding immediate return of their belongings.

Zilsel, Ellenbogen, and Parker were promptly subpoenaed to appear before the grand jury.[42] They sued the government to quash the subpoena. In the proceedings, the police department's explanation of the chain of events that had led to the "accidental" raid on the activists disintegrated. A man who fitted the description of the one the officers had said they had been pursuing when they charged into the apartment building testified that, while the arrests and seizure were taking place, he had leaned out of his window and asked the police: "What's going on?" They had ignored him and never returned to conduct an interview. The actual driver of the stolen car was apprehended. Police had said that upon arrest, he had pointed in the direction of the apartment and said another participant in the crime had run in that direction, thus beginning the chase. The detainee testified for the "Left Bank 3" that he'd never done any such thing.

Federal District Judge Sharp threw out the radicals' motion. "We didn't really expect them to rule in our favor," Zilsel remarked afterward. "But what was striking about Judge Sharp's ruling was its blatancy, its total contempt of the legal issues."[43] "They are trying to portray us as 'terrorists,' but the real terrorists are in the government," the Left Bank statement concluded.[44]

Increasing evidence that a nascent guerrilla cell overlapped with the Left Bank Collective, combined with the fact that Whitnack knew Bruce and Ed from past prison activism, transformed her, in the eyes of investigators, from a potential source of information into a criminal suspect. She was re-subpoenaed when the jury reconvened in early June. She refused to testify or to provide fingerprints or handwriting samples. The judge had refused to jail her for contempt for her refusal to testify before the first grand jury, but confined her in July when she continued to do so the second time around.[45] Laurie Raymond, the sister of Jill, who had been jailed for over a year for resisting a grand jury in Lexington, Kentucky, called out to her fellow courtroom observers: "Are you just going to sit politely by while they take us all away? *We've got to show some resistance to this!*" She approached Michelle, was pounced upon by a U.S. marshal, and the two women were dragged off together, Laurie by her hair, Michelle by her handcuffs. Raymond was later convicted of assaulting the officer.[46]

Whitnack was then accused not only of having information on the Brigade but of being a member. She refused to appear before a police lineup in connection with the probe into the New Year's Eve Laurelhurst bombing, and, as she told the *Women's Press* in Eugene, Oregon, "was dragged by five marshals to a lineup, where a 'witness' identified me as 'the woman who climbed up a tree' by the substation the afternoon before [the explosion]."[47]

"Witness" in quotation marks because the woman had been shown pictures of Whitnack previous to the lineup. When she first heard of the positive identification by a suburban housewife Whitnack queried Mead, with whom she managed to have contact at the jail: "I wouldn't ask you this if I didn't need to know, but was there anybody who looked like me in the Laurelhurst bombing?"

"Nope," he replied truthfully. "There were no women involved."

Sherman called Wright again to state that Whitnack "knows nothing. I can tell you now that she's not involved." He sent Wright duplicate samples of his handwriting, fingerprints, and samples from the typewriter used to write Brigade communiqués from Laurelhurst on. He asked that one set be given to the authorities and the other be retained for independent verification.[48]

Whitnack's allies investigated the site of the Laurelhurst bombing and discovered that it was completely unnecessary to climb a tree to get a good look at the City Light substation and that the only tree sufficient to hold a grownup's weight had no branches for its first ten feet. Whitnack noted: "at 5'6" and 195 pounds, I'm not the most athletic, proficient tree-climber you'll ever meet."

In her own defense, Whitnack pointed out that her "critical support for the GJB has included some pretty scathing public criticism in the past, before they cleaned up their act with regard to people's safety." This critical perspective did not cause her to denounce the Brigade, as many of her supporters urged her to do. According to Left Bank members, the Left Bank Collective, the primary anti-authoritarian voice in the Committee to End Grand Jury Abuse, had recently been forced out of the group by Prairie Fire Organizing Committee (PFOC) members. These were the same people who, in the past, had insulted all who declined to commence domestic armed struggle, but now the national leadership had issued new orders to combat the practice. It was, they declared, an indulgence that alienated "the masses." PFOC members refused to be in the same organization with people who voiced critical support for the GJB.

The PFOC people hadn't been the only ones to give Left Bank members grief for not only rhetorically supporting armed struggle but preparing to engage in it themselves. One Left Bank Collective statement remarked irritably, "Numerous folks have expressed interest in why we owned [the] seized guns and literature. We have no intention of giving any information to the government which will aid them in their attempts to frame us now or in the future, and will not answer any questions about the specifics of our activities. If they want to spy on us and our friends, they will have to do their work the hard way."[49]

The longer Whitnack's ordeal continued, the more positively she spoke of the Brigade: "You look a *whole* lot better from my perch today than you did ten months ago," she commented enthusiastically. She was a member of the Left Bank Collective at the time it issued its disavowal of the Brigade's first Safeway bombing. She observed that the collective had addressed the criticism to the mainstream media because they had had no "expectation that anyone who could do something that wrong was going to be receptive to criticism." When the Brigade criticized itself, she reevaluated her opinion upward.[50]

Aside from the first Safeway bombing, Whitnack rated the Brigade's actions as "good to real good. The real good was breaking out John Sherman," she told *Open Road*, a Vancouver-based anti-authoritarian paper, that winter. She also liked the destruction of the City Light transformer: "I'm real glad that if the Feds are going to try and hang one of your actions on me, it was at least one of the real nice ones," she wrote in a note to the Brigade composed in King County Jail and printed in *Dragon*. She added: "I have to cop that I think a part of the respect I receive in here is due to a belief by some of the sisters that I *am* with you despite my protestations!"[51]

Jill Raymond, who had come to Seattle after her sister Laurie's arrest at Michelle's contempt hearing, commended Whitnack for her principled stance. "It has been to the prosecution's advantage in most of these cases that the people it was calling to offer up information were not people who would be likely to have been so connected up with the original 'crimes' that they would have their own personal or political interests at stake in defending those crimes," she observed.

> In other words, the government hopes to play on our own real difficulties with an act like the bombing of a Safeway store in which people were injured, or with bank robberies [and] shootings [—] simply with "adventurism." The problem with that, in the most pragmatic terms, is that the system is not all that interested in bank robberies, or even in the bombing of grocery stores, difficult though that may be for the law and order factions to live with. If whole communities were investigated every time a bank was robbed there would be little time for anything else. The system's own actions are what stamp each of these cases as politically motivated investigations.

By refusing to comply with the government's divide-and-conquer strategy, Whitnack refused "the dividing up, the isolating, the typing, the black-and-whiting of the movement into distinct and separate camps to use each one to discredit and invalidate the other."[52]

In public, Whitnack was not shy about her radical politics. She told a reporter from the *Seattle Times* that she was an anarchist who believed the government should be destroyed so as to let "people control their own lives." To this end, she supported "people who do bombings as long as there is a regard for people's lives."[53]

The prosecutor's motives in insinuating Whitnack's involvement with the Brigade—"to scare me to testify, to make me a 'warning' to other witnesses, and to justify jailing me without charge or trial to the press and public"—were transparent enough to be met with skepticism by the mainstream media. He didn't attempt to press charges, leaving her in legal limbo.[54]

Once in jail, Whitnack provided the impetus for a collective effort to improve health care in the institution. On August 10, thirty-three female inmates signed a petition saying that "we are not receiving even the minimum medical care to which we are entitled under the sheriff's own rules and regulations . . . never mind what people on the streets expect as decent and right medical treatment." In September, the gay women's coalition Leftist Lezzies organized a demonstration attended by 150 people providing outside support for the demands of the inmates. In retaliation, Whitnack was shipped to the Tacoma jail. King County women prisoners staged a hunger strike demanding her return. One of her lawyers, John Ziegler, finagled the transfer.[55]

On December 20, Michelle was taken from her cell to the lobby of the jail, where she was met by three federal marshals, three ATF agents, one SPD officer, and a jail matron. They showed her an order authorizing them to obtain her fingerprints and mug shot, using "reasonable force" if necessary.

"I wish to consult with one of my attorneys!" Michelle cried as the agents menaced her. This request was ignored and, as they had chosen a day when the magistrate and primary supervising officer were off duty, there was no other recourse. The agents choked Whitnack until she passed out, then took her fingerprints while she was unconscious. They also took her mug shot forcibly. After that she was abruptly released.

The prosecutor's office issued a press release stating that the prints had been obtained "without injury to the prisoner." It continued that the prints would be compared to those found on the unexploded pipe bomb planted in the downtown Federal Building September 12 of the previous year. Michelle and her comrades saw this as a face-saving measure: "If they thought I'd planted that bomb, wouldn't it be better to keep me in custody until *after* they compared the prints?"[56]

Mead, observing from his perch on the tenth floor of the King County Jail, was pleased by the cohesion the Left community was demonstrating in the face of persecution. "Good old uncle Ho [Chi Minh] said that adversity is a true test of a people's fidelity," he commented. Invoking imagery straight out of George Jackson's *Blood in My Eye*, he reminded the politically conscious that the situation "is not so difficult as what might be in the future . . . barbed wire, and National Guard patrols on Capitol Hill and the Central Area. House to house searches, doors being kicked in."[57] Mead's prophecy did not come to pass, but the vision he projected onto Capitol Hill did resemble his own conditions inside the jail, which were as stark as could be.

## 20

# Diverging Paths to a Common Dream

*In which Seattle's communist, socialist, and anarchist revolutionaries exchange dueling polemics regarding the propriety of the Brigade's activities*

In his second month in jail, Ed Mead publicly acknowledged his membership in the George Jackson Brigade. Resolved to use his trials as a forum for his politics, Mead left the broad contours of the charges against him uncontested. With little to hide, he became the de facto public spokesperson for the organization, doing his best to convey collective goals and his own personal motivations. He granted interviews to the *Post-Intelligencer* and the *Seattle Times* and engaged in a lengthy discussion with Seattle's left-wing community in the pages of the countercultural biweekly *Northwest Passage*.

Mead's jailhouse interview with two contributors to the *Passage* was the first opportunity for the city's aboveground Left to present their questions and concerns to a member of the Brigade. The first question of the interview was: "I'd like you to comment on whether you consider yourselves a terrorist group."

"My thoughts are constantly changing as I learn things," Mead responded. "Initially my thinking was more 'you fight Fascist terrorism with revolutionary counterterror.' Terrorism is traditionally the weapon of the weak. . . . As the Brigade grew stronger it drew further and further away from terrorist acts."

Mead's dissatisfaction with the city's aboveground Left was immediately apparent. It was only "[o]ver a lot of resistance from the Left" that he had "joined with others" to develop a capability for "revolutionary violence." "There's a real tendency for people to say: 'There's two kinds of people—there's those doing armed work, and they can take all the risks and make the sacrifices and we can sit back and criticize them. . . . [W]e can just go about our work and revolution is some nebulous hope or passing fad.'"

Mead's critique applied to the country as a whole, but he regarded the situation in his adopted city as particularly acute. "Seattle has traditionally been 'laid back,' kind of a nice place where lefties go because of the mountains and hiking. The struggle should come other places before it comes here." Now that the grand jury had returned "the Seattle left has to deal ... just like the San Francisco community had to learn to deal" after the Symbionese Liberation Army, New World Liberation Front, and others started blasting all over the city. Mead predicted that "the Brigade is going to totally bypass the left."

Mead introduced himself as "a person who has done years of mass work," inside prisons and out. In Seattle, he had become involved in the local chapter of Prairie Fire, and had experienced an immediate identification with the Symbionese Liberation Army. "The SLA inspired me, though ... they went too far too fast. The Brigade has tried to go further and faster than Weather, but not to go as far and as fast as the SLA. To maintain some sort of balance, we always have to be testing the outer limits of struggle: we don't want to go beyond what is sustainable. There's no clear line. The only way to find out what is the sustainable level of struggle is to get your feet wet." Up to the present, the Brigade, in Mead's estimation, had "done a pretty good job of measuring and defining what is sustainable." The organization was "doing just fine. I can think of nothing I would suggest they do differently than what they're doing right now." The Brigade had demonstrated a capability of resisting being drawn into self-defeating disputes with power. Specifically, Mead pointed to the "gauntlet" thrown down by John Reed, the FBI's special agent in charge in Seattle, after the Sherman jailbreak. "The Brigade is not responding to the media," he observed. "[T]hat's a real credit."

Ed shared the concern voiced by others that the poem attached to the International Women's Day communiqué revealed too much about the makeup of the Brigade and its implied constituency: "[T]here's always an important line to be drawn between the need for security and the need to educate. It's important that people know that the Brigade is made of people of different races and sexes. And different sexual orientations, within those races and sexes."

"What kind of support do you think you have among working and poor people?" one of the interviewers asked.

"Some people think that in order to have the support of people, poor people should organize themselves and march around in circles with signs saying 'We support the George Jackson Brigade.'" This was a conceptual rut. "In terms of food, shelter, guns, money—that's support. And we're getting it. The Brigade couldn't exist without it."

Mead wished to correct an earlier comment he had made that was misinterpreted to the effect "that everybody should be doing armed work." His position was more nuanced: "[W]hat Communists should be doing right now is to strengthen their weakest point[:] ... the armed front. That's not to say that there isn't very important work being done at the mass level." The aboveground work, however, was solely defensive in nature; physical confrontation with power was a crucial "supplement" that would give the Left the opportunity to achieve positive changes.

The priority Mead gave to armed action was uncontestable: "As things continue to decay, how are we going to be able to overturn this thing if not by armed force?" Are those who hold power "going to peaceably give it up?" he demanded. Those who saw a possibility of significant change by peaceful means were deluded. Those in the First World who conceded that revolutions inevitably involved violence, and who condoned its use by their Third World counterparts yet indefinitely delayed deploying force themselves, were racist. Mead summarized their position with bitter sarcasm: "[I]t's alright to wage armed struggle in other countries, but when it comes to waging armed struggle at home, then that's a different thing . . . our lives are more important than those gooks or niggers."

Doesn't being situated in "the heart of imperialism . . . call for different tactics?" an interviewer inquired. "How long, how long do you think we should wait?" Mead retorted—until those struggling against U.S. imperialism abroad "invade our borders to destroy the class enemy of all humanity?" He continued: "The best way that we can help the people of Puerto Rico, the people of South Africa, of South America, all the oppressed people of the world is not by marching, not by mouthing anti-imperialist slogans, but by waging armed struggle against the common enemy."[1]

Roxanne Park, one of Mead's interviewers for the *Northwest Passage*, penned a response to his comments and the discernible ideology of the Brigade. This, in turn, sparked further debate in the following issues of the paper, primarily from the Left Bank Collective and Mead himself.

Park began by defining the Brigade as an organization engaged in "terrorism," a pejorative, as opposed to one waging "armed struggle," as they claimed. The latter, for Park, "implies highly organized, extensive resistance." She did not consider these conditions prevalent in the United States, so any organization engaged in armed confrontation was categorically "terrorist." Park's distinction between "terrorism" and "armed struggle" was an odd one to find in a movement paper: it was the one favored by law enforcement and printed in the mainstream media.[2] In this view, the state was presented as a neutral arbiter between conflicting parties; the police acted to cap passions that threatened to boil over. The interests of the oligarchy, with its integral ties to the business world, were conflated with those of the country's people. From this perspective, detonating a bomb in the unoccupied offices of a particular corporation or state agency was identical to setting one off in a crowded public square. In the early 1970s, William Olson, assistant attorney general for the Internal Security Division of the Justice Department, stated the case this way: "In recent years, because of the Vietnam War, there has developed the feeling that what is important is the motive for which the crime is committed. As a result, we come to the term 'political crime' which we don't have in this country, in my opinion. We don't have crimes related to people's political beliefs or statements. We have protections in the Constitution, such as the First Amendment, that protect those adequately. It's hard for me to see the difference between the bombing of a bank for the purpose of obtaining money or the bombing of a bank for the purpose of protest against the establishment."[3] Lee Moriwaki, one of the *Seattle Times*'s reporters on the Brigade, concurred: "When you start using guns and bombs, 'terrorism' becomes an accurate descriptor."[4]

The conventional distinction between "armed struggle" and "terrorism" in Left-inclined publications concerned an organization's selection of targets: did it concentrate closely on the state or corporate opponents, or did it seek to inflict pain upon and sow fear among the populace? In an article entitled "We ... Support Armed Action ... Now," the Left Bank Collective corrected Park: "Armed struggle is *not* of necessity a mass uprising, but rather includes a whole spectrum of militant resistance to the ruling class, including bombings, armed occupations of buildings and land," like the prison uprising in Attica, and those which took place on Menominee land and at Wounded Knee, as well as "prisoner breakouts, armed robbery, kidnapping, assassination, assaults on police and military installations, etc." It also included a range of vocations. The underground consisted of: "technicians, writers, printers, forgers, harborers, drivers, suppliers, and a host of others." This path was "one way ... in which revolutionaries can make militant demands on the system, put cracks in the walls, and break down the capitalist system." The "central proviso," for them, was "that the revolutionary *must always* make concern for the welfare of innocent people a vital part of the planning and execution of actions." In contrast, "terrorism" was "armed action which deliberately or callously ignores the welfare of the people, and is not focused on the groups and individuals against which the actor is fighting." It was "primarily a right-wing phenomenon" that complemented the "*institutionalized* terrorism" of those in power.[5] Mead himself confused the Brigade's place between these two semantic camps. He called the organization's initial bombings against the Bureau of Indian Affairs and the FBI terroristic because they "were not accompanied by any warnings." In contrast, in Mead's eyes, the Brigade's attack against Safeway on Capitol Hill, in which numerous people were injured while completing a daily chore, was less so because the injuries inflicted were unintentional. The Left Bank Collective readily conceded that the Brigade's first Safeway bombing "was not defensible," but said that the George Jackson Brigade had "publicly criticized themselves" and "learned from" their mistake. By way of comparison, the Left Bank Collective asked: "When was the last time you heard a police agency apologize for its acts of terror against the people?"[6]

Park's criticisms of the Brigade were tactical, not political: both she and the Brigade wanted to see communists and socialists in power. Park did not even differ on means: "I believe that force, or the threat of force, will be the only way a revolution will succeed in this country." Her problem with the Brigade was not "that they engage in illegal action or are willing to defend their beliefs with guns, or that they commit armed bank robberies, or even that they shoot police." It was a matter of timing. Though "convinced that there will come a time when we need to be ready with arms, with our lives, if we intend to radically transfer power in this country," Park contended that more consciousness-raising needed to be done to create a viable prospect of success. Brigade members opted for confrontation because they did "not have the energy to sustain their political commitment." They were the contemporary equivalent of those Lenin condemned with the words: "Calls for terror are merely forms of *evading* the most pressing duties that now rest upon Russian revolutionaries."

Park made the questionable assertion that: "It is relatively easy to hold up a bank, shoot police, bomb a few buildings." Brigade members had "chosen to turn their backs to" the challenging work of "changing people's minds about the viability of capitalism" and "organizing workers."

Left Bank collective members defended the organizing credentials of the known members of the Brigade: "People like Bruce Seidel, Ed Mead, and John Sherman came from long backgrounds of doing aboveground organizing, and clearly see their armed work as a natural extension of their past work." Claiming a privileged place for either above- or underground work was counterproductive: both were necessary, and complemented one another. What made one more "difficult" than the other was a matter of individual inclination.

The Brigade's take on the organized Left offended Park. "Listening to Ed Mead I sometimes thought he considered the Left a greater danger than capitalism," she recalled of their interview. While scorning the aboveground, the Brigade's actions had brought police repression crashing down on the heads of others. "Mead *chose* to engage in illegal activities, so he knew what consequences he was facing. Other people were merely friends of Po's, or went to a hearing, or answered a telephone call: they did not make a similar choice."

The bombings themselves did not constitute an intelligible form of propaganda. Ordinary people experienced "confusion," "a mild horror," and "an implicit fear" around such activities and their perpetrators, encouraging them to cling to the police as protectors.

"The arrogance of the Brigade seems most obvious," she complained. "They think they know what is needed . . . at this point and they intend to involve all the rest of us in their decision." She quoted one of the Capitol Hill subpoenees: "Every time Mead opens his mouth, he hurts someone."[7]

The person who provided the quotation was certainly not Michelle Whitnack. Though she had recently been a member of the Left Bank Collective, Whitnack composed her own passionate excoriation of Park's piece, which she called "the most offensive article I've ever read in what's usually a real fine paper." "You say that you 'do not see this country even close to a state of armed struggle.' Just who are you talking to? Other lefties? Do you have any contact to speak of with the people locked up in prison anywhere across the country? Do you hear the Black or Native American communities unanimously voting to 'postpone violence until a receptive time'?" These are among the communities for whom "every day is next to intolerable"; people whom Park wasn't "even considering." "What I do hear you saying," Whitnack continued, echoing Mead's rhetoric, "is that it's all right for poor and oppressed people to fight—just so long as the fighting's not close to home."

Whitnack acknowledged that, inasmuch as persuasion alone couldn't convince the defenders of a certain regime to abandon the interests of those who gave orders in favor of their own best interests, "use of violence is an admission of powerlessness." But indefinitely postponing a comprehensive campaign for social change until such an ideal condition was reached revealed a comfort with the status quo and an insensitivity toward others who suffered every day in order that their comfort be maintained.

As to the arrogance of the Brigade, Whitnack offered no defense: "I'll be the last to take issue with you . . . . I feel real strongly that the tendency of people doing armed stuff to become arrogant and 'heavier than thou' is the greatest danger of that kind of work. What we aboveground can do to cut down this tendency and make the underground more answerable to the aboveground—as well as vice versa—is to offer principled constructive criticism." Park's criticism, in Whitnack's estimation, was too self-righteous to be considered as such.

Beyond prioritizing armed struggle over public organizing (which the Brigade did not do in their communiqués), the criticism that they were intending to involve others in their actions appeared to Whitnack nonsensical. "[E]veryone who is trying to be part of a revolution . . . has an idea of what they think is needed at any given point." Did Park's case for inaction affect others any less than the Brigade's forward charge?

Whitnack took Park to task for presenting those who were called to testify before the grand jury as naïve innocents. "I for one have spent the last several years of my life trying real hard to tromp on the Government's toes any way I could—mostly by doing prison work. Considering that, if I had been really surprised to eventually get a subpoena for my efforts, I'd feel pretty damn sure I either wasn't too bright, or was at least real naïve, and never really had any idea of just what kind of beast it was I'd been fighting against all along. . . . If we don't want trouble from the government, we don't belong on the Left, we belong in the suburbs."[8]

Left Bank was not particularly fazed by the grand jury: "The events in Seattle are acquainting many white radicals with the nature of police repression which the Black, Chicano, Native American, and Puerto Rican communities have lived under constantly for decades." Bemoaning the plight of those who had been called before the grand jury ignored the regularity of this repression in other communities, repression that "will continue until the state which sponsors these outrages is destroyed, a process from which further repression and abuse can be expected in abundance."

The importance of the Brigade, and others like them, could be judged, in part, by the reaction of police. "We believe that . . . the ruling class takes the threat which groups like the G.J.B. pose to the continued existence of the state extremely seriously . . . the indications are that such groups are growing, and that the state is nearly powerless to halt their activities. This fact in itself is an indication of a 'base of support' in the community, and one which, if not destroyed, may grow into a permanent base of operations for the guerrillas."[9]

It was easy for Park's opponents to cast her in the camp of overprivileged whites who identified as socialist revolutionaries but delayed the actual revolution indefinitely because it would not only inconvenience them personally, but would, in its combustive violence, prompt troubling ethical questions as well. To resolve this internal dilemma, these intellectually inclined individuals created an idealized path to a more just world, one that, if followed in every detail, would bring victory with only infinitesimal casualties. If anyone disturbed this vision, the visionary balked, and, if possible, ignored the intruder or, when groups such as the SLA and the Brigade brought down repression that forced the issue, denounced the interlopers.[10]

As the murder of the Kennedy brothers and Martin Luther King Jr. had done in the United States, the U.S.-backed coup in Chile brutally murdered the vision of bloodless revolution in the international arena. In the aftermath, people such as Park acknowledged the place for force, but only under appropriate conditions.

"This particular litany has been repeated over and over again by dogmatists since the successful revolution of 1917 in Russia," the Left Bank Collective (or, put more accurately, probably their strongest personality Paul Zilsel) chastised, "in other countries in every stage of technological development, and has been proven wrong repeatedly by armed militants who were not prepared to wait for the 'right time.'" The most prominent example of successful revolutionaries who had refused to conform to textbook protocols was the Chinese Communist Party. In mobilizing from a peasant base, Mao Zedong's "people's army" had ignored Comintern dictates that a country must pass through an industrialized stage so as to create an urban proletariat, which could then seize power. "In Vietnam, in Laos, in Angola, Mozambique, Algeria, etc., the pattern of guerrilla warfare has invariably involved a very small group of fighters, outside the doctrinaire left, growing with their successes to become popular revolutionary movements." Cuba was the clearest example: of the eighty-two people on the initial boat to the island only twenty-two managed to regroup in the mountains, where they began accumulating military successes while being denounced by the country's official Communist party until victory was imminent.

A number of other groups in Latin America employed tactics similar to the Brigade's:

> The legendary Tupamaros (M.L.N.) of Uruguay, whose numbers were believed to be in the thousands, were begun by a group of no more than 12 people, whose first actions included theft of food trucks and food giveaways, bombing of office buildings, and a gun club robbery. The Movement of the Revolutionary Left (M.I.R.), now considered *the* resistance to Chilean fascism, was rejected by the traditional left during the Popular Unity period because of its "extremism". The People's Revolutionary Army (ERP), которая is now waging outright guerilla war against the Argentine junta, began as a small urban "terrorist" organization.[11]

Just as "[a]rmed struggle may use the same spectrum of tactics here in Seattle as in Latin America, Europe, Palestine, or Vietnam," practitioners came in for the same criticisms regardless of locality. These organizations hadn't come into being passively: they had taken the initiative. "People simply do not learn these sorts of skills in the abstract against some later time when they might want to use them. The only time people have the time or the interest in developing such skills is when they are preparing to wage war immediately, or are already engaged in it. Thus preparation and ability to carry out armed struggle begins when people are ready to fight, so that if people *are* ready to fight, there is no 'better' time than the present."

In none of these countries was the development of an armed component unproblematic. It was a constant battle to maintain an effective balance between the cultural and diplomatic fronts and that of the military. Indeed, a particular movement's success in doing so dictated not only their ability to win the war, but how they fared in the peace that followed. Timeliness was certainly an issue. The position of Franz Fanon on incipient anti-colonial struggles in Angola and Guinea-Bissau is illustrative. Fanon was a French-trained Martiniquean psychiatrist who, in the mid-1960s, was embraced by politicos in the United States for his assertion that violence on the part of the oppressed against the oppressor had a therapeutic quality. In 1959, at a conference in Rome, Fanon, acting as an advisor to the Provisional Government of the Algerian Republic, urged a delegation from the Popular Movement for the Liberation of Angola (MPLA, after its name in Portuguese), the most established anti-colonial organization in the oil-rich West African country, to initiate guerrilla warfare against their Portuguese colonizers as soon as possible. The MPLA delegation agreed in principle, but reality had circumscribed their options: many MPLA members were in jail. The MPLA demanded time to plan its insurgency properly. Fanon, disapproving, directed Algerian aid instead to the Union of Peoples of Angola, the creation of Holden Álvaro Roberto, who was widely believed to be in the pay of the United States, but was ready to initiate violence. Roberto quickly launched a bloody guerrilla offensive, which elicited harsh repression in turn: the estimated death toll was 20,000–30,000. More important, the ill-conceived effort set the stage for both a continuously bloody anti-colonial campaign and, before victory could be enjoyed, a dismal civil war.[12]

In 1960, Fanon provided Amílcar Cabral, the leader of the African Independence Party for the liberation of Guinea and the Cape Verde Islands (PAIGC), with the same charge he had given to the MPLA (of which Cabral was a founding member). Cabral declined, saying that the preparatory work for a rurally based armed campaign had not yet been completed. Fanon excoriated Cabral, who replied: "It is better to begin the armed struggle with an apparent delay, but with guarantees of being able to continue, than to start at some premature moment, before we have established all the conditions to ensure its continuity and victory for our people." This preparation allowed the struggle in Guinea-Bissau to become one of the "cleanest" of the continent's decolonization campaigns: it was the most surgical in targeting representatives of the colonists, the least involved in gratuitous, unfocused violence. This was in sharp contrast to Angola, which, partially as a result of Fanon's involvement, quickly became a bloodbath and remained a gory quagmire for decades.[13]

The difference between Cabral and Roxanne Park and her ilk was that Cabral had been preparing for a campaign, whereas Park and those who thought as she did were simply waiting indefinitely, and protested vehemently when events developed independently. Marighella had an injunction for those in doubt: "It is better to err acting than to do nothing for fear of erring. Without initiative there is no guerrilla warfare." This was the advice heeded by the Brigade.

Unlike Mead, Park, and nearly all the organizations they themselves cited as exemplary, the Left Bank Collective members were anarchists. The armed activities they were endorsing had been denounced as "adventurist," an "anarchistic" strain, related to "infantile disorders" like "'left-wing' communism," by orthodox communists. The Collective asserted "we do not seek to have anyone 'in control' and the armed struggle cannot wait for the formation of a 'vanguard party' under which we have no intention of being subjugated." They reiterated the Brigade's frustration with the aboveground Left while articulating their own critique. "People are looking for concrete ways to change the conditions of this society, to bring about social control of the means of production and individual liberation. The 'leadership' of the sectarian left instead offers the people the chance to join any one of 17 different vanguards, each of which claims to be the true one, and all of which spend most of their energy arguing among themselves over doctrinal disagreements."[14]

The Left Bank Collective's statement identified one cause of Park's arguments: "fear." It could be terrifying to dip into illegality, and potentially to face the wrath of the police and prosecutors. The solution wasn't to sublimate anxiety, and transform it into an ideological construction that could be wielded against those who had overcome (or were acting despite) their own fear. "Facing up to our own fear openly and honestly, and dealing with each other's fear in a loving and comradely manner goes a long way toward overcoming" it. "People need to be able to say: 'I'm willing to struggle for revolution, but such and such is just more risk than I can deal with.'" This way, they both won't get themselves involved in a situation they'll despise, and won't interfere with those who are willing to engage in clandestine activities.[15]

*Northwest Passage*'s readers followed this extended debate avidly. "The Forum on Armed Struggle / Terrorism has sparked the hottest debate from our readers since the legendary Passage debate over two years ago on the subject of Monogamy," the editorial collective member Eileen Kirkpatrick wrote. "Does this represent progress? Perhaps."[16] Even the *Seattle Times* felt compelled to cover the debate, quoting dueling positions in order to provide its readers with "a close-up look at radical thought today."[17]

## 21

# Ed Mead Gets His Day in Court

*In which the Tukwila robber puts U.S. imperialism on trial but is himself convicted*

> *There is no lawyer who can adequately present the type of defense I intend to. If there was such a lawyer, he would've been in the bank.*
>
> —ED MEAD

On February 26, 1976, as Mead sat eating in the cafeteria of the King County Jail, an inmate passed by and dropped a note on the floor. By the time Mead realized that it might be intended for him, however, a sharp-eyed guard had already intercepted the missive.

Once placed in segregation—a unit called "the Annex"—Mead was informed of the contents of the note: it was a proposal to riot, take hostages, and escape. Over the next six months, he was also able to fill in why he'd been the intended recipient. The author of the proposal was both a committed comrade and a serial bumbler. Mark LaRue had been involved in the takeover attempt at the Washington State Penitentiary on New Year's Eve of 1974. The takeover was intended to enforce the collective demands of the inmates—the same demands that the Brigade would make six months later when it bombed the offices of the Washington Department of Corrections in Olympia. LaRue was paroled from the state penitentiary in 1975, but before departing, he promised his colleagues—the other participants in the takeover attempt, who remained in the prison's Intensive Security Unit—that he'd rob a bank and use the proceeds to break them out of prison. He was caught in a burglary attempt in the spring of 1975 and had his parole revoked in February 1976. When Mead, obviously a member of the George Jackson Brigade, was placed in the same jail, LaRue counted him as a new ally. The note—an invitation to conspiracy—was LaRue's way of introducing himself.

"I had been doing my best to come up with an escape plan," Mead remembers of his time in the King County Jail directly after the escape of John Sherman, "but it certainly hadn't included Mark." Mead had noticed that a false ceiling covered both sides of the inmate-attorney divide in the legal visiting room. If he could get hold of some civilian clothes, he figured, he could pop up and over the divide and simply walk out of the visiting room. Mead's visitor wouldn't be in on the plan but, ideally, wouldn't thwart it either. Once confined in the Annex—a steel tomb sealed off from the rest of the jail—Mead's visiting privileges were severely curtailed and the visits that were permitted occurred in a different room. He didn't give up on the possibility of escape, but he had no immediate prospects.

In the Annex, Mead was denied access to newspapers, the telephone and visitors other than his two lawyers. David Allen, Mead's public defender on state charges, and David Shelton, his advisor on the federal case, were friendlies Mead knew from his days in the progressive legal community. The two men maintained a professional focus on the cases, with their slight prospects of success, and declined to keep their client up to date on developments regarding the George Jackson Brigade. Legal details interested Mead, but he found that to receive information on the Brigade, he had to become a source of information himself.

Despite the front-page coverage in the *Post-Intelligencer*—a banner headline proclaiming "Seattle's New Radical Threat" drew attention to a feature titled "Destruction, Bloodshed, Threatened by Radicals"[1]—Mead's first exposure to the International Women's Day communiqué was when *Post-Intelligencer* reporter Walt Wright brought him a copy on Monday March 28.

Mead's eyes lit up as he read the document. When he got to the portion of the statement on meeting police violence with revolutionary violence he exclaimed: "Far out!" When he read his comrades' considerate words: "Take heart, Mead, we miss you and we continue fighting," he melted.

"*All right!*" he proclaimed as he set the paper down, radiating contentment.

"How does it make you feel?" Wright inquired.

"It makes me feel good!" Mead replied. "I want to send a greeting back." He paused. "Love and struggle to comrades on the outside. Keep the faith."

Mead was feeling expansive, confident. He volunteered to Wright: "There are a lot of actions that were never claimed by the Brigade—such as the FBI bombing in Tacoma and the bombing of the BIA offices in Everett, and others."

Wright tried not to let his pleasure at receiving this information show, so as to prevent Mead from clamming up. He continued questioning: "Why do you think they picked this time to deliver this communiqué?"

"I'd guess that the primary reason is what it says: International Women's Day. To let people know the role of women in the Brigade, the leading role of women."

"It's the first time a communiqué hasn't accompanied an action," the reporter observed.

"There had been a tendency on the part of the Left, prior to the advent of the Brigade, to do a lot of talking without a lot of action behind your words. The George Jackson Brigade changed that; when they spoke, they spoke with deeds as well as words. Now, having established their right to speak, it's not necessary that every action be accompanied by a communiqué, or vice versa."

"Are you a member of the Brigade?" Wright inquired pointedly.

"I won't deny it and I won't say it," Mead equivocated.

"So you are a member of the Brigade?"

"This communiqué would appear to clearly say that the Tukwila bank robbery was an action of the George Jackson Brigade. And there is no question I was involved in that action."

"Does the information revealed in this communiqué affect the defense you've planned for your upcoming trial?"

"No, it coincides with the defense I've planned, which will be on the basis of the action's politics."

Wright continued with other questions, which Mead turned away. Ed's final statement was: "The aim of the Brigade is to empower the powerless."[2]

Three days later, in an interview with John Arthur Wilson of the *Seattle Times*, Mead declared: "What we did in the bank we had an absolute right to do in order to further political goals."[3] He was enthusiastic about his upcoming trial: "I'm going to put the issue of revolution on the agenda. It's the government that needs to be tried, not me."[4]

The state of Washington charged Mead with first-degree assault on police officers Joseph L. Abbott and Robert W. Mathews. Though he had indeed shot at the men, Mead claimed he was not guilty as charged. He had not shot with "intent to kill," so it was *second*-degree assault of which he was guilty. "At no time did I have any police officers in my sights," he later insisted. By shooting his pistol, "I was just making noise. It was a stalling action, until more police showed up, or television cameras, or whatever. To let them know: this isn't going to be a massacre."[5] Mead's defense would be that: (1) he had not been trying to harm anyone; and (2) in the United States at that time, it was reasonable to assume that the police would arrive on a crime scene shooting, so it was within a person's inalienable right to self-defense to fire back. Joe Remiro, one of the Symbionese Liberation Army defendants accused of killing Oakland Superintendent of Schools Marcus Foster, had recently used such a defense.

Proceedings surrounding a captured member of an active guerrilla cell prompted some changes at the Federal Courthouse. On Wednesday March 31, guards scoured the courtroom of Lloyd W. Bever for bombs in preparation for Mead's appearance to make pretrial motions. Visitors were searched for weapons. Mead arrived with David Allen, his defense attorney. Allen requested the personnel records of officers Abbott and Mathews, imagining that they might contain citizen's complaints relevant to his client's case. He also asked for $500 of state funds to hire an independent ballistics expert, indicating that the expert would, by examining bullet trajectories and fragments, provide evidence proving that Mead had only fired in self-defense. Deputy County Prosecutor Phillip Y. Killien successfully argued that inasmuch as the Brigade had threatened the lives of the two officers—the "International Women's Day" communiqué stated: "we fully intend to get justice for Bruce's murder, but we prefer to retaliate against the murder[er]s themselves: officers Abbott and Matthews [sic]"—Mead should not be given access to their records. The defense did get the $500.

The defense also filed for dismissal of charges on the grounds of prejudicial pretrial publicity. Allen contended that publicity had reached "intense proportions" the previous Sunday, with the publication of the *Post-Intelligencer*'s article on the "International Women's Day" communiqué. "He wants to have his cake and eat it too," Killien complained, pointing to the interviews Mead had granted. Bever declined to issue a decision on the motion.

The heavy security was absent when Allen appeared, *sans* Mead, in the court of Warren Chan. Allen relayed Mead's appeal for a hearing on his relegation to the jail segregation unit. Deputy Prosecutor Robert Stiere presented affidavits by jail officials, asserting that the February 26 conspiracy proposal intended for Mead was a serious threat to institutional security. Jail officials also cited the Brigade's claim of responsibility for Sherman's escape, and its embrace of Sherman and Mead as "members." Judge Chan opined that Mead was being "saddled with a particular burden by reason of others' actions" and ruled that the inmate was entitled to a disciplinary hearing like those received by inmates segregated for disciplinary reasons.

"What sort of hearing would be necessary?" demanded the irritated prosecutor. "Would it be necessary to bring in a member of the George Jackson Brigade and ask them if they intend to break into the jail, or stage another rescue, or shoot another officer?"

"But what can the plaintiff do?" Chan countered. "Does he have no remedy when an officer simply says, 'You're too much of a risk'? This inmate should have had a hearing in jail before bringing this grievance to my court. The inmate is also entitled to a institutional hearing in which he will have a chance to deny suspicions on behalf of the jail administration that he is a member of the George Jackson Brigade."

"The inmate had an opportunity to deny his membership in the interview in the *Post-Intelligencer* and specifically declined to do so!" a frustrated Stiere pointed out.

"I am not at liberty to consider statements reported in a newspaper—an article which, in any event, has not been included in the prosecution's affidavits," Chan snapped back.[6]

Mead's trial on two charges of first-degree assault on police officers opened on Monday April 5. At Mead's urging, David Allen had filed a successful motion of prejudice against Judge Erle W. Horswill, who had a reputation as being friendly to the prosecution. That success resulted in Superior Court Judge James W. Mifflin hearing the case.

According to the *Post-Intelligencer,* the trial began "under the heaviest courtroom security experienced in King County." A dozen police officers lined the corridor leading to the 10th floor courtroom, and all but two entrances to the floor were locked. The courtroom itself was searched carefully for anything that might contain a bomb. Visitors were frisked by Seattle's "Crime Specific Unit" and scanned with a metal detector by county officers before being admitted. The court proceedings were videotaped by one county and one city officer—in case the trial should be marked by a violent incident, one of the cameramen explained. Defender Allen asked the judge to halt the filming and order the erasure of the videotape, on the grounds that Mead's friends would be discouraged from attending out of fear that their photos would end up in police intelligence files. Mifflin declined to do so.

The first order of business was the defense's motion for dismissal on the grounds of prejudicial pretrial publicity. The prosecution introduced the printed results of Mead's interviews with the *Post-Intelligencer* and the *Seattle Times,* published as "'Brigade Bombed FBI': Jailed Comrade Speaks" and "The Psychological Anatomy of a Revolutionary," respectively.[7] *Times* reporter John Arthur Wilson was subpoenaed by the defense.

"How would you rank this case in terms of news significance?" Allen asked the journalist.

"It has received more coverage than any similar recent crime, but it would be impossible to weigh it against all other major stories since the first of the year," Wilson replied.[8]

"The jurors have been so saturated with coverage of this case that it will be impossible to select an impartial jury," Allen told the court. But when he began interviewing prospective jurors, the vast majority promised that they ignored news and that whatever publicity the case might have received rolled right off of them. Only two out of thirty-two said they had learned of the case from the press. Allen's other questions included: "Do you have any deep-rooted dislike of firearms?" "Will you put added weight on the testimony of police officers?" and "Will the defendant's political views have any bearing on your verdict?"

Judge Mifflin accepted the prosecution's argument and denied the motion for dismissal. "The publicity has been created by Mr. Mead substantially himself.... Nobody is going to come in and create publicity and then not be tried because of the publicity he created." The jury would not be sequestered to shield them from press coverage of the case; they would simply be ordered to continue avoiding media reports.

Once the jury was selected, the defense challenged its composition—all white and middle-class, with nine out of twelve jurors female and only one who was not middle-aged or older—as unrepresentative of the county's demographics. This challenge was dismissed.

There was a collective sharp intake of breath in the courtroom when, in announcing the witnesses it planned to call, the defense listed "John Sherman." Allen quickly added that Sherman would be testifying only via his previous testimony at the inquest into Seidel's death. "To admit second-hand testimony you must prove that the witness himself is unavailable to you," Judge Mifflin reminded, as if insinuating that a line of communication remained open between Mead and the George Jackson Brigade.

"I don't foresee a problem with that," responded Allen.[9]

Deputy Prosecutor Killien opened the state's case against Mead with the testimony of Detective Mathews and Officer Abbott of the Tukwila Police Department. The officers were hustled into the courtroom, very aware of the Brigade's threat to kill them. Mathews testified, as he had at the inquest, that he had driven into a parking lot alone, pulled out his badge and gun, and yelled "Hold it, police!" as Seidel stepped onto the bank's front porch. "An arm came up under the poncho" Seidel was wearing, Mathews related, and he saw the muzzle of a gun flash. He heard one or two shots, then yelled, "Drop it!" as Seidel started back into the bank. When Seidel turned toward the policeman and shot at him again, Mathews shot back.

Almost immediately, Mathews continued: "Somebody else seemed to fire at me from the left side of the bank, and I turned and fired a second time." Still receiving fire from the bank, Mathews ducked behind his car, but felt bullets whizzing by from across the street. He saw another man shooting at him. Mathews began to move around the car for cover when he realized that "the guys in the bank would be shooting at me again, and they were closer." So he knelt down and fired two shots at the gunman across the street, who then fled in a car.

Abbott testified that when he arrived at the bank, he saw a figure raise his right hand toward him, and then felt dropping glass when a bullet blasted out a light atop his patrol car. Abbott said he fired once at the man, apparently hitting him.[10]

On Wednesday, Mark Wallbom, the manager of the Pacific National Bank in Tukwila, testified. He described a moment when, for a few seconds after the gunfire started, he and Sherman were inches apart, head to head on the floor of the converted trailer. Suddenly, Wallbom continued, "Sherman's face exploded with blood when he was hit by the bullet that came through the wall." At this point in his testimony, Wallbom drew several deep breaths and glanced at Mead, and plunged ahead. "After I opened the safe, the defendant and others began yelling, 'Pigs! Pigs! Pigs!' I heard two shots just outside the bank, then a third from outside, and then a fourth shot from inside the bank, right over our heads."

Excerpts from Sherman's testimony at the inquest were read into the record by Dan Kirkpatrick, a member of Mead's defense team. Sherman said that the first shot was fired by Officer Mathews and that it hit Bruce in the lower back. It was not until after police had fired several more shots, hitting Bruce a second time, that Mead "kind of held his gun up in the air and shot through the south window." Sherman said he was "convinced at the time that [the police] were determined to kill us . . . because they kept shooting into the bank."[11]

On Thursday, the jury heard Mead's own story. "The state sees me as a dangerous person. I am—to the state," he opened. He introduced himself as "a poor person and a communist," who, like many other poor people, had been forced into crime by "the ruling class." Often this crime was aimed at others of the same class. Mead, in contrast, urged others to "go after banks and big businesses." He qualified the exhortation with a garbled quotation from Chairman Mao: " . . . but do it with it in mind not to hurt a single thread of the people."

Mead proclaimed his membership in the Brigade for the first time and called the attempted robbery "an action of the George Jackson Brigade." Though he explained that the "expropriation" was an expression of his "desire for social change," he focused on the military aspects. "We anticipated we might come into problems with the police. We were heavily armed but our heaviest armaments were not at the scene of the bank, but in one of the cars."

Mead insisted that he and his comrades were not guilty of the "terror in the bank": the police were. Bruce was "gentle and loving." He had been murdered "resisting the excessive use of force by the police."

While candidly describing clicking the action back on his gun to intimidate the manager into compliance, he claimed that he had "never hurt anyone in my life" and hadn't intended to begin with the manager of the Pacific National Bank—though he acknowledged having considered shooting Wallbom in the leg when he was slow to open the safe.

"Did you attempt to kill the two police officers?" Allen asked his client.

"I didn't want to kill. I didn't see the sense," Mead replied. "I wasn't trying to kill anybody."

The prosecution pressed the point: "Were you not attempting to kill officers Abbott and Mathews?"

"I only began firing after Bruce had been hit twice and John once. I shot into the air out a window then two or three times at a police car."

Under continued cross-examination, Mead swelled with obvious pride. The robbery was training for "bigger and better things." Proceeds were to have been used to help the poor and to "further political ends" by buying any arms available, preferably automatic weapons and "explosives . . . for doing things like when workers go on strike . . . like the City Light Laurelhurst bombing."

"So it's all right to kill rich kids in a bomb blast?" Killien demanded.

"The most extreme precautions were taken," Mead countered. "Police were there 20 minutes before the bomb went off."

"Would you kill a police officer who got in your way?"

"It was only over objections that a Brigade member shot the man who was guarding John at Harborview."

"That doesn't answer my question."

"I wouldn't be above it."

In his closing statement, Killien summarized Mead's defense: "It's all right to rob banks, and if police show up, they don't have the right to take action."

"Who did Mead think he was, talking about holding the bank manager hostage to 'negotiate' a surrender?" Killien demanded. "Does he think he's Henry Kissinger? Or is he some political messiah with a fanatical obsession with violence, hurting others, death?"

"In his classic adherence to Marxist strategy," Killien continued, "Mead sees himself leading the 'vanguard' toward the 'dictatorship of the proletariat' on the grounds that 'we know what's best for them, and we make the rules: for some reason we are better than others.' He accepts the right to bomb rich neighborhoods on the grounds that shrapnel and glass are less dangerous to rich three-year-olds than to poor three-year-olds.

"The defendant is not simply dangerous to the state, as he claims, but to anyone who happens to get in his way, from a policeman trying to stop a bank robbery to a child who might be killed in a blast from a bomb planted by his paramilitary 'Brigade'. The defendant's 'comrade' across the street," Killien reminded, "was attempting to shoot Officer Mathews in the back. 'Peaceful, loving, gentle' Mr. Seidel, the economist, went into the bank with his belt of ammunition on and carrying his long-barreled gun.

"I'm not arguing about Mead's politics. He can believe anything he wants as long as he leaves other people alone . . . I don't care how revolutionary he wants to be, but his idea he can shoot people on his own choosing isn't politics—it's intent to kill."

"This self-anointed deliverer of life and death," Killien perorated, "is a dangerous fanatic not possessed of an orderly, logical and reasonable mind. His perverted sense of right and wrong gives him an absolute, total callous lack of concern for others."[12]

At 4:03 P.M. the jury retired for deliberation. Five hours later they returned with a verdict of "guilty" on two counts—each with a possible twenty-year sentence and a mandatory minimum of seven and a half years on each count, because a firearm had been used. (In November the State Board of Prison Terms and Paroles confirmed that Mead must serve at least fifteen years on his state sentence.)[13] Mead immediately declared that the verdict would be appealed.[14]

On April 21, the day before sentencing, Allen spoke with Judge Mifflin. "I'm going to impose a single life sentence on your client," Mifflin told the counselor. The next day, during the proceeding, the Court asked Mead if he had anything to say before the sentence was declared. Mead, bitter at the severity of the term he was about to receive, retorted: "I have been framed and railroaded—like all poor people who appear before this court! I don't have anything else to say—do what you're going to do!" The judge, livid, blurted: "*Two* consecutive life terms!"[15]

Mead was headed to the Washington State Penitentiary in Walla Walla. He felt the same injustice he had known in the courts before. "I got one life sentence for the assault, and the other for the crime of having a smart mouth!" he complained to himself. "This country espouses free speech but *I certainly paid!*"

In the time intervening between his conviction on state charges and sentencing, Mead requested several delays in his federal trial. On Monday, April 12, in U.S. District Court, he cited the time that was taken to prepare for his state defense. Assistant U.S. Attorney Jack Meyerson argued that a long delay would be hard on several of the witnesses; they had faced death during the robbery, and, while the trial continued, lived in an "aura of fear." Mead replied: "I don't think witnesses need to fear anything."

Mead also reiterated his concerns regarding prejudicial pretrial publicity, arguing that, while he did grant an interview each to the *Post-Intelligencer* and the *Seattle Times,* he had "no control" over many other things that had been published about him.

Judge Donald Voorhees responded: "[T]he Watergate and Hearst trials indicated that the courts do feel that despite widespread publicity, a fair trial can be given. Publicity will continue because the case is noteworthy. This is not a reason to forfeit a trial. I have a great deal of confidence in the jurors. I'm sure they can give you a fair trial."

Voorhees continued the trial to April 26, giving Mead an extra week, a small concession in light of the additional three months the convict had requested.[16] On April 22, however, Voorhees conceded the indefinite delay Mead had been requesting. He also severed the cases of Cook and Mead, which Cook's attorney, Robert Czeisler, had been requesting since Mead's initial conviction; Voorhees's words were: "The prejudice to defendant Cook arising out of a joint trial outweighs the benefits of judicial economy and convenience to witnesses."[17]

What had changed the judge's mind was a new defensive tack by Mead. On April 21, in the course of appearing before Judge Voorhees to ask for another continuance, Mead cited a court ruling that a defendant lacked capacity to appreciate the wrongfulness of his conduct "if he knows the act to be criminal but commits it because of a delusion that it is morally justified." He announced that he planned to plead not guilty by reason of insanity. In the course of the state trial, Mead declared:

"We are crazy enough to believe that it is morally right what we did, and that we have a right to defend ourselves in the process of doing it."

In support of this new strategy Mead submitted an affidavit by Dr. Dan Kelleher, who had met with him briefly at the jail. Kelleher was a former collective mate of prostitutes' union organizer Janine Bertram, who, unbeknown to Mead, was then being courted for Brigade membership herself. Kelleher's document stated in part: "There is certainly substantial reason to believe [Mead] may have, due to psychological pressures in his background, lacked substantial ability to appreciate the wrongfulness of his act.... I would cite a long history of behavior that, besides being unlawful, has many earmarks of psychological disturbance suggestive of irrational and psychotic processes."

The predictable result appeared in the next day's *Post-Intelligencer:* "Mead, a member of the revolutionary George Jackson Brigade, may be planning to use an insanity defense as a showcase for his Marxist-Leninist political views."[18] In an interview with the *Seattle Times,* Mead called the insanity defense "The best possible use of a public platform for demonstrating the need for armed struggle."

Mead's friends had counseled him that the insanity defense would "reinforce the government's characterization of revolutionaries as 'crazies.'" Interpreting the law narrowly, Mead thought he could make it work for his purposes. He quickly found that he could not. On Friday, June 18, he announced that he would not cooperate with any psychiatrist the government hired to examine him, saying he considered it a violation of his Fifth Amendment rights against self-incrimination. Judge Voorhees replied that he would not allow Mead to plead "not guilty by reason of insanity" unless he did cooperate: "You can't have it both ways. If you use an insanity defense, you have to give the government the right it has to oppose the insanity defense."[19]

The conditions in which Ed was confined in "the Annex" were not conducive to effective legal work. Mead was denied access to a law library; as a consequence, he simply recalled prevailing interpretations of the Constitution and left out exact Code citations. He proceeded to appeal the jury verdict on the Tukwila case on the grounds that his confinement in jail prevented him from preparing and presenting an adequate defense on his own behalf.[20] The appeal was denied.

Tensions were high between inmates and guards. On March 28, a guard made racist slurs over the loudspeaker. Several Annex prisoners responded by badmouthing the officers in the control room. Guards entered the walkway behind inmates' cells and sprayed in mace. Their positioning hid their identity: individual charges could not be filed against them.

Any inmate solidarity in the Annex was quickly punished. Mead observed a fellow inmate request treatment for a sick person one cell over. As the inmate lay in his bunk afterward, thinking of other matters, a guard entered the cell and maced him in the face. The inmate, Mike Dunaway, drafted a second-degree assault charge against the two guards who participated.

The next day, Mead told Superior Court Judge Chan of the incident and the charges. "I'll immediately refer the matter to the prosecutor's office," the judge stated decisively. Instead, he had a chat with the guards involved; no changes were immediately forthcoming.

Inmates initiated a collective protest. Due to guard hostility, their conditions declined rapidly. The walls and ceilings of the cells were metal; frustrated inmates discovered that, when struck in the proper place with the proper force, they resonated at the same frequency as the ten-story building itself. As a protest picked up, the inmates began banging in concert. Judges in the courtroom below began complaining to the guards. "Are you going to do something about this?"

Sunday May 16, while the courts were closed, the guards did take action. Several prisoners rang the buzzer placed outside the first cell in the unit for the purpose of calling the deck officer. When guards refused to respond, several inmates pounded on the walls in a short burst. When this elicited no response, they pounded again.

It was at this point Mead noticed a stream of white liquid squirting into his cell from the lower vent on the rear wall. It seared his lungs first, then set his eyes on fire: mace. He grabbed a towel and wrapped it over his head but, as the liquid continued to come in, moved to put the towel over the vent. As he tried to cover the lower vent, the officer on the other side of the wall began shooting it out the top one. Mead switched to covering the upper vent, at which point white liquid squirted back through the one close to the floor. Mead picked the top vent and continued to plug it.

The other dozen or so prisoners on the tier received the same treatment. The guards used pressurized gallon jugs fitted with a spray nozzle. By the time the discharge ceased, the floors were wet, the walls dripping, and the inmates' mattresses, sheets, and blankets were drenched. Their skins burned and their hair was matted.

Prisoners didn't need access to the instruction manuals to know that the agent, which was also in use on the streets to disperse rioters, was only intended to be employed in open spaces. There was no air circulation in the Annex; the entryway, a solid steel door, which was usually open, was closed. The protesters cooked for nearly twenty-four hours, their plight exacerbated by the midsummer heat.

"The annex was like a gas chamber, several prisoners were in fear of death and experienced harmful symptoms resulting from the lingering effects of the mace," Mead wrote the next day in a letter of public protest. At the time of writing, the unit had still not been aired out and inmates continued to be denied cleaning materials or new bedding. Mead wrote a report of the incident and attempted to file a petition charging cruel and unusual punishment. He also informed the appropriate officer at the jail, a Sergeant "Randell," and sent details of the incident to the *Post-Intelligencer* and the *Seattle Times*. With other channels blocked, Mead, writing with five other Annex inmates, appealed directly to the public. "We as prisoners are near powerless. We have exhausted available remedies in our attempt to end the terrorism of guards (only one aspect of which is mentioned here). We urge people on the outside to demand an investigation be conducted and the guilty guards be charged with first degree assault."[21]

On July 6, 1976, Sergeant Mike Nault was suspended from the King County Police Department for three days without pay as punishment for directing the macing incident. Four other officers who participated were given written reprimands. The matter was referred to County Prosecuting Attorney Christopher Bailey for consideration of possible criminal charges, but nothing came of it. Sheriff Lawrence Waldt explained to the press that Nault, a third-generation King County police officer, was a "good sergeant," but that he made an error in judgment.[22]

Mead's federal trial finally got under way the same day as the official reprimand. There were few friendly faces in the crowd: "The community is paranoid, not without reason," Michelle Whitnack commented in a letter from jail.[23] Among the few who showed up were Paul Zilsel and Helen Ellenbogen, Left Bank Collective members who had already been subpoenaed. Mead grumbled as, again, an all-white and predominantly middle-aged jury was seated.

"Are you ready to begin?" Judge Voorhees asked Mead, after the selection was completed.

"As ready as we'll be, considering the circumstances," the surly convict replied. Mead's hope for the insanity defense was that it would allow him broad leeway to discuss his mental condition—that of a communist revolutionary—and thus provide a platform for his ideas. "If successful this will be a major trial in terms of political impact," he wrote optimistically in *Dragon* that April.[24] Judge Voorhees, for his part, had promised to be "very flexible" in permitting the introduction of material relating to the defendant's mental condition. As a means of circumventing Mead's refusal to be assessed by a government psychologist, he permitted the professional to sit in the courtroom and observe Mead, so that, should he be needed by the prosecution to refute Mead's case, he would be available.

Mead took the stand acting as his own attorney, and solicited the jury's sympathy: "Be patient with me. This is the first time I've done this." He then conceded the facts of the case: "I came into one of your banks and was caught with my hand in the cookie jar." He was not concerned with the outcome of the case, he declared, he simply wanted to communicate why "I felt it was morally right to rob the bank."

When Mead began relating, as he had in his state trial, the conditions of his early life, his planned defense crashed into a wall of judicial obstinacy. Voorhees cut him off, ruling that Mead's childhood did not directly impact his mental condition when he attempted to rob the Pacific National Bank.

"I tell you that living in a racist, sexist and imperialist society has had a direct effect on my emotional development," Mead protested.

"It's not a defense of insanity if a person simply has a different philosophy of life," the judge countered.

"You can do what you want, I'm not going to dance at the end of your string," Mead shot back, and, from that point on, refused to participate in the trial. He did not cross-examine the prosecution witnesses, who identified him as one of the gunmen in the bank. The proceeding ended quickly. The next day, after forty minutes of deliberation, the jury convicted Mead of bank robbery and using a firearm in the commission of a felony, potentially adding thirty-five years to his two life sentences.[25] Mead remains chagrined by this episode. "I saw the insanity plea as very risky, yet worth taking the chance in order to present my case to the jury and hopefully to others," he states, adding somewhat defensively: "I was not trying to sleaze my way out from under the federal charges as I already was serving two consecutive life sentences for the state of Washington, with a mandatory minimum of fifteen years on each."[26]

Assistant U.S. Attorney Jack Meyerson announced that "the government has successfully prosecuted the ringleaders of the Brigade," but cautioned: "That's not to say that there aren't more persons around who were involved in one or more of the Brigade's actions."

Mead's outlook wasn't much more optimistic: "The Brigade may be, in effect, dead—I don't have any idea. We'll just have to wait until the next time they decide to speak." It was unlikely, in any case, that they would carry out an action in response to his conviction: "The Brigade has seemed to develop an appreciation for not doing things on an emotional basis."[27]

On August 6, Mead was sentenced to thirty years in federal prison: twenty-five for the bank robbery, and another five on the related weapons charge. After his sentencing, he made a bitter reference to President Gerald Ford's words, on September 16 of the previous year, when he pardoned Richard Nixon: "I feel that Richard Nixon and his loved ones have suffered enough and will continue to suffer, no matter what I do, no matter what we, as a great and good Nation, can do together to make his goal of peace come true." Mead told the court: "It would be utterly unrealistic for me to expect the same kind of justice that Nixon received by saying that I've suffered enough already, so go ahead and do what you're going to do." He continued: "I have been through these courts a lot of times, and I cannot help but notice two levels of justice. One is for people who don't have much money, and another is for people like Boeing."[28]

After being convicted Mead told reporters that he had a "90 percent chance" of winning at least a new trial on appeal. When Walter Wright of the *Post-Intelligencer* met with Mead for an interview he remarked that Mead had looked haggard and worn during his federal trial, but already "appeared at ease, reconciled to the prospect of prison time, and even anxious to get it under way."

Mead told Wright: "The State Parole Board has told me that after some long period of time, 7 or 10 or 15 years, they would consider me for release—if my political opinions were to change. I told them I'd drop dead first and walked out." He added: "I hope my conviction will be reversed on appeal." Then he continued, more fancifully: "Or, perhaps, with the deepening crisis of capitalism, there will be a shift in public opinion, and I'll be released earlier."

"Do you have any messages for the George Jackson Brigade?" Wright asked.

"Keep moving. I love you all."

"What is left of the Brigade?"

"The defeat at Tukwila substantially weakened the Brigade," Mead replied. "It's licking its wounds. How serious those wounds are, I can't say."

Wright opined that Mead, for his part, was "probably already at work attempting to organize fellow prisoners." He then quoted an acquaintance of Mead's and others associated with the Brigade, whom he'd interviewed several months earlier: "Their minds are still in prison. They can hardly wait to get to prison. The prisons contain 'the armies of tomorrow.'"[29] Mead said as much in the *Northwest Passage* interview: "To me . . . what's the difference between the inside and out. . . . It's all the same. . . . The work I do is the work I do."[30]

## 22

# Underground in Oregon

*In which the Brigade licks its wounds and debuts "The Gentleman Bank Robber"*

The collective decided that it was time to get out of the city. John and Therese left first. Initially just posing as a couple, they had quickly become one in actuality. The partners crossed over to coastal Route 101 and drove south until they arrived in Coos Bay, Oregon, a sleepy town beginning to awaken for the summer tourist season. The couple decided that they'd spent as much as they could afford to on gas and moved no further.

Rita stayed on a little longer in Seattle to clean up the Brigade's tracks. She spent a few days at the 10th Street Collective burning papers from Women Out Now and other potentially incriminating documents in the house's massive fireplace. She picked up a Volkswagen van from Brenda's Autoshop, the first such woman-owned business in the Seattle area. While Rita was a student she had worked at Brenda's part-time, on that particular Volkswagen as well as on other vehicles. Rita told Brenda that she would sell the car, though she intended to use it for Brigade purposes without compensating the owner. "I lied a bit on that one," Brown admits today. "I figured, 'She's not gonna turn me in.'" She confesses: "I kinda feel bad about it."

In the company of Janine and her housemate Marta, Rita gestured to her belongings and announced: "This shit's going to disappear. I'm leaving." The three filled the van with Rita's discards before Rita sent a broader call out to the political women's community via word of mouth. "This weekend y'all need to come in here and clean out my house. Everybody take everything. Take my dog and find him a home somewhere. This house will be cleaned out by Sunday." The community obliged. When the feds checked it out three months later, there was nothing left for them to find.

To Janine Rita made a declaration of a more personal nature: "After I move out of here, I'll need a place to stay." Janine offered her own place, and the two spent their second night together.

Rita stayed in phone contact with Therese and John via a prearranged series of dates in public phone booths. At each phone call, Rita gave three more numbers for other booths. The code was simple: a number decided upon earlier was added to each of the digits. Once her belongings were dispersed, Rita let the other two members of the Brigade know that she was ready to join them.

Rita invited Janine to accompany her on the drive down the coast. The trip was intended to be a honeymoon, a break from the manic activity of the preceding days and months, but it was marred by an injury. Their first night a torrential downpour forced them off the road. They holed up in a small hotel. Settling in for a movie, Rita slid the TV closer to the bed. It fell and smashed her foot. She passed out. Janine revived her, then gave Rita the sedatives she had had on hand for her own use. Janine spent the night icing her lover's foot. By morning the swelling had been reduced sufficiently that Rita could fit her injured foot in her boot, but the pain continued to bother her for another year. The couple never had their honeymoon.

Before parting, Rita invited Janine to join the Brigade.

"Perhaps," Janine responded haltingly.

Approaching Coos Bay, Rita put Janine on a bus back to Seattle. The two said their good-byes.

At the new Brigade headquarters, Rita told John and Therese that she'd invited Janine to join. The news riled them. "That wasn't part of the plan," one chastised.

"I don't care," Rita replied defiantly.

Chronically short of cash, one of the first topics on the collective's agenda was potential sources of income. John's first suggestion was: "I play a good hand of poker. Maybe I could win us some money at the card table." Therese and Rita exchanged cautious glances. John clearly liked to gamble, and cards were a notoriously unreliable income-generator. But neither of them had a better idea. John was allotted a portion of the Brigade's dwindling "kitty," as they called their store of cash on hand. Over the first few nights, to the pleasant surprise of his companions, John won a significant sum.

Since Therese was cast in the role of John's wife, Rita was forced into playing the role of his sister, "Anna Blakely." Later John and Rita took the names "Karl Joseph Newland" and "Carol Alice Newland." So as not to draw attention to themselves, Rita agreed to play straight, submitting to the indignity of wearing dresses for the first time since she had initially arrived in Seattle.

These trips to the bars broke the monotony of a directionless small-town existence, yet—especially for Brown—they were still quite dismal. Already irritable from the painful circumstance of living in close quarters with her ex-girlfriend Therese and Therese's new lover John, Brown was quickly aggravated when hit on by what she later characterized as "hick hets." She directed incendiary thought-beams to those who tried to pick her up: "I want to kick you in the balls!" Observing the pleasure Sherman derived from gambling, she mused sourly that she had conceded to one of John's personal compulsions, not to a money-making scheme for the collective. "This could be a problem," she concluded. If Therese realized the same thing, the distance between the two women prevented them from discussing it.

As summer dawned in 1976, the threesome took an exploratory trip down the Oregon coast, looking for other places to live and banks to rob. Near Eugene, they were pulled over by a police officer. John was driving, Therese was in the passenger seat, and Rita was in the back with her hand on the pistol she had acquired from Virgil Johnson, the unfortunate police officer who had been escorting John at the time of the jailbreak (John had filed off the serial number). Each person's false identification cards held up under cursory scrutiny, but the incident made the collective wary of continuing to live in Coos Bay and of using the same van, which was registered under one of their false IDs. When they returned home, the three decided to rob a bank in Coos Bay and use the proceeds to relocate.

John had the most experience with armed robbery, but was gun-shy from the blast in the face he had suffered in the Tukwila robbery in January. Not only that, but any bank robber fitting his description would immediately give away the location of the Brigade remnants to law enforcement. In order to prevent an impasse, Rita volunteered to be the trigger person.

John walked her through the process: preparing a demand note, being cool in the bank, and passing the note to a teller while flashing a weapon. After the lesson, John and Therese hit the bars. Rita stayed home, got drunk and practiced her opening lines in the mirror: "Put the money in the bag!" She didn't practice quick draws: having grown up playing cowboys and Indians, she already knew that game well, and she was hoping to prevent enacting it in real life.

On June 8, Rita entered the Empire branch of the Western Bank with John behind her as backup. Impersonating a man and sporting a false mustache, she informed the teller that she had a gun. He handed her $2,095, all that he had in the drawer. The drag ruse seemed to work, and Brown used it for the rest of her days as a bank robber.[1] The three then decided that John and Therese would remain in Coos Bay, while Rita would made a quick visit to Seattle to tie up a few loose ends—such as disposing of the van—and to keep the line of communication open with their supporters.

With a few hundred dollars in her pocket, Brown headed up the coast. After a couple hours of driving, she pulled over and got herself a room in a motel. She luxuriated in her own company. Over dinner, she resolved to procure some company for herself before returning to her dysfunctional family–cum–vanguard cell. Conveniently, she had already initiated her love interest Janine as a Brigade supporter.

Once in Seattle, Rita checked in with "base," as the Brigade termed its primary safe house. All was quiet in Coos Bay. Rita then contacted Janine. Rita scoped out a safe place for them to meet in the wooded outskirts of Seattle. She worked out elaborate directions that allowed her to observe Janine approach on a trail before making contact, so as to make sure she was not being followed.

Nervous about the encounter for both personal and legal reasons, Janine brought a friend for company. She and her young gay male friend carefully followed instructions from one public phone to the next. As they climbed the last leg of the journey, Rita observed that one of them was carrying a rifle—presumably for protection in case of a confrontation with the police. Rita too was armed.

Rita emerged dramatically from the underbrush as Janine and her friend climbed the forest path. The two women greeted one another joyfully. That night, in a hotel room, the young man popped pills until he passed out; Janine and Rita took advantage of the privacy.

The next day they parted. Janine and her companion disposed of the van by running it off a cliff. Brenda, the owner of the van, who had reported it stolen, then received a visit from police. After Rita was declared a suspected member of the George Jackson Brigade the following year, federal investigators would visit her as well.

Rita's quick visit to Seattle kept the Brigade's contacts in their home town alive. Brigade members regularly contacted several supporters in Seattle by phone, to hear reports of what was being said about the Brigade in political circles. These phone calls were recorded so as to be shared with other members of the Brigade, then destroyed the next day.

Back in Coos Bay, the collective opened up a map of the state to choose where they wanted to operate. They decided that they needed a moderately sized city to support their activities. Oregon offered limited choices: Portland, Salem, Medford, Grants Pass, and Eugene. Eugene they ruled out quickly: it was too well-known for radical activism. They decided that, initially, further away was better, and opted for Medford, a city in the south of the state that had no countercultural presence to speak of. By June 13, they were already 200 miles south, where phone company records indicate John placed three calls from a phone booth in the resort town of Seaside, using fraudulent billing information.[2] One of the people John called was his wife Joanne, who hung up immediately upon recognizing his voice, certain the FBI had a tap on her phone.[3]

Establishing themselves in Medford, they went to work quickly. On July 13,

Brown hit the South Ashland branch of the Crater National Bank for $1,331. On August 2, Rita and a partner hit the Rogue River Valley Branch of the Oregon Bank at 1025 Cort Street in Medford for $4,405. Both robberies went off without difficulty, though in Medford, a witness saw all three of them fleeing the scene, and in Ashland, Rita had to run three blocks over railroad tracks and through bushes to get to the getaway car.

Personal relations between Rita and both Therese and John continued to deteriorate. A vigorous schedule of casing banks, maintaining vehicles, and doing other errands permitted little respite from one another. In one collective meeting, Rita finally declared: "I need a day off and a little money to myself. Ten bucks, whatever, I don't care, but something I don't have to answer to you two about." The others accepted this as a new policy.

On her days off, Rita went down to the Rogue River, which passed through Medford on its way from the Cascade Mountains to the sea. Enjoying the heat of the summer, she would bring along a quart of beer and do a little swimming. But she was still lonely and continued to desire that Janine join the group.

Therese had pressing personal problems as well. That summer the FBI discovered that she had been using her mother Nancy's Union Oil credit card. Agents contacted Nancy's ex-husband Victor and asked him to get the number of the card from his former spouse without telling her why. They also contacted Therese's 22-year-old brother, urging him to go into his mother's financial records without her knowledge. Agents asked the men the last time they had seen Therese. Both declined the inquiries and requests. On August 2, the FBI subpoenaed the records from Union Oil. Nancy Coupez got in touch with Michael Withey, the attorney to whom the Brigade had turned after Bruce Seidel was injured and taken into police custody. Withey was able to temporarily block the request.

On August 19, 1976, the FBI visited Nancy Coupez for the first time. "[S]ince the reputation and credibility of the FBI have been questionable in the past few years, I did not wish to talk with them," Coupez later explained. "They very belligerently told me I could talk to them or I could talk to a grand jury." On August 25, Coupez was called before a federal grand jury in Portland. The first inquiry was: "Do you have a daughter?" Coupez refused to answer.

"For the next two hours, they kept asking me, 'Where's your daughter?'" Coupez complained to *Northwest Passage* after the ordeal. "I guess they figure I'm a straight middle class person who's going to go in and talk," she continued. "I haven't done anything, but I suppose I could go to jail because I won't talk about my daughter."

Coupez conveyed her indignation to the jurors. Reading to them from a prepared statement, she said: "I am shocked that a judicial body such as the grand jury would expect me to violate the very profound and sacred trust relationship that exists between parent and child." To *Northwest Passage* she added: "In a time when the family structure is disintegrating anyway, here's the grand jury contributing to it . . . I thought I was living in the United States in 1976, but I feel like I'm in Germany in 1935."[4]

After carrying out two bank robberies and passing some bad checks, the trio concluded that they had reached the limits of what they could safely pull off in Medford. They headed back north, to the largest city in the state, Portland. There they cased practically every bank in the city and its suburbs. Their criteria were the same as ever: few customers and quick access to a freeway.

Rita's continued surliness made John and Therese receptive to the idea of resuming contact with Janine, who had fallen off the radar by missing scheduled phone calls to public phones shortly after Rita's last visit to Seattle. The question remained of how exactly to get back in contact. Therese remembered she had once dropped Janine off at her aunt's house in Vancouver, Washington, just across the Columbia River.

"Do you think you could find the house again?" Rita asked, trying to conceal her excitement.

"I think I could," Therese replied.

On October 9, the threesome drove up to Vancouver together. Therese found Janine's aunt's house without difficulty. In case whoever might open the door knew of Rita, John and Therese knocked on the door while Rita waited in a park nearby. Janine's mom, who happened to be visiting her sister with Janine, greeted them at the door. They introduced themselves as Janine's friends "Bill and Rachel."

A surprised Janine accompanied John and Therese to the park where she and Rita were reunited. After discussing the reasons they'd lost contact, they quickly turned to the immediate question, directed to Janine: "Will you join us?"

She answered hesitantly: "Yes."

Rita was unconvinced. "Is this what you want to do?" she insisted.

Janine clearly didn't know herself. She was torn between the opportunity to help people she admired and cared for and her daily life. Having left the position with COYOTE years earlier, she did not have politically important responsibilities tying her to aboveground life. She was infatuated with Rita and had been greatly impressed by Therese, despite the fact that the latter treated her condescendingly. She felt that physical violence was an inevitable part of the struggle against oppression. "It's not everyone who's invited into an urban guerrilla cell," she told herself. Though not being guilt-tripped by the others, she felt the need to challenge herself, demanding: "Am I just paying lip service or am I really a revolutionary?"

"Yes," Janine answered with a display of conviction.

She returned to her aunt's house, gathered her belongings, and told her mom that she was going to the library with her friends. Later that day, she called her mom and said: "I'm going to California with Bill and Rachel." Her mother was a little taken aback, but not particularly concerned. She didn't hear her daughter's voice again for another year and a half.

In the second week of October, the collective decided that John should call *Post-Intelligencer* reporter Walt Wright again. They wanted to know what the authorities were up to, and how Mark Cook and Ed Mead were doing in custody. "It probably wouldn't be a bad idea to dispute the accounts linking the Brigade to a string of Oregon bank robberies," Sherman decided. As a preventative measure against the tracking device that must, by this time, have been installed on Wright's phone by law enforcement, John promised Rita and Therese that he would limit his call to three minutes, which they considered too brief a period for the call to be traced.

When John returned after making the phone call, Therese asked: "What's the news?"

"Not much," John replied. "Mark's still in King County. Ed's been shipped to Walla Walla."[5]

On Sunday November 7, 1976, Sherman placed his fifth call to Wright.

"Where are you?" Wright asked, as well as: "Are you involved in these bank robberies that have been occurring in Oregon?"

John refused to answer the questions, and had little new to tell Walter.

The next day, Wright phoned the FBI, informing them of Sherman's call. An agent discouraged him from continuing to report on his conversations with the fugitive: "He keeps calling in order to gain publicity and to get information about the investigation of the bombings. Do you really want to *encourage* that?" the agent demanded.[6]

Janine volunteered to be the getaway driver for the next Brigade robbery, on October 28, when they hit the Sunset branch of the First State Bank of Oregon on 805 NW Murray Road in Cedar Mill, a suburb west of Portland. It went off without difficulty.

That winter John and Therese decided to take a trip by themselves. The ostensible political motivation was to find a like-minded organization in California with which they could link: ideally, this would be the same New World Liberation Front that Ed Mead had worked with in 1974. Ed had never disclosed the names of the group's membership, or a way to contact them; thus, as a federating effort, the trip was a bust.

The couple was back in town for the next robbery, carried out January 4, 1978, at the Raleigh Hills branch of the U.S. National Bank of Oregon on 4870 SW Seventy-sixth Avenue, which netted $5,054. On January 11, a grand jury in Portland handed down secret indictments against Brown and Sherman, charging the former with the Ashland and Medford robbery and with the one in Coos Bay. The charges were not made public until May 14, the day after a spectacular Brigade attack announcing its return to the Seattle area.

On Monday February 7, 1977, Rita entered the U.S. National Bank of Oregon in the Portland suburb of Wilsonville with John behind her, handed the teller a note demanding money, and opened her jacket to reveal a revolver tucked in her waistband. The teller passed her $7,753. Outside, Janine sped to the parking lot of a restaurant at the nearby Stafford exit off I-5. As they headed to the switch-off spot, they heard police sirens approaching in the opposite lane. Janine, who was again acting as the getaway driver, unconsciously pressed the gas.

"Slow down!" Rita exclaimed. With concentrated effort, Janine complied.

They were trailed to the drop-spot by a passerby who had seen the robbery occur. He called the police, but Rita and John escaped from the restaurant's rear door before the police arrived, and Janine had already departed separately.

The next day's *Oregonian* indicated that Brown's drag ruse was still effective. It reported: "The suspect was described as a white male about 30 years old with gray hair and mustache and a stocky build. He was wearing a plaid shirt, a blue windbreaker and a black stocking cap. There was no description available of his companion."

Another bank robbery had occurred in Portland on the same day. Two men in their twenties barged into the East Gate branch of the Oregon Bank. Both were wearing ski masks; one carried a shotgun, the other a pistol. One of them announced loudly: "This is a holdup!"[7] Compared to the competition, the Brigade was practically subtle.

## 23

# Back with a Bang!

*In which the Brigade returns to Seattle with a high-profile string of bombings*

> The suburban guerrilla must be considered as situated in exceptionally unfavorable ground.
>
> —CHE GUEVARA, GUERRILLA WARFARE

In returning to Seattle, the Brigade was careful to choose a residence in a neighborhood in which they were unlikely to run into past acquaintances. They decided on a place in South Seattle, near the Seattle-Tacoma airport. Since it was directly under the flight path, the house was unpleasantly noisy.

While there was much work in relocation and the selection of new targets, weekly days off were mandated. On these, Rita and Janine began fishing at a spot just north of the ferry docks in Edmonds. They cast their lines and crab trap directly off the pier into a calm inlet shielded by a breakwater. The fisherman's culture of dignified quiet and, when fortunate, generosity, fit their need for privacy perfectly. The depth of Puget Sound allowed them to catch good-sized perch and flounder, as well as vibrantly colored crabs.

One day, after catching a small shark, Janine asked a local: "What can I do with this?"

"You can eat the meat and boil down the liver for oil," he replied.

Back at base, Janine cooked down the shark liver and used the oil to lubricate everyone's guns. The smell was horrible, but the episode fused her nascent identity as an urban guerrilla with her love of the land.

In another indication of a desire for personal stability, Rita got a dog. She had seen a notice in the classified ads for a Doberman named "Dillinger," presumably named after the gangster and bank robber John Dillinger, whom the FBI had declared "Public Enemy Number One" in 1933. "Cool!" she thought.

The perennial issue of prison struggle cropped up again in the late spring. As with the Brigade's first bombing—that in support of prisoners on June 1, 1975—the long-term isolation unit at the State Penitentiary in Walla Walla was the flash point. A triumvirate of interests was in conflict: prisoners, caged for indefinite periods in dismal circumstances; guards, who despised and feared their charges and complained of a lack of support from their superiors; and policy makers in Olympia, whose dreams of reform became nightmarish realities when implemented.

The guards, who were as resistant to rehabilitation as the most hardened criminal, were the greatest obstacle to the Olympia planners' push for cleaner, more therapeutic institutions. The advent of "the new prisoner" in the 1960s—prone to rebellion and partial to hard drugs—saw its counterpart in the 1970s as a resurgence of rank-and-file prison guard unionism. "Correctional officers," as guards were fighting to be called, demanded more control over their working conditions. More control meant more "security"—that is, less mobility for prisoners. They were thus diametrically opposed to both the realization of prisoners' dreams of freedom and the reformists' plans to grant prisoners greater power over their own lives. Washington prisoners showed a strong hand in the disturbances of 1977, but they were, as always, limited by their own isolation, a problem compounded by public disinterest in and disdain for their plight. Guards, in contrast, if not warmly embraced by the public, were at least perceived as men in unenviable positions who deserved the support of administrators.

On April 5, 1977, a guard at the Washington State Penitentiary lost three fingers and suffered facial and chest wounds after using a cigarette lighter that had been filled with improvised gunpowder. Penitentiary Superintendent B. J. Rhay ordered a thorough shakedown of the entire institution. The search for contraband began in the Intensive Security Unit, where incarcerated Brigade co-founder Ed Mead and some newfound friends had been waging a bitter struggle over their conditions of confinement. On April 10, Easter Sunday, cognizant that the changes coming down would mean a more Spartan regime for all the institution's residents, inmates in the general population set small diversionary fires in the Protestant chapel and elsewhere and raided the prison commissary. By one count, three hundred of the prison's more than 1,600 inmates participated in the looting; nothing was left in the store but its shelves.

Prisoners formulated fourteen demands, the first of which was improvement of conditions in the isolation wing, and declared a strike, refusing to leave their cells. The administration obliged and the entire institution was put on lockdown. Prisoners were only allowed two showers, then one, a week; other than that, they remained in their cells twenty-four hours a day. At first, Superintendent Rhay claimed that he was the instigator of the entire affair. The Resident Council (RC), as the Residents Governance Council was referred to after being stripped of its self-governing role, insisted that, to the contrary, the inmate body had voluntarily confined itself: they were on "strike." The campaign against contraband translated into confiscation of their few amenities, stripping them, as it did, of the curtains that provided them with their only modicum of privacy, as well as other belongings. From April 12 on, the RC refused to deal with Superintendent Rhay directly, smuggling out a letter to a special governor's committee investigating the chronic problems in the institution and requesting the intercession of Governor Dixy Lee Ray. By early May, the disruption had become the longest lockdown in state history. Rhay then conceded that the inmates might have started it, but, he vowed, "I'm going to finish it."[1]

The press initially covered the conflict dispassionately, but as it persisted, the *Seattle Times* began deploying more prejudicial language. In an early piece on the strike, the *Post-Intelligencer* used the phrase "prisoner unrest" and objectively described the events of April 10 as "a demonstration, a fire in a chapel, and a break-in at the prisoner store."[2] The *Seattle Times* initially spoke of "an Easter fire in a chapel and looting of a prison store," but soon began calling the disturbance "a small riot."[3]

On May 7, the tone of the *Seattle Times*'s coverage changed sharply. Staff writer Paul Henderson wrote of "an Easter Sunday rampage," adding the previously undisclosed incriminating information that, not only had prisoners engaged in burning and looting, but "Inmates also stormed the prison kitchen and packed out 700 pounds of raw chicken."[4] In a different article in the same issue, Henderson echoed guards' fears of retaliation from prisoners when the institution opened up again. He recalled their memories of the state penitentiary as "a jungle of violence," and cited the way in which "a mob of inmates burned the prison chapel and looted their own store" as an ominous harbinger of things to come.[5]

The governor's "blue-ribbon commission," led by the director of the Department of Health and Rehabilitational Services, Harlan McNutt, met with inmates to discuss their concerns. Guards took this as a serious slight. The commission quickly recommended that James Harvey, associate superintendent of custody and a disciplinarian despised by inmates, be fired. Superintendent Rhay, however, defended his right-hand man, declaring: "He is one of the best associate wardens I've seen in my entire career in corrections. Jim Harvey is tough but he is eminently fair."[6]

On May 5, Director McNutt announced the changes the committee would institute. The controversial James Harvey would be transferred to Shelton, a lower security institution in western Washington, where he had worked before being sent to Walla Walla. Wary of being perceived as bending to inmate demands, McNutt took pains to assert that this change was voluntary: "It may sound contrived," he told the press, "but Mr. Harvey actually requested this transfer a year ago, and again last month, before the lockup even went into effect." Other promised changes were the transfer of the mentally ill prisoners to the Eastern State Hospital in Medical Lake (McNutt stated that the sight of deranged men in a maximum-security prison "turns my professional stomach"); acceleration of work release opportunities; increase of the minimum-security population; addition of a second dentist; and institution of regular sanitary inspections.

Not everything at the prison would change. McNutt declared that he could find nothing to substantiate the inmates' complaints of racial discrimination (a simple walk down the cell block would have revealed racial segregation, with the race inhabiting the cell indicated by a colored sticker at the entrance). In another important concession to guards, McNutt declined to ban anal and vaginal searches of visitors, instead asking that they be conducted "discreetly." "I'm not forbidding orifice searches, but there must be reasonable cause," he stated.

These modest changes were met with relief by prison guards, who had feared wide-reaching reforms like the ones they blamed for bringing in the disruptive openness of 1970.[7] On the Harvey issue, Paul Dever, spokesman for the guards' union, Local 621, conceded: "I feel comfortable that the Olympia officials did not bow to pressure. Nonetheless inmates are going to think that they were responsible for the associate warden's transfer and that's the problem we are facing."[8] A potential flare-up between politicians and professors operating out of the state capital and the rank-and-file guards in the most eastern part of the state was thus avoided. Prisoner cohesion flagged after inmates were confined to their cells for an unprecedented period, and it appeared that their major concerns would be glossed over with minor concessions masking a greater deprivation of rights. With Ed Mead, one of their own, in the eye of the storm, the George Jackson Brigade resolved to do what they could to carry prisoners' demands into the public arena.

Drawing on the structural analysis pioneered by C. Wright Mills, an intellectual godfather of the New Left, the Brigade looked into the corporate anatomy of the *Seattle Times*.[9] They discovered an interlocking directorate joining the *Times*, among other regional corporations, to Rainier National Bank. Partial to banks as targets—what clearer symbol of capitalism?—the Brigade decided to use actions against Rainier National Bank branches as a launching pad for its objections to the circumscribed public debate over prisoners' rights.

In the first week of May 1977, John and a female partner, and then Janine and John, rented safety deposit boxes at the Rainier National Bank branches at Overlake Park, at 2245 NE Bellevue–Redmond Road in Redmond and the Midlake office, 1815 One Hundred Sixth Avenue NE, in Bellevue. The pairs posed as a couple, with the women sharing the same false ID.

On Thursday May 12, one of the Brigade women returned to the Overlake Park branch while Janine visited the Midlake one. Each woman placed a pipe bomb in her respective box; the banks' policy of allowing its patrons total privacy ensured that they were unobserved. At 3 P.M. a collective member placed a call to the Redmond bank, notifying them that a bomb would go off between 3:15 and 3:45. The bank immediately called the police, closed the heavy vault door so as to contain the damage, and evacuated the building. The bank in Bellevue and the Bellevue police received a similar warning.

The pipe bomb in Redmond detonated at 3:35 P.M. Half a dozen safety deposit boxes were damaged and an interior wall was knocked down, causing approximately $20,000 worth of damage. The Bellevue bomb, however, was a dud, likely suffering from a defective clock or faulty soldering. Three Bellevue police bomb squad members worked for three hours to disassemble the 3" × 12" gunpowder-filled pipe bomb.[10] They were rewarded with a piece of evidence that would later be useful in Janine's prosecution: a crisp set of fingerprints.

At 3:40 P.M., KZAM radio station received a call from a woman identifying herself as a member of the George Jackson Brigade. The woman announced that two branches of Rainier National Bank had been bombed, and that a communiqué explaining the reason was in a telephone booth near the Dairy Queen adjacent to I-405 in Bellevue. The caller then requested that the station play two songs decided upon earlier by the collective. Not one to violate procedure by pandering to an urban guerrilla, the receptionist informed the caller that she would have to hang up and place a separate call to the station's request line.

The communiqué was recovered and turned over to the police. Befitting the Brigade's first action in Seattle in fourteen months, it was longer than most of their other compositions, running three single-spaced pages. "We chose Rainier National Bank as a target because of its links to the *Seattle Times,* a bourgeois daily newspaper ... [which] has led the propaganda campaign in Seattle against the prisoners," it declared. Rather than being the "independent and objective" entity it presented itself as, the *Seattle Times* was "a weapon used by the ruling class to lie to us." The Brigade excoriated the paper for having "printed long diatribes by paranoid guards who are fearful of retaliation for their crimes," and asserted: "By not printing the RGC [*sic,* RC] grievances, the *Times* has refused to even pretend to be objective."

The Brigade singled out William Pennington, president of the *Times* and a director of Rainier National Bank, who, they claimed, was also tied to "Sea-First, SafeCo, Boeing, Weyerhaeuser, Paccar, etc. etc." They proclaimed: "The owners and bosses of these companies are the real criminals—the real enemies of society. Capitalism and capitalists cause crime and prison." (Pennington was contacted by the Associated Press but declined to comment; he only told the AP reporter that he had not read the communiqué. A spokesman for the *Seattle Times* denied the Brigade's accusation that the newspaper disregarded legitimate inmate complaints, and announced that it was taking security precautions.)

The communiqué retold the prison lockdown from the perspective of inmates, calling the looting of the commissary "a well-planned and executed raid," after which maximum-security prisoners went into their cells, "starting a strike." They disclosed that prisoners had specifically requested not to see Director McNutt and denounced his changes as "three attacks and four empty promises."[11]

Making the idealistic claim that "[i]f people knew what really goes on in prison and understood what their true effects on society are they would shut them down tomorrow," the Brigade demanded that the *Seattle Times* print the entire text of the Resident Council's grievances, the Brigade's own communiqué, and every one they issued in the future. Finally; "We also demand that the *Seattle Times* interview prisoners in struggle in the hole at Walla Walla and print those interviews."

The next day on its front page the newspaper printed a story on the bombings and the communiqué that accompanied it, along with the charge that it was "a bourgeois newspaper" that foisted off propaganda as objective reportage. Another story, on page A20, included longer quotations from the Brigade's challenge but did not respond with editorial comment, or print either the communiqué or the Resident Council's demands in full.[12] Interviews with prisoners did, however, begin to appear in both the *Seattle Times* and the *Post-Intelligencer*.

In a review of the "Mayday Communique," as the missive about the Rainier National Bank bombing was titled, the *Post-Intelligencer* reporter Paul O'Connor wrote "the polemical rhetoric dies away and is replaced by a kind of folkeyness when the press release moves into the section called 'the Brigade' which begins: 'so, the GJB is back.'"[13] The section reads:

> "There are two things to remember about revolution: we are going to get our asses kicked, and we are going to win."
> 
> So the GJB is back. We got our asses kicked real bad at Tukwila a year ago, and we've spent this last year licking our wounds and learning our trade. We've accumulated a lot of equipment and an enormous amount of experience. We've done 6 teller robberies in Oregon banks for more than $25,000. Without firing a shot. In the course of this, we've learned a lot about the police, the front line troops of capitalism.
> 
> Although we are armed and will defend ourselves if attacked, we are not crazy. We do not, as the FBI has claimed, "Believe in shooting it out with an army of police". We understand that we are vastly outgunned and out numbered and, if we are trapped, we will make a positive effort to surrender. But we have corrected the error that we criticized at Tukwila. We have a higher level of combat training and will never again be caught unprepared by the violence of an individual police officer. If captured, we will continue to fight wherever we end up.
> 
> Overall, we live pretty much like everybody else. We have landlord hassles, the car needs repair, the wiring in our home is bad. We are stunned (like everybody else) by the prices when we buy groceries.
> 
> For several months now we have been concentrating on political study and struggle to clarify what we think about revolution in this country. As individuals we have many disagreements. We will have more to say in the future about political struggle within the Brigade. We need criticism and analysis of our words and our actions.
> 
> We believe that capitalism is the source of all oppression at this time, and that revolution requires that it be overthrown by force of arms by the masses of poor and working people in this country. We believe that the struggle against racism, national oppression and sexism in all its forms are part of the struggle against capitalism. We are firmly united on these points.

The communiqué ended with a hyperbolic quotation from the tenth Symbionese Liberation Army communiqué that clashed with the relative level-headedness of the rest of the missive: " . . . if people on the outside do not understand the necessity of defending them (prisoners) through force of arms, then it is because these people on the outside do not yet realize that they are in an immediate danger of being thrown into concentration camps themselves, tortured, or shot down in the streets for expressing their beliefs."[14]

On Wednesday May 18, the Left Bank Collective resumed its earlier defense of the Brigade by putting out a press release that demanded: "[I]s it any wonder that in the face of inhumanly violent conditions inside the prison walls, ex-prisoners would resort to counter violence as a way of drawing the public eye to their plight?"

Warm words also came from the locked-down prisoners in the Intensive Security Unit in Walla Walla. A statement entitled "Message to the Progressive Community on the Media and the George Jackson Brigade" read in part:

> The reaction of ISU prisoners upon learning of the [May 12] bombing[s] was positive, enthusiastic and unanimous. The target was perfect and the timing ideal. [The George Jackson Brigade] showed themselves familiar with the essence of our struggle as well as the identity and nature of the enemy. We view the Brigade action as another level of the support we so urgently need. They were able to put the rulers on the spot for their criminal abuse of the power of the press, and they did so in a manner that could not have been as quickly and effectively accomplished by conventional means. We see the Brigade action as an example of armed propaganda at its best.

Though signed "The Walla Walla Brothers," the statement was written by Ed Mead. (His personal copy of the printed document bears the words: "Our finest hour. The truest reason for the existence of GJB.")

The same day someone claiming to represent the Brigade called Rainier National Bank announcing that bombs had been placed at three of their facilities: a computer center, a bank under construction, and an operating branch. The three sites were evacuated but no bombs were found.[15] Asked nearly thirty years later if Brigade members were responsible for this call, Brown replied: "I don't know. If we didn't, I'm sure we were pleased to read about it!" Thus unfolded what former Brigade members consider, along with the City Light attack, one of their great victories, in which grand detonations drew attention to a communiqué that essentially served as an editorial presenting an oppositional perspective.

A ripple effect of costly and dangerous copy-cat actions was one of the reasons the Washington Bankers Association was eager to see the Brigade apprehended. After the Rainier National Bank bombings, the trade group announced a reward of

$25,000 for information leading to the arrest of John William Sherman and Rita Darlene Brown, the two publicly confirmed, indicted Brigade members. The association's announcement describes them both as "extremely dangerous."[16] The collective was nonplussed: the Brigade stole $4,200 from the Factoria branch of Rainier National Bank three days after the reward was made public, and in a letter to the American Friends Service Committee claimed credit both for this and for a May 21 heist at a Newport Hills liquor store, where the manager's purse was returned the next day still containing $45.[17]

In the wake of the Rainier National Bank bombings, the FBI told the press that they had known the Brigade "remnants"—John Sherman and "two ladies"—were in town. They knew because John had told them: the collective decided to call the police and have John impersonate someone who had done time with him, report spotting him so as to draw police away from a robbery site, and give the Brigade an opportunity to once again observe the workings of the Seattle police.

The Bureau no longer perceived the Brigade as an amorphous entity with vast resources. Rather, the FBI now believed correctly that the organization it sought consisted of five people at most. Yet FBI agents were still blinded by sexist tunnel vision, one telling a reporter that, although a woman (in fact, women) had planted the bombs in the two safety deposit boxes, Sherman was probably behind the latest incidents.

John Reed, special agent in charge of the FBI in Seattle, quickly conformed to the collective will of Washington State bankers. He added more agents to the hunt for Sherman and Brown and began to collaborate more closely with the FBI office in Portland in the hopes of apprehending the outlaws. He also released a series of photos of Brown and Sherman so as to secure assistance from the public, and exposed Brown's practice of robbing banks in drag.[18] To avoid the impression of incompetence and impotence, a Portland grand jury's indictments of Brown and Sherman, kept secret since January 11, were made public on May 13.[19] The FBI had not yet identified Coupez or Bertram.

A complication in the Brigade's next robbery provided them with an opportunity to display the way in which they differed from common criminals. On May 21, the Brigade robbed the Newport Hills state liquor store of $1,300. In a typewritten letter mailed to the American Friends Service Committee (AFSC) afterward, they explained: "When we robbed the liquor store, it was necessary to take the manager's entire purse because the liquor store money was in it. The day after the robbery we returned the manager's purse with all her own personal money, about 45 dollars." This was consistent with the Brigade's principle: "[We] won't steal as much as a penny from the small businesses or working people."

The Brigade continued in the same vein of transparency, stating that they needed the money from the liquor store heist and the June 20 robbery of the Factoria branch of Rainier National Bank for "weapons, ammunition, explosives, medical supplies, vehicles, etc." The letter—which referred to the recent "strike" of prisoners at Walla Walla as part of a "continuing struggle against feudal conditions" in the "hole"—was made public by Janice Lien, a staff member of the AFSC's Justice Program. Lien told the press: "I assume the Committee received the letter because we've been working to improve conditions at the State Penitentiary."[20]

On the night of Sunday July 3, Rita dropped John and his partner off near the corner of Sixteenth and Cherry in Olympia, where the Puget Sound Power and Light Company substation that supplied the Washington State Capitol complex was located. The pair cut through the chain-link fence surrounding the station, shielded by trees from the view of passersby. They placed a brown satchel containing a triple pipe bomb—three metal pipes filled with gunpowder wired to an electronic timing device—beside one of two main transformers and departed.

Around 11:30 P.M., a woman identifying herself as a member of the George Jackson Brigade called the Olympia Police Department. She gave the location of the pipe bombs and said they would explode in about half an hour. The caller did not explain why the bombs had been planted.

City and state police rushed to the site and evacuated fifteen to twenty people from nearby residences. The officers discovered the pipe bomb and the State Patrol Bomb Squad cautiously deactivated it, taking two hours to complete the job. At 6 A.M., the evacuees were permitted to return to their homes. The FBI joined city and state police in their investigation.

A State Patrol spokesman estimated that, had the bomb gone off, it would have sent shrapnel over a 300-foot radius, damaging the two main transformers enough to plunge the Capitol's administrative office into darkness. Ignoring the fact that the pipe bomb had been carefully placed on the side of the transformers and away from houses (across a field and a highway), the policeman continued: "They could have maimed nearby residents." Amplifying such assertions, the *Tacoma News Tribune* called the Brigade "the Northwest's most notorious band of terrorist bombers and bank robbers."[21]

The bomb had been placed in support of the inmates of the Walla Walla State Penitentiary. The Brigade made ten demands on behalf of the inmates, including an end to arbitrary punishment; release of all prisoners from segregation unless the administration could show "clear and present danger"; and remission to general population of all prisoners who had spent ten consecutive days or more in isolation. The Brigade pledged to continue "armed support . . . until all of these demands are met."[22]

In a letter to a Seattle radio station following the dismantling of the Olympia pipe bomb, the Brigade explained the problem that confronted it: "Now we are faced with the dilemma of either being willing to see some police officer killed trying to disarm a bomb that is truly booby trapped, or to be willing to watch them disarm our bombs with impunity." The Olympia action, an effort to disrupt state government, "was clearly a failure in this regard." The letter continued that police were given ample time to evacuate surrounding areas—"as it should be"—but this presented "one of the many contradictions in any bombing."[23]

## 24

# Winding Down

*In which the Brigade continues on its course for lack of a more-appealing option*

In the fall, the collective relocated from their working-class digs in southern Seattle to the more middle-class North Seattle. Given that Brigade members had spent nearly all of their time in Seattle before joining the group on or near Capitol Hill, they felt anonymous in the neighborhood. As usual, the banks they robbed were far away from their home.

On Thursday September 8, Rita handed a note to a female teller at the Old National Bank on 13233 One Hundredth Avenue NE in Juanita, a suburb north of Bellevue. She pulled a handgun partially out of her belt. The note identified the bearer as a member of the George Jackson Brigade and demanded that the teller fill a drawstring bag with cash. The teller emptied the drawer and passed the contents—$1,100—to Brown, who fled in a green Plymouth with a black top.

The Associated Press account of the holdup stated: "The robber was described as a white male, 5-foot-9, 180 pounds, with a mustache and light, wavy hair." By this time, however, the drag ruse was wearing thin. The wire service noted that the FBI suspected Brigade member Rita D. Brown had posed as a man in a string of bank robberies in Washington and Oregon.[1] Rita was not surprised to learn that her disguise had been penetrated. What caught her interest was "the way I always gained a few inches in witness reports," the 5'6" Brown remembers.

Shortly after noon on Monday September 19, Rita, again in drag (the *Post-Intelligencer* remarked on her "false-looking mustache"), handed a teller at the Skyway Park branch of People's National Bank, located at 12610 Seventy-sixth Avenue South, a typewritten note that was nearly a haiku:

This is a hold up
I have a gun
The George Jackson Brigade

Brown didn't flash her weapon in the course of the robbery. The take, the Brigade later claimed, was a whopping $8,200, quite a sum in contrast to the $1,000–$3,000 the FBI said was average for a bank robbery at the time.[2] She was driven off in a 1967 maroon Ford station wagon, license number OBK 508, by a collective member waiting outside. The car had been stolen in the morning, and was abandoned in Renton after the robbery.[3]

The proceeds from this and other recent robberies funded a new campaign, one in support of automotive machinists in Bellevue who had been on strike since May 18.[4] Brigade members walked with picketers at five different dealerships and, as with the City Light workers two years before, concluded that the workingmen would be amenable to some old-fashioned American labor violence.

The Brigade's first attempt against car dealers was inauspicious. On October 6, they modified their technique somewhat, creating a firebomb—a gallon jug of gasoline mixed with other chemicals and capped with a timing device and battery igniter—rather than a pipe bomb. The target was the Westlund Buick-Opel-GMC dealership in North Seattle, Warren Westlund having been the spokesperson for King County new car dealers since the beginning of the strike. John planted the device outside of a recreational vehicle, waited for it to ignite, and when it didn't, he later told the *Seattle Times*, "We went back and retrieved it and spilled it around the R.V." He then created a makeshift fuse using a cigarette and a matchbook, but that didn't work either.[5] At this point they gave up and called the dealership: "This is the George Jackson Brigade. We have placed a bomb but it has failed to go off. We want to let you know that we are in sympathy with the strikers." An employee rooted out the device around 3:30 A.M.

Police initially discounted the Brigade's claim of responsibility. Major Ray O. Connery stated: "We're not convinced that it was the George Jackson Brigade. There were some similarities but also some dissimilarities from the Brigade's former work." Westlund and Pat Goodfellow, the former chairman of the automobile dealer's association, both made comments to KOMO TV that strikers said linked them to the attack, prompting their union to file a half million dollar slander suit.[6]

Early in the morning of October 13, an explosive damaged vehicles at S. L. Savidge Dodge in downtown Seattle. A communiqué entitled "Bust the Bosses" followed:

> Tonight we bombed the S. L. Savidge new car dealership in support of the four month long strike by the Automotive Machinists Union, Lodge 289. Sheet metal, Teamsters and Automotive Painters unions have also been on strike against the dealers for sev-

eral months. We chose S. L. Savidge in particular because he was identified by striking workers as one of the leaders of the car dealers' attempts to break the union.

Also, on October 6, we attempted to test an incendiary bomb at Westlund Buick as punishment for Westlund's role as president of the 52 member King County Automobile Dealers' Association. The device failed to detonate. (To verify that we placed the device: the timer was a white plastic, 60 minute kitchen timer with red numbers; and the gallon bottle of gasoline and sulfuric acid was wrapped with cheesecloth containing a potassium chlorate solution.)

It is clear that the bosses only want more profit for themselves at the expense of their workers. In this particular strike, the bosses are clearly trying to break the union in an attempt to get more profit for themselves. The best strategy against this union busting attempt is to cost the bosses more than they gain by employing scabs.

We therefore encourage all people to support this workers' struggle. There are many ways to express support, some are more comfortable than others. Choose one of the following and act.

1. Don't cross a picket line for any reason! Take your business elsewhere or wait until the strike is settled.
2. Tie up the dealers' phones! Call in as a concerned person and complain, or call from a phone booth and leave the line hanging.
3. Put sugar in the gas tanks of dealers' new cars, or potatoes in the tailpipes! This will destroy the engine.
4. Break the dealers' windows! Use bricks, slingshots, small arms, etc. Slash their tires too!
5. Lock the bosses out! Put super glue in any and all locks of buildings or cars. (This is easy and it works great!)

We are not members of any of the striking unions, but we have talked (anonymously) with striking workers all over town. We are claiming these actions so that the workers will not be blamed for them.

AN ATTACK AGAINST ONE OF US
IS AN ATTACK AGAINST ALL OF US!

THE BOSSES NEED US,
BUT WE *DON'T* NEED THE BOSSES!

At 11:15 P.M. on Saturday October 15, bombs exploded on the hoods of two Dodge Aspens and in the trunk of a third Aspen at the BBC Dodge dealership, a non-union shop on 14650 First Avenue S in Burien. Shrapnel damaged two other cars nearby. The bombings caused an estimated $2,500 in damage. There was no warning before the detonations, which were promptly denounced by union officials.[7]

The Brigade sent a letter addressed to the Automotive Machinists Union claiming responsibility for the three automobile dealership bombings. The letter was intended to exonerate union members of the bombings. Like the letter sent by the Brigade a year earlier seeking to exonerate the women subpoenaed to appear before the grand jury, it was authenticated by John's right thumbprint. The correspondence read:

Friends:

We were responsible for the fire bombing last night at BBC Dodge in Burien. We were also responsible for the pipe bombing of S. L. Savidge earlier this week, and the attempted fire bombing at Westlund Buick on October 6.

In last night's action we used three gallon juice bottles containing a gasoline sulphuric acid solution. The bottles were wrapped with cheesecloth saturated with potassium chlorate and sugar as an igniter. A small pipe bomb was taped to the bottles to break them. Each of the bombs were detonated by a Westclox Travelalarm; two of the clocks were still in the red plastic cases they came in, one of them was taped in a piece of styrofoam. At least two of the timers were recovered by the King County Police.

We gained entry to the storage lot by cutting a chain link fence on the North side of the lot, about 20 feet east of a cluster of blackberry bushes. One bomb was placed on the hood of a sedan parked against the chain link fence; and the third was on the hood of a station wagon parked toward the center of the lot next to a large recreational vehicle.

We are certain that there is enough specific information in this letter to completely clear the union and its membership of any complicity in these actions. This letter itself is being typed on a typewriter used extensively by the Brigade, and the FBI has samples of this type, including bank robbery notes. To eliminate *all* question, we are including two copies of the right thumbprint of John Sherman, a known member of the Brigade. One thumbprint is at the bottom of this letter, and the other is on the enclosed xerox copy of this letter. You should give this letter to the police and keep the xerox for your own protection.

Also attached is a copy of our October 12 communique which sets forth our reasons for these actions.

We wish you complete success in your efforts to hold the line against ever increasing and ever sleazier attacks by the bosses.

*Love and Struggle,*
*The George Jackson Brigade*

Copies of the letter were sent to BBC Dodge, Seattle FBI Special Agent in Charge John Reed, the King County Automobile Dealers Association, and KOMO TV News. Previous to the letter, it had been rumored that the Brigade was responsible for the bombings, but law enforcement officers had expressed skepticism, preferring to cast blame on disgruntled machinists. The FBI now acknowledged to the media that they believed the letter to be authentic. Union officials were advised by their lawyers not to comment on the bombings.[8]

Despite the communiqué, it was clear that not all actions against the auto dealers were by the Brigade. On October 18, in what the *Post-Intelligencer* called one of "many incidents of property damage at many Seattle-area auto dealerships since the mechanics went on strike," over eighty tires on new cars, vans and pickup trucks were punctured at the Foothills Ford dealership in Eastgate. Bellevue police estimated the damage to be at least $5000.[9]

While the Brigade took its potshots at the owning class in the United States, a parallel formation in West Germany was shaking the country to its foundations. Like the Weather Underground, the Red Army Faction (RAF) grew out of the country's largest student group, which shared an acronym with SDS. But whereas the Weather Underground turned away from violence against people after it lost three of its own in a devastating accident in 1970, the RAF—also known as "the Baader-Meinhof Gang" after two famous founding members, Andreas Baader and Ulrike Meinhof—became notorious for bloody kidnappings and murders.

In April 1977 Baader and fellow RAF members Gudrun Ensslin and Jan-Carl Raspe were found guilty of four murders, twenty-seven attempted murders, and forming a criminal association. That September, other RAF commandos kidnapped one of the country's most outspoken industrialists, Hanns Martin Schleyer, president of the Employers' Association of the Federal Republic and of the Federation of German Industry, demanding the release of their three recently convicted collaborators and eight other imprisoned comrades. Schleyer had been a mid-ranking member of the Nazi Party and SS member and was one of numerous officers to have served in Czechoslovakia under Reinhard Heydrich, one of the architects of the "Final Solution." To his captors he thus embodied what they conceived to be an unbroken link between the Third Reich and the contemporary German nation. When they killed him in October, they felt little regret.

Before this murder the RAF had upped the stakes of their demands by collaborating with a Palestinian commando to hijack a Lufthansa flight carrying ninety-one people. On October 16, the hijackers shot and killed the pilot. On the night of October 17, a special German force raided the plane in Mogadishu, Somalia, killing three hijackers and wounding a fourth, while incredibly protecting all the hostages. That evening RAF prisoners Baader and Raspe died of gunshot wounds in their cells in Stammheim prison and Ensslin died by hanging. Another RAF captive, Irmgard Möller, was nearly killed with a knife. The government made the unconvincing claim that the three had committed suicide while Möller had failed in a similar attempt. That the authorities had said the same thing when Meinhof was quite likely killed in custody the previous year further strained credulity. It was in retaliation for these deaths that Schleyer was killed.[10]

Just as after the capture of the last members of the Symbionese Liberation Army two years earlier, the Brigade felt compelled to respond. The collective already had materials assembled for another bombing; since they'd been doing auto dealerships, they decided to continue. They picked the Phil Smart Inc. Mercedes-Benz and BMW dealership in Bellevue because of the company's links to German industry.

On the night of Sunday October 31, so as not to disturb the calm of downtown Bellevue, Brown walked three or four pipe bombs to their destination: 10515 Main Street. She planted them near the dealership office building and under a blue Mercedes sedan. At 8:52 P.M. Brown called the Bellevue radio station KZAM and, identifying herself by name, warned that bombs would explode in fifteen minutes. She declared that the bombings were dedicated to the Lufthansa hijackers who had been killed by the West German commando force. She also dedicated the bombings to those fighting in the streets of Europe in protest of the German government's apparent attempt to liquidate incarcerated Red Army Faction members. (Militant demonstrations and anti-German firebombings occurred in a dozen cities in France and Italy in response to the prison deaths and West German anti-terrorist crackdown.) Brown, described as calm by the announcer, repeated the dedication and told the announcer to call the police.

No one was in the Phil Smart building when the bombs went off, and no one was hurt, but a large fragment of pipe was found on the porch of an apartment building on a bluff overlooking the back lot. Another fragment had blown clear over the building and landed in the front parking lot.[11] Police reported that the blasts caused slight damage to the building—"pock marks"—and to the $12,000 Mercedes 450SL under which one of the pipe bombs was placed, as well as several nearby. Three to four reports shook the ground and were heard three blocks away at the Bellevue police station.[12]

The accompanying communiqué "You Can Kill a Revolutionary, but You Can't Kill the Revolution!" declared:

> This punitive action is in solidarity with the thousands of freedom fighters throughout Europe and around the world who have taken up the counter attack against the real terrorists: the international imperialist ruling class and all its instruments of terror.
> This action was dedicated to:
> Ulrike Meinhof, a political prisoner who was raped and strangled in her maximum security isolation cell in Stammheim, the special fortress prison in Stuttgart, Germany on May 9, 1976. The official coroner's verdict was suicide.
> Andreas Baader and Jan Carl Raspe, political prisoners who were shot in the back of the neck in their separate isolation cells in the same prison on October 13, 1977. The official coroner's verdict was suicide.
> Gudrun Ensslin, a political prisoner who was hanged from an electric extension cord in her isolation cell on the same day that Baader and Raspe were shot, in the same fortress prison. The official coroner's verdict was suicide.
> We send a special message of support and revolutionary greetings to Irmgard

Moller. She is a political prisoner at the same prison in Stuttgart, Germany. The state failed in its attempt to stab her to death with a bread knife. However[,] her statement, made from her hospital bed [saying] that she did *not* try to kill herself, means that her life is still in danger. The ruling class freely uses murder and torture to silence people who expose their terrorism.

All four murdered freedom fighters, as well as Moller, were captured urban guerrillas, members of the Red Army Faction (referred to by the ruling class media as the "Baader-Meinhof gang"). They were tried and convicted under "exceptional" laws—laws designed to give the German ruling class a freer hand in crushing popular dissent. These people were subjected to increasing physical and mental torture, sensory deprivation and isolation from each other, their friends and their lawyers. The German government's excuse for the torture was the charge that these guerrillas were directing armed activity in Germany from inside the prison.

The German ruling class has a bloody history of disposing of their political enemies. In the early days of Hitler Germany, the Nazis began this murderous practice by herding their enemies into concentration camps, shooting them, and labeling it "an escape attempt". (Just like the murder of George Jackson at San Quentin.) Because the internationalist capitalist class wants us to forget its experiment with fascism, they now murder enemies through "suicides", instead of staged "escape attempts".

. . .

We chose Mercedes-Benz as a target because it is a German luxury car which is a favorite item of conspicuous consumption for ruling class bosses, and because of its association with Hans Martin Schleyer, late captain of German industry and unpunished Nazi war criminal.

Schleyer was president of Daimler Benz, the manufacturers of Mercedes Benz. He was also head of the Union of German Employer's *[sic]* Association (a combination national chamber of commerce and manufacturer's Association.). He was also an economic advisor and close personal crony of the boss of the West German government. During World War II, he was a high ranking Nazi SS officer in charge of war industries in Nazi occupied Czechoslovakia. He was the perfect representative of "democratic" German capitalism.

Schleyer was taken hostage by the Red Army Faction to win freedom for eleven of their captured comrades, including Ensslin, Baader and Raspe, who were murdered two weeks ago. Schleyer was executed in retaliation for those murders.

LOVE AND RAGE—FIRE AND SMOKE<br>REMEMBER THE STAMMHEIM MASSACRE[13]

Toward the close of the auto dealership bombings, the Brigade began to plan something more ambitious. What they had in mind was unprecedented in the United States: the kidnapping of a public official. Though the Schleyer episode certainly encouraged such thinking, it was the Tupamaros in Uruguay, their early inspiration, who provided the model. On July 31, 1970, the Tupamaros kidnapped and murdered Dan Mitrione, a CIA police advisor who provided instruction in physical interrogation techniques to the counterguerrilla forces.[14] In 1974, in the midst of the Symbionese Liberation Army brouhaha, Kirkpatrick Sale, the definitive chronicler of Students for a Democratic Society, commented: "A sensible thing to do would have been to kidnap a Bob Haldeman type and get him to confess, Dan Mitrione-style, to his crimes. Then, after putting out the information you want to put out, let him go."[15] This is what the Brigade aimed to do.

The Brigade considered that their target, like Mitrione, was guilty of torture, though less by design than by complacency. They planned to seize Harlan McNutt, director of the Department of Social and Health Services, the person who oversaw the prison system. Other potential kidnap victims discussed by the collective included Lynn P. Himmelman, retired board chairman of Western International Hotels; Governor Dixy Lee Ray, the former chairperson of the Atomic Regulatory Commission and the state's first female governor; and C. Davis Weyerhaeuser, Charles W. Bingham, Robert Scheyler, and F. Lowry Wyatt, executives of Weyerhaeuser, the huge timber product company based in Federal Way, Washington.[16]

"We'll interview him about the conditions in the hole at Walla Walla, see what he has to say about that. Then we can mail the tape to the press," Brown suggested.

"Yeah," said John, enthusiastically. "We'll ask him about the money that he says isn't available for improvements at Walla Walla."

"I don't want to keep a hostage for any period of time," Janine interjected.

"We'll keep him for a day, or twelve hours—*hell, I don't care!*" Brown cried. "As long as it takes to get him to talk. The main thing is that the people responsible for these crimes know they'll no longer be ignored."

While heaping more work on themselves—eight to ten hours a day, six days a week, to carry out three times more activity than when in Oregon—the collective continued to be polarized into two couples. Rita and Janine stuck together as much as possible, while John and Therese did the same.

A dispute between Rita and John highlighted the poor state of personal relations within the group. In one collective meeting John declared that he had found a wad of cash in Rita's coat pocket. Often responsible for losing the collective's money during gambling binges, John was seeking to sow confusion as to the source of these mysterious disappearances. Rather than challenge his word directly—Rita had no cash on hand to speak of—she barked: "Well you shouldn'ta been diggin' through my pockets! I guess you're trying to steal my pot again!"

The Brigade's aboveground supporters had, of late, been supplying them with small quantities of marijuana. Janine didn't smoke, so the stash would be divided between John, Rita, and Therese. "John would smoke all his, smoke all of Therese's, and then come for mine," Brown recalls with undiminished indignation. So she hid her portion, moving it to a different place each day, but John would root through all her belongings until he found it. After the collective blowup, she planned to buy a mousetrap to leave in her pocket for the next time he came snooping.

There was little division of labor in the Brigade; everyone did what they could as the need arose. The frantic pace concealed a deep anomie: the revolution they had hoped to build when joining the group was drawing further away each day. As if mutually agreeing not to bring up this painful subject, collective meetings focused on day-to-day tasks. Brown recalls of this time: "If nothing had changed for another year or so, we would have stopped and done something else. As it was we were trying to get enough money together to split town and take a break." But the "break" would have come *after* the kidnapping.

The group planned to do one more bank robbery while in North Seattle, then either leave town or relocate to another part of the city. For this reason they aspired to do more than one drawer in the bank. They also planned to do a bank very close to their house, so they could go "straight to ground."

The North Seattle house, at 13746 Roosevelt Way, was adjacent to Jackson Park, where Rita and Janine enjoyed walking Dillinger, Brown's Doberman. Though they were in the city, at night it was easy to imagine that they were in the woods.

On Saturday, November 4, Rita drove the collective's station wagon—a 1968 Rambler—over to the bank she was casing near the Highland Medical Plaza on North One Hundred Seventy-fifth Street. Brown put in a load of laundry in a nearby Laundromat and walked into the bank on the pretense of breaking a $100 bill. After viewing the layout inside the bank and getting a sense of the customer presence at that time of day, she took Dillinger for a walk on the beach. She collected the laundry, threw it in the back of the car, and drove to the mouth of the plaza to observe the traffic.

On her way out she passed a hamburger joint. A number of men dropped their food, piled into a black sedan, and followed her out of the lot. She remembers:

> I looked in my rear view mirror and saw four guys crammed into a black Ford Fairlane, and I knew right away who they were. I started making turns, going around blocks, and they did everything I did. I was trying to work my way back to highway 99 so I could go north. I was just going to drive to Canada, because we were living very close to where I was, and I wanted to steer them away from the others. I cut through a parking lot which turned out to have been blocked off since I'd been through it last. I had to make a U-turn: I was trying to come out as they were coming in. They threw down on me.[17]

The bust occurred around 1:30 P.M. The feds discovered a pistol in her car: the .357 that Mark Cook had taken from Virgil Johnson. Police told the press that the arrest was based on one of hundreds of tips. Yet relations were so bad between

Rita and John that she couldn't help wondering if he was the one who had called them.

Brown appeared before federal Magistrate John Weinberg, who set her bond at $100,000. She was charged with violating the Federal Firearms Act and with committing five bank robberies occurring in Oregon between July 1976 and February 1977, and ordered to stand trial.[18]

Janine and Therese listened to the police scanner as they went about their household duties. "Two Adam 23, meet the FBI agent at 175th and Aurora impounding [plate number]." Therese's head snapped up: the FBI was zeroing in on Rita.

"*Janine!*" Therese shouted. "*The pigs have captured Bo!*" she yelled, using the term of endearment by which Janine often referred to Rita.

Janine rushed over and listened in. She was shocked by the potential loss of her lover and comrade.

"We need to go get her!" Janine cried.

"How?" Therese demanded. "John's got the car. He's not due to be back"—she glanced at the clock—"for another hour and a half."

"Ohmigod!" Janine wailed.

"Oh shit!" Therese cut in. "Dillinger's tags give this address!"

Therese began frantically gathering the most essential items from the house. The two women waited for John for an hour, then, deciding the risk was too great to dally any longer, burned some incriminating documents and set off—lugging papers, tools, and weapons—on foot. They gave up and turned back after a block—the materials they were carrying were just too heavy.

Just then John returned. They loaded up the Dodge with weapons, ammunition, and a few clothes, then rushed over to a hotel room in another part of town and unloaded it. By this time it was past 3:00.

John looked at his watch. "It's only been a couple hours since they got her. Do you think it's worth going back to the house for another load?"

"I'll go!" Janine exclaimed, her face wet with tears.

"You stay here," Therese commanded. To John she announced: "I'll go with you, but we have to be *careful!*"

They approached the house cautiously and immediately noticed four or five unmarked vehicles in an adjacent school parking lot.

"That's the spot we always said they'd use as a staging ground for a raid of our house," Therese remarked quietly. "Are these all feds?"

"Let's see," John replied. One of the cars was pulling out of the parking lot. John pulled in close behind it and read out its license number: "IVU 004. Isn't that almost the same as the fed car we spotted downtown a while back?"

"IVU 001. Yeah, they're all feds. Let's get out of here!"

Law enforcement agents stayed outside the house until evening, shouting through a bullhorn for whoever might be inside to come out. After they lobbed in teargas, it finally became apparent that the house was empty.

Seattle area FBI spokesperson Ray Mathis told the press that the Bureau believed Sherman and a Miss Therese Coupez, aged twenty-four—not yet charged with any crime—had driven away from a house around 3 P.M. near the site where Brown had been arrested. Law enforcement still didn't know about Janine. A search of the Northside Seattle home turned up a pistol and a "pipebomb-type device" incapable of detonation, as well as, among other things, "radio type–equipment believed to be used in monitoring police radios." A pickup truck also thought to have been used by the Brigade was left at the address.

Agents alerted other law enforcement agencies that the remaining pair of Brigade members were believed to be driving a blue 1970 Dodge Dart with Washington license plate number OUC 635.[19] When the car, registered to "Martin Elliot"—one of Sherman's aliases—was seized in downtown Seattle, a block from the Greyhound depot, it sowed great confusion.[20]

The FBI hunt for Coupez and Sherman involved from thirty to thirty-five agents in several Washington cities. Agents in Oregon were also put on notice to be on the lookout for the pair. "A lot of leads and look-alikes" had been checked out since the arrest, SAC Reed told the *Post-Intelligencer* a few days later. On Monday November 7, in response to questions from the Associated Press, Seattle FBI spokesperson Mathis quipped: "They're in Seattle, they're out of Seattle. They're in Washington, they're out of Washington."[21] A source at the FBI leaked to the press that a subpoena had been issued for Coupez. The FBI refused to confirm or deny the report.[22]

The predictable neighbor interviews conducted by reporters after the Seattle flight hint at the tone of Brigade members' day-to-day life. "They never mentioned their names, even when you introduced yourself," one said. "They were very cool to whatever was going on," offered another. A third stated: "They were always home. They never went anywhere." The collective's only apparent concession to neighborhood spirit was to put out a jack-o'-lantern and dispense candy to trick-or-treaters on Halloween.[23]

The last three Brigade members resumed their isolated lives in a rented house on a hill overlooking Tacoma. As soon as they had a free moment, they sat down to analyze the mistakes that had cost them Brown, the North Seattle home and most of its contents. They identified a series of small errors, such as their failure to remove the dog's rabies tags and the absence of a clear emergency plan, but they didn't flinch from larger mistakes as well. "Overall, we made the mistake of too much doing with too little thinking and discussion," they wrote in "An Open Letter to Bo (Rita D. Brown)." They signed the document "The rest of the Brigade," and sent it to the *Seattle Sun* for publication.[24]

To prevent the reoccurrence of such disasters, they resolved to:

> develop and implement a realistic division of labor based on the number of people we have and logical definitions of areas of responsibility in our work . . . ; set aside one day each week solely for meeting. We will use these meetings for political struggle, for discussion and analysis of our strategic development, and for reports, practical criticism, and planning of next week's tasks . . . ; immediately develop a set of evacuation plans, establish priorities for the removal of supplies and equipment, and, from time to time, conduct evacuation drills so that we all understand what is to be taken, and how, for every possible situation.

"In this way," they continued, "we will transform the raid and your capture from a defeat into a solid foundation for the new base." They quoted Chairman Mao: "We learn a thousand times more from a defeat than we do from a victory." "This is true," they observed,

> but only to the extent that we make it true in our practice. And we will make it true because we love you, and we love freedom, and because we are part of the masses of people and a handful of sleazy capitalists and their lackeys are not a match for us.
> So take care of yourself and hold on. Victory is certain.

Janine composed a nostalgic lament in poetic form for her lost lover. John and Therese agreed to tack it onto the missive as a sop to comfort their heartbroken and quasi-catatonic comrade. Janine signed the poem "Jory" for "Jory Uhuru," her nom de guerre ("uhuru" being Kiswahili for "freedom"). In contrast to the cooler letter, Janine's poem exuded desperation: she was clearly making an effort to drive herself on. It closed:

> Aches turn to comfort
> Bodacious sister woman you are
> In my mind as I
> Plant bombs, rob banks
> Your strength and discipline will
> Keep me fighting.[25]

Among the papers found by the FBI at the Northside Seattle residence of the Brigade were the names, addresses, and telephone numbers of the prominent state and corporate individuals whom the Brigade had considered kidnapping. The FBI notified the individuals that they might be targets for kidnapping or murder, as well as local police agencies and the State Patrol, but kept this information from the press.

On November 21, 1977, Adele Ferguson of the *Bremerton Sun* broke the story (the FBI blamed the State Patrol for the leak). FBI SAC John Reed told the press that the existence of the papers had been kept secret "because we don't want to give the George Jackson Brigade people any more publicity. That's what they're after." He continued: "We're not calling it a list. We're issuing a disclaimer that any list exists. We're still going through half of the stuff we got at that house." Assistant FBI District Director Jack Pringle confirmed that papers bearing these particular names, addresses, and telephone numbers had been seized after Brown's arrest.

The *Tacoma News Tribune* reported: "Paraphernalia that might be used in a kidnapping also was found in the Seattle house raided by the FBI Nov. 4." They were referring to a straitjacket and goggles. Security was increased for Governor Ray and Department of Social and Health Services Secretary McNutt. A trooper was assigned to guard Secretary McNutt's home and another to take over as his driver (his original driver continued to accompany him on trips). McNutt told the press: "I feel comfortable. This sort of thing goes with the job."[26]

Increased security at the Governor's Mansion came to the attention of the press on November 14, the date of a press conference for an event hosted by the governor's sister Marion Reed (Ray herself wasn't present). In contrast to earlier events, every reporter was forced to wait for one of two state troopers guarding the front door to unlock it. State Patrol policeman Bob Landon refused to say if additional precautions were being taken because of what the press was calling the George Jackson Brigade's "hit list": "When you discuss security measures in the press, you cease to have security," he quipped.

A map of Tacoma with sites marked, photos of the Brigade members firing pistols at a Skynomish-area shooting range, and a log of police radio broadcasts were also found at the deserted Brigade safe house. There was also a list of rental garages including one in Federal Way, where officers found a complete outfit of camping equipment—one pack for each collective member—"as if the owners were ready to head for the hills," imagined a *Tacoma News Tribune* reporter. More ominously, the trio who left the house were believed to have taken with them weapons including a 9 mm automatic pistol, a .38 caliber revolver, a 12-gauge shotgun, tear gas, mace, and a 30–30 rifle (this last was actually a .30 caliber semi-automatic). Police did not know that Sherman also had a 7 mm hunting rifle.

# 25

# Crying a River

*In which the disintegration of the Brigade is related through the diary entries of a heartbroken Janine*

Janine was devastated by the capture of Rita—her darling "Bo," as she called her affectionately. Compounding the pain of the abrupt loss of her partner was her isolation from her friends and loved ones in the community in Seattle. Further, she was alienated from John and Therese both conjugally, and, as an ideologically cloudy person in contrast to their crisp doctrine, politically.

During the period directly following Brown's capture, Bertram kept a diary. The document offers an invaluable look at the Brigade's most dismal period. With its numbers clipped by attrition and at a loss for campaigns to which they could contribute in the manner in which they had become accustomed, the collective proved unable to nourish one another's ideals and visions. A conspicuous absence of popular support for their work only compounded the problem.

Each entry of Janine's diary was addressed to Rita. It opened with a poem of recommitment in which Therese is referred to by her alias "Nora":

> It takes time and
> the people[']s will
> to rebuild a base
> We evacuated with weapons
> a change of clothes
> and Nora remembered
> our pipes, bulbs, timers and wires (bombmaking tools)
> So, sister, still in business
> We take each step carefully now[1]

Janine closed the poem with a Swahili verse and signed it "Jory." In a poem called "Picking Up the Pieces," Janine lamented, "why you, sweet love? . . . why do I keep on keepin' on / when you're gone? only last night I rolled over in fitful sleep / to hold you / tonight there's only air."

It is clear in every entry of the journal that, absent Rita's solid presence and forceful logic, Janine was tapping deep reserves to push herself through the torpor of depression. On November 28 she wrote: "wake up / hurting that don't matter gotta work—exercises." John and Therese chastised her for moping. "[S]ubjective feelings have no part in revolution," she related, complaining to her jailed lover. "[W]hen i say i want you—I'm told its sniveling. Fuck, don't need that support." She fantasized about freeing "Bo" as the Brigade had freed John: "[S]till want you & keep going til the time we get you."

As a continuing member of the perpetually broke Brigade Janine was compelled once again to participate in bank robberies. In her diary she refers to these with the coded phrase "going to see Morris." She volunteered to act as the trigger person—"I could go in okay"—but the other collective members didn't accept. They were right to be cautious: Janine's hopelessness would have made her a danger to herself and others. "Now more than ever there is nothing to lose," she stated bleakly.

Regardless of who was to play the central role, the Brigade needed the money a bank robbery would bring in. All of the funds in their "kitty" took an unexpected plunge for reasons undisclosed. Janine obviously had a strong suspicion. The night she discovered the loss she referred to John starkly: "Thief's back." Betraying a lack of faith in either John *or* Therese, she continued: "Wonder which of them it is that disposed of $150." She didn't trust herself either, due to substance abuse and reflexive self-blame: "Maybe me but with no recollection of blanking out." Either way, it was clear that Rita, whom John had accused of misallocation of funds shortly before her arrest, was vindicated. "Well babe, yer cleared," Janine commented with forced irony.

Janine made no mention of the emotional impact of participating in the next robbery. On November 29 she only jotted laconically: "we got a little $- more than 10 dollars we had." That same day, the collective members were reminded that they were not the only bank robbers in the city. In the course of routine monitoring of the police scanner they overheard the interception by law enforcement of another band of thieves. "[S]hots fired, no injuries," Janine reported. "[C]owboys"—the police—"got real excited but didn't do well. Gentleman from bureau"—the FBI—"think they have a positive solution for case." Janine's sympathies were with the outlaws: "Hope not."

Outside a Laundromat, a man from a local radio station doing "person on the street" interviews asked Janine if she would say her name and "Merry Christmas!" in an original way. "Would have liked to do a little rap on solstice & patriarchal christianity ripping off the people's holiday but thot I best be silent lest my voice be recognized," she wrote after returning home. It made her melancholy that she was unable to communicate with others openly in such an elementary way.

Janine attempted to comfort herself with the self-management techniques she had employed before going underground: reading and watching movies, meditating and doing yoga. Her reading that winter was of politically conscious but less-than-doctrinaire writers: Marge Piercy's *Woman on the Edge of Time*, Margaret Atwood's *Surfacing*,[2] and B. Traven's *The Death Ship*. She judged the last a "good book," commenting that the "writer has high regard for workers; no regard for a state & bureaucracy. anarchist outlook—real faith in people."

As if justifying the slack time required for viewing, she likewise commented on the political content of the films she saw. *The Gauntlet* was "a real good Clint Eastwood flick—almost as good as *[The Outlaw] Josie Wales*. He was fighting a corrupt pig that was trying to have him killed because he was transporting a strong woman/whore who once tricked with the pig official. The real target was the ♀. She was incredible—real aggressive."

Several months later, the group watched *Bonnie and Clyde* on TV. "It's one of my all time favorite movies," Janine gushed, then mused to Rita: "Too bad we didn't see it together. Altho our movies shared record is pretty good, *The Getaway*, *[The Outlaw] Josie Wales*, *The Great White Hope*." Spirits raised by popular culture, the threesome went out the next day to see *Close Encounters*, but were disappointed. "It was a mediocre movie," Janine reported. "Nowhere near as good as *Star Wars*."


Janine's yoga practice was a stress reliever. The meditation, however, was primarily an effort to contact Rita in her jail cell. These spiritual efforts bore some fruit, but it was the fruit before Tantalus. "[M]editate—try for contact," Janine wrote. "See you sometimes. Usually once or twice a day for a split second. [N]eed to feel you more."

Her isolation pressed on her constantly, all the more so because she was so ambivalent about the political efficacy of the small cell guerrilla tactic that made it necessary. Outright despair pounced on her November 30, and she pined for drugs to fill the void inside herself. "[F]eel dispirited, walking dead, want dope to take pain away." She knew this craving was not, however, what she truly desired: "Need a dose of people's spirit & strength. Just as THE Man would have it, I seriously doubt there is enough strength in me to help build revolution. It seems hopeless, we just get picked off one at a time, w/o doing significant damage. Isolated as we are, i don't know if there's much support among real people for us. If not, where do we get off doing this? There ain[']t been much indication of support from regular people (cept W2 bros.)".

The counting of mutinous maximum-security inmates as "regular people" speaks volumes about the desperation with which Janine sought to find value in her position. She didn't succeed. Her lament continued: "Oh, babe, the state struck hard & now i can't find the courage, strength & determination [to continue] fightin'. Don't wanna keep on keepin on. What for?" Janine closed the entry: "70 $ of our last 130 got ripped off today." She did not name the culprit.

Though far fewer than she would have liked, there were good days in which Janine felt the elation of "the people's spirit" and a deep satisfaction in being able to place herself on the continuum of organizers and rebels who had come before her. One of these days was prompted by a viewing of the documentary *Union Maids*. "[P]oignant morale-builder that put the struggle in better perspective and renewed my determination to fight capitalism/imperialism, sexism, racism & all oppression. Incredible sisters have struggled, died, been locked up before us." Exhibiting a still functional "gaydar," she took a particular interest in a sister who had been active in union organizing in the 1930s: "She looked like a dyke and mentioned she had time to struggle w/in the unions because she wasn't married. . . . Our herstory makes me proud."

In contrast, Janine wrote of herself disparagingly: "a little ashamed that I am always so down & feel a near overwhelming need to do dope to take personal loss & pain away." These cravings came, in part, because the victories were so few and far between. Her intimates were just as out of reach. A people person, Janine suffered sorely from her lack of contact with others. "Day to day work is so slow, hard to see progress. Mostly it is hard to keep a clear view of the necessity of this work when I am completely isolated." She pitied and mocked herself for it: "Snivel—not a friend in the world." Janine closed the entry with a cry so hollow it could only have deepened her depression: "Hasta la Victoria!"

December 3, 1977, was a heart-stopping day for the three remaining Brigade members. In the morning, Janine and John set out to find a "dirty car," their name for the getaway vehicle, which would almost inevitably be seen by witnesses. They ditched the "dirties" immediately after each robbery—usually within five minutes of the heist—at a spot where a "clean" car was waiting. "Jory" and "Frank"—Janine and John's aliases within the collective (they had others for the outside world)—planned to steal the car from a used car lot. One of them would take it for a test drive and, instead of bringing it back, would simply take it home. The other would quietly trail behind in case any difficulties developed.

"Jory" wasn't permitted to do any test driving at the first three lots the pair visited. "Frank" was given a set of keys at the next one and promptly headed home, Janine following in a separate car. "In a fluke the dealer's friend was at a gas station & dealer came swooshing up behind in a fancy T-bird," Janine wrote after the event. With the assistance of someone he had flagged down, the dealer followed John off I-5. Janine ditched John's pursuers but lost John in the process. She looked for him on "the rd most likely," but could find "no sign." She called home, but Therese hadn't seen or heard from him, so Janine went out looking again. "[F]ound car w/ wasps [white men] and no him. Terrified & freaked out," she again called Therese, who forced her to be calm. "Would have lost my shit if I hadn't been able to call home," Janine observed with concern.

On the third call home, Therese had new information: John was at the police station in downtown Tacoma. He was initially jailed for running off with the car but, impressively, talked his way out of it: the police had bought a story he had concocted. Upon his return home, Therese inflicted a severe tongue-lashing on John and declared, with Janine's approval, John was, in effect, grounded: He was not to go to town "except for important work."

December 4, the following day, was the one-month anniversary of Rita's arrest. Rita's case had been in the press only very little—nothing compared to the publicity garnered by the male Brigade members Ed and Mark in their respective arrests. The accounts that did appear revealed little. "Wonder how you are doing," Janine reflected. "[Y]ou look real unhappy & angry in the two pictures I've seen. Mostly figure your [you're] o.k. & doing pretty well in general population."

To distract her mind from the anniversary and recover from the previous day's close call, Janine vegged, reading and watching TV. Inevitably she succumbed to the pain of her lover's absence. "[R]eal bad," she scrawled desperately. Sharing her desire that the Brigade obey the aboveground injunction to "Free Rita Brown!" Janine continued: "Gotta get you. Must see you again."

The rest of the collective rejected as unfeasible the proposal to "liberate" Rita before or during her upcoming trial in Portland. Janine urged that the collective should at least *be* in Portland: "The pigs could slip up!" she contended. "It'd be wrong to miss it!" Janine jotted the response to her pleas in her diary: "They, particularly Nora, seem resigned to never see you—or any locked down comrade—again. That's wrong, too. People escape all the time. We should, whenever possible, case trials since that[']s suppose[d] to be the easiest time. Be real hard gettin you if they send you to Alderson."[3]

Soon after, as if consoling herself, Janine dreamt that Rita was out on furlough with her three companions. Rita was obligated to return to prison. Janine pleaded with her lover to stay, but Rita was determined. "That was far from reality!" Janine exclaimed in her diary upon waking: "Bo" was hardly one to return to prison voluntarily. It pained Janine to see a picture of her girlfriend "visibly shaken" after a pretrial hearing. These and other photographs exacerbated Janine's longing for her partner.

The furlough dream recurred in the early morning of January 7, 1978. Janine pictured the three remaining Brigade members, plus Rita, staying at her mother's house. Rita was on a furlough again, and about to report back to prison. Janine couldn't find her to talk her out of it. With Rita gone, Janine tried to decide whether to stay with her mom or with the Brigade sans Rita.

It seemed that a reconnection with any other Brigade member would have alleviated some of her depression. On January 6, referring either to Ed or Mark, Janine had written: "Hank was on the news tonite. It's real hard to see people confined & not be able to get to them. He's real strong."

Early in December the collective got word that at least one of their supporters in the aboveground community was not as trustworthy as their underground complement would have liked. On December 2, Janine wrote: "[H]eavy words that disappointed from a trusted friend of yours. You'll be blown away."[4]

On December 5, a drop of materials from a Seattle supporter brought "Bad news. An old friend of yers talked to the Feds at least 50 times in the last year & ½," Janine informed Rita, to whom her diary was still addressed.

When Janine and Therese returned from their meeting with their Seattle contacts Janine sank into a lethargy, which was soon followed by unconsciousness. She dreamed that she and Therese had uterine cancer and woke up abruptly, alarmed and paranoid. She dreaded the Brigade's "next visit to Morris," the ever-impending heist for the destitute outlaws. "Knew I couldn't do it[,] knew we'd get busted." Janine was so rattled that she "[h]ad to wake people up so i didn't go screaming down the street or out to find dope."

More positively, Janine and John conversed on armed struggle, Rita, and the problems he had had with the Revolutionary Union. Tensions ran high, however, between John and Therese. While the two argued heatedly, Janine, caught in between, tried desperately not to chain-smoke. "Dinner time meant another one of their fights," she recorded that night. "Drives me batty. Don't know whether to keep walking on eggshells and assume that it's between them (which it mostly is) or say what seems true to me. Last nite they were both right. He was defensive about his work being criticized & she was uncomradely in her method of criticism. Altho last night she was friendlier than usual, less condescending."

The situation had declined since Rita's capture. Rita, even when angry and irritated, insisted on keeping discussions productive; she rarely permitted them to degenerate into insult exchanges under the guise of political disagreement. Likewise, in her and Janine's relationship the fights had never become particularly bitter. "When we had disagreement, and even in our one fight, we could analyze what was happening pretty well 'cuz we knew that both of us contributed to the problem," Janine recalled. John and Therese, in her view, "seem to think that one of them is all right & the other full of shit—at least that's how they act."

Janine's anxious nightmare—minus the cancer—was a creeping reality: the next bank job was slated for December 8. On December 6, Janine busied herself with "errands related to Morris," such as taking the car in for a paint job, a minor disguise that ideally would conceal that the collective was responsible for not one, but several, bank robberies.

That same day, news of the capture of Joanne Little, the African American woman who had killed a white jailer who had tried to rape her in a North Carolina jail, caused Janine to cry: "It's sad news. They keep locking up fighting women." She moaned to Rita: "Sweet sister why don't you walk out of that place," promising: "We'll come pick you up." She then added dismally: "If you could wait a bit until we have more than $20.00, we'd even help."

The diary entry for December 7 reads: "Am scared shitless. I don't think I'll lose my shit. There's no dirty driver"—someone to take the robber from the scene of the crime to the clean getaway car—"& no backup" listening in on police scanners or accompanying the person with the holdup note into the bank. "[I]t's a long way out of the area in the clean car. . . . Hope I'm around to write tomorrow."

The job came off okay the next day, with Janine inside the bank for the first time. She procured $3,966 from the Northeast branch of the Puget Sound National Bank in Tacoma. "I only did a single [drawer]," she confessed, and fretted that she had lost a pen—one that Rita had given her—in the course of the operation. She slept poorly that night. "Real lonely—missed you. The feel like giving up came flooding over & hung around." Around 3 or 4 A.M., she calmed down.

On December 10, friends from Seattle visited with gifts. Janine received a flannel nightgown, heating pad, and a vibrator, and found the pen she thought she'd lost in the bank—"Another small comfort that reminds me we loved fine for 1 year & 1 mo." She continued wistfully: "Wish the strength of commitment to this work would reach what it has been in the past."

Janine never dropped the nostalgia for an instant. She headed each entry of her diary with the length of time that had passed since Rita's capture. Over the entry for December 11 were the words: "5 wks 2 days." The following night she watched, as she slumbered, Rita in a prison yard. Another prisoner tried to start a fight with her incarcerated partner. Though obviously pissed, Rita knew better than to respond to the provocation. She shoved her hands in her pockets and walked past the offending inmate. As she did so, a guard shot her in the back. The dream was, Janine stated, "to put it mildly, unsettling."

Janine coaxed herself back to sleep and was greeted by the image of a cat in her lap. Fiddling with a pair of scissors, she accidentally stabbed the "kitty." A hissing sound escaped from the wound: she had punctured a lung. The feline cried and cried and cried. Someone else finally wrung its neck.

Clearly in need of relief, Janine took the next day off. She declined to perform her exercises, made a banana cream pie, and took a walk to the Puyallup River. She charted her biorhythms into the spring. This mini-vacation helped reestablish her equilibrium. She closed her diary entry for the day sounding more centered than she had in over a month: "yep I miss you babe but for a few hours it hasn't been agony."

On the night of December 12 Janine and Therese woke in the wee hours of the night, anxious and irritated. John, due back at 10:00 P.M., had not yet returned. The collective took time commitments seriously. Any breaking of an obligation could signify not only a comrade's capture but, depending on the circumstance, an impending raid on those still outside of police custody. The irritation was compounded by the knowledge that John had been irresponsible and inconsiderate in the past: they had no way of knowing how to interpret his absence.

John came back the next afternoon. He claimed to have "lost" $800 from the collective's small stash. "I dropped my wallet and spent the night walking the streets looking for it," he told the women. But his sugar-coated cover stories had already given his companions cavities, and this new lie hit a nerve. The greater insult was that he hadn't called the previous night to let them know that he hadn't been arrested. "The fact that he didn't give a shit about us has totally overridden his callousness regarding money," Janine vented in her diary. "Total disregard for his comrades. One more time he leaves people climbing the walls wondering what the fuck has happened. It's always real bad but it's now much worse.... It's truly inexcusable."

Janine blamed herself in part for John's ill behavior: "I haven't expressed my anger so it's part my responsibility that he'll probably get away with it again and again and again." When she did voice her upset, she found that she and Therese actually agreed on something: that John should not go out alone or with sizable amounts of money. The elephant in the room that no one found the courage to identify was that John was a gambling addict. Though Janine hoped precautions and increased supervision would improve the situation, she confessed to Rita, "especially without your support, my dear, I doubt my passivity will stop."

It didn't. Several days later she complained about Therese. "This group is getting held up by her arrogance & I'm being passive, not saying anything—just listening to snide, condescending trash. Ah, fuck it."

The next week Janine recorded: "I'm having a hard time with her [Therese] these days.... The arrogance gets no better—maybe worse?" The day before John "was where he wasn't supposed to be" and got harassed by police—their beat-up car had attracted attention. This time, John called home to let the others know. Therese screamed at him, hung up, and, when questioned by Janine, refused to divulge any information.

"Was he joyriding?" Janine asked blandly.

"He doesn't joyride!" Therese flared defensively. She continued poisonously, "Your view of us is disgusting" and took Janine to task for such lapses in faith as the time, during one of John's unexplained disappearances, when she called card rooms around town asking if someone of his description was present.

"She is so off the wall," Janine complained. "[W]e found him once in a card room—*she's* called card rooms before when he was gone!" Janine then struck with the weapon of her collaborators: attributing political significance to personal failures. "Sometimes I really question her motivation for revolutionary work," she wrote of Therese.

On Sunday December 18, the day after a draining collective meeting, a friend of the collective's visited from Seattle. Janine got some respite from her prolonged isolation by cuddling with this person and speaking of one another's lives: of Rita, dope, unhealthy habits, and new meditation practices. Janine was pleased to learn of the support for her captured partner in the Seattle women's community. "Many ♀ are sending you white light," she informed her lover. "That's another way of concentration & support—which you have alot of. It's a real good combination of spiritual and revolutionary." Her own efforts in this arena were promising: "Have been trying to contact you myself and it looks like we're making some connections." By midweek the collective was back to "target hunting" and bomb construction.

Janine didn't mention it in her diary, but the collective had decided to bomb the Puget Sound Power & Light substation at the intersection of One Hundred Eighty-fifth Street and the West Valley Highway, in Tukwila close to the Renton border. The transformer there supplied power to the Southcenter and Andover Park Industrial Complex, which was the Brigade's true target. On the evening of December 23, the group planted the pipe bomb.

At about 8:20 P.M., one of the women in the Brigade called KOMO TV in Seattle and requested the journalist Ruth Walsh. The caller then identified herself as a member of the Brigade and announced that a bomb planted at the Puget Sound substation to "protest the growth of capitalism in the Andover Park Area" would detonate in twenty minutes. Walsh immediately called the police. The bomb exploded soon thereafter. Renton Police Captain Jim Bourasa later complained: "They gave us 20 minutes notice, but it only took 14 to go off. They cheated." The few minutes could have made a deadly difference, as a police officer was within a couple hundred feet of the station when the explosion occurred.

Around noon the next day, Christmas Eve, one of the Brigade women called the *Seattle Sun* to inform them that a communiqué intended for publication was taped to the inside of a toilet seat cover dispenser in the men's room of an all-night restaurant on Fourth Avenue.[5]

The communiqué was addressed to King County Executive John D. Spellman and public safety official Lawrence G. Waldt.[6] It proclaimed that the aim of the previous night's bombing was "to protest the criminal and inhuman conditions at the

King County Jail." Their rationale was: "Sounthcenter / Andover Park Industrial Complex . . . is a center of capitalist activity in King County. Capitalism causes crime with unemployment, poverty and oppression, and the capitalists are responsible for the conditions in their jails." Thus, one of the Brigade's last bombings sounded a theme very similar to its first.

The communiqué set out general objections to jail conditions, such as overcrowding and fire code violations, and decried the excessively long period—twenty-one months—Mark Cook had been confined in the jail's segregation unit. In comparison, captured Brigade members Ed Mead and Rita Brown—who, unlike Cook, did not maintain their innocence—were in the general population in the Washington State Penitentiary in Walla Walla and the Marion County Jail in Salem, Oregon, respectively. The communiqué attributed the discrepancy to "blatant racism," which, rather than being an anomaly, they contended was the norm in prisons and jails.

The Brigade issued four "initial demands," one for the immediate release of Cook into the general prison population and the other three for reports they wanted to see published in the *Post-Intelligencer* and *Seattle Times*. The latter were to catalogue what fire codes were being violated and what was being done to comply with them; plans for the emergency evacuation and rescue of prisoners in the jail in case of fire; and medical conditions in the segregation unit. This last report was to be written by an investigatory team of "licensed medical personnel from outside the jail," including "people from the alternative medical community."

The Brigade ordered Spellman and Waldt to "inform your capitalist bosses that we hold them responsible for these demands," continuing: "[I]f they are not met within a month's time, we will continue attacking ruling class institutions, capital equipment and persons throughout the Pacific Northwest." The threat against people, as opposed to property, was only the second in the life of the Brigade. (The other was the unfulfilled promise of revenge against the policemen who had killed Bruce Seidel issued in the "International Women's Day" communiqué nearly two years earlier.)

At this point, the communiqué addressed itself to "all progressive people in Oregon and Washington," whom the Brigade urged "to join with us in this campaign to bring the King County Jail up to minimum standards of human decency." They asked people to do everything from calling the fire marshal to complain about jail conditions to sabotaging "any and all ruling class institutions (banks, supermarkets, insurance companies, etc.) and their capital equipment."

In an interesting comment on their own perception of the efficacy of their methods, the communiqué closed with the assertion that phone calls and small-scale sabotage were "by no means petty. If they were taken up by enough of us, they would mean a hundred times more than any bomb."[7]

Even a few phone calls would have done more than the bomb planted at the Puget

Sound Power & Light substation. "The bomb went off, but it caused no serious damage and power was not cut off," Captain Bourasa informed the press. Apparently, the device exploded in an open area of the substation, leaving the transformers that ringed it unscathed. "I guess it was improperly placed," Bourasa concluded. "It was quite a large substation. I don't know if they couldn't get in and had to toss the thing over the fence or what." On the morning of December 24, FBI agents joined local police in an effort to determine the nature of the device employed,[8] presumably a simple task as there was very little technical variation in the Brigade's pipe bombs.

At 6:25 P.M. on December 24, a woman identifying herself as a Brigade member again called KOMO TV, this time stating that a bomb would explode in fifteen minutes at the Convoy Company, a Kent trucking firm. The device had been planted, the woman declared, in support of the auto machinists, who were still on strike. The bomb was placed in a 1978 Mercury on a freight car loaded with automobiles near the railroad tracks at South Two Hundred Seventy-second Street and Seventy-second Avenue South. After the 6:40 P.M. detonation, FBI agent Jim Schaffer told the press that damage was limited to that one car.

The accompanying communiqué was titled "Bust the Union Busters." It decried the efforts of the King County Automobile Dealers' Association to break the strike, and lauded "the workers who have stood firm against these attacks and continue to build support for the struggle throughout their long and courageous strike." It drew attention to other regional efforts against unions by employers and reminded that Seattle was one of the last islands of trade unionism on the West Coast: auto dealers in Portland had broken the unions two years previous; those in Spokane had done so five years earlier; while all of southern California "has no auto machinists unions left at all." The authors of the communiqué—most certainly John and Therese, given the strident workerist tone of the document—tied these changes to the crisis of diminishing profits faced by corporations in the United States: "As the capitalists scramble to increase their declining profits, strikes everywhere are becoming longer and harder fought.

"The best strategy against the Dealers' union-busting attempt is to cost the bosses more than they gain by employing scabs," the communiqué contended. To this end, they advocated boycotts, harassment, and vandalism against both dealers and news media that didn't cover the strike properly.

Lloyd Wilson, business representative for the Auto Machinists' Local 289, rebuked the Brigade, as he had in the past. "We're opposed to the bombings," Wilson stated. "They don't settle any strike . . . violence doesn't settle anything. I think they use any kind of excuse they can to go ahead and do it." In the opinion of Brigade members, Wilson was likely one of the "local union hacks [who] haven't done much better than the dealers," as they wrote in the communiqué.[9]

After two bombings in two days, law enforcement remained alert for any recurrences. "It's something we can't predict," FBI Agent Schaffer told the press. "But

I am sure the sheriff's office and police departments are awake for any trouble."[10] Law enforcement still viewed the Brigade through a lens distorted by sexism, and the media, in turn, spoke of the FBI's search for "the Brigade's reputed leader, John Sherman, and a woman thought to be traveling with Sherman."[11] As far as the police and the press could see, Therese was less a driving member of the collective than a passive adjunct.

The day after Christmas, the group had a harrowing encounter, in which they appeared to have been identified while driving by at least one FBI agent. The next day Janine returned home from an errand and found that John was absent. She looked for a note telling her where he was but there was none to be found. Two hours later John returned smiling. When she berated him for his inconsideration, he protested that he *had* left a note for her—in his pocket!

John's explanation of what he had been doing further infuriated Janine. Listening in on the police scanner, he had heard that the feds were in the same place they had seen him the day before. The collective had already decreed that John was not to go out alone, and that they would replace the car in which he had been seen as quickly as possible, leaving it unused in the meantime. Yet John got in the same vehicle in which he'd been recognized the day before and drove over to observe the agents who were presumably searching for him. "Is that just bad judgment or insanity?" Janine demanded of her diary. "I am so sick of waiting & fretting & worrying about where he is i want to throw up."

Therese was also angry. The women's criticisms upset John, who huffed "I'm going for a walk." Aware of his short leash, he added hurriedly, "I'll only be in the back yard." Two hours later, Therese went looking for him, but couldn't find him. Hours later, she went out again and brought him back. He claimed he didn't hear her screaming and crying his name. "Jesus—[']I am sorry['] ain't gonna cut [it] much longer," Janine wrote.

On December 29, 1977 John "got lost" again. Pegging him for a burglary suspect, three policemen pulled guns on him and took him into custody. "Another agonizing 8 hrs" passed before they cut him loose and he returned to his comrades. "This can't go on. He or me has gotta stop being in this life."

A little after New Year's Eve, Janine visited "Suzy," presumably a code name for a Brigade supporter, for the first time. "What a flash," she writes. "She wasn't nearly as scary as you all portrayed her." Suzy gave Janine a "real pretty choker" she'd stitched herself.

The following entries were terse:

1.1.78: "Got followed today. Don't know bout [*sic* by] who."
1.2.78: "Hims [John] gone since 2:00 PM yesterday. Came back around 3:00 PM. He doesn't remember anything. He lost all our money again."

The next night Janine fantasized about Rita meting out poetic justice to John. "You were gone all day on Sat. I think cuz you were trying to show him how it feels. When you came back we held each other for a long time—then I went to another room crying & angry."

The following evening Janine had trouble sleeping. She continually demanded of herself, "Is armed struggle *wrong* at this time?" and couldn't help responding with an emphatic "yes!" "I think it is wrong, arrogant (maybe) & individual(small group)istic. In this period of development towards revolution, a small group of people should not be 'professional revies.' People should be in touch with & organizing others. Military skills should be learned along with other work—not in an isolated underground itty biddie group."

The collective had a long discussion about an article on the Brigade in *Open Road*, a Vancouver-based anarchist paper. "It is pretty unfair to the group," Janine complained, though she didn't identify her objections. In the same sitting, collective members "Also talk about what we hate in each other."

A bank robber in Tacoma caught Janine's attention. The perpetrator entered a bank the police had under surveillance and collected money from three tellers. Once outside, the police shouted "Freeze!" to which he responded with gunfire, which was immediately returned. Shot in the leg, the man continued to fire on the officers and struggled to his getaway car. "That takes courage or insanity," Janine commented. Grasping for the implications of the episode, she decided it was "encouraging to anyone interested in bank robbery."

With Rita's trial coming up on January 11, Janine was apprehensive. She thought it would be good for Rita to see her supporters in the courtroom and difficult for her to get sentenced to life in prison. "Think, breathe & plot escape my love," Janine exhaled onto her paper. "Keep fighting. We'll make it."

On the January 10, the group did another bank. A Brigade woman, dressed as a man and bearing a revolver, carried it out, entering the Westgate branch of the Great Northwestern Federal Savings & Loan Association at 1:56 P.M. and seizing $2,518. They ditched the dirty car in the driveway of a home near North Twenty-first and Bennett Streets. The car was registered to one of the Brigade's former Seattle safehouses, allowing the FBI to readily identify the robbery as the work of the group.[12]

On January 11, television news covered what was to have been the first day of Rita's trial. The Brigade members learned to their surprise that Rita had pled "guilty."

This displeased them. Defiance was considered proper revolutionary conduct: a plea of "guilty" implied that what one had done was wrong, and thus undermined the political "rightness" of the Brigade's very existence. "Heard about your guilty plea & am upset," Janine acknowledged. "Can't understand a reason for telling people guilty. Cried alot about that. It's a big mistake. Yer not guilty. Your [sic] strong & righteous." Rita had read an incendiary statement at the hearing, but only a fraction of it was quoted on television. "It's good that you said yer glad you did it," Janine commented, adding "but people associate guilty w/ wrong."

The next day a greater portion of Rita's statement was printed in the paper. Reading it, Janine understood that her lover had not recanted. The document, in her opinion, conveyed a "good, strong message. It may have been enough to make it clear that you don't feel guilty or feel that you did wrong."

That same evening a scenario from one of Janine's old anxiety dreams was realized in a circuitous way: Therese received word that her mother had been diagnosed with cancer. Janine, always empathetic, was deeply saddened. "That would cause me to feel pain, trapped & lost [sic] my shit." "She's been strong," Janine wrote of Rita. While less serious than the troubles faced by Therese, Janine's own situation took a plunge: the FBI made it be known that, as part of the Brigade investigation, it was searching for a woman using the pseudonym "Jory." Previous to this announcement, Janine had been able to retain the illusion that she was under the FBI's radar.

In an effort to lift their spirits, the harried group played the quintessentially capitalist board game Monopoly. It was a disaster. "Ended up in a fight over whether to play strictly by the rules," Janine reported. "Disgusting."

The next day they managed to play Monopoly *and* Yahtzee without fighting. They all went car shopping, and made plans to look for mattresses, because all their backs were sore from sleeping on the floor since they'd fled North Seattle. John taught Janine cribbage, which she liked, and the collective members decided that it was worth allocating a portion of their precious resources on Risk. It had become clear to each and all that if they were to continue on their chosen path, it was imperative to improve their interactions with one another. Just as such war games encourage militarism in the dominant society, collective members never dropped their combative perspective. "Played a game," Janine stated after the purchase. "It's great. . . . [I] am coming to understand strategy & tactics better."

With a new bed, Janine settled into her room. She decorated it with dried flowers and seedlings and a poster of the Hindu pantheon. The only constant book in her collection was Rita's copy of George Jackson's *Blood in My Eye*, treasured more for its past owner than for its content. The location of the house was remote enough that she never had to close her drapes; her sleep was sometimes cloaked in moonlight, and her mornings were met with a bucolic vision of woods, pastures, and, on clear days, mountains. The lights of the city shone at night. "Yes, love, I'm beginning to enjoy some times alone here. Meditating helps." She sketched a childish depiction of the front view of the house to share with the intended recipient of the diary.

On the evening of January 20, 1978 "the folks"—a handful of supporters from Seattle—came. They brought the full text of Rita's plea statement and informed the collective that their colleague was in segregation at the federal prison in Alderson, West Virginia. "[Y]our statement at sentencing was real fine & strong—like you," Janine wrote in her diary. "Am impressed at the clarity & power of your words. Love, strength & determination." Janine took comfort cuddling with a friend she called "Sandy": "felt happy felt all warm & comfortable."

The day after the visit was a free day for everyone in the collective. Janine burned through the *Autobiography of Mother Jones*, which she found inspiring. Then it was back to casing banks. Collective members listened to the police scanner frequently and, possibly as a precaution against one of their own, took all the money they had with them each time they left the house.

On January 23, the *Seattle Times* printed a picture of the fishing dock where Janine and Rita had passed the time on their days off. Janine clipped it with the intention of sending it on to Rita once she again became able to communicate with her. Janine hadn't given up on the escape fantasy, and considered, more as a wish than a practicality, moving to West Virginia to explore such possibilities.

Janine got the blues near the quarter-year anniversary of Rita's bust. She still dated her journal by counting the days since the arrest—"2 mos. & 30 days"—and had never ceased to address her diary to Brown. It took her another day to emerge from the funk.

February 7: "It's been a real bad day. They had a fight over her arrogant behavior. He had a macho tantrum. Yelled at me cuz there was no dog to kick." Janine too felt the lack of a convenient punching bag. She, however, took her frustrations out on herself, smoking until she experienced recurrent chest pain. A lament in her diary highlights the extent of the problem: "If I could only be disciplined about cigarettes and only smoke (one an hr.), my health would improve."

*King*, a TV special on the life of Dr. Martin Luther King Jr., stimulated Janine's ongoing internal dialogue about appropriate strategy, but her comments on the program in her diary have the feel of regurgitations intended to please her ideal reader, Rita. "i keep asking was he self[-]serving—did he really believe that turn the other cheek crap? . . . Ain't no inner peace when your belly is empty." As the third and final installment of the *King* series aired, Janine imagined what could have happened if both Malcolm X and King had lived and joined forces. "Can you imagine?" Janine demanded. "Had they stayed alive long enough, working together could have meant heavy material change."

On February 19, Janine had another of her recurring Rita furlough dreams. She found the episodes frustrating but, as they were her only opportunity to pass time with her beloved, poignantly pleasant as well.

On February 21, the day of Rita's sentencing, the collective watched the nightly news. To their chagrin, there was not a word on the case of their comrade. The next morning they learned from the paper that Brown had been sentenced to twenty-five years. Janine was impressed by her lover's statement. "Your words still turn my head around," she wrote in her diary. Janine makes no mention of it, but Brigade members were later indicted for taking $865 from the Ninety-ninth Street and Pacific Avenue branch of Union Bank in Tacoma on February 23.

February 27 was a day before an action: "constant companion insomnia," an anxious and sleep-deprived Janine recorded. The following day went well enough—$1,899 from the University Place branch of Puget Sound National Bank—but was followed by more disappointing evidence of the collective's failure to inspire others. March 2, she jotted: "Had a phone call. It sounds like the folks are abandoning us. Ah well . . . that's life." A mail drop the next day, however, lifted group spirits. "We were deluged with mail," Janine delighted. One letter even resuscitated the prospect of replenishing the organization, as opposed to simply continuing until they, the last three, were caught: a woman bank robber who was to be released from prison in a year said she would like to hear from people outside of prison. Apparently, the Brigade's support people thought the guerrillas could be a good contact.

The collective also received the thoughtful feedback that they had solicited in a lengthy political statement they issued only days before Brown's arrest the previous fall. It was in the form of a document signed by the "Valerian Coven." The communiqué primarily concerned itself with how to improve the relationship between the above- and underground. The Coven—an anonymous collection of politically active workers and students in the Seattle area—shared their take on the Brigade's actions in support of Walla Walla prisoners and the automotive machinists' strike. The contrast between the two campaigns, they opined, illuminated the best points of the Brigade and the aspects of the organization that were cause for concern. The Coven felt:

> your most effective work has been around prison issues. We give the following reasons:
>
> a. Violent aggressions call for violent retaliations. The prisons are full of violent dehumanizing conditions. The pipebombing of the Wash. State Dept. of Corrections offices in Olympia, the 1977 attempted bombing of the main substation supplying power to the State Capitol in Olympia were clearly warranted actions against state institutions and mobilized support for the Walla Walla strike—on both sides of the prison walls.

b. The communiqués that followed these actions and the jail letter dated Dec. 23 were excellent examples of effective communication in an area where the aboveground can and is working to end the brutalizing conditions suffered by inmates.

In the bombings in support of the Automotive Machinists' Union, on the other hand, the Brigade clearly lacked a connection with the constituency they sought to aid, an omission so glaring that their work in this area verged on being counterproductive, the Coven opined. This problem was caused by the Brigade looking at the struggle too narrowly. By focusing on workers in an all-white, male guild, the Brigade lost out on connections with all the others excluded from the union. For example:

> One of the struck dealers is on property robbed from older poor residents of a neighborhood that is struggling daily to survive and keep big business from suffocating them out of existence. The visible striking workers are only a small percentage of people affected by the bosses that "we are trying to bust". We criticize you for not taking into account other people who suffer from the greediness of the profitmakers. The residents of that neighborhood are too poor, too old, and too sick to ever walk a picket line and for some ever to hope to see the possibility of having a job to strike at.

The most important question the Coven asked the Brigade members was whether they were "open enough to hear the non-support and reevaluate your work [?]" Unlike self-identified radicals who secretly feared that they were liberals and consequently cheered positions more dangerous than their own, the Coven writers were confident in the importance of their political work and felt no need to pander to the claims of superiority made by some proponents of clandestinity:

> We must do our work differently than you do yours. We . . . take daily risks in providing services to poor and working class young and old people. We feel we do not confine our politics to meetings and organizations. We take them with us to the job. Which means putting ourselves on the line one day and going back the next to face the consequences of our overt actions. We cannot hide our identity or make hit and run attempts at change. We believe our aboveground work is essential and vital to a revolutionary overthrow of Amerikkka.
> 
> We also see underground work as an essential and necessary part of the whole, entire struggle. We need to know if you're into struggling and acknowledging our work. Will our input about the usefulness and timing of armed support for our struggles and work be heeded?

Despite the considerate tone of the missive, the remaining Brigade members only heard the criticism. "We don't support sexist hiring/work practices!" Janine vented in her diary. "Really (harumph)." Though the Brigade had solicited such feedback, the Coven's letter went unanswered for months.

From Janine's perspective, the best part of the drop was copies of two letters: one from Rita to Ed and the other from Ed back to Rita. Each decried the temptation of succumbing to fear and urged the other to "FIGHT BACK." "Yer letter along with Ed's . . . are helping me to deal with fear," Janine wrote to Rita appreciatively. "If the pigs knew what a job they did on this tug [The Urban Guerrilla], they'd smile constantly." She decided she would reread Ed's "when I feel scaredy cat about getting caught. . . . Someday I'll be a strong ♀ freedom fighter 'stead of a fretful, hesitant student."

In the next installment of her dreamtime prison motif, Janine pictured herself inside rather than imagining that Rita was out. She and her girlfriend, both inmates, encountered one another in the course of a transfer between institutions. The lovers hugged and Janine awoke grinning.

March 8 was a warm spring day. Janine was domestic, cooking dinner and baking a chocolate cake for dessert, while John and Therese picked up their aboveground support visitors and brought them home. "We talked a little 'bout where we're at & where the folks should be at—which is rebuilding while they take 2–3 mo.s to decide what they're going to do. They're having heart trouble," she recorded of the aboveground support.

The doubts were well founded. The aboveground collaborators, unbeknown to anyone but likely sensed by all, would not be called on much longer. Within a few weeks, the Brigade would cease to exist.

# Coda

Tuesday, March 21, 1978, was a day of dramatic change for the final Brigade members. Janine, Therese, and John sat in their 1965 Buick Electra—John in the driver's seat—in the parking lot next to the Jubilee Hamburger Restaurant, 858 South Thirty-eighth Street, in Tacoma. Each wore a disguise: Janine, a scarf and an ill-fitting wig; Therese, drag; John, a priest's collar. Therese had a stickup note on her; they were preparing to rob the Thirty-eighth and J Street branch of the United Mutual Savings Bank, across an alley from the restaurant.

At 1:55 P.M., while chewing their burgers and slurping their milkshakes, an unmarked sedan pulled up behind them, blocking their exit. Almost instantaneously, a horde of federal agents and police officers leapt into view with weapons drawn.

"Get out of the car! Hands up!" an agent barked. All three exited the car slowly, hands in the air. Once spread-legged against the Buick, Therese informed the agent patting her down "I've got a gun in my waistband."

"*Gun!*" the man cried, causing all the other agents to jump. Janine flinched: "We're all gonna die!" she remembers thinking.

Therese's piece was a 9 mm. Agents found another just like it in a cardboard box just to the right of the driver's seat, and a third the day after when they searched the car more thoroughly. On Janine, they discovered an ammo clip fitting Therese's pistol. There was also a police scanner in the car.

The feds were delighted by their catch. The *Post-Intelligencer* observed: "FBI officials were elated that their long, often frustrated man hunt for Sherman was over." The women in the Brigade were an afterthought.

Most federal prisoners considered dangerous by authorities were whisked quickly and covertly into the U.S. Courthouse in Seattle directly after capture. But the FBI paraded Sherman before the press. His two female companions, whom they clearly considered less significant, were carried behind in a second car.

Once inside the Courthouse, the three outlaws refused to confirm or, in Bertram's case, reveal their identities. John was identified by FBI agents and Therese by agents, as well as by her father, Victor. Authorities, however, were initially unable to determine Janine's identity. On March 22, 1978, she was thus charged under the pseudonym "Jori Uhuru" with "harboring a fugitive," John Sherman. Other charges would soon follow.

U.S. Attorney Robert Westinghouse requested that Sherman's bail be raised from the original $200,000, where it had stood just over two years ago before his escape, to $1 million. John and Therese glanced at each other and chuckled sarcastically at this overblown figure, but Magistrate Phillip Sweigert granted the request. Reflecting the sexism of the press coverage of the George Jackson Brigade members' arrest—prioritizing Sherman and characterizing him as the "leader" despite the Brigade's protestations to the contrary—Magistrate Sweigert let Coupez's bail stand at $250,000, where it had been set by the grand jury that indicted her the previous fall. Bertram's bail was $100,000. All three defendants were held in King County Jail in Seattle.

FBI Agent Ray Mathis told the press that Sherman and Coupez were "the only members we know about remaining in the GJB." *Post-Intelligencer* reporter Neil Modie wrote that this arrest "apparently would close the books on an elusive band of radical terrorists."[1] The *New York Times* was more circumspect reporting on March 24, under a San Francisco byline: "Attacks on Government and corporate property by radical groups in the West are expected to continue despite the arrests" of those believed to be the last three members of the Brigade. Of particular concern was the New World Liberation Front, which, as recently as March 14 of that year, had claimed responsibility for bombing a PG&E substation in Contra Costa County, California. The attack caused a blackout affecting 40,000–60,000 people; the NWLF had committed similar acts in the past, demanding low-cost or free utilities for the poor. "There is a lot of interaction and support between these groups," a spokesperson for the Seattle Police Department told the *Times*. "There is a lot of interaction between those suspected of bombing in Northern California and up here."[2]

Press coverage was both exultant and mocking. In an article titled "Brigade Makes Explosive Appearance, Fizzles on Arrest," a *Tacoma News Tribune* reporter stated: "The brigade had established a reputation as a shadowy, elusive network of sophisticated urban guerrillas, but the capture of Sherman and his two companions came in almost comic-opera fashion."[3]

Several hours after the initial arrests, Agent Mathis acknowledged that the Bureau was trying to determine if there was a connection between the captured Brigade members and a cream-colored van that sped away from the drive-in when the agents sprang from their Buicks. The authorities were concerned that the vehicle might have contained Brigade members of whose existence they were not aware.

A group of the Brigade's support people intentionally inflamed this anxiety by composing a communiqué called "Our Losses Are Heavy but We Are Still Here and We Intend to Keep On Fighting." The missive, dated "Easter Sunday" March 26, 1978, was postmarked Longview, Washington, March 28. The authors quoted from the "Political Statement" of the George Jackson Brigade:

> We have no "Mastermind" and no single leader. The ruling class and its authoritarian, sexist media can't understand this. All they know is "command and obey," bosses and sheep, masterminds and followers, superstars and groupies. They desperately want to believe that in capturing our comrade John Sherman they have destroyed us.... Our losses are heavy but we are still here and we intend to keep fighting!

The communiqué brought to public attention what the FBI had not: that people close enough to the Brigade to have known the whereabouts of their safe house remained active outside of custody.

> On the night of the Tacoma bust, a couple of us went to the safe house to clean up. We didn't have the key so we got in by breaking the glass in the patio door. We had no idea if the Feds were onto the location so we had to hurry but we got everything that was important: the weapons, the equipment, the important documents. Everything but the cat which we couldn't find.
> The Feds found the house on Thursday. The media has said nothing about it being cleaned-out. They desperately want this to be the end of the Brigade but the GJB won't die. As long as there are rich and poor, as long as people are starving, rotting in prisons and being shot on the street, as long as we are denied the power to control our own lives, the GJB will live![4]

As proof of the endurance of the direct action anti-capitalist spirit, the writers of the communiqué pointed to occurrences on the most recent International Women's Day. A crew calling itself "The Umbilical Corps" made a mess in the Nestle's section of a Safeway store in protest of Nestle's pushing of infant formula in the African and Latin American countries, and the resulting deaths caused by a lack of access to clean drinking water with which to prepare the formula. Another organization calling itself RIOTSONG tossed paint on a couple of "rich white intrusion" establishments on Capitol Hill. They declared: "We resent the influx of rich people from the suburbs and other wealthy sections of town. If you must cater to a decadent lifestyle, do it in your own neighborhoods.... This placement is NOT our idea of urban renewal." RIOTSONG proceeded to list the names of stores and restaurants they found obnoxious, urging: "We encourage people to loiter around these establishments and make these intruders feel uncomfortable with obnoxious behavior at peak business hours." They concluded, "Feel free to harass the owners at their homes or businesses," and provided addresses for this purpose.

The "Our Losses Are Heavy" communiqué closed:

> There is a lot of anger being felt these days.... We have decided that the focus of our work right now will be to encourage that anger, to get more folks in touch with it, and to share in expressing it whenever possible.
> Love and Struggle,
> The George Jackson Brigade (the rest of us)[5]

Brigade-related hallucinations continued to pop up periodically, though with declining frequency. One scattershot communiqué was relayed in a May 15 press release from Political Support–George Jackson Brigade (PS–GJB), a group consisting largely of people who had been friends and comrades of Brigade members before they went underground.

GJB LIVES

Greetings to the George Jackson Brigade

The F.B.I. and the news media would like to make the public believe that they have broken the back of the GJB and that the support that is left is minimal.

This is a fallacy! The aims and aspirations of the Brigade have wide if unexpressed support.

When more political arrests of courageous fighters for social and economic change occur, the more the unknown ranks come forward.

Ideas cannot be jailed and the fight for freedom and justice is an innate heritage of all poor, working, and third world people.

We wish to inform the media, and the members of the Brigade that there are many working, and poor people who are behind and in support of their goals. With our love to all of you.

In struggle,
Soldiers of the Rainbow

Despite these claims to the contrary the George Jackson Brigade no longer existed as an urban guerrilla cell. The trials and Coupez and Sherman (Bertram quietly accepted a plea bargain) featured prominently in the regional press through the winter of 1978, providing a public forum for their views. But after capture any tangible organizing efforts by Brigade members would have to take place where, for many of them, it had for the first time: in prison.

Brigade members remained politically active in prison, confronting prisoner-on-prisoner rape, the rise of control unit isolation, and institutional racism and homophobia, among other issues.[6] Bertram, Coupez, and Brown were released in the early-to-mid 1980s (1983, 1985, and 1986, respectively); Mead and Sherman were freed in 1993 and 1996.⁷ In January 2000, Mark Cook was released from the minimum security facility at the Washington State Reformatory in Monroe, less than two months after the protests against the World Trade Organization in Seattle displayed the power of a new generation of anticapitalist activism.

NOTES

ABBREVIATIONS

| | | | |
|---|---|---|---|
| BB | Berkeley Barb | SFE | San Francisco Examiner |
| DJA | Daily Journal American | SP-I | Seattle Post-Intelligencer |
| EH | Everett Herald | SS | Seattle Sun |
| NP | Northwest Passage | ST | Seattle Times |
| NYT | New York Times | TNT | Tacoma News Tribune |
| oob | off our backs | TTLG | Through the Looking Glass |
| OR | Open Road | TUG | The Urban Guerrilla |
| PO | Portland Oregonian | WP | Washington Post |
| SFC | San Francisco Chronicle | WSJ | Wall Street Journal |

ACKNOWLEDGMENTS

1. Donald Lemen Clark, *Rhetoric in Greco-Roman Education* (New York: Columbia University Press, 1957), 219.
2. See, e.g., Jack Hopkins, " 'Proud Of Everything'—Coupez," *SP-I*, 6 July 1978, A1.

PRELUDE

1. Dick Clever, " 'Brigade' Takes Credit for Blast at State Office," *SP-I*, 2 June 1975, 1, back page.
2. John Wilson, " 'Brigade' Says It Set Off Explosion," *ST*, 2 June 1975.
3. "After Hearst Arrest: Drive to Root Out U.S. Terror Gangs," *U.S. News & World Report*, 6 Oct. 1975, 22.
4. "Seattle Bombings in the Past 5 Years," *SP-I*, 20 Sept. 1975.

5. Larry Roberts, "The New Year's Bombers: Who and Why?" *SS*, 14 Jan. 1976, 6.
6. Walter Wright, "Jailed Comrade Speaks: 'Brigade Bombed FBI,'" *SP-I*, 30 Mar. 1976, A1.
7. Quoted in Erik Lacitis, "Downtown March Protests Police Hollow-point Bullet," *ST*, 15 Dec. 1974, B5.
8. Todd Gitlin, *The Sixties: Years of Hope, Days of Rage* (New York: Bantam Books, 1987), 393.
9. "RE: GEORGE JACKSON BRIGADE," Federal Bureau of Investigation, Seattle, WA, 4 Jan. 1978, 4. In U.S. Department of Justice, Federal Bureau of Investigation. "George Jackson Brigade." File #105-295956.
10. See the overview in Max Elbaum, *Revolution in the Air: Sixties Radicals Turn to Lenin, Mao, and Che* (New York: Verso, 2002), 1-2.
11. Malcolm X, with Alex Haley, *The Autobiography of Malcolm X* (New York: Grove Press, 1966), 366.
12. Tom Hayden, *Partisan Review*, 1965. Quoted in Hayden, *Reunion: A Memoir* (New York: Collier Books, 1989), 142.

CHAPTER 1

1. Quoted in *Robert and Mabel Williams Resource Guide* (San Francisco: Freedom Archives, 2005), 17.
2. For Mauney's threatening remark, see Robert Williams, quoted in Timothy B. Tyson, *Radio Free Dixie: Robert F. Williams & the Roots of Black Power* (Chapel Hill: University of North Carolina Press, 1999), 280.
3. Quoted in *Robert and Mabel Williams Resource Guide*, 18.
4. The preceding account of events in Monroe draws on James Forman, *The Making of Black Revolutionaries* (Washington, DC: Open Hand Publishing, 1985), 158-211; Truman Nelson, "People with Strength," in *Robert and Mabel Williams Resource Guide*, 41-81; and Tyson, *Radio Free Dixie*, 81; 262-86.
5. Martin Luther King Jr., "The Social Organization of Non-Violence," in *The Eyes on the Prize Civil Rights Reader: Documents, Speeches, and Firsthand Accounts from the Black Freedom Struggle, 1954-1990*, ed. Clayborne Carson et al. (New York: Viking, 1991), 112-13. This essay first appeared in *Liberation*, October 1959.
6. Roy Wilkins, with Tom Mathews, *Standing Fast: The Autobiography of Roy Wilkins* (New York: Viking, 1982), 265.
7. Tyson, *Radio Free Dixie*, 305.
8. This comment was made to Peter Rose, a former American Independence Movement member in New Haven, CT. Interview, November 2005.
9. Tom Wells, *The War Within: America's Battle over Vietnam* (New York: Owl Books, 1996), 96.
10. Clayborne Carson, *In Struggle: SNCC and the Black Awakening of the 1960s* (Cambridge, MA: Harvard University Press, 1981), 51; 53.
11. Hayden, *Reunion*, 74; 102. On the relations of early elite student activists with the Kennedy Administration, see also Todd Gitlin, "Uneasy in an Anteroom in Camelot," in *The Sixties: Years of Hope, Days of Rage*, 85-97.

12. Kirkpatrick Sale, *SDS* (New York: Vintage Books, 1973), 206.
13. James Russell quoted in Todd Gitlin, *The Whole World Is Watching: Mass Media in the Making and Unmaking of the New Left* (Berkeley: University of California Press, 1980), 130.
14. Quoted in Sale, *SDS*, 317–18; 325.
15. Ibid. This episode is also discussed in Gitlin, *Whole World*, 183–85.
16. Gerald Horne, *The Fire This Time: The Watts Uprising in the 1960s* (Charlottesville: University Press of Virginia, 1995), 16.
17. Roxanne Dunbar-Ortiz, *Outlaw Woman: A Memoir of the War Years, 1960–1975* (San Francisco: City Lights, 2001), 51–52.
18. Quoted in Horne, *Fire This Time*, 165.
19. *Scanlan's* "Suppressed Issue: Guerrilla War in the USA" didn't come out until January 1971. When the editors sent the issue to their printer, right-wing unionists refused to print the publication, deeming it "detrimental to the interests of the United States." The editors tried to have the issue published in Colorado, then Missouri, but the orthographers' union had put the word out across the country. *Scanlan's* looked north, eventually getting the issue printed in Quebec, which, ironically, was under martial law in order to suppress the clandestine guerrilla Quebec Liberation Front. The editors remarked ruefully that even under such conditions, Canada was "eminently more conducive to the publication of *Scanlan's* than the hardhat state of America." *Scanlan's*, January 1971, 1.
20. *Report of the National Advisory Commission on Civil Disorders* (New York: Dutton, 1968), 68.
21. A young man named James Rutledge was shot at point-blank range according to Tom Hayden, *Rebellion in Newark: Official Violence and Ghetto Response* (New York: Vintage Books, 1967), 82; "kill them," ibid., 100. For other pro-genocidal remarks by National Guardsmen, see ibid., 46, and Hayden, *Reunion*, 154.
22. *Report of the National Advisory Commission on Civil Disorders*, 80. The violent recklessness of the black youths in Plainfield contrasted sharply with the mature community control in Elizabeth. There, local officials permitted a respected colleague of the late Malcolm X to use his paramilitary force to police the black community, which was close to eruption. The Kerner Commission reported: "As the peace keepers began to make their influence felt, the police withdrew from the area. There was no further trouble." Ibid., 73.
23. Ibid., 106–7.
24. Dan Georgakas and Marvin Surkin, *Detroit: I Do Mind Dying* (New York: St. Martin's Press, 1975), 37.
25. See, e.g., Sam Greenlee, *The Spook Who Sat by the Door* (1969; repr., Detroit: Wayne State University Press, 1989); a film of the same title based on the novel, directed by Ivan Dixon, was released in 1973 (on DVD, 2004).
26. In January 1968, *Seattle Magazine* reprinted one of the grimmer passages from *The Crusader* under the title "How to Rub Out Seattle." The editors explained, "Not long ago, [we] became aware that copies of this revolutionary manual were being circulated locally" (33–36).
27. *Robert and Mabel Williams Resource Guide*, 29. I don't question Williams's veracity, but his host was undoubtedly flattering him, given that the Vietnamese communists had been engaged in urban warfare against the French at least as early as 1947 (in Haiphong and Hanoi).

I find it significant, however, that the Vietnamese chose to do so. Williams's earliest call for guerrilla warfare in the United States was "USA: The Potential of a Minority Revolution," *The Crusader* (Havana) 5, no. 4 (May–June 1964): 1–7.

28. "Create Two, Three, Many Vietnams (Message to the Tricontinental)," in *Che Guevara Reader: Writings on Guerrilla Strategy, Politics & Revolution*, ed. David Deutschmann (New York: Ocean Press, 1997), 316; 327.

29. The phrase was first coined by Ben Jonson in *Bartholomew Fair* (1614), in reference to a drum, but by the 1960s the United States was associated with Martí based on a passage in the last letter he ever composed, to Manuel Mercado. Esther Allen translates the relevant portion without the catchy alliteration: "I have lived in the monster and I know its entrails." José Martí, *Selected Writings*, ed. and trans. Esther Allen (New York: Penguin Books, 2002), 347.

30. Guevara, "Socialism and Man in Cuba," ibid., 211.

31. Guevara, "Create Two, Three, Many Vietnams," ibid., 325.

32. Régis Debray, *Revolution in the Revolution? Armed Struggle and Political Struggle in Latin America*, trans. Bobbye Ortiz (New York: Monthly Review Press, 1967), 27–28.

33. Ibid., 45. Debray arrived at this conclusion at the cost of what Williams cared for so passionately: protecting one's women and children (ibid., 29; 44–45). In contrast to the family man of the Union County NAACP chapter, Guevara and his guerrillas often operated in regions—and even countries and continents—to which they were alien. Though they relied on the support of locals, they sought to minimize contact with them as much as possible: they wished both to protect the communities from reprisals by repressive forces and to protect themselves from informers.

34. Ibid., 30.

## CHAPTER 2

1. The "Day" lasted thirty-six hours. For the speeches of notables at the event, see National Coordinating Committee to End the War in Vietnam, *We Accuse: A Powerful Statement of the New Political Anger in America* (Berkeley, CA: Diablo Press, 1965).

2. This account of the preparations for the march on the Pentagon draws on Norman Mailer, *The Armies of the Night: History as Novel, the Novel as History* (1968; repr., New York: Plume, 1994), 220–43.

3. Lance Hill, *Deacons for Defense: Armed Resistance and the Civil Rights Movement* (Chapel Hill: University of North Carolina Press, 2004), 260. On nonviolence and black patriarchy, see also Tyson, *Radio Free Dixie*, 141; 143; 268. Tyson also provides a portrait of a militant black woman who refused nonviolent discipline: 190.

4. Dave Dellinger, *More Power Than We Know: The People's Movement toward Democracy* (Garden City, NY: Anchor Books, 1975), 56–57.

5. Sale, *SDS*, 444–46.

6. Dellinger, *More Power Than We Know*, 104–5.

7. "Eight Experts on Violence," *Seattle Magazine*, August 1968, 29.

8. Cleaver, "Requiem for Nonviolence," in *Eldridge Cleaver: Post-Prison Writings and Speeches*, ed. Robert Scheer (New York: Vintage Books, 1969), 76; 74.

9. Cleaver's account of the events leaves out the belligerent intention of their mission: Cleaver, "Affidavit #2: Shoot-Out in Oakland," in *Eldridge Cleaver*, ed. Scheer, 80–94. David Hilliard made the disclosure in *This Side of Glory: The Autobiography of David Hilliard and the Story of the Black Panther Party* (Boston: Little, Brown, 1993), 182–95.

10. Patrick Douglas, "Black Panthers on the Prowl," *Seattle Magazine*, October 1968, 38.

11. Chicago police killed Jerome Johnson, a young Amerindian from Sioux Falls, South Dakota, who had come to Chicago to participate in the counter-convention. See Daniel Walker, *Rights in Conflict* (New York: Signet Books, 1968), 113; Dellinger, *More Power Than We Know*, 100.

12. "The cops didn't like the 12-hour shifts, but most of them liked their work," Chicago resident John Schultz asserted in his *No One Was Killed: Documentation and Meditation: Convention Week, Chicago—August 1968* (Chicago: Big Table Publishing, 1969), 27.

13. Hayden, *Reunion*, 316–17. Hayden inaccurately places Oglesby's talk before the police charge. See Schultz, *No One Was Killed*, 176; Walker, *Rights in Conflict*, 203.

14. This also instilled into the press a fear of covering future protests. Journalists were willing to brave war zones, but their editors caved under the tremendous political pressure leveled against them by Richard Nixon and Spiro Agnew—soon to be president and vice president—and Chicago Mayor Richard Daley, among others, because of their "prejudicial" coverage of the convention violence. Dellinger, *More Power Than We Know*, 101–3; Walker, *Rights in Conflict*, 255–96.

15. Schultz, *No One Was Killed*, 68.

16. The Walker Commission, which investigated the events for the National Commission on the Causes and Prevention of Violence, characterized the convention week disturbances as a "police riot." Critics from the Left complained that this characterization didn't go far enough: it rendered what was clearly policy into a collective phenomenon of rogue officers. This criticism was borne out by the Chicago Police Department's rank-and-file Confederation of Patrolmen, which was disgusted that several officers had been suspended for covering their name tags and stars of rank during the protest. The *C.O.P. Newsletter* fumed about the way officers were forced to "take the heat" alone despite the fact that "the men WERE given DIRECT ORDERS in regard to the nametags and stars.... Further, they were GUARANTEED that NO MAN would be SUSPENDED for any action taken at the time of the riots" (quoted in Schultz, *No One Was Killed*, 291; capitalization as in original).

17. "Introduction," *Rights in Conflict*, vi.

18. Robinson, like many other potential defense witnesses in the Chicago conspiracy case, was denied permission to testify. Hayden, *Trial*, 62.

19. Walter Wright, "Slain Man's Document: Self-Implication in Three Bombings," *SP-I*, 21 April 1976.

20. David Davis and Stephen Talbot, *The Sixties: The Years That Shaped a Generation* (New York: Public Broadcasting System, 2004).

21. Quoted in Hayden, *Trial*, 22.

22. *United States Statutes at Large*, vol. 82, chap. 102 (Washington, DC: Government Printing Office, 1969), 175–77.

23. The defendants maintained that "the real conspiracy" was between the executive and

judicial branches of the federal government, which collaborated in convicting them. The intermediary in this second "conspiracy" was the Federal Bureau of Investigation.

24. Gitlin, *The Sixties: Years of Hope, Days of Rage*, 394–95.

25. Cited in Hayden, *Reunion*, 409. There were, in effect, two "TDAs": on 17 February, after the contempt sentences, and on 19 February, after the jury's verdict. Highlights of the latter protests included a 5,000-person march in Boston, from which 1,000 broke away and fought with riot police. In Washington, DC, 300 protesters broke windows and splattered paint on the Watergate Hotel, where Attorney General John Mitchell and other officials of the Nixon Administration resided. As they approached George Washington University, police pounced on marchers, effectively dispersing the crowd. "120 Arrested in Washington March," *SFC*, 20 Feb. 1970, 1.

26. "2000 in N.Y. Streets—Police Snowballed," *SFE*, 17 Feb. 1970, 7; "Berkeley Rampage: 1000 Run Wild after Protest Rally," *SFC*, 17 Feb. 1970, A1.

27. David Brewster and Ardie Ivie, "Right On!" *Seattle Magazine*, May 1970, 23–24; Susan Stern, *With the Weathermen: The Personal Journal of a Revolutionary Woman* (Garden City, NY: Doubleday, 1975), 232–34.

28. "Berkeley Police Bombed; 6 Cops Hurt; Scores Saved by Fluke; 3 Autos Wrecked in Blast; Fragments Only Clues," *SFE*, 13 Feb. 1970, 1, 12.

29. Margot Adler, "My Life in the FSM: Memories of a Freshman," in *The Free Speech Movement: Reflections on Berkeley in the 1960s*, ed. Robert Cohen and Reginald E. Zelnik (Berkeley: University of California Press, 2002), 121. This distinction is contested by another participant at the same sit-in: "As they were arrested, a lot of people were thrown down the stairs [by police] and the women in particular were grabbed by the hair and thrown down the stairs. I was on the top floor and saw many people brutalized like that." Bob Avakian, *From Ike to Mao and Beyond: My Journey from Mainstream America to Revolutionary Communist* (Chicago: Insight Press, 2005), 133.

30. On the Third World Strike, see W. J. Rorabaugh, *Berkeley at War: The 1960s* (New York: Oxford University Press, 1989), 154, 162.

31. "Grim Reagan Calls It 'Insurrection,'" *SFC*, 21 Feb. 1969, 8.

32. Rorabaugh, *Berkeley At War*, 162–63. The organizers of the initial occupation planned it as a way to politicize hippies, whom they regarded as perversely obtuse and ignorant. They anticipated repression and were not disappointed. Ibid., 156.

33. Camus' "ideal healer" was an unlikely goal for primarily healthy youth who had not yet experienced the potentially irrevocable consequences of violence. On Camus' ideal, see Tarrou's deathbed soliloquy in *The Plague* (1947), trans. Stuart Gilbert (New York: Vintage International, 1991), 253–54.

34. Marley's hit first became known to Americans and Britons when the cover by Eric Clapton topped the charts in both the United States and the United Kingdom in 1974.

CHAPTER 3

1. Along with the "currency" of legitimacy that blacks and Third Worlders were perceived by their white American counterparts as possessing, the young toughs had a "street cred" that appealed to Newton, whose own socioeconomic status was relatively comfortable. As

the Panthers succumbed to external pressures brought on by the boldness of their own demands, they evinced a pandering to thuggishness that further alienated their dwindling number of supporters. Chris Booker, "Lumpenization: A Critical Error of The Black Panther Party," in *The Black Panther Party, Reconsidered,* ed. Charles E. Jones (Baltimore: Black Classic Press, 1998), 337–62.

2. Karl Marx, *The Eighteenth Brumaire of Louis Bonaparte* (1852; New York: International Publishers, 1963), 75. Marx included not only "vagabonds, discharged soldiers, discharged jailbirds ... pickpockets, tricksters, gamblers ... brothel keepers, beggars" in the lumpenproletariat, but also "ruined and adventurous offshoots of the bourgeoisie" (the emperor Napoleon III, the "chief of the Paris lumpenproletariat," being one such). Here, in contrast, is the definition of "Lumpen proletariat" from the "Political Dictionary" of the Black Liberation Army: "The under class, unemployed, marginally employed and those who live outside of the law, i.e. criminal element. The aged, infirmed, and disabled are also part of this class because they are marginally employed, therefore, not a secure part of the productive process. Those on welfare, social security are also members of this class." If the Panthers had consented to Marx's original definition, it would have implied that educated white radicals of their day who abandoned their class privileges could participate in the revolution on equal footing. But this would have been to relinquish the Panthers' own claim to "vanguard" status, which they were unwilling to do.

3. Like the vast majority of important players in the radicalism of the 1960s and 1970s, the Panthers were ideologically eclectic. One might describe them as communist "Malcolmists" who read the Little Red Book a lot. On "Malcolmism," see Mumia Abu-Jamal, *We Want Freedom: A Life in the Black Panther Party* (Cambridge, MA: South End Press, 2004), 80–82.

4. Hannah Arendt gave voice to the consternation with which older radicals regarded the intellectual confusion of their younger counterparts: "The new undeniable glorification of violence by the student movement has a curious peculiarity. While the rhetoric of the new militants is clearly inspired by Fanon, their theoretical arguments contain usually nothing but a hodgepodge of all kinds of Marxist leftovers. This is indeed quite baffling for anybody who has ever read Marx or Engels. Who could possibly call an ideology Marxist that has put its faith in 'classless idlers,' believes that 'in the lumpenproletariat the rebellion will find its urban spearhead,' and trusts that 'gangsters will light the way for the people'?" Arendt, *On Violence* (New York: Harcourt, Brace, 1969), 19–20.

5. "Word Play," in *Ho Chi Minh on the Revolution: Selected Writings, 1920–66,* ed. Bernard B. Fall (New York: Praeger, 1967), 136.

6. The best history of the BLA is Akinyele Omowale Umoja, "Repression Breeds Resistance: The Black Liberation Army and the Radical Legacy of the Black Panther Party," in *Liberation, Imagination, and the Black Panther Party,* ed. Kathleen Cleaver and George Katsiaficas (New York: Routledge, 2001), 3–19. For a patrolman's-eye view of the BLA, see Robert K. Tanenbaum, *Badge of the Assassin* (New York: Pocket Books, 2001) and Robert Daley, *Target Blue: An Insider's View of the N.Y.P.D.* (New York: Delacorte, 1971), 75–86, 170–83, 402–45.

7. Eric Cummins, *The Rise and Fall of California's Radical Prison Movement* (Stanford, CA: Stanford University Press, 1994), 164.

8. George Jackson, *Blood in My Eye* (New York: Bantam Books, 1972), 67.

9. Ibid., 47.

10. William Gilday, one of the ex-convicts, hit the police officer, Walter Schroeder, with a blast of fire from a submachine gun several minutes *after* his collaborators safely fled the bank. See Lucinda Franks, "Return of the Fugitive," *New Yorker*, 13 June 1994, 51.

11. By my count, they were the fifth and sixth women to receive this distinction in the twenty-year history of the list. Two contemporary communist women preceded them: Angela Davis and Weather spokesperson Bernardine Dohrn.

12. The others included Raymond Procunier, head of the California Department of Corrections, and fourteen manufacturers and business leaders from Bank of America, ITT, Kaiser Industries, Safeway, Standard Oil, and other prominent corporations. A fuller list appears in John Bryan, *This Soldier Still at War* (New York: Harcourt, Brace, Jovanovich, 1975), 182–83, 205.

13. The San Francisco civil rights lawyers Charles Garry claimed after Foster's death that the latter had considered the plan "a police state action . . . an example of fascist forces trying to take over." Bryan, *This Soldier Still at War*, 187.

14. See "SLA's Field Marshall Cinque: Revolutionary or Police Agent?" *The Black Panther*, 3 April 1974, 3, 10; Mae Brussell and Stephanie Caruana, "Is SLA's Cinque the First Black Lee Harvey Oswald?" *BB*, 19–25 April 1974, 1, 11; Tom Thompson's series in the *Los Angeles Free Press*: "The SLA—Revolutionaries or Agents?" 31 May 1974, 1, 4–5, 26; "Police Cover Up Shootout Facts," 19 July 1974, 1, 4, 28; "Recruitment for Terror," 26 July 1974, 1, 5; and "How the SLA Was Born," 9 Aug. 1974, 1, 6, 17. First incarcerated as a juvenile, by his late twenties, DeFreeze had a long record not only of thefts, burglaries, and assaults (several against women) but of collaboration with the police. After originally being politicized by black nationalists, he abandoned racial exclusivity and collaborated with primarily white Berkeley radicals, who sheltered him when he escaped in 1973 and appointed him "Field Marshal" of the SLA. DeFreeze was not the only one in the nine-person SLA with real-world experience of violence; Joe Remiro was a Vietnam combat veteran. All shared an enthusiasm for guns. One conspiracy theory identified the SLA as a CIA excuse to stage a Pinochet-style military coup and liquidate dissidents and minorities.

15. M. F. Beal and friends, *Safe House: A Casebook Study of Revolutionary Feminism in the 1970's* (Eugene, OR: Northwest Matrix, 1976), 24.

16. Quoted in Bryan, *This Soldier Still at War*, 290.

17. Several months earlier Governor Reagan had made it clear that he felt that those who benefited from the program of the putative urban guerrillas deserved the same unpleasant demise. A luncheon of prominent supporters of the Republican Party, at which Reagan was the prime celebrity, coincided with the commencement of the SLA's "People In Need" program. As a precondition for negotiation, the guerrillas had demanded that Hearst distribute $2 million worth of food to the state's poor. After Reagan and his cohorts completed their plush meal, the governor allegedly grumbled: "It's just too bad we can't have an epidemic of botulism." Ibid., 239.

18. Carlos Marighella, *Mini-Manual of the Urban Guerrilla* (Montreal: Abraham Guillen Press, 2002), 4, 10. The first English-language edition was published as the *Mini-Manual of Urban Guerrilla Warfare* by the San Francisco-based Red Guerrilla Family in 1969, the same

year it was published in the Cuban journal *Tricontinental*. The "New World Liberation Front U.S.A.," also active in San Francisco, reprinted the pamphlet under its more common name in 1970. Marighella died on April 11, 1969, in a police ambush in Brazil after his disciples kidnapped U.S. Ambassador C. Burke Elbrick.

19. Sale, *SDS*, 636–37.

20. "New Day—Changing Weather," in *The Weather Eye: Communiques from the Weather Underground, May 1970–May 1974*, ed. Jonah Raskin (San Francisco: Union Square Press, 1974), 28.

21. Hoover made this remark at a congressional hearing on 10 February 1970. U.S. Senate, *The Weather Underground: Report of the Subcommittee to Investigate the Administration of the Internal Security Act and Other Internal Security Laws of the Committee on the Judiciary* (Washington, DC: Government Printing Office, 1975), 38.

22. Bernardine Dohrn, interview quoted in Varon, *Bringing the War Home*, 184. "[W]e dreaded the possibility of two, three, many Townhouses, and we hoped to use our celebrity in the lunatic left as well as the gathering Weathermyth in the larger world to persuade others to pull back, " Bill Ayers writes in his memoir *Fugitive Days* (Boston: Beacon Press 2001), 228.

23. "New Day—Changing Weather," in *Weather Eye*, ed. Raskin, 30.

24. Jones, "An Open Letter to the People, the Emiliano Zapata Unit, and New Dawn," *Berkeley Barb*, 16–22 Jan. 1976, 9. The Zapata Unit, like the SLA, was initiated by an informer, but their "Chepito," unlike Cinque, remained on the payroll and set up the group's members for arrest. Before their capture, the Unit declined to provide information that would have enabled others to corroborate its claim to have attacked the prison guard.

25. "International Women's Day Communiqué," in *Creating a Movement with Teeth: Communiqués of the George Jackson Brigade* (Montreal: Abraham Guillen Press, 2003), 18–19. All the Brigade communiqués, their political statement, and a range of articles from the underground and mainstream press are collected in *Creating a Movement with Teeth: A Documentary History of the George Jackson Brigade*, ed. Daniel Burton-Rose (Oakland: PM Press, 2010).

26. The "armed and incompetent" crack was made to Ayers by a fellow Weatherperson when he visited New York City directly after the Townhouse explosion. Ayers, *Fugitive Days*, 194.

27. Umoja, "Repression Breeds Resistance," in *Liberation, Imagination, and the Black Panther Party*, ed. Cleaver and Katsiaficas, 12–13.

28. "Bombs Go Off in 3 Cities," *SP-I*, 27 Oct. 1975, A1; "10 Blasts Claimed by Puerto Ricans," *SP-I*, 28 Oct. 1975, A2.

29. John Springer, "LaGuardia Christmas Bombing Remains Unsolved 27 Years Later," Court TV, 24 Dec. 2002, http://archives.cnn.com/2002/LAW/12/24/ctv.laguardia (accessed 29 Aug. 2009).

30. Charles Raudebaugh, "The Bay Area Bombings Have Lawmen Stumped," *SFC*, 18 Feb. 1975, 4.

31. "Editorial: 'Systematic State Terror on a Global Scale Makes Armed Resistance Inevitable . . . But Some Serious Mistakes Have Been Made,' " *BB*, 16–22 Jan. 1976, 7.

## CHAPTER 4

This chapter draws on chapters 1–5 of Ed Mead's unpublished autobiography (copy of draft dated January 2009 in author's possession). It is supplemented with interviews conducted between 1998 and 2007. Only direct quotations are followed by citations.

1. Lee Moriwaki and John Arthur Wilson, "The Psychological Anatomy of a Revolutionary," *ST*, 1 April 1976.
2. Mead, "Autobiography," 46.
3. Jim R. Mott, 1976 probation report (copy in author's possession), 6.
4. Mead, "Autobiography," 18.
5. Mott, 1976 probation report, 8.

## CHAPTER 5

1. Mead, "Autobiography," 152.
2. Ibid., 152.
3. Ibid., 155.
4. Jim R. Mott, 1976 probation report (copy in author's possession), 10.
5. Mead, "Autobiography," 175.
6. Ibid., 196.
7. Ibid., 202.

## CHAPTER 6

1. In *Doherty v. United States* (404 U.S. 28 No. 71–5679), decided 9 November 1971, Mead helped a friend from McNeil Island challenge his denial of counsel in petitioning the U.S. Supreme Court. The Supreme Court vacated the lower court's dismissal of the claim and advised its inferiors to consider relevant federal law. A similar occurrence took place with an inmate named Weber whose case Mead took to the Supreme Court after the Court made a favorable ruling regarding a similar case involving Dr. Timothy Leary, presumably in *Leary v. United States*.
2. www.law.umkc.edu/faculty/projects/ftrials/price&bowers/Bowers.htm (accessed 4 May 2009).
3. Mead, "Autobiography," 212.
4. For more of Sherman's backstory, see John Sherman, "Autobiographical Sketch," www.johnsherman.org/truth_is_all_that_matters/autobiographical-sketch-1.html (accessed 29 Aug. 2009).
5. For a national overview of the Moratorium, see Tom Wells, *The War Within: America's Battle Over Vietnam* (New York: Owl Books, 1996), 370–75. On the events in Seattle, see "5,000 in Anti-War Rally Here" and "Moratorium Blankets Nation," *ST*, 16 Oct. 1969, A1.
6. "Subject: Weatherman," an "Intelligence Report" received by Deputy Chief of the Department of Public Safety Robert Steele from W. Falk and L. A. Ferreira, dated 7 June 1971 (copy in author's possession).
7. Meldon Acheson, "McNeil," in *When Can I Come Home? A Debate on Amnesty for Ex-*

*iles, Anti-War Prisoners and Others*, ed. Murray Polner (Garden City, NY: Anchor Books, 1972), 169.

8. In Susan Stern's telling description, the meeting participants were so at odds that their indictment made a mockery of the concept "conspire": Stern, *With the Weathermen*, 216–18.

9. For Stern's account of the trial, see *With the Weathermen*, 283–324. Lerner is the prolific rabbi who currently edits *Tikkun* magazine in Berkeley, California.

10. Don Hannula and Stephen Dunphy, "Judge Orders Jail First to Halt Disruption," *ST*, 15 Dec. 1970, A1. For Lippman's own recollection of the Seattle Seven case, see his pamphlet "Looking Back on the Seattle Conspiracy Trial" (Seattle: Security Index Press 1990), http://terrasol.home.igc.org/trial.htm (accessed 4 May 2009).

11. Stern, *With the Weatherman*, 60. Lippman objects that Stern's depiction is "flattering, but not true," characterizing it as the flip side of criticism that could be equally exaggerated. He also says their first meeting was in 1967 or 1968. Interview with the author, 24 Jan. 2009.

12. Chuck Armsbury, interview, May 2005; Chuck Armsbury, "In Memory of Ray Eaglin," http://www.itsabouttimebpp.com/Memorials/pdf/InmemoryofRayEaglin.pdf (accessed 4 May 2009), and Jaja Anderson, "Short History of the Black Panther Party in the Eugene, Oregon Chapter," www.itsabouttimebpp.com/Chapter_History/Eugene_Oregon_Chapter.html (accessed 4 May 2009).

13. *Paul Bailleaux, Charles Armsbury, Armando Vargas, Larry Crews, Gerald A. Thompson, and Willie Brazier v. Jacob J. Parker, Paul T. Walker, and A. C. Mobley*, United States District Court, Western District of Washington, Southern District, Civil # 4223, 1, 2, 6 (copy in author's possession).

14. "Six McNeil Prisoners File Suits," *TNT*, 22 Jan. 1971; Rick Anderson, "Terrorism at McNeil Charged," *SP-I*, 27 Jan. 1971, 1; Rick Anderson, "McNeil Petition: 'Our Hope Is Society Will Show Interest,'" *SP-I*, 27 Jan. 1971; "Six McNeil Inmates Sue Top Officials," *TNT*, 27 Jan. 1971, A2.

15. Mead, "Autobiography," 218.

16. Rick Anderson, "McNeil Felon Now 'Prophet': Prison Strike Leader Held in 'Solitary,'" *SP-I*, 28 Feb. 1971, 9.

17. Mead, "Autobiography," 221.

18. Stephen Dunphy, "Jane Fonda Uses 'Leverage' to Aid Cause of Indian Rights," *ST*, 8 Mar. 1970, A20.

19. Boldt did not remain a reviled figure for regional social justice activists. In February 1974, in what came to be called "The Boldt Decision," he courageously upheld indigenous fishing rights in the Pacific Northwest. See, e.g., Peter Matthiessen, *In the Spirit of Crazy Horse* (1983; repr., New York: Viking, 1991), 137. For background on the indigenous struggle for fishing rights in the Northwest, see *Uncommon Controversy: Fishing Rights of the Muckleshoot, Puyallup, and Nisqually Indians* (Seattle: University of Washington Press, 1970).

20. "Jane Fonda, Demonstrators Support McNeil Island Strike," *ST*, 1 Mar. 1971, D4.

21. Jessica Mitford, *Kind and Usual Punishment: The Prison Business* (1971; repr. New York: Vintage Books, 1974), 12, 216.

22. Armsbury interview.

23. Mead, "Autobiography," 222.

24. "Some Prisoners Return to Work," *ST*, 4 Mar. 1971, A6.

25. Mead, "Autobiography," 224.

26. "Ed Mead Speaks from Prison," *NP,* 24 May–7 June 1976, 4–5.

27. One of these other prisoners, Jerry F. Desmond, was shot to death on Capitol Hill in Seattle during the period in which Mead received his greatest publicity as a member of the George Jackson Brigade. This prompted police to investigate possible Brigade involvement in the murder, which turned out to be a dead end. "Slain Man Had Role in Prison Hunger Strike," *ST,* 23 July 1976.

28. John Arthur Wilson, "'2 Armies' Share Bond of Revolution," *ST,* 23 Apr. 1976.

29. The total death toll in the uprising was forty-three, as one guard died from injuries sustained in the seizing of the yard and three inmates were killed, presumably by other prisoners, during the course of the occupation.

30. *Mead v. Parker* (464 F.2d 1108, No. 71-2462), was decided in favor of the plaintiffs on July 20, 1972.

CHAPTER 7

Epigraph: George Jackson, *Soledad Brother: The Prison Letters of George Jackson* (New York: Bantam Books, 1970), 86.

1. Bruce Olson, "SDS Rally Draws 6–7,000," *University of Washington Daily,* 7 Mar. 1969, 1.

2. George Katsiaficas, *The Imagination of the New Left: A Global Analysis of 1968* (Cambridge, MA: South End Press, 1987), 123.

3. Sale, *SDS,* 503.

4. John Arthur Wilson, "Old West Fades, but Not Bank-Robbing," *ST,* 6 Mar. 1977. See also Evelyn A. Schlatter, "'Extremism in the Defense of Liberty': The Minutemen and the Radical Right," in *The Conservative Sixties,* ed. David Farber and Jeff Roche (New York: Peter Lang, 2003), 47, and www.historylink.org/index.cfm?DisplayPage=output.cfm&file_id=1464 (accessed 29 Aug. 2009).

5. Roger Lippman, interview, 24 Jan. 2009.

6. John Irwin, *Prisons in Turmoil* (Boston: Little, Brown, 1980), 87.

7. Charles Statsny and Gabrielle Tyrnauer, *Who Rules the Joint? The Changing Political Culture of Maximum-Security Prisons in America* (Lexington, MA: Lexington Books, 1982), 87–88.

8. Other prisoners' unions are reported to have existed in Georgia, Kansas, Oklahoma, and Washington, D.C.

9. Wilson, "'2 Armies' Have Bond of Revolution," *ST,* 23 Apr. 1976.

10. Martin Works, "A Former Convict Tells Why the Prisoners at Monroe Want a Union," *SP-I,* 22 Oct. 1973, A1.

11. Mitford, *Kind and Usual Punishment,* 39.

12. Bryan, *This Soldier Still at War,* 231. Hearst quickly replied that the demand was beyond his means: initial estimates placed the cost of compliance at $400 million. The SLA, via a recorded message from Patty, dropped the demand; "whatever you come up with basically is okay," as Patricia put it in her first, coached, audio missive: communiqué #5, reprinted in Leslie Payne and Timothy Findley, with Carolyn Craven, *The Life and Death of the SLA* (New

York: Ballantine Books, 1976), 350. Between February 19 and March 25, the Hearst interest gave away $2.3 million worth of food. A countercultural account of the distribution appears in Bryan, 239–42.

13. On the symbolism of the cobra, see the SLA's "7 Aims" and " ... Cobra ... " in Bryan, *This Soldier Still at War*, 321–24.

14. Ed Mead, "Jailhouse Lawyers Attack Parole Standards," *Contempt*, Oct. 1974, 15–16.

15. Examples of these posters appear as end papers in Bryan, *This Soldier Still at War*, and in Beal, *Safe House*, 120; 137.

16. Bryan, *This Soldier Still at War*, 244.

17. *Ramparts* called the November 1970 Folsom strike "the most resilient show of inmate solidarity in recent California history" (Frank Browning, "Organizing behind Bars," *Ramparts*, Feb. 1972, 40–41). The strikers' demands were echoed across the country, most commonly by the Attica rebels—so much so that the demands of their New York counterparts were at first written off by New York Corrections Commissioner Oswald because he thought them a simple copy of those of the Folsom prisoners. See Tom Wicker, *A Time to Die* (New York: Quadrangle / New York Times Book Co., 1975), 25.

18. Cummins, *The Rise and Fall of California's Radical Prison Movement*, 215–17.

19. "United Prisoners Union Editorial: we must unite," *Anvil* 1, no. 1 (Apr. 1974): 2.

20. "The Chinese Revolution and the Russian Counterrevolution," *TUG* 1 (n.d. [1976]): 20.

21. Ed Mead, "Sexism in the New World Liberation Front," *Dragon* 9 (June 1976): 28–31.

22. For a profile of Zilsel, see Regina Hackett, "Paul Zilsel Really Knows How To Rile Young Leftists; He Calls Them Hip," *SP-I / Northwest Magazine*, 29 Mar. 1981, 5–6.

23. Steve Long, "'Prairie Fire' Now for Sale at Bookshops," *Berkeley Barb*, 13–19 Sept. 1974, 4.

24. *Prairie Fire*, 3. This document is now available in *Sing a Battle Song: The Revolutionary Poetry, Statements, and Communiqués of the Weather Underground, 1970–1974*, ed. Bernardine Dohrn, Bill Ayers, and Jeff Jones (New York: Seven Stories Press, 2006). Subsequent page numbers refer to this edition.

25. Dohrn et al., *Sing a Battle Song*, 234.

26. Ibid., 233–34.

27. Roxanne Park and John Brockhaus, "Ed Mead Speaks from Prison," *NP*, 24 May–7 June 1976, 5.

28. Roger Lippman, interview, 24 Jan. 2009.

29. Matthiessen, *In the Spirit of Crazy Horse*, 49; 136–37. Matthiessen's comprehensive biography places Peltier in Seattle, on the run, in September 1974. Though Ed remembers the incident described above clearly, he also clearly remembers being in Buffalo for a couple of weeks leading up to the Attica Day demonstration on September 13, 1974. Others remember him in Buffalo as well (Liz Fink, ABLD attorney, interview, Spring 2002). Subsequently, he went to San Francisco before returning to Seattle.

30. "Flames from Protest at Bank Here," *ST*, 10 Sept. 1974, A1.

31. ABLD routinely supported Arthur O. Eve, a black assemblyperson from Buffalo, who had been an observer on the yard at Attica and who was a consistent supporter of ABLD, both in terms of funding for their criminal defense cases and by testifying on prisoners' be-

half. That same year, at the behest of the Attica survivor Herbert X. Blyden, the organization also supported former Attorney General Ramsey Clark, who was running for the U.S. Senate. Liz Fink, personal correspondence, 3 Nov. 2006.

32. Mead and I have both been unable to locate this statement in Jackson's sole published works, *Soledad Brother* and *Blood in My Eye*, so either Jackson said it in an interview or Mead erred in his attribution.

CHAPTER 8

Epigraphs: Russell Banks, *Cloudsplitter* (New York: HarperCollins, 1999), 378; George Jackson, *Blood in My Eye* (New York: Bantam Books, 1972), 28–29.

1. Eric Lacitis, "Downtown March Protests Police Hollow-Point Bullet," *ST*, 18 Dec. 1974, B5.
2. Lee Moriwaki and John Arthur Wilson, "The Psychological Anatomy of a Revolutionary," *ST*, 1 Apr. 1976.
3. "Menominees Steadfast in Abbey," *ST*, 12 Jan. 1975, A14.
4. Matthiessen, *In the Spirit of Crazy Horse*, 117; 137.
5. Lee Moriwaki, "Another Job-Site Protestor Given Jail Sentence," *ST*, 14 Mar. 1975, A8.
6. Ed Mead, interview, May 31, 2005. These acts of sabotage are described (though not linked to Mead or Seidel) in Lee Moriwaki, "Tyree Scott: 'We don't retaliate,'" *ST*, 3 Oct. 1975, A6.
7. Eric Lacitis, "Angry Judge Challenges Protestors," *ST*, 24 Mar. 1975, A1.
8. Moriwaki, "Tyree Scott." As an example of the appeal of Scott and the UCWA to white politicos, the bulk of a 1975 issue of *Contempt: A Magazine of News and Analysis of the National Lawyers Guild, Seattle Chapter* is devoted to reproducing a speech Scott delivered at a demonstration on the University of Washington campus on May 15, 1975: Tyree Scott, "Get to Know Who Your Friends *Really* Are!" *Contempt* 4, no. 3 (n.d. [1975]): 1, 12–24. For more on Scott and the UCWA, see the extensive archive of the Seattle Civil Rights and Labor History Project: http://depts.washington.edu/civilr/ucwa.htm (accessed May 2009).
9. Danny Atteberry, interview, 1999. Atteberry was present at the RGC meeting described above.
10. For Atteberry's backstory, see Andy Stack, "The Life-or-Death Ordeal of Seven Seattle Hostages," *Master Detective*, March 1974, 26–29; 52–54; and Charles Aweeka, "'He was a polite dope addict,' says hostage" (n.p., n.d.; copy in author's possession).
11. Don Hannula, "Walla Walla Loosest It's Ever Been, Says Guard," *ST*, 12 Jan. 1975, A19.
12. "Prison Nearly Normal," *ST*, 1 Jan. 1975, A11.
13. Hannula, "Walla Walla Loosest It's Ever Been."
14. "Hostages Thought They Would Die," *ST*, 31 Dec. 1974, B8; Hannula, "Walla Walla Loosest It's Ever Been."

CHAPTER 9

Section epigraph, p. 96: George Jackson, *Soledad Brother: The Prison Letters of George Jackson* (New York: Bantam Books, 1970), 18–19.

1. Rita Brown, "A Short Autobiography" (n.d. [Winter 1977]). Unless otherwise noted all subsequent quotations from Brown in this chapter come from this document.
2. "Funding Proposal," Women Out Now Prison Project, 30 Nov. 1974.
3. Rita Brown, interview, Spring 2001.
4. "Indictment," *U.S.A. v. R. D. Brown*, USDC Western District of Washington at Seattle, No. 52178, 9 Mar. 1971.
5. *U.S.A. v. R. D. Brown*, USDC Western District of Washington at Seattle, No. 52178, 10 Sept. 1971.
6. *U.S.A. v. R. D. Brown*, USDC Western District of Washington at Seattle, No. 52178, 15 Mar. 1971.
7. Jackson, *Soledad Brother*, 173.
8. Ibid., 213.
9. Bob Dylan composed a lament that captures the mourning, and the pride, of many who admired Jackson. Bob Dylan, *Lyrics, 1962–1985* (New York: Knopf, 1985), 302.
10. "Women Prisoners Revolt," *Off Our Backs*, September 1971. The *Washington Post* identified the overflow prison as the Federal Correctional Institution in Seagoville, Texas, a somewhat less plausible option. See Ben Bagdikian and Leon Dash, *The Shame of the Prisons* (New York: Pocket Books, 1972), 94–95.

## CHAPTER 10

1. John Arthur Wilson, "Brigade Suspect Was Devoted, Says Family," *ST*, 23 Mar. 1978, A14.
2. Brigade member Mark Cook later claimed that the name of the assassin was divulged to him in the early 1990s while he was incarcerated for Brigade-related activities. Dan Raley, "A Call to Reopen the Pratt Case," *SP-I*, 10 Nov. 1994, A1, A13.
3. Walter Crowley, *Rites of Passage: A Memoir of the Sixties in Seattle* (Seattle: University of Washington Press, 1996), 298.
4. Women Out Now, "Constitution," Feb. 1974 (copy in author's possession).
5. Women Out Now, "Funding Proposal," 30 Nov. 1974 (copy in author's possession).
6. The bar was so named because its owner, Shelly, had established it with money she had won in a lawsuit against the city after a memorial cannon detonated and blew off her leg.

## CHAPTER 11

Epigraph: Karlene Faith, "Education for Empowerment: California 1972–1976," in *Unruly Women: The Politics of Confinement and Resistance* (Vancouver: Press Gang Publishers, 1993), 297.

1. This presentation contained material published in Bergman's *Women of Viet Nam*, 2nd ed. (San Francisco: People's Press, 1975).
2. Resources for Community Change, *Women Behind Bars: An Organizing Tool* (Washington, DC: self-published, 1975), 22–23.
3. Cook was captured December 12, 1957, after robbing the Pay 'n Save Drug Store at 319 Pike Street in downtown Seattle of $120. In a signed confession, Cook also admitted to

the robberies of the Caledonia Coffee Shop at 1328 Seventh Avenue on October 15 and the Richelieu Café at 703 Union Street on November 6. He was convicted of all three robberies on April 15, 1958, and given a minimum prison sentence of four years. On March 25, 1965, Cook again robbed a Pay 'n Save, this time the one at 2707 Rainier Avenue South, for over $50. He was sentenced to three terms of thirty years, to run concurrently. "Captured Bandit Confesses Two Other Robberies," *SP-I*, 15 Dec. 1957, 12; "Man Convicted of 3 Robberies," *SP-I*, 16 April 1958, 18; "Sets Minimum Parole Board Monroe Terms," *SP-I*, 9 Sept. 1958, 35; "3 Men Charged with Robbery in Two Cases," *SP-I*, 20 March 1955, 8; "Prison Terms Are Set," *SP-I*, 18 July 1967, 34.

4. This account of Black's ordeal comes from Jan Hoffman, "For Survivor of Prison Rebellion, the Agony of Attica Never Ends," *NYT*, 20 Aug. 1999.

5. Rita and Therese, among other outside organizers, accompanied Smith to the Reformatory in Monroe. Rita entered the prison with a pin on her chest proclaiming "Attica Is All of Us." A guard stopped her, proclaiming: "You can't wear that in here!" Rita got behind Smith and moved the pin and some others to the inside of her shirt. When the lights went out for the documentary, she began distributing them to prisoners.

6. David Cortright, *Soldiers in Revolt: GI Resistance during the Vietnam War* (1975; repr., Chicago: Haymarket Books, 2005). Shelter Half is also discussed in the 1971 proceedings of the House of Representatives' Committee on Internal Security, "Investigation of Attempts to Subvert the United States Armed Services," and David Zeiger's 2005 documentary film *Sir! No Sir! The Suppressed Story of the GI Movement to End the War in Vietnam.*

7. Resources for Community Change, *Women Behind Bars*, 39.

## CHAPTER 12

1. Beal, *Safe House*, 24.
2. "Tania" was actually her alias. Her real name was Hayde Tamara Bunke Bider. See, e.g., Ulises Estrada, *Tania: Undercover with Che Guevara in Bolivia* (New York: Ocean Press, 2005).
3. Bryan, *This Soldier Still at War*, 124.
4. Fragments of this poetry are contained in ibid., 125–26. I haven't been able to identify the original book of poems.
5. Ibid., 284.
6. Quoted in Beal, *Safe House*, 73.
7. *Blood in My Eye*, 20.
8. Min S. Yee, "Guerrillas at the Marin County Courthouse," *The Melancholy History of Soledad Prison: In Which a Utopian Scheme Turns Bedlam* (New York: Harper's Magazine Press, 1973), 157–74.
9. Phyllis Chesler, *Women and Madness* (1972; repr., New York: Avon, 1973), 288.
10. Beal, *Safe House*, 87–88.
11. Monique Wittig, *Les Guérillères*, trans. David Le Vay (1971; repr., New York: Avon, 1973), 89.
12. Ibid., 111.
13. Ibid., 134.

14. Ibid., 127.
15. E.g., "Friends of Bill Walton under Investigation in Hearst Case," *ST,* 14 Mar. 1975. In what came to be called their missing year, after hunkering down in the Bay Area during the initial fallout from the massacre, the SLA remnants—Bill and Emily Harris and their ward Patty—were shuttled east by the sportswriter Jack Scott, where they holed up in a Pennsylvania farmhouse until they decided that inevitable capture on the West Coast was preferable to going stir-crazy.
16. Faith, *Unruly Women,* 297.

### CHAPTER 13

1. Resources for Community Change's *Women Behind Bars* lists Action for Forgotten Women as a prison activist organization with contact info in Durham. The organization is described as an electorally/legislatively-inclined "citizen interest group"—i.e., one that organized letter-writing campaigns and petitions: 24.
2. "Women in Prison at N. Carolina," *Dragon,* no. 6 (Jan. 1976): 33–34.
3. "Sisters Fight On," *Midnight Special: Prisoners News* 5, no. 1 (Jan. 1975): 1–2.
4. "Attica Brothers Support Bedford Hills Women," ibid., 3; "Bedford Hills Sisters," ibid., no. 2 (Mar. 1975): 20.
5. "Three Men at Attica" (n.d.; copy in the author's possession).
6. Alpert tells it differently. She says that after reading newspaper accounts of her own surrender and Pat's arrest, Lonnie volunteered information on his travels with the women to the FBI. Though he was a witness in Swinton's trial, everything he had to say about the relevant charge—the bombing conspiracy—was hearsay, so it didn't aid the prosecution. Jane Alpert, *Growing Up Underground* (New York: William Morrow, 1981), 367.
7. Ibid., 343–44.
8. Alpert, "Letter from the Underground," http://scriptorium.lib.duke.edu/wlm/mother (accessed 1 May 2009).
9. Alpert, *Growing Up Underground,* 361.
10. Ibid., 355–56; 363.

### CHAPTER 14

Epigraph: snapdragon, letter to the George Jackson Brigade, *Dragon,* no. 9 (June 1976): 47.
1. I have been unable to locate any issue of *The Sunfighter* after vol. 3, no. 2 (July–Aug. 1975), which carried the "Olympia Bombing" communiqué. Considering the changing focus of Ed and Bruce's activism, and the key role they played in maintaining the organization, this may have been the last issue.
2. Ward Churchill and Jim Vander Wall, *Agents of Repression: The FBI's Secret Wars against the Black Panther Party and the American Indian Movement* (Boston: South End Press, 1990), 103–4.
3. Ibid., 120–21.
4. Ibid., 123. For an extensive account of the march, see: Vine Deloria, *Behind the Trail of Broken Treaties: An Indian Declaration of Independence* (New York: Delacorte, 1974).

5. Rex Wayler, *Blood of the Land: The Government and Corporate War against the American Indian Movement* (New York: Vintage Books, 1984), 72–73.

6. Churchill and Vander Wall, *Agents of Repression*, 123.

7. Ibid., 165, 425n119.

8. Ibid., 170.

9. Ibid., 175.

10. Ibid., 188.

11. Ibid., 238.

12. Ibid., 245.

13. The description of the NWLF, People's Forces Unit IX, introduced below, as a "guerrilla group that overlapped with the Left Bank Collective" is based on overwhelming circumstantial evidence and confirmation by a former Left Bank Collective member to Ed Mead.

14. *The Power of the People Is the Force of Life: Political Statement of the George Jackson Brigade* (1977; repr., Montreal: Abraham Guillen Press, 2002), 24.

15. In 1976, the NWLF clarified its affiliation process.

16. Maribeth Morris, "U.S. Offices Guarded: Bomb Alert in Seattle," *SP-I*, 16 Sept. 1975, A1, A16.

17. Paul Boyd, "Bomb Planter Believed Killed in Safeway Blast," *SP-I*, 16 Sept. 1975; "Man Killed by Bomb Identified," *ST*, 16 Sept. 1975; "Supermart Blast Victim Identified," *SP-I*, 17 Sept. 1975.

18. Lee Moriwaki, "Man Killed by Safeway Bomb 'gentle, polite . . . concerned,'" *ST*, 20 Sept. 1975. One friend of Po's told the press that he was "very absent-minded. That's probably what killed him" (Larry McCarten and Fred Brack, "Bomb Victim Was Activist," *SP-I*, 20 Sept. 1975, A14). Ed Mead knew, however, that Po's death hadn't been his own fault. He was certain that Po had not been the one who had made the bomb. The person who had made it constructed it quite poorly, using alligator clips where he should have soldered components. Ed contends that it was Zilsel who made it. Zilsel passed away on May 27, 2006.

19. Witnesses later provided a fairly accurate description of him to police. David Birkland, "Man in 40s Listed as Bombing Suspect," *ST*, 23 Sept. 1975.

20. "A Poor Way for Them to Be Noticed," *ST*, 17 July 1976.

21. "Several Hurt in Safeway . . . ," *ST*, 19 Sept. 1975; Eric Nalder, "SLA Reprisal? Bomb in Seattle Store Hurts Five," *SP-I*, 19 Sept. 1975, A1.

22. Dave Birkland, "Store Bomb Meant to Kill, Say Police," *ST*, 19 Sept. 1975, A1.

23. "Communique from the George Jackson Brigade," in *Creating a Movement with Teeth*; Lee Moriwaki, "Safeway Bombing: Retaliation, Love," *ST*, 24 Oct. 1975.

24. By January 1976, Safeway had received so many bomb threats that the company enacted a policy dictating that customers must pass through checkout during evacuations, so that no items left the store without being paid for. The most concerted bombing campaign against Safeway was that of the "Emiliano Zapata Unit," which included an attack in San Jose on January 27, 1976, and another in Oakland close to the same time; "Zapata Unit," *TUG* 1, no. 3. See also "Bomb Hits Safeway in Oakland," *ST*, 24 Oct. 1975; Lee Moriwaki, "No Network Seen in Safeway Bombings," *ST*, 30 Dec. 1975.

25. "Bombing Shows Need for Strong Safeguards," *SP-I*, 21 Sept. 1975, B2.

26. Lee Moriwaki, "Local Leftists Condemn Bombing of Safeway as 'irresponsible,'" *SP-I*, 3 Oct. 1975, A8.
27. Left Bank Collective, "Left Bank Statement," *NP*, 29 Sept.–13 Oct. 1975, 11.
28. Don Hannula, "Police Fear 'bombing increase,'" *ST*, 20 Sept. 1975.
29. "History of Violence: Seattle Bombings in the Past 5 Years," *SP-I*, 20 Sept. 1975, A4.
30. Dellinger, *More Power Than We Know*, 78–82.
31. Ardie Ivie, "Act II," *Seattle Magazine*, June 1970, 24–29.
32. John Wilson, "Shootout Was to Be Last Act," *ST*, 7 Apr. 1975, A1; John Wilson, "March Led Not to Peace but to Terror, Prison Cell," *ST*, 7 Apr. 1975, B4; John Wilson, "'We scouted for a target,'" *ST*, 8 Apr. 1975, C16; John Wilson, "Another Bomb, Another Target," *ST*, 9 Apr. 1975, G1; John Wilson, "A New Life as Ronald J. Scheller," *ST*, 10 Apr. 1975, G6; John Wilson, "Time to Head for Seattle," *ST*, 11 Apr. 1975, B1; John Wilson, "'The one thing for which I am truly sorry,'" *ST*, 13 Apr. 1975, A28.
33. "Guards Conducting Searches at Bombed Capitol Hill Safeway," *ST*, 26 Sept. 1975; Fred Brack, "A Lot of 'bits and pieces': Store Bombing Clues Sifted," *SP-I*, 25 Sept. 1975, A3.
34. Maribeth Morris, "U.S. Offices Guarded: Bomb Alert in Seattle," *SP-I*, 16 Jan. 1975, A1.
35. Brack, "A Lot of 'bits and pieces,'" *SP-I*, 25 Sept. 1975, A3.
36. Nalder, "SLA Reprisal? Bomb in Seattle Store Hurts Five," *SP-I*, 19 Sept. 1975, A1.
37. McCarten and Brack, "Bomb Victim Was Activist," *SP-I*, 20 Sept. 1975, A14.
38. "Bomb Threats Sweep the Seattle Area," *SP-I*, 20 Sept. 1975, A1.

CHAPTER 15

Epigraph: Jill Johnston, *Lesbian Nation: The Feminist Solution* (New York: Simon & Schuster, 1973), 97.
1. Brown, Cook, Mead, and Sherman recall Coupez joining the organization at this time. Coupez insists, however, that it was not until the group fled to Oregon the following spring.
2. Communiqué dated June 1, 1975, *Sunfighter* 3, no. 2 (July–Aug. 1975), reprinted as "Olympia Bombing," in *Creating a Movement with Teeth*, 11–13.
3. The *Post-Intelligencer* said the call went in to the wrong Safeway (Brack, "A Lot of 'bits and pieces'"; Left Bank Collective, "Left Bank Statement"). Mead insists he called the right one, but that the warning was disregarded.
4. M. F. Beal, for example, observed, in an article published several years later, that men's "sexual monopoly system" was disintegrating as a result of the consciousness raising of the women's liberation movement. "[U]nder the new rules," she declared, "men will have to redefine their own sexuality and face the prospect of loving one another." "What Men Fear," in Beal et al., *Safe House*, 77–78.
5. Elbaum, *Revolution in the Air*, 95–102.
6. Roxanne Dunbar-Ortiz, *Outlaw Woman: A Memoir of the War Years, 1960–1975* (San Francisco: City Lights, 2001), 295.
7. U.S. House of Representatives, Committee on Internal Security, *America's Maoists: The Revolutionary Union; The Venceremos Organization* (Washington, DC: Government Printing Office, 1972).
8. Dunbar-Ortiz, *Outlaw Woman*, 299.

9. Dunbar-Ortiz, *Outlaw Woman*, esp. 316–38.

10. The internal organizational debate is preserved in *Proletarian Revolution vs. Revolutionary Adventurism: Major Documents from an Ideological Struggle in the Revolutionary Union*, The Red Papers 4 (San Francisco: Revolutionary Union, 1972).

Future members of the Symbionese Liberation Army had been involved in Venceremos to such an extent that some speculated that the SLA was a continuation of Venceremos by another name. On October 6, 1972, some Venceremos members killed a guard in the course of freeing an inmate whom they had recruited from the prison in Chino. The prisoner, Ronald Beaty, then testified against those who had helped him escape. Venceremos collapsed as an aboveground organization. Bryan, *This Soldier Still at War*, 102–9.

11. John Sherman, interview, 19 Jan. 2004. Subsequent Sherman quotations are also from this interview.

12. Dunbar-Ortiz confirms that there were "weapons kept in all RU houses." *Outlaw Woman*, 295.

13. These are late 1980s, early 1990s-era quotations from the propaganda of the Revolutionary Communist Party, as the RU was renamed in the mid-1970s. For an elaborated critique of this organization, see Greg Jackson, "Mythology of the White-Led 'Vanguard': A Critical Look at the Revolutionary Communist Party, USA," http://illvox.org/2007/06/22/mythology-of-the-white-led-vanguard-a-critical-look-at-the-revolutionary-communist-party-usa (accessed 29 Aug. 2009).

14. A contemporaneous gay protest against the RU's position is "Is Genocide the Answer—To Contradictions among the People?" in *The Lavender & Red Book: A Gay Liberation/Socialist Anthology* (Los Angeles: Lavender & Red Union, 1976), 27.

15. Roger Lippman, interview, 24 Jan. 2009.

## CHAPTER 16

Epigraph: William Upski Wimsatt, *Bomb The Suburbs: Graffiti, Freight-Hopping, Race, and the Search for Hip-Hop's Moral Center* (Chicago: Subway and Elevated Press, 1994), 11.

1. "City Light Workers Meeting over Offer," *SP-I*, 28 Dec. 1975, B4.

2. Eric Nalder, "Woman Testifies on City Light," *SP-I*, 20 Apr. 1976, A4; "Women Fight City Light," *NP*, 10–24 May 1976, 20. For a broader contemporary account of gender integration in blue-collar Seattle, see the series "Women in the Trades," by Karen West in the *SP-I*, Dec. 28–31, 1975.

3. Popular opposition to the new Safeway store was particularly strong in June of 1971. See Stephen H. Dunphy, "Police Clash with Protesters," *SP-I*, 17 June 1971, A1; Charles Aweeka, "Protesters Doused at Supermarket Site," *ST*, 19 June 1971, A5.

4. "We Cry and We Fight!" in *Creating a Movement with Teeth*, 16–17.

5. The Weather Underground's *Prairie Fire* quoted this too. Dohrn et al., *Sing a Battle Song*, 353.

6. "We Cry and We Fight!" in *Creating a Movement with Teeth*, 16–17.

7. John Arthur Wilson, "Sherman Tells of Joining Brigade," *ST*, 6 July 1978.

8. Younger urged that all states pass legislation forbidding the payment of ransom demands; he had lobbied for a similar law in California after the Patricia Hearst kidnapping.

He had also attempted to establish a "war games project" within the state, but had met with resistance from federal officials. ENS, "Guerillas 'Planning a Violent Birthday' in 1976," *BB*, 4–10 Oct. 1974.

9. David Birkland, "Threats of Terrorism Weighed," *ST*, 2 Jan. 1976. See also "Weather Underground Behind Bombings?" *ST*, 2 Jan. 1976. The former Weatherwoman Susan Stern balked at the assertion of Weather involvement, calling it "an outrageous attempt to malign the political left, specifically the Weather Underground." As for conflating the Weather Underground with the Brigade, and thus implicating it in the September 18 Safeway attack, she pointed out: "It is totally out of character that they [the Weather Underground] would go in and bomb where innocent people would get hurt." "57 Bombings Here since 1969," *ST*, 3 Jan. 1976.

10. George Foster, "City Police Fear More Bombings," *SP-I*, 2 Jan. 1976, A1.

11. Martin Works, "Bomb Fragments to Be Analyzed," *SP-I*, 3 Jan. 1976, back page.

12. It was initially reported that police retained a recording of this call, but if they did so, to the best of my knowledge it was never used in court. See Lee Moriwaki, "Bomb Threat May Be on Police Tape," *ST*, 2 Jan. 1976.

13. "Transformer Bombed," *ST*, 1 Jan. 1976.

14. "Fire Explosion Jolts City Light Substation," *SP-I*, 1 Jan. 1976, A1.

15. Billie Jackson, a staff person at the hospital, wrote a public letter to the Brigade berating them for endangering the infants in the intensive care unit. See "Editor, The Times," *ST*, 6 Jan. 1976.

16. "Laurelhurst Residents Asked to Curb Power Use," *ST*, 1 Jan. 1976.

17. "City Light Substation Rebuilt," *ST*, 20 March 1976.

18. John Wilson, "Laurelhurst 'getting by,'" *ST*, 2 Jan. 1976.

19. John Wilson, "Residents Still Face Total Outages," *ST*, 2 Jan. 1976.

20. Don Hannula, "Support Denounced," *ST*, 2 Jan. 1976.

21. "Bomb Damage Repair: Strikers Refuse to Help, City Says," *SP-I*, 3 Jan. 1976, A1; "No Pickets at Power Site," *ST*, 4 Jan. 1976.

22. "None Need Help from Bomb Brigade," *SP-I*, 7 Jan. 1976, A8.

23. City Light's linewoman, telephone interview, Winter 2004.

24. "None Need Help from Bomb Brigade."

25. The most comprehensive surveys of violence and militancy in the U.S. labor movement are Louis Adamic, *Dynamite: A Century of Class Violence in America, 1830–1930* (Gloucester, MA: P. Smith, 1960), and Jeremy Brecher, *Strike!* 2nd ed. (Boston: South End Press, 1997).

26. Del Castle quoted in Bill Patz, "Captured Brigade Members Discuss Their Politics," *NP*, 13 June–10 July 1978, 18.

## CHAPTER 17

1. Ed Mead, "The Theory and Practice of Armed Struggle in the Northwest" (self-published, 1981), 12.

2. Walter Wright, "Jury Convicts Mead in Bank Robbery Case," *SP-I*, 9 Apr. 1976.

3. In a casually probing conversation with a police officer after his arrest, Sherman remembers being told that all the officers at the Tukwila station had gone out to respond to the Brigade's diversions, except for Detective Mathews, who was in the bathroom. "He came

out as the bank alarm was coming in, and he elected to go there instead," Sherman relates. Interview, 19 Jan. 2004.

4. A ballistics expert testified in Seidel's death inquest that the slug removed from Sherman's jaw did not come from a police pistol, indicating that it came from Cook's across the street. A slug from the same gun was later offered as authentication of the International Women's Day communiqué. See Walter Wright, "Destruction, Bloodshed. Threatened by Radicals," *SP-I*, 28 Mar. 1976, A1.

5. This account is a composite of Mark Reed Wallbom's initial police report, taken 24 Jan. 1976, by Detective Desmul of the Tukwila Police Department for Case 76-0151; press accounts of testimony at the inquest and state trial (the original transcripts of the inquest, along with those of Mead's subsequent trial on state charges, were lost by the court in the early 1990s); and Mead and Sherman's "On the Death of Bruce," dated 26 Jan. 1976, *Dragon* no. 8 (Apr.–May 1976): 3–5. Press accounts include: "Inquest Jury to Weigh Bank Shoot-Out Evidence," *SP-I*, 18 Feb. 1976, A4; W. Wright, "Jury Clears Tukwila Policeman in Fatal Shooting," *SP-I*, 20 Feb. 1976, A4; W. Wright, "Officers Tell of Gun Battle," *SP-I*, 7 Apr. 1976, A5; W. Wright, "Accounts of Gun Battle Differ Widely," *SP-I*, 8 Apr. 1976, A5; J. A. Wilson, "Mead Says Police Fired First," *ST*, 8 Apr. 1976.

6. Lee Moriwaki and John Arthur Wilson, "Of Life and Death in Radical Circles," *ST*, 30 Mar. 1976.

7. John Arthur Wilson, "Dead Radical's Roommate Sought," *ST*, 21 Apr. 1976.

8. Michael Woo, interview, 11 Jan. 2006.

CHAPTER 18

Epigraph: Quoted in "Law Agencies on Brigade's Trail," *SP-I*, 27 Mar. 1976, A11.

1. "Inquest Jury to Weigh Bank Shoot-Out Evidence," *SP-I*, 18 Feb. 1976, A4; Walter Wright, "Jury Clears Tukwila Policemen in Fatal Shooting," *SP-I*, 20 Feb. 1976, A4.

2. John Brockhaus, "Grand Jury in Seattle: 'I'm a-goin fishin' . . . ,'" *NP*, 15–29 Mar. 1976, 3.

3. "On the Death of Bruce," 26 Jan. 1976, repr. in *Dragon*, no. 8 (Apr.–May 1976): 3–5. Nearly three decades later, Sherman was more circumspect about the charge that police deliberately allowed Seidel to die. "It was in the nature of things that we would claim they did it on purpose, but how can you know? Incompetence reigns everywhere," he said. Interview, 19 Jan. 2004.

4. In response to the events of March 10, the Department of Rehabilitative Services began refusing to transfer inmates to court-ordered medical appointments at Harborview. William Gough, "Security Rules Cancel Medical Appointment," *ST*, 4 Apr. 1976, B5.

5. John Arthur Wilson, "Shot Officer Testifies about Escape Attempt from Hospital," *ST*, 17 June 1976.

6. "Radical Wounds Officer to Help Inmate Escape," *SP-I*, 11 Mar. 1976, A1.

7. In an interview with the author in 2001, Cook insisted that the SPD did not question him about Harborview at the time of this initial arrest. The police, however, told the press that they had done so. Martin Works and Walter Wright, "A Quiet Arrest . . . the Tukwila Bank Robbery Case Develops," *SP-I*, 13 Mar. 1976, A11.

8. Mark consistently maintained his innocence from his initial arrest and trial up until he was granted a definite release date in 1999. A number of his supporters didn't learn of his actual guilt until he revealed it in an interview with a reporter from the alternative newsweekly *The Stranger*: Phil Campbell, "Day of the Panther," 14 Oct. 1999, 11.

9. Works and Wright, "Quiet Arrest."

10. Walter Wright and Martin Works, "Escape Case Hunt Intense," *SP-I*, 12 Mar. 1976, A1.

11. Walter Wright, "FBI Fumes over Threats by Radicals," *SP-I*, 29 Mar. 1976, A4.

12. John Arthur Wilson, "Sherman Had Lived 'next door,'" *ST*, 4 Apr. 1978.

13. Saxe was a lesbian activist at Swarthmore who, in 1971, robbed a National Guard Armory and a bank to fund anti-war activities. In the course of the bank robbery, one of the male ex-convicts with whom she was collaborating killed a police officer. Saxe and her friend Katherine Power hid out in women's communities, stumping the FBI, who hardly had any female agents, let alone ones willing to engage in lesbian acts in order to infiltrate. To compensate for this "failure of intelligence" the FBI launched grand juries in women's communities where Saxe and Power were believed to have visited. Jill Raymond was jailed for months in Lexington, Kentucky, resisting one of these grand juries. Martin Sostre was a black prisoner on the East Coast who wrote powerful anarchist propaganda and physically and legally challenged oppressive institutional practices. On his case, see Vincent Copeland, *The Crime of Martin Sostre* (New York: McGraw-Hill, 1970).

14. The Brigade was deliberately inflating its numbers. "Comrade" would have been more accurate, because Cook was the only member across the street.

15. "International Women's Day Communique," in *Creating a Movement with Teeth*, 18–21.

16. John Arthur Wilson, "Terrorist Unit Says It Shot Officer," *ST*, 28 Mar. 1976; Walter Wright, "Brigade's Promised Proof; Station Gets Dental Evidence," *SP-I*, 31 Mar. 1976.

17. "Text of Brigade Communique," *SP-I*, 31 Mar. 1976, F6.

18. John Arthur Wilson and Lee Moriwaki, "Brigade Deserves Respect, Say Leftists," *ST*, 31 Mar. 1976.

19. Bay Area Radical Collective, "George Jackson Brigade," *Dragon*, no. 8 (Apr.–May 1976): 10.

20. Wright, "FBI Fumes."

21. Ibid.; AP, "FBI Chief Warns Against Too-Tight Curbs on Bureau," *SP-I*, 12 Feb. 1976, A2; "Kelly Cites Brigade," *SP-I*, 12 Feb. 1976, A2.

22. "'Brigade Is a Challenge,'" *SP-I*, 30 Mar. 1976, A12.

23. Bay Area Radical Collective, "George Jackson Brigade."

CHAPTER 19

1. Dick Lilly, "The Grand Jury v. the Jackson Brigade," *The Weekly* (Seattle), 5 May 1976, 7–8.

2. "Bank Robbery Probe Halts for a Week," *SP-I*, 5 Mar. 1976, B4.

3. Wright and Works, "Escape Case Hunt."

4. Walter Wright, "Grand Jury Defied by Two Witnesses," *SP-I*, 24 Mar. 1976, A6.

5. Walter Wright, "New Twist In Tukwila Bank Case," *SP-I*, 25 Mar. 1976, A6.

6. Ed Mead, interview, Spring 2005.

7. Harry Gombe, "Grand Juries: The New American Inquisition," *OR*, Spring 1977, 13.

8. Robert H. Gibbs, "Abusing Grand Jury in Seattle," *ST*, 27 Mar. 1976, A8; John Arthur Wilson, "Affidavit Pushes for Testimony by Lawyer," *ST*, 2 Apr. 1976, A8; "Grand Jury Calls Attorney in Tukwila Case," *SP-I*, 4 Apr. 1976, A4; "Bar Group Backs Lawyer in Dispute," *ST*, 2 May 1976; Lilly, "Grand Jury v. the Jackson Brigade."

9. In Gombe's "Grand Juries," the figure is 100 cities. *OR*, Spring 1977.

10. John Arthur Wilson, "Federal grand jury under fire again," *ST*, 18 May 1976, A10.

11. Ronald J. Ostrow, "Have Jury, Will Travel," *WP*, 11 Feb. 1973, D4.

12. Quoted in Brockhaus, "Grand Jury in Seattle: 'I'm a-goin fishin' . . . ,'" 4.

13. Eighty-eight members of the Pressmen's Union were subpoenaed in an investigation into the destruction of *Washington Post* presses in a strike in 1975. Fifteen unionists were indicted for rioting and destruction of machinery, among other offenses. A grand jury was convened in Sioux Falls, South Dakota, after the death of two FBI agents on the Pine Ridge Reservation. Three people were jailed for refusing to discuss the shootout. In Denver, Colorado, a grand jury purporting to investigate a 1974 bombing that killed six Chicano men was essentially an assault on the Chicano movement in that city. One Chicana activist spent seven months in jail for refusing to talk. In Tucson, Arizona, four Chicana community workers were indicted for aiding illegal immigrants (*Quash*, "Four Women Indicted," *NP*, 24 Jan.-6 Feb. 1977, 16). As for gays, there were grand juries in Lexington, Kentucky, and New Haven, Connecticut, chasing the FBI's "Most Wanted" women, anti-war activists Katherine Power and Susan Saxe (Gombe, "Grand Juries: The New American Inquisition," *OR*, Spring 1977, 13).

14. Brockhaus, "Grand Jury in Seattle: 'I'm a-goin fishin' . . . ,'" 3-4.

15. Susan B. Jordan, "The SLA: A Recurring Nightmare," *Guild Practitioner* 59, no. 2 (Spring 2002): 112.

16. "Seattle under Attack," *Dragon*, no. 9 (June 1976): 43-45.

17. Quoted in Brockhaus, "Grand Jury in Seattle: 'I'm a-goin fishin' . . . ,'" 3.

18. George Foster, "Police Treated to Unusual Demonstration," *SP-I*, 1 Jan. 1976, A3.

19. Larry Roberts, "Police Raid Hill Apartment," *SS*, 28 Apr. 1976, 1; 4; Laurie McCarten, "Revolutionary Hideout Sought: Hoax Calls Trigger Police Raid on a Peaceful Couple," *SP-I*, 30 Apr. 1976, A10; Paul Henderson, "Hoax: But Versions of What Happened Are Vastly Different," *ST*, 1 May 1976; Larry Roberts, "Police Department Changes Story on Apartment Raid," *SS*, 5 May 1976. Wright was given a suspended fine of $25 by the municipal court for obstructing police during the search of his home, but the conviction was overturned on appeal. "Man Fined $25 in Search Incident," *ST*, 15 July 1976; "Laddie Wright Not Guilty of Obstructing Capitol Hill Search," *ST*, 16 Dec. 1976.

20. John Arthur Wilson, "Radical, Seized Items Subpoenaed," *ST*, 22 June 1976; Tony Collins, "George Jackson Brigade Probe Leads to Subpoena of Two Women," *UW Daily*, 5 May 1976, 4.

21. The reflections of several members of that year's Seattle delegation to Cuba are recorded in "behind the blockade," *NP*, 18 June-19 July 1976, 13. For a present-day retrospective of the Venceremos Brigade, see Elizabeth Martinez, "The Venceremos Brigade Still Means 'We Shall Overcome,'" *Z Magazine*, July-Aug. 1999, 56-62.

22. John Arthur Wilson, "Federal Agents Raid House," *ST*, 2 May 1976; John Arthur Wilson, "Possible Residence of Radicals Is Searched," 3 May 1976; AP, "New Raid Made in

'Brigade Case,'" *TNT*, 3 May 1976; "Agents Will Seek to Link Brigade," AP, 3 May 1976, A14; Walter Wright, "3 Deny Link to Brigade," *SP-I*, 4 May 1976, A5; John Arthur Wilson, "Agents Seize Typewriters, Wire," *ST*, 5 May 1976.

23. The anonymous expert's credibility was as tenuous as that of Smith. The only thing he was able to state with certainty was that all three notes were written by the same person. According to *Northwest Passage* the *SP-I*'s Walt Wright, who got a look at the papers, contended that even his layman's eye could see "significant differences" between them (Roxanne Park and Emmett Ward, "Grand Jury: 3 Who Refused to Speak," *NP*, 28 June–19 July 1976.) I have not been able to locate the original statement by Wright.

24. At 7:45 A.M. on a March morning, four FBI agents visited Mark Cook's on-and-off-again girlfriend Sandra Hastings at her Capitol Hill home. Hastings was taking care of Cook's son, making her, in effect, another single mother. Two agents began firing questions at her, pinning her against the kitchen sink as they sought information as to Cook's whereabouts. She refused to answer, and was soon served with a subpoena. Susan Chadwick, "The Grand Jury: Why Are Those People Refusing [to] Testify," *SS*, 12 May 1976, 8.

25. "Government Accused of 'fishing,'" *ST*, 5 May 1976; "Search, Seizure, and Subpoenas on Capitol Hill," *NP*, 10–24 May 1976, 19; residents of the searched Capitol Hill house, "Press Release," 3 May 1976, and "For Immediate Release," 4 May 1976 (copy in author's possession).

26. Walter Wright, "Capitol Hill Home Search Defended," *SP-I*, 7 May 1976, A7; "Review Ordered of Material Seized in House," *ST*, 7 May 1976; Walter Wright, "Search Items: A Review," *SP-I*, 8 May 1976, A11; John Arthur Wilson, "Seized Items . . . ," *ST*, 8 May 1976, C8; John Arthur Wilson, "More Items Taken from House Sought," *ST*, 11 May 1976; AP, "Agents Went beyond Limits," *TNT*, 18 May 1976.

27. John Arthur Wilson, "Government Still Probing Activist, Unsolved Bombings," *ST*, 22 Dec. 1976.

28. David Birkland, "Burglary Suspects' Release Hurt Bomb Case, Says Chief," *ST*, 4 Oct. 1975, A3; "Another Woman Subpoenaed in Grand Jury Bomb Probe," *SP-I*, 9 May 1976, A11; Walter Wright, "Brigade Probe Twist: Woman Sues U.S." *SP-I*, 20 May 1976, A8; "Seattle Grand Jury—'Fighting It Every Inch of the Way,'" *NP*, 24 May–7 June 1976, 17.

29. See John Arthur Wilson and Lee Moriwaki, "Sent to Newspaper; Tests Fail to Show Bullet Was Fired in Attempted Bank Robbery," *ST*, n.d., A6.

30. Walter Wright, "Revolutionary Phones *PI*: Mystery Call From a Fugitive," *SP-I*, 11 May 1976, A1.

31. John Arthur Wilson, "Federal grand jury under fire again," *ST*, 18 May 1976, A10.

32. Walter Wright, "U.S. Wants Sherman's Handwriting," *SP-I*, 14 June 1976. A handwriting sample from Capitol Hill is reprinted next to one from the International Women's Day communiqué in "Sleuths on the Write Track?" *ST*, 18 May 1976.

33. "Brigade Communique Finding," *SP-I*, 19 June 1976, A3.

34. Due to an editing error at the *SP-I*, several editions printed the opposite of the assertions. It was corrected the next day. "Four Denied Meeting Sherman," *SP-I*, 13 May 1976, A4.

35. Walter Wright, "No Telltale Fingerprints," *SP-I*, 12 May 1976, A1.

36. John Brockhaus and Roxanne Park, "Ed Mead Speaks from Prison," *NP*, 24 May–7 June 1976, 5.

37. Walter Wright, "Grand Jury Hands Out New 'Brigade' Charges," *SP-I*, 19 May 1976, A11.

38. Walter Wright, "Brigade Probe Twist: Woman Sues U.S." *SP-I*, 20 May 1976, A8.

39. Ross Anderson, "Ruling on Radicals: Police Justified in Entering Apartment," *ST*, 25 Aug. 1976.

40. The titles of the books were *Demolition Materials, The Four Faces of Tania, Hand to Hand Combat, Lock Picking Simplified, Special Forces Operations and Techniques, Total Resistance, Unconventional Warfare Devices and Techniques, The War of the Flea and How Guerrilla Fighters Could Win the World*, and one on firearms silencers. John Arthur Wilson, "Search Nets Guns, Radical Literature," *ST*, 21 June 1976; John Arthur Wilson, "Lists Seized in Raid on Radicals' Home," *ST*, 13 July 1976.

41. Ross Anderson, "Grand Jury May See Evidence, Judge Rules," *ST*, 11 Sept. 1976. Some of the weapons and other belongings were quietly returned the following spring: John Arthur Wilson, "Seized Weapons Returned to Activists," *ST*, 21 Apr. 1977.

42. Walter Wright, "Leftist Called in Bomb Probe after Accidental Raid," 22 June 1976, C14; John Arthur Wilson, "Radical, Seized Items Subpoenaed," *ST*, 22 June 1976; Neil Modie, "Seattle Women Defy Jury in Bombing Probe," *SP-I*, 23 June 1976, A10; "More Subpoenas in Seattle," *NP*, 28 June–9 July 1976, 20; "Grand Jury Goings On," *NP*, 19 July–2 Aug. 1976, 13.

43. "Left Bank vs. Grand Jury," *NP*, 30 Aug.–19 Sept. 1976, 19; "Left Bank Subpoena Holds," *NP*, 20 Sept.–4 Oct. 1976, 21.

44. John Arthur Wilson, "Radicals Charge Illegal Search," *ST*, 24 June 1976.

45. "Judge Refuses to to [sic] Hold Contempt Hearing for Grand-Jury Witness," *ST*, 29 June 1976.

46. On November 4, Laurie was convicted with Jo Maynes (another Left Bank Collective member) and Alice Ray-Keil of illegally entering the Trident Nuclear Submarine Base. The three had done so as part of a direct action organized by the Pacific Life Community, a regional pacifist organization. The three women were each sentenced to thirty days in jail. Raymond was allowed to serve her nonviolent direct action sentence concurrently with the one for "assaulting an officer." Earlier in the year, Judge Voorhees had sentenced the same three women to thirty days in jail for illegalities they had committed at a demonstration at the Keyport Naval Torpedo Station outside of Bangor, Washington. Voorhees called their sentence a "deterrent to others." Michelle Whitnack, "Compañeras y Compañeros," *Dragon*, no. 10 (Sept. 1976): 35; "Whitnack Jailed," *NP*, 9–29 Aug. 1976, 14–15; "Raymond Convicted," *NP*, 8–21 Nov. 1976, 10; "Alice, Jo, Lori Sentenced," *NP*, 30 Aug.–19 Sept. 1976, 19.

47. "Officials Want Woman in Bombing-Case Line Up," *ST*, 24 July 1976; John Arthur Wilson, "Woman Appears in Line-up in Bombing of Substation," *ST*, 26 July 1976; John Arthur Wilson, "Woman Picked from Line-up in Bombing Case," *ST*, 28 July 1976; John Arthur Wilson, "Radical Fears 'frame-up' in Bombing," *ST*, 4 Aug. 1976, E14.

48. Walter Wright, "Sherman Calls to Say He'll 'clear others,'" *SP-I*, 25 June 1976, A6.

49. "Grand Jury Goings On," *NP*, July 19–Aug. 2, 1976, 13.

50. Michelle Whitnack, "On Armed Struggle: A Continuing Dialogue," *NP*, 28 June–19 July 1976, 2.

51. Whitnack, "Compañeras y Compañeros," 37.

52. Jill Raymond, "repression," *oob*, Nov. 1976, 3. A portion of this article was reprinted in *Northwest Passage* as "Michelle Whitnack, Grand Juries, & the Left," 8–21 Nov. 1976, 9, 22.

53. Wilson, "Radical Fears 'frame-up' in bombing."

54. "Letter from Michelle Whitnack: Caught in the Grand Jury Whirl," Oct.–Nov. 1976, *Women's Press* (Eugene, OR). This article is included in the FBI's file on the Brigade. Portions of the same letter appear as "whitnack letter excerpts," *oob*, Nov. 1975, 18–19.

55. "News from Michelle," *NP*, 20 Sept.–4 Oct. 1976, 5; Karin Strand, "Women Protest Jail Conditions," *NP*, 20 Sept.–4 Oct. 1976, p. 20; "whitnack letter excerpts," *oob*, Nov. 1975, 19; "changes for Michelle," *NP*, 11–25 Nov. 1976, 3.

56. "Whitnack out of Deep Freeze," *OR*, Spring 1977, 12–13; cad, "whitnack fingerprints forced," *oob*, Feb. 1977, 5.

57. Brockhaus and Park, "Ed Mead Speaks," 5.

## CHAPTER 20

1. Brockhaus and Park, "Ed Mead Speaks," 4–5; 20.

2. The theoretical guide for Park's piece was Walter Lacquer, an expert on terrorism and unconventional warfare closely linked with the American national security establishment.

3. Ronald J. Ostrow, "Have Jury, Will Travel," *WP*, 11 Feb. 1973, D4.

4. Lee Moriwaki, interview on June 27, 1983, by Robert Bruce Barnum, in Barnum, "Terrorism as a Silent Form of Protest Communications: A Retrospective Look at the George Jackson Brigade" (M.A. thesis, Communications Program, University of Washington, 1983), 36.

5. Left Bank Collective, "We . . . Support Armed Action . . . Now," *NP*, 19 July–8 Aug. 1976, 18.

6. Ibid.

7. Roxanne Park, "Terrorism and the George Jackson Brigade," *NP*, 7–28 July 1976, 5–7.

8. Michelle Whitnack, "On Armed Struggle: A Continuing Dialogue," *NP*, 28 June–19 July, 1976, 2.

9. Ibid.

10. Susan Saxe lampooned such individuals with a sing-songy poem called "Risk My White Ass? Not On Your Life, Baby," *TTLG* 3, no. 3 (Apr. 1978), 6.

11. Left Bank Collective, "We . . . Support Armed Action . . . Now," 18. Quotations in the next paragraph of text are also from this source.

12. David Macey, *Franz Fanon: A Biography* (New York: Picador USA, 2000), 270; 290–92.

13. Sylvester Cohen, "Amilcar Cabral: An Extraction from the Literature," *Monthly Review*, Dec. 1998, 39–47.

14. Left Bank Collective, "We . . . Support Armed Action . . . Now," 19.

15. Ibid., 20.

16. Eileen Kirkpatrick, "Staff Comments," *NP*, 19 July–8 Aug. 1976, 2.

17. John Arthur Wilson, untitled, *ST*, 17 July 1976.

## CHAPTER 21

Epigraph: Ed Mead, *ST*, 20 Mar. 1976, quoted in *Dragon*, no. 8 (Apr.–May 1976): 7.

1. Walter Wright, "Destruction, Bloodshed, Threatened by Radicals," *SP-I*, 28 Mar. 1976, A1.
2. Walter Wright, "'Brigade Bombed FBI': Jailed Comrade Speaks," *SP-I*, 30 Mar. 1976, A1; A12.
3. Lee Moriwaki and John Arthur Wilson, "The Psychological Anatomy of a Revolutionary," *ST*, 1 Apr. 1976, C5.
4. Wilson, "Bank Manager Testifies on Gunfire," *ST*, 7 Apr. 1976, B7.
5. Mead, interview, January 2005.
6. Walter Wright, "Mead Case Gets Action in 2 Courtrooms," *SP-I*, 1 Apr. 1976, A4; AP, "Drop Charges, Bank Suspect Asks," *TNT*, 1 Apr. 1976, C12; AP, "'Comrade' on Trial in Seattle," *TNT*, 5 Apr. 1976; Larry Brown, "Officers' Files Ruled 'off limits,'" *ST*, 1 Apr. 1976. Brown's account stated that Mead had been in isolation since March 10, the date of Sherman's escape, when in fact the interception of the note from LaRue on February 26 provoked his isolation.
7. Walter Wright, *SP-I*, 30 Mar. 1976, A1 (the same article also appeared under the title "'Brigade' Bomb Link: Comrade Says FBI Hit"); Lee Moriwaki and John Arthur Wilson, *ST*, 1 Apr. 1976, C5.
8. "Times Reporter Is Subpoenaed," *ST*, 6 Apr. 1976, A15.
9. Walter Wright, "Security Tight as New Trial Starts," *SP-I*, 6 Apr. 1976, A10; John Arthur Wilson, "Jury Selected in Mead Assault Trial," 6 Apr. 1976, A15; AP, "Judge Denies Dismissal of Mead Assault Charges," *TNT*, 6 Apr. 1976.
10. Walter Wright, "Officers Tell of Gun Battle," *SP-I*, 7 Apr. 1976, A5; AP, "Tukwila Police Tell of Holdup," *TNT*, 7 Apr. 1976, B6.
11. Walter Wright, "Accounts of Gun Battle Differ Widely," *SP-I*, 8 Apr. 1976, A5; John Arthur Wilson, "Mead Says Police Fired First," *ST*, 8 Apr. 1976; AP, "Trial 'hears' Escapee," *TNT*, 9 Apr. 1976.
12. Walter Wright, "Ed Mead: 2 Faces of a Dangerous Man," *SP-I*, 11 Apr. 1976, A6; John Arthur Wilson, "Mead Convicted of Assault; Faces Federal Charges," *ST*, 9 Apr. 1976, A10.
13. "Jackson Brigade Member Draws 40-year Minimum," *ST*, 3 Nov. 1976; AP, "Bank-Robbing Radical Gets 40-year Term," *TNT*, 4 Nov. 1976.
14. Wright, "Jury Convicts Mead in Bank Robbery Case," *SP-I*, 9 Apr. 1976.
15. Walter Wright, "Mead Gets Prison Sentence," *SP-I*, 23 Apr. 1976, A7; AP, "Mead Trial Continued One Week," *TNT*, 13 Apr. 1976; Mead, interview.
16. J. A. Wilson, "Mead Granted Trial Delay," *ST*, 12 Apr. 1976; "Mead Trial Delayed to Give Him Time to Prepare Case," *SP-I*, 13 Apr. 1976, A6.
17. "U.S. 'Intimidation' Charged in Bank Case," *SP-I*, 10 Apr. 1976, A3; John Arthur Wilson, "Radical Gets 2 Life Terms for Shooting in Robbery Try," *ST*, 22 Apr. 1976; Walter Wright, "Mead Gets Prison Sentence," *SP-I*, 23 Apr. 1976, A7.
18. Walter Wright, "Mead Says He'll Plead Not Guilty Due to 'Insanity,'" *SP-I*, 22 Apr. 1976, A4.
19. John Arthur Wilson, "Federal Bank-Robbery Trial of Edward Mead Delayed," *ST*, 23 Apr. 1976; Wilson, "Mead Sticks to Insanity Plea," *ST*, 19 June 1976; "Bank Robbery Defen-

dant Refuses Psychiatric Test," *SP-I*, 20 June 1976, H5; AP, "Radical Will Plead Insanity," *TNT*, 20 June 1976.

20. "Edward Mead Loses Plea," *SP-I*, 24 Sept. 1977, A3.

21. Walter Wright, "Grand Jury Hands Out New 'Brigade' Charges," *SP-I*, 19 May 1976, A11; "A Letter from Ed Mead," *NP*, 7-28 June 1976, 9.

22. "Policemen Reviewed for Mead 'Macing,'" *SP-I*, 7 July 1976, A7.

23. Michelle Whitnack, "Compañeras y Compañeros," *Dragon*, no. 10 (Sept. 1976): 34.

24. Ed Mead, letter dated Apr. 14, 1976, *Dragon*, no. 8 (April–May 1976): 11.

25. John Arthur Wilson, "Jury Chosen, 'Brigade' Member's Trial Begins," *ST*, 6 July 1976; AP, "Mead Trial Opens in Bank Robbery," *TNT*, 6 July 1976; Wilson, "Judge Refuses to Allow Mead to Plead Insanity," *ST*, 7 July 1976; Wilson, "Mead Convicted of Bank Robbery," *ST*, 7 July 1976; Walter Wright, "Jury Finds Mead Guilty of Armed Robbery Try," *SP-I*, 8 July 1976, A12; AP, "Brigade Member Guilty of Bank Job," *TNT*, 8 July 1976.

26. Mead, personal correspondence, 2 Jan. 2009.

27. John Arthur Wilson, "George Jackson Brigade May Be Dead, Says Mead," *ST*, 8 July 1976.

28. "Jackson Brigade's Mead, Cook Get 30 Years," *SP-I*, 7 Aug 1976, A9.

29. Walter Wright, "'Revolutionary' May Be 60 after Prison," *SP-I*, 8 Aug 1976, F6.

30. John Brockhaus and Roxanne Park, "Ed Mead Speaks from Prison," *NP*, 24 May–7 June 1976, 5.

CHAPTER 22

1. Brown recalls being referred to as "The Gentleman Bank Robber" in the Oregon press, due to her politeness to tellers. I have not encountered any such references, but I have used only *The Oregonian*, the largest paper in the state, rather than local press in Coos Bay, Medford, etc.

2. John Arthur Wilson, "Brigade Member Tied to Oregon Bank Robberies?" *ST*, 1 Oct. 1976, B3.

3. Walter Wright, "Sherman Hunt: FBI in Oregon," *SP-I*, 27 July 1976.

4. Michelle Celarier, "Activist's Mother Subpoenaed: 'I feel like I'm in Germany 1935,'" *NP*, 30 Aug.–19 Sept. 1976, 22.

5. W. Wright, "Fugitive Sherman Denies Oregon Robbery Link," *SP-I*, 12 Oct. 1976, B4.

6. "Fugitive Phones *PI* Fifth Time," *SP-I*, 9 Nov. 1976, A13.

7. "Wilsonville, Eastgate Bank Branches Robbed," *Oregonian*, 8 Feb. 1977, A9.

CHAPTER 23

Epigraph: Ernesto "Che" Guevara, *Guerrilla Warfare* (1961; repr., Lincoln, NE: Bison Books/University of Nebraska Press, 1998), 36.

1. Marjorie Jones, "Prison Panel to Talk with Staff," *ST*, 4 May 1977, G7.

2. Mike Layton, "Prison Unrest Laid to Overcrowding," *SP-I*, 13 Apr. 1977, A3.

3. "Hostility Increasing in Prison Lockup," *ST*, 22 Apr. 1977, A17; Peter Rinearson, "Prisoner Leaders Ask Attention to 'basic needs,'" *ST*, 24 Apr. 1977, B9.

4. Paul Henderson, "Prison Lockup: Tension Mounts under Enforced Calm," *ST*, 7 May 1977, A1.

5. Paul Henderson, "Guards Fear Reform Will Mean 'replay' of Prison Violence," *ST,* 7 May 1977, A4.
6. Paul Henderson, "State-Prison Aide Defended," *ST,* 5 May 1977, D2.
7. Paul Henderson, "Changes Pledged at Prison," *ST,* 8 May 1977, A1.
8. Paul Henderson, "Guards Back Changes at Prison," *ST,* 9 May 1977, D1.
9. For an early effort to map "the power elite" of Seattle, see Editors, "The Establishment," *Seattle Magazine,* Apr. 1968, 19–23. For a follow-up article a decade later, in which the *Seattle Times* appears prominently, see Ed Newbold, "A Look at the Power Elite," *NP,* 20 Mar.–10 April 1978, 11–14.
10. S. L. Sanger, "Redmond Bank Bombed; Bellevue Bomb Diffused," *SP-I,* 13 May 1977, A1.
11. They continued: "The involuntary transfer of 'mental patients' to Eastern State is a fascist attack on prisoner resistance. Involuntary transfer of any kind allows the administration to ship out 'trouble-makers' and break up prisoner organization."
12. John Arthur Wilson, "Radicals Blame Bombing on Abuse of Inmates," *ST,* 13 May 1977, A1; John Arthur Wilson, "Bombs: Jackson Brigade Speaks Out Again," *ST,* 13 May 1977, A20.
13. Paul O'Connor, "Brigade Is Back with a Bang," *SP-I,* 13 May 1977. An anarchist periodical greeted this communiqué as "remarkably free of rhetoric." "GJB Blasts Media Blackout," *OR,* Summer 1977, 5.
14. "Mayday Communique," in *Creating a Movement with Teeth,* 22–26.
15. AP, "Leftist Group Defends Jackson Brigade's Latest Bombings," *TNT,* 19 May 1977, B11.
16. "Bankers Offer $2,500 Reward," *SP-I,* 18 June 1977, A12; "Bankers' Group Offers Reward for 2 Fugitives," *ST,* 19 June 1977.
17. "Summer Solstice Communique," in *Creating a Movement with Teeth,* 26–27; "Jackson Brigade Claims Robberies," *ST,* 24 June 1977.
18. John Arthur Wilson, "F.B.I. Steps up the Hunt for Brigade Members," *ST,* 25 June 1977; AP, "FBI Terrorist Hunt," *TNT,* 27 June 1977.
19. John Arthur Wilson, "Bank-Robbery Charge: Brigade Fugitive Indicted," *ST,* 14 May 1977, A1.
20. "Brigade: We Did It," *SP-I,* 23 June 1977, A5; AP, "Brigade Takes Credit for Bellevue Holdups," 24 June 1977, A5.
21. John Gillie, "Brigade Bomb Disarmed in Olympia," *TNT,* 4 July 1977; "State Capital Bomb Plot Foiled," *SP-I,* 5 July 1977, A1; "Bomb Defused in Olympia Power Station," *ST,* 5 July 1977; "Investigators Seeking Clues to Bomb Planting," *TNT,* 5 July 1977.
22. "Capitalism Is Organized Crime," in *Creating a Movement with Teeth,* 27–29; "George Jackson Brigade Bombers May Get Nastier," *TNT,* 7 July 1977.
23. "Self-Criticism and Other Thoughts," in *Creating a Movement with Teeth,* 29–31; John Arthur Wilson, "F.B.I. Studying Defused Bombs," *ST,* 6 July 1977.

CHAPTER 24

1. Steve Miletich, "Juanita Bank Hit, Brigade Claims Credit," *DJA,* 9 Sept. 1977; AP, "Brigade Robber Hits Bank," *TNT,* 9 Sept. 1977. The *Seattle Times* account did not mention

the probability of the suspect gender-bending: "Jackson Brigade Suspect in Eastside Robbery," *ST,* 9 Sept. 1977.

2. Wilson, "Old West Fades, but Not Bank-Robbing," *ST,* 6 March 1977.

3. "Bank Heist a 'Brigade' Hit?" *SP-I,* 20 Sept. 1977, D12; "Jackson Brigade Note Left in Bank Robbery," *ST,* 20 Sept. 1977.

4. "Two More Automobile Dealers Hit," *ST,* 25 May 1977.

5. John Arthur Wilson, "Support for Auto Strike: Sherman Admits Fire-Bombings," *ST,* 27 Apr. 1978.

6. Dave Birkland, "Unexploded Bomb Found at Car Agency," *ST,* 7 Oct. 1977; "Gasoline Bomb Found at Seattle Auto Dealership," *ST,* 8 Oct. 1977; "Striking Auto Mechanics File Slander Suit against Dealers," *ST,* 27 Oct. 1977.

7. Paul Henderson, "Pipe Bombs Damage 5 Cars," *ST,* 17 Oct. 1977; "Bomb Probe Stepped Up," *ST,* 18 Oct. 1977, A3.

8. John Arthur Wilson, "Fugitive's Thumbprint on Letter, Says F.B.I." *ST,* 19 Oct. 1977, D7; "FBI Says 'Brigade' Letter Real," *TNT,* 19 Oct. 1977.

9. Martin Works, "Brigade Linked to Bombings," *SP-I,* 19 Oct. 1977, A1.

10. On the Stammheim deaths, see J. Smith and André Moncourt, *The Red Army Faction: A Documentary History,* vol. 1: *Projectiles for the People* (Oakland, CA: PM Press, 2009), 511–20; on Meinhof's death, see ibid., 381–432.

11. Diane Alters, "Bomb Explodes at Car Dealership after Jackson Brigade Call," *ST,* 2 Nov. 1977; Steve Miletich, "Bombs Explode in Bellevue Car Lot," *DJA,* 2 Nov. 1977.

12. "The Brigade Again," *SP-I,* 3 Nov. 1977; "Brigade Says Bombing Backed Terrorists," *TNT,* 2 Nov. 1977, B8.

13. "You Can Kill A Revolutionary, But You Can't Kill The Revolution!" in *Creating a Movement with Teeth,* 37–39.

14. The Tupamaro leader Raul Sendic later gave a different account, saying Mitrione had "been selected as a target for kidnapping because he was helping to teach riot control procedures to the Uruguayan police." See www.nytimes.com/1987/06/21/world/uruguayan-clears-up-state-of-siege-killing.html (accessed 29 Aug. 2009). My thanks to Peter Dreyer for bringing this article to my attention.

15. Kirkpatrick Sale, "How SDS Seeded SLA," *BB,* 8–14 Mar. 1974, 8.

16. "Brigade Tells of Fantastic Scheme to Kidnap McNutt," *TNT,* 2 May 1978.

17. Daniel Burton-Rose, "Queering the Underground: An Interview with George Jackson Brigade Veterans Rita 'Bo' Brown and Ed Mead," in *That's Revolting: Queer Strategies for Resisting Assimilation,* ed. Mattilda [a.k.a. Matt] Bernstein Sycamore, 2nd ed. (Brooklyn, NY: Soft Skull Press, 2006), 26.

18. "Jackson Brigade: Bombing Suspect Seized Here," *SP-I,* 5 Nov. 1977, A1; John Arthur Wilson, "Jackson Brigade Suspect Arrested Here," *ST,* 5 Nov. 1977;"Member of Revolutionary Group Arrested by the F.B.I. in Seattle," *NYT,* 6 Nov. 1977; John Arthur Wilson, "Rita Brown Ordered to Stand Trial," *ST,* 14 Nov. 1977.

19. "FBI Pursues Jackson Brigade Man, Friend," *SP-I,* 6 Nov. 1977; Martin Works, "Sherman's Car Found Near Bus Depot," *SP-I,* 7 Nov. 1977, A9; Peter Rinearson, "Few Clues Found in Car Linked to Brigade," *ST,* 7 Nov. 1977; "FBI Still Seeking George Jackson Pair," *TNT,* 6 Nov. 1977.

20. "Brigade-Suspect Search Fruitless," *TNT*, 7 Nov. 1977.
21. "Alleged Brigade Chief's Pal Sought," *TNT*, 8 Nov. 1977.
22. "Sherman Friend Subpoenaed?" *SP-I*, 8 Nov. 1977, A3.
23. Peter Rinearson, "North End Home Yields Jackson Brigade Clues," *ST*, 6 Nov. 1977.
24. "Paper Studying F.B.I. Request for Letter," *ST*, 4 Dec. 1977.
25. "An Open Letter to Bo (Rita D. Brown)," in *Creating a Movement with Teeth*, 39–43; John Arthur Wilson, "Jackson Brigaders Relate Flight from N. End House," *ST*, 1 Dec. 1977.
26. "Ray among Brigade Targets?" *SP-I*, 22 Nov. 1977; John Arthur Wilson, "Suspected Brigade List Names Local Officials," *ST*, 22 Nov. 1977; Jack Pyle, "FBI Warns People on 'kidnap list,'" *TNT*, 22 Nov. 1977.

## CHAPTER 25

1. Quotations appear throughout as they do in the original document with erratic capitalization, punctuation, and spellings. Brackets provide clarifying information where necessary.

2. Joyce Carol Oates describes Atwood's Canadian novel *Surfacing*—which is interspersed with bitter references to "Bloody fascist pig Yanks" and "Rotten capitalist bastards"—as a "minutely introspective" work, in which "the self-absorbed, rather generic young-woman narrator" progresses from "delusion" to "enlightenment." She embarks on a trip that is actually a "journey into . . . the demons of the self," thus enabling her to "come to terms with her distorted and self-lacerating memories." Throughout much of the narrative the protagonist is confined in isolation with "a singularly disagreeable married couple." It is clear why Janine found it appealing. Joyce Carol Oates, "Margaret Atwood's Tale," *New York Review of Books*, 22 Nov. 2006, 18–19.

3. The phrases "pigs could slip up," "people escape all the time," and "we should, whenever possible, case trials since that's supposed to be the easiest time" were underlined by investigators after the discovery of Janine's diary.

4. Oddly, none of the former Brigade members I interviewed remembered who this person may have been. Brenda, the owner of the auto shop Brown had once worked for, did speak with federal investigators. The agents contacted her about the van Brown had stolen from her and then had Janine run off a cliff, but Brenda didn't know enough to incriminate any Brigade members. Nor was she a "trusted friend" of Brown's, though it is possible Janine perceived her as such. It's difficult to conceive who might have spoken to the FBI "at least 50 times in the last year & ½" without causing the arrest of a Brigade member, unless this collaboration *did* lead to Brown's arrest.

5. "Brigade Bombs in Renton and Kent," *SS*, 28 Dec. 1977.

6. The Republican John D. Spellman was elected governor of Washington in 1980, riding the right-wing backlash epitomized by the presidential victory of Ronald Reagan. As governor, Spellman eased prison overcrowding in Washington—by building more prisons. Kit Oldman, "Spellman, John D. (b. 1926)," www.historylink.org/index.cfm?DisplayPage=output.cfm&file_id=7674 (accessed 12 May 2009).

7. "Horse's Mouth," *SS*, 28 Dec. 1977, 2.

8. "Bomb Explodes at Renton Substation," *SP-I*, 24 Dec. 1977, A14; "Small Bomb Explodes at Renton Substation," *ST*, 24 Dec. 1977 (an abbreviated "bulletin" printed the same day in an earlier edition was titled "Small Bomb Set Off at Renton Power Station"); "Bomb Explodes at Renton Power Station," *EH*, 24 Dec. 1977; "Ineffectual Bomb Linked to Brigade," *DJA*, 24 Dec. 1977; "Bomb Was Retaliation for Capitalist Activity," *TNT*, 25 Dec. 1977; "Investigation Continues into Local Bombings," *ST*, 26 Dec. 1977.

9. "Bust the Union Busters," in *Creating a Movement with Teeth*, 48–49.

10. "A Second Bomb Blast," *SP-I*, 25 Dec. 1977, A1, A19; "Kent Bombing Follows Brigade Call," *ST*, 25 Dec. 1977; "Jackson Bunch Claims Bombs," *TNT*, 26 Dec. 1977; "Radicals Say They Set Off 2 Bombs," *EH*, 26 Dec. 1977; "2 Bombings Have Police on Alert," *DJA*, 26 Dec. 1977; "Law 'Alert' for More Bombings," *SP-I*, 26 Dec. 1977.

11. *EH*, 24 Dec. 1977; *SP-I*, 26 Dec. 1977.

12. "FBI Ties Holdups to Jackson Bunch," *TNT*, 11 Jan. 1978.

## CODA

1. John Arthur Wilson, "Long Hunt for Remnant of Elusive Brigade Ends Quietly," *ST*, 22 Mar. 1978, A1; Neil Modie, "Brigade Leader Captured: Sherman, 2 Women Seized by FBI at Tacoma Drive-In," *SP-I*, 22 Mar. 1978, A1; A20; "FBI Nabs Leader of George Jackson Brigade," *EH*, 22 Mar. 1978; "Radical Held on $1 Million Bail," *DJA*, 22 Mar. 1978, A1; "FBI Arrests Fugitive Radicals," *PO*, 22 Mar. 1978, A1; "FBI Hunt Clues to Radical Suspect's Past," *PO*, 23 Mar. 1978, A14; "Sherman Preparing to Rob a Bank?" *TNT*, 25 Mar. 1978; Jack Hopkins, "Jury Given 2 'Pictures' of Brigade Pair," *SP-I*, 24 June 1978.

2. Les Ledbetter, "Coast Bombing Expected to Go On Despite Arrests," *NYT*, 24 Mar. 1978, A7. Relying on police sources, this *New York Times* article inaccurately stated that the California NWLF had been linked to the Brigade in the past. The police regarded the proximity of the Safeway bombings carried out by the Left Bank Collective NWLF cell and the George Jackson Brigade on September 15 and 18, 1975, respectively, as evidence of active collusion between both the Brigade and the Seattle NWLF upstart and the Brigade and the California NWLF, an error on both counts.

3. "Brigade Makes Explosive Appearance, Fizzles on Arrest," *TNT*, 23 Mar. 1978; Kerry Webster, "Indictments Due in Brigade Bust," *TNT*, 27 Mar. 1978.

4. "Letter Claims Radicals 'fight on,'" *PO*, 31 Mar. 1978, Metro, back page. An affidavit filed by federal agents corroborated this information, acknowledging that the patio door window had been broken before they searched the house and saying that they had, among other things, recovered radical left-wing literature, a "demand note," a sawed-off shotgun, and a homemade radio scanner, items perhaps missed in a hasty cleanup.

5. John Arthur Wilson, "F.B.I. Expected Letter from 'rest of' Brigade," *ST*, 31 Mar. 1978.

6. I have drafted an account of former Brigade members' activities behind bars and since their release titled "Enemy Combatants: Captured Domestic Guerrillas in America's Gulag Archipelago."

7. Sherman's sentence was extended by an escape from 1979 to 1982. See "At 40, Sherman Says Reality Has Intruded," *SP-I*, 25 Apr. 1982, H9.

# SELECT BIBLIOGRAPHY

### INTERVIEWS

*I conducted numerous interviews with former Brigade members Janine Bertram, Rita "Bo" Brown, Mark Cook, and Ed Mead from 1998 to February 2009. I conducted one extensive interview with John Sherman on 19 Jan. 2004. All interviews were conducted in person unless otherwise noted.*

Chuck Armsbury, May 2005 (telephone)
Danny Atteberry, 1999
Liz Fink, Attica Brothers Legal Defense attorney, Spring 2002
Roger Lippman, Fall 1999, 24 Jan. 2009 (telephone)
Michael Woo, 1 Jan. 2006 (telephone and electronic correspondence)

### GOVERNMENT DOCUMENTS

U.S. Congress. House of Representatives. Committee on Internal Security. *America's Maoists: The Revolutionary Union; The Venceremos Organization.* Washington, DC: Government Printing Office, 1972.
———. "Investigation of Attempts to Subvert the United States Armed Services." Washington, DC: Government Printing Office, 1972.
U.S. Congress. Senate. *The Weather Underground: Report of the Subcommittee to Investigate the Administration of the Internal Security Act and Other Internal Security Laws of the Committee on the Judiciary.* Washington, DC: Government Printing Office, 1975.
U.S. Department of Justice, Federal Bureau of Investigation. "George Jackson Brigade." Files 105-295956 and 174-7843.

## NEWSPAPERS

*Daily Journal American*
*Everett Herald*, Everett, WA
*New York Times*
*Portland Oregonian*
*San Francisco Chronicle*
*San Francisco Examiner*
*Seattle Post-Intelligencer*
*Seattle Times*
*Tacoma News Tribune*, Tacoma, WA
*Wall Street Journal*

## UNDERGROUND, OPPOSITIONAL, AND OTHER PERIODICALS

*Anvil*, CA
*Berkeley Barb*
*Berkeley Tribe*
*Contempt: A Magazine of News and Analysis of the National Lawyers Guild, Seattle Chapter*, Seattle
*Crusader*, Monroe, NC, Havana, Cuba, and Beijing, China
*Dragon*, Bay Area Radical Collective, Berkeley, CA
*Midnight Special*, New York City
*Northwest Passage*, Seattle
*off our backs*
*Open Road*, Vancouver
*Ramparts*
*Seattle Magazine*
*Seattle Sun*
*Sunfighter*
*Through the Looking Glass*, Seattle
*TUG: The Urban Guerrilla*, New World Liberation Front, San Francisco

## BOOKS AND SELECTED ARTICLES

Abu-Jamal, Mumia. *We Want Freedom: A Life in the Black Panther Party*. Cambridge, MA: South End Press, 2004.
Adamic, Louis. *Dynamite: A Century of Class Violence in America, 1830–1930*. Gloucester, MA: P. Smith, 1960.
Alpert, Jane. "Letter from the Underground." http://scriptorium.lib.duke.edu/wlm/mother (accessed 29 Aug. 2009).
———. *Growing Up Underground*. New York: William Morrow, 1981.
Arendt, Hannah. *On Violence*. New York: Harcourt, Brace, 1969.

Armsbury, Chuck. "In Memory of Ray Eaglin." www.itsabouttimebpp.com/Memorials/pdf/InmemoryofRayEaglin.pdf (accessed 29 Aug. 2009).
Avakian, Bob. *From Ike to Mao and Beyond: My Journey From Mainstream America to Revolutionary Communist.* Chicago: Insight Press, 2005.
Ayers, Bill. *Fugitive Days: A Memoir.* Boston: Beacon Press, 2001.
Bagdikian, Ben, and Leon Dash. *The Shame of the Prisons.* New York: Pocket Books, 1972.
Barnum, Robert Bruce. "Terrorism as a Silent Form of Protest Communications: A Retrospective Look at the George Jackson Brigade." MA thesis, Communications Program, University of Washington, 1983.
Beal, M. F., and friends. *Safe House: A Casebook Study of Revolutionary Feminism in the 1970's.* Eugene, OR: Northwest Matrix, 1976.
Bergman, Arlene. *Women of Viet Nam.* 2nd ed. San Francisco: People's Press, 1975.
Brecher, Jeremy. *Strike!* Boston: South End Press, 1997.
Brown, Dee. *Bury My Heart at Wounded Knee: An Indian History of the American West.* New York: Holt, Rinehart & Winston, 1971.
Browning, Frank. "Organizing behind Bars." *Ramparts,* Feb. 1972.
Bryan, John. *This Soldier Still at War.* New York: Harcourt, Brace, Jovanovich, 1975.
Burton-Rose, Daniel. "Queering the Underground: An Interview with George Jackson Brigade Veterans Rita 'Bo' Brown and Ed Mead." In *That's Revolting! Queer Strategies for Resisting Assimilation,* ed. Mattilda [a.k.a. Matt] Bernstein Sycamore, 2nd ed. Brooklyn, NY: Soft Skull Press, 2008, 19–28.
Cabral, Amílcar. *Unity and Struggle: Speeches and Writings.* Translated by Michael Wolfers. New York: Monthly Review Press, 1979.
Carson, Clayborne. *In Struggle: SNCC and the Black Awakening of the 1960s.* Cambridge, MA: Harvard University Press, 1981.
Carson, Clayborne, et al., eds. *The Eyes on the Prize Civil Rights Reader: Documents, Speeches, and Firsthand Accounts from the Black Freedom Struggle, 1954–1990.* New York: Viking, 1991.
Chesler, Phyllis. *Women and Madness.* 1972. Reprint. New York: Avon Books, 1973.
Churchill, Ward, and Jim Vander Wall. *Agents of Repression: The FBI's Secret Wars against the Black Panther Party and the American Indian Movement.* Boston: South End Press, 1990.
Cohen, Robert, and Reginald E. Zelnik. *The Free Speech Movement: Reflections on Berkeley in the 1960s.* Berkeley: University of California Press, 2002.
Cohen, Sylvester. "Amilcar Cabral: An Extraction from the Literature." *Monthly Review,* Dec. 1998.
Cortright, David. *Soldiers in Revolt: GI Resistance during the Vietnam War.* 1975. Reprint. Chicago: Haymarket Books, 2005.
*Creating a Movement with Teeth: Communiqués of the George Jackson Brigade.* Montreal: Abraham Guillen Press, 2003.
Crowley, Walter. *Rites of Passage: A Memoir of the Sixties in Seattle.* Seattle: University of Washington Press, 1996.
Cummins, Eric. *The Rise and Fall of California's Radical Prison Movement.* Stanford, CA: Stanford University Press, 1994.

Daley, Robert. *Target Blue: An Insider's View of the N.Y.P.D.* New York: Delacorte, 1971.
Debray, Régis. *Revolution in the Revolution? Armed Struggle and Political Struggle in Latin America.* Translated by Bobbye Ortiz. New York: Monthly Review Press, 1967.
Dellinger, Dave. *More Power Than We Know: The People's Movement toward Democracy.* Garden City, NY: Anchor Books, 1975.
Deutschmann, David, ed. *Che Guevara Reader: Writings on Guerrilla Strategy, Politics & Revolution.* New York: Ocean Press, 1997.
Dohrn, Bernardine, Bill Ayers, and Jeff Jones, eds. *Sing a Battle Song: The Revolutionary Poetry, Statements, and Communiqués of the Weather Underground, 1970–1974.* New York: Seven Stories Press, 2006.
Dunbar-Ortiz, Roxanne. *Outlaw Woman: A Memoir of the War Years, 1960–1975.* San Francisco: City Lights, 2001.
Elbaum, Max. *Revolution in the Air: Sixties Radicals Turn to Lenin, Mao and Che.* New York: Verso, 2002.
Faith, Karlene. *Unruly Women: The Politics of Confinement and Resistance.* Vancouver, BC: Press Gang Publishers, 1993.
Fall, Bernard B., ed. *Ho Chi Minh on the Revolution: Selected Writings, 1920–66.* New York: Praeger, 1967.
Forman, James. *The Making of Black Revolutionaries.* Washington, DC: Open Hand Publishing, 1985.
Franks, Lucinda. "Return of the Fugitive." *New Yorker,* 13 June 1994.
Georgakas, Dan, and Marvin Surkin. *Detroit: I Do Mind Dying.* New York: St. Martin's Press, 1975.
Gitlin, Todd. *The Whole World Is Watching: Mass Media in the Making and Unmaking of the New Left.* Berkeley: University of California Press, 1980.
———. *The Sixties: Years of Hope, Days of Rage.* New York: Bantam Books, 1987.
Greenlee, Sam. *The Spook Who Sat by the Door.* New York: R. W. Baron, 1969. Reprint. Detroit: Wayne State University Press, 1989.
Guevara, Ernesto "Che." *Guerrilla Warfare.* 1961. Reprint. Lincoln, NE: Bison Books / University of Nebraska Press, 1998.
Hayden, Tom. *Rebellion in Newark: Official Violence and Ghetto Response.* New York: Vintage Books, 1967.
———. *Trial.* New York: Holt, Rinehart, & Winston, 1970.
———. *Reunion: A Memoir.* 1988. Reprint. New York: Collier Books, 1989.
Hill, Lance. *Deacons for Defense: Armed Resistance and the Civil Rights Movement.* Chapel Hill: University of North Carolina Press, 2004.
Hilliard, David, and Lewis Cole. *This Side of Glory: The Autobiography of David Hilliard and the Story of the Black Panther Party.* Boston: Little, Brown, 1993.
Horne, Gerald. *The Fire This Time: The Watts Uprising in the 1960s.* Charlottesville: University Press of Virginia, 1995.
Irwin, John. *Prisons in Turmoil.* Boston: Little, Brown, 1980.
Jackson, George. *Soledad Brother: The Prison Letters of George Jackson.* New York: Bantam Books, 1970.
———. *Blood in My Eye.* New York: Bantam Books, 1972.

Jameson, Fredric. "Periodizing the 60s."In *The 60s Without Apology*, ed. Sohnya Sayres et al. Minneapolis: University of Minnesota Press, 1984.

Johnston, Jill. *Lesbian Nation: The Feminist Solution*. New York: Simon & Schuster, 1973.

Jones, Charles E., ed. *The Black Panther Party, Reconsidered*. Baltimore: Black Classic Press, 1998.

Jordan, Susan B. "The SLA: A Recurring Nightmare." *Guild Practitioner* 59.2 (Spring 2002).

Katsiaficas, George. *The Imagination of the New Left: A Global Analysis of 1968*. Cambridge, MA: South End Press, 1987.

Macey, David. *Franz Fanon: A Biography*. New York: Picador USA, 2000.

Mailer, Norman.*The Armies of the Night: History as Novel, the Novel as History*. 1968. Reprint. New York: Plume, 1994.

Marighella, Carlos. *Mini-Manual of the Urban Guerrilla*. 1969. Montreal: Abraham Guillen Press, 2002.

Marx, Karl. *The Eighteenth Brumaire of Louis Bonaparte*. 1852. New York: International Publishers, 1963.

Matthiessen, Peter. *In the Spirit of Crazy Horse*. 1983. Reprint. New York: Viking, 1991.

Mead, Ed. *The Theory and Practice of Armed Struggle in the Northwest*. Self-published, 1981. San Francisco, 2006.

———. "Autobiography." Draft dated January 2009 in author's possession.

Mitford, Jessica. *Kind and Usual Punishment: The Prison Business*. 1971. Reprint. New York: Vintage Books, 1974.

National Coordinating Committee to End the War in Vietnam. *We Accuse: A Powerful Statement of the New Political Anger in America*. Berkeley, CA: Diablo Press, 1965.

Payne, Leslie, and Timothy Findley, with Carolyn Craven. *The Life and Death of the SLA*. New York: Ballantine Books, 1976.

Polner, Murray, ed. *When Can I Come Home? A Debate on Amnesty for Exiles, Anti-war Prisoners and Others*. Garden City, NY: Anchor Books, 1972.

*The Power of the People Is the Force of Life: Political Statement of the George Jackson Brigade*. Montreal: Abraham Guillen Press, 2002. First released in 1977.

Raskin, Jonah, ed. *The Weather Eye: Communiques from the Weather Underground, May 1970–May 1974*. San Francisco: Union Square Press, 1974.

*Report of the National Advisory Commission on Civil Disorders*. New York: Dutton, 1968.

Resources for Community Change. *Women Behind Bars: An Organizing Tool*. Pamphlet. Washington, DC, 1975.

*Robert and Mabel Williams Resource Guide*. San Francisco: Freedom Archives. 2005.

Rorabaugh, W. J. *Berkeley at War: The 1960s*. New York: Oxford University Press, 1989.

Sale, Kirkpatrick. *SDS*. New York: Vintage Books, 1973.

Scheer, Robert, ed. *Eldridge Cleaver: Post-Prison Writings and Speeches*. New York: Vintage Books, 1969.

Schlatter, Evelyn A. "'Extremism in the Defense of Liberty': The Minutemen and the Radical Right." In *The Conservative Sixties*, ed. David Farber and Jeff Roche, 37–50. New York: Peter Lang, 2003.

Schultz, John. *No One Was Killed: Documentation and Meditation: Convention Week, Chicago–August 1968*. Chicago: Big Table Publishing, 1969.

Smith, J., and André Moncourt. *The Red Army Faction: A Documentary History*. Vol. 1: *Projectiles for the People*. Oakland: PM Press, 2009.

Statsny, Charles, and Gabrielle Tyrnauer. *Who Rules the Joint? The Changing Political Culture of Maximum-Security Prisons in America*. Lexington, MA: Lexington Books, 1982.

Stern, Susan. *With the Weathermen: The Personal Journal of a Revolutionary Woman*. Garden City, NY: Doubleday, 1975.

Tanenbaum, Robert K. *Badge of the Assassin*. New York: Pocket Books, 2001.

Tyson, Timothy B. *Radio Free Dixie: Robert F. Williams & the Roots of Black Power*. Chapel Hill: University of North Carolina Press, 1999.

Umoja, Akinyele Omowale. "Repression Breeds Resistance: The Black Liberation Army and the Radical Legacy of the Black Panther Party." In *Liberation, Imagination, and the Black Panther Party*, ed. Kathleen Cleaver and George Katsiaficas, 3–19. New York: Routledge, 2001.

*Uncommon Controversy: Fishing Rights of the Muckleshoot, Puyallup, and Nisqually Indians*. Seattle: University of Washington Press, 1970.

Varon, Jeremy. *Bringing the War Home: The Weather Underground, the Red Army Faction, and Revolutionary Violence in the Sixties and Seventies*. Berkeley: University of California Press, 2004.

Walker, Daniel. *Rights in Conflict: Convention Week in Chicago, August 25–29, 1968. A Report to the National Commission on the Causes and Prevention of Violence*. New York: Dutton, 1968.

Weather Underground Organization. *Prairie Fire: The Politics of Anti-Imperialism: The Political Statement of the Weather Underground*. [San Francisco]: Communications Company, 1974.

Wells, Tom. *The War Within: America's Battle Over Vietnam*. New York: Owl Books, 1996.

Weyler, Rex. *Blood of the Land: The Government and Corporate War against the American Indian Movement*. New York: Everest House, 1982.

Wilkins, Roy, with Tom Mathews. *Standing Fast: The Autobiography of Roy Wilkins*. New York: Viking, 1982.

Wittig, Monique. *Les Guérillères*. 1969. Translated by David Le Vay. 1971. Reprint. New York: Avon Books, 1973.

X, Malcolm, with Alex Haley. *The Autobiography of Malcolm X*. New York: Grove Press, 1966.

Yee, Min S. *The Melancholy History of Soledad Prison: In Which a Utopian Scheme Turns Bedlam*. New York: Harper's Magazine Press, 1973.

## DOCUMENTARIES AND FILMS

Davis, David, and Stephen Talbot. *The Sixties: The Years That Shaped a Generation*. New York: Public Broadcasting System, 2004.

Dixon, Ivan. *The Spook Who Sat by the Door*. 1973. DVD, 2004.

Zeiger, David. *Sir! No Sir! The Suppressed Story of the GI Movement to End the War in Vietnam*. 2005.

# INDEX

*Italicized page numbers refer to illustrations.*

Abbott, Robert W., 168, 172–73, 180, 212–13, 215–16
Abeles, Michael, 56
Action for Forgotten Women (Durham, N.C.), 127–28, 293n1
Africa, decolonization of, 4, 207–8
African Americans: and Attica Correctional Facility (N.Y.) uprising, 112–13, 127; and Bertram, 114–15; and Black Liberation Army (BLA), 37, 159; Brown's experiences with, 98–100, 103, 111; in Central District (Seattle), 82, 111, 144; and civil rights movement, 3–4, 11, 13; and construction worker demonstrations, 82–83, 148–49; at CONvention, 112–14; Cook as, 112, 155, 165, 175–76, 264; Foster as, 33, 286n13; and GJB, 3, 155, 165, 175–76, 181; and guerrilla warfare, 15–16; Herbert as, 173; at Hilltop Community Center (Tacoma), 114–15; Jackson as, 31, 62, 98–99, 121; Left's views of, 201, 205–6; Little as, 127; in Monroe (N.C.), 9–11; patriarchal duty of, 21, 282n33; and prison reform, 30–31, 235, 284–85n1; at riots in response to King assassination, 22; and Safeway bombing (Seattle), 143; at Seattle Central Community College (SCCC), 103; and Sherman's jailbreak, 175–76; Smith, Frank "Big Black," as, 112–13; Sostre as, 301n13; "The Super Crew," 112; at Terminal Island penitentiary (San Pedro, Calif.), 98; at University of California at Berkeley, 28; and urban riots, 15–16, *17*, 281nn21,22; Ward as, 144
Afro-American Patrolmen's League (Chicago), 25
Agnew, Spiro, 185, 283n14
Alaska Supreme Court, 49–50
Alcatraz Island (San Francisco Bay), 136
Alderson (W.Va.) Federal Reformatory for Women, 129, 259, 269
Alexian Brothers Novitiate property (Gresham, Wis.), 81, 203
Algeria, 31, 121, 206–7
Allen, David, 211–18
Allen, Esther, 282n29
Alligood, Clarence, 127
Alpert, Jane, 130–31, 295n6
*Amazon One* (Beal), 121–22
Amazon Women's Music Festival (Santa Cruz), 125
American Brotherhood Alliance, 187–88
American Civil Liberties Union (ACLU), 63, 118
American Correctional Association, 72–73, 82
American Friends Service Committee (AFSC), 136, 165, 239–40
American Indians, 4, 21, 55, 85, 135–36, 283n11; American Indian Movement (AIM), 78–79, 82, 135–37, 183; fishing rights of, 60, 136,

319

American Indians *(continued)*
154, 289n19; grand jury investigations of, 185; Hunkpapas, 135; Independent Oglala Nation, 136; Indians of All Tribes, 136; Kootenai band (Idaho), 79; Left's views of, 203, 205–6; Menominee land, 81, 203; Minneconjou, 135; Modocs, 91, 120; Oglala Sioux, 135–38; Pine Ridge Indian Reservation (S.Dak.), 135–38, 183, 302n13; Rosebud Indian Reservation (S.Dak.), 135–36, 138; at Seattle Central Community College (SCCC), 103; "Trail of Broken Treaties," 78, 136; and Wounded Knee siege, 135, 137–38, 183, 203, 302n13. *See also* Amerindians
*American Way of Death, The* (Mitford), 60
*Amistad* (slave ship), 34
anarchism, 13, 61, 63, 76, 123, 138, 180, 198, 208, 257, 301n13
Andersen, Jerry, 160, 162
Anderson, Nicky L., 142
Angola, 206–8
anti-communism, 28, 48, 54, 58
anti-war movement, 12, 20–30, 282n1; Berkeley bombing of police headquarters, 27–28; and Bertram, 115; "Bring the War Home" call, 120; and Chicago 7 conspiracy case, 25–26, 283–84nn18,23; "counter-convention" in Chicago, 1968, 23–25, 283nn11,14; and The Day After (TDA) demonstrations, 26–27, 27, 284n25; and Dunbar-Ortiz, 151; and "festival of life," 24; "From Protest to Resistance," 21; and GJB, 202–3; grand jury investigation of, 184–85; at Kent State University, 35; Mead's response to, 54–55; and Melville, 130; Moratorium to End the War in Vietnam Day, 26, 55; and participatory democracy, 4, 30, 62; and prison reform, 30–32, 62, 111; rallies for, 12, 20–26, 282n1; response to Nixon's announcement of Cambodian bombing raids, 32, 35; and Saxe, 301n13; at University of Washington, 105; and Women Out Now (WON) programs, 111; and Yoshimura, 141
*Anvil, The* (UPU), 75
Aquarian Foundation, 187–88
Arendt, Hannah, 285n4
Argentine People's Revolutionary Army (ERP), 207
armed struggle. *See* firearms/armed struggle; self-defense, armed
Armsbury, Charles "Chuck," 56–59, 63
Armstrong, Karl, 25

Armstrong, Louis "Satchmo," 99
Army Math Research Center (Madison, Wis.) bombing, 36, 128
arson attacks, 9, 15, 24, 35, 42–43, 144
Asian Americans, 4, 103, 143
Associated Press, 236, 242, 252
Atteberry, Danny, 83–84
Attica Correctional Facility (N.Y.) uprising, 62, 69, 79, 99, 112–13, 127–30, 173, 203, 290n29, 291–92nn17,29,31; *Attica* (documentary), 114, 294n5; Attica Brothers Legal Defense (ABLD), 79, 113, 291–92n31; Attica Day demonstrations, 79, 127–28
Atwood, Margaret, 257, 310n2
*Autobiography of Malcolm X*, 23
*Autobiography of Mother Jones*, 269
Automotive Machinists Union, 243–46, 265, 270–71
Avakian, Bob, 151–53
*Awakened China* (Greene), 48
Ayers, Bill, 77, 130, 287n26

Baader, Andreas, 246–48
Bacon, Leslie, 185
Bailey, Christopher, 221
Bakunin, Mikhail, 61
bank robberies: Brighton (Mass.) bank robbery, 32–33, 286n10; by campus radicals, 67; by LaRue, 210; Old National Bank robbery, 242; in Oregon, 226, 228–31, 237, 251, 307n1; Park's views on, 204; People's National Bank robbery, 242–43; Puget Sound National Bank, 261, 270; Rainier National Bank robberies, 239–40; by SLA, 74; in Tacoma, 256, 260–61, 267, 270, 273; Tukwila bank robbery, 2–3, 156, 165–74, 176, 179–80, 212–13, 215–16, 221–23, 237, 300nn3,4, 301n13; Union Bank in Tacoma robbery, 270
*Bartholomew Fair* (Jonson), 282n29
Basher, Philip T., 145
BBC Dodge car dealership bombing, 244–45
Beahler, Chris, 116–17
Beal, Mary F., 121–22, 297n4
Beaufort (N.C.) County Jail, 127
Beauvoir, Simone de, 115
Bedford Hills (Westchester, N.Y.) women's prison uprising, 128–29
Beeks, William T., 95
Bellevue (Wash.): Bellevue Sniper, 69–70, 84; car dealership bombings in, 243, 247; KZAM radio station in, 161, 180, 236, 247; New Year's

Eve bombing in, 161–62; Police Department, 235–36, 246–47; Rainier National Bank bombings in, 235–37
"belly of the beast," 18, 282n29
Bergman, Arlene Eisen, 111
Bergman, Liebel, 151
Berkeley (Calif.), 34, 119–20; bombing of police headquarters, 27–28; The Day After (TDA) demonstrations in, 26–27, 56. *See also* University of California at Berkeley
*Berkeley Barb*, 33, 37, 139
*Berkeley Tribe*, 139
Bertram, Janine, 114–18, 239; alias of, 258, 268, 274; arrest of, 274; and bank robberies, 256, 260–61, 273; and bombings, 235–36; and COYOTE, 111, 114, 117–18, 219; diary of, 254–63, 266–72, 310nn2,3; and fishing, 232, 269; flight from Seattle, 251–53; and International Women's Day communiqué, 178–79; and kidnappings (proposed), 249–50; and meditation, 257, 263, 269; in Oregon, 224–25, 227–31; plea bargain of, 277; reading of, 257, 268–69, 310n2; release from prison, 276–77; and Sherman's jailbreak, 177–78; in Tacoma, 255–63, 266, 268–73
Bever, Lloyd W., 212–13
Bicentennial, U.S., 158, 160
biker bars/bikers, 125, 151
Bingham, Charles W., 249
bin Miriam, Faygele, 158
Birmingham (Ala.) riots, 15
bisexuals, 3, 44, 74, 76, 115, 119, 150
Black Cultural Association, 58–59
Black Guerrilla Family, 37
"Black Intelligence Test of Cultural Homogeneity" (Williams), 103
Black Liberation Army (BLA), 31, 37, 128–29, 159, 185, 285n2
*Black Panther*, 33
Black Panther Party for Self-Defense, 22–23, 37, 283n9; community service work of, 56; declaration of war, 22–23; in Eugene (Ore.), 56; and GJB, 170, 176; issue of "armed struggle" in, 22–23, 31; "lumpen" ideology of, 31, 68, 285nn2,4; and National Guard Armory (Fairbanks, Alaska) robbery, 51; prison chapters of, 112, *113*, 155; and prison reform, 31, 85, 284–85nn1–3; and Revolutionary Union (RU), 152; and Shakur, 129; "Ten Point Program" of, 56
Black Power movement, 3, 11, 30

Blackstone Rangers (black youth gang), 21
Blakely, Anna. *See* Brown, Rita D.
*Blood in My Eye* (Jackson), 121, 123–24, 199, 268, 292n32
Boldt, George, 56, 60, 289n19
bombings, 27; Army Math Research Center (Madison, Wis.), 36, 128; of Berkeley police headquarters, 27–28; bombs through mail, 36; and bomb threats, 143–44, 146, 155, 167, 182; of Capitol Building, U.S., 62; of car dealerships, 243–48, 271; of City Light public utility, 159–64, 196–97, 216–17, 238; and construction worker demonstrations, 83; of Convoy Company, 265; of Division of Corrections (Olympia), 1–2, 62, 85–87, 135, 138, 145, 147–49, 210, 295n1; of Everett BIA offices, 138, 145, 211; by GJB, 1–3, 25, 38, 86–87, 138–39, 141–43, 145–49, 153–55, 157–64, 170, 194, 196–97, 203–4, 211, 216–17, 235–41, 243–48, 263–66, 287n25, 297n3; by New World Liberation Front (NWLF), 36–37, 76, 139–40; on New Year's Eve, 158, 160–65, 194, 196; by New Year's Gang, 25, 36; of New York commissioner of corrections office, 62; of Pacific Northwest Ball Building (Seattle), 144; by People's Forces Unit IX (NWLF), 139–41; of Puget Sound Power and Light Company, 240–41, 263–65; of Rainier National Banks, 235–39; response to Nixon's announcement of Cambodian bombing raids, 35–36; of ROTC buildings, 66, 144; of Safeway, 140–43, 145–47, 149, 158–62, 188, 197, 203, 296nn18,19,24, 297n3–98n3, 299n9; Seattle Federal Building (attempted), 139–40; second wave of, 36–38; of Tacoma FBI offices, 138, 145, 211; as terrorism, 202–3; by Weatherman/Weather Underground, 35–36, 62; by white supremacists, 5, 54
Bond, Stanley, 32
*Bonnie and Clyde* (film), 257
Bourasa, Jim, 263, 265
Bowers, Sam, 54, 59
Brandeis University, 33
Brazilian Communist Party, 34
*Bremerton Sun*, 254
Brenda's Autoshop, 224, 227, 310–11n4
Brezhnev, Leonid, 24
Brighton (Mass.) bank robbery, 32–33, 286n10
Brinks truck (Nyack, N.Y.) attempted robbery, 128

Brown, Frank (father), 91–92, 96, 102, 121
Brown, Ina (mother), 91–92, 121
Brown, Kenny (brother), 92
Brown, Rita D., 91–114, *106*, *107*, 117–31; alias of, 225; arrest of, 250–55, 259–61, 269–70, 310–11n4; at Attica Day demonstration, 127–28; and bank robberies, 167, 169, 226, 228–31, 239, 242–43, 251, 307n1; Bertram's diary addressed to, 254–63, 266–72; and bombings, 157–58, 161–62, 238–40, 247; in Buffalo (N.Y.), 127–28; as butch, 93, 96–97; childhood of, 91–92, 120–21; and Cook, 112; and COYOTE, 118; dogs of, 102, 124, 232, 250–52; in drag, 226, 231, 239, 242, 309n1; as drug dealer, 94, 103, 118; education of, 92, 102–3; employment of, 92–95, 99–100, 102, 124; and feminism, 121–23; and firearms/armed struggle, 149, 226–27, 231, 242–43, 250; and fishing, 232, 269; "Free Rita Brown!" campaign, 259; as "The Gentleman Bank Robber," 307n1; at Holly Near concert, 171; and International Women's Day communiqué, 178–79; Jackson's influence on, 98–99, 123–24; and kidnappings (proposed), 249–50; in Klamath Falls, 91–92, 120–21; as lesbian, 91–97, 101–3, 105, 114, 118, 225–27, 229, 253; and meditation, 97, 257; in New York City, 128–31; in Oregon, 224–31, 259; parole of, 95, 99, 101; petty crimes of, 93, 95; as prisoner, 95–101, 104, 148, 254–69, 272, 276–77; queer family of, 94, 126; reading of, 121–23, 148; recruitment for GJB, 147–50, 297n1; release from prison, 276–77; response to Safeway bombing, 147, 149; and Revolutionary Union (RU), 154; and Sherman's jailbreak, 174–78; and SLA, 119–20, 124; and Smith, Frank "Big Black," 113–14, 294n5; state liquor store robbery of, 155; trial of, 259, 267–70; vacations of, 124–26, 228; and Women Out Now (WON), 105–6, 108–12, 114, 117, 124, 224
Bryan, John, 120
Buffalo (N.Y.), 79, 113, 127–28, 291–92nn29,31
Bunke Bider, Hayde Tamara. *See* "Tania"
Bureau of Alcohol, Tobacco and Firearms, U.S. (ATF), 2, 160, 162, 188–89, 194, 198
Bureau of Indian Affairs, U.S. (BIA), 78, 136–38, 145, 203, 211
Bureau of Prisons, U.S., 55, 111
Burgess, Tim, 187
butch, 93, 96–97. *See also* lesbians

Cabral, Amílcar, 208
California Bureau of Prisons, 96–97
California Department of Corrections, 31, 62, 286n12
California Highway Patrol (CHP), 28, 33–34, 119, 160
California Institution for Women, 125
California Senate Internal Security Subcommittee, 160
Calvert, Greg, 14
Camus, Albert, 29, 284n33
capitalism, 3, 12; and Brown/Coupez, 124–25; capitalist-owned press, 135, 235–36, 238; and GJB, 147, 149, 203–4, 237, 263–65, 268; and homosexuality, 154; and Left Bank Collective, 203; and Mead, 43–44, 65, 67, 223; and Seidel, 147, 149; and Shakur, 159; and Sherman, 153–54; and unemployment, 68, 72, 264; in West Germany, 248
Capitol Building, U.S., bombing, 62, 185
Capitol Complex Building (Wash. State) bombing, 1–2
Captain Jack (Kintapuasch), 91, 98, 120
Carlson, Duane I., 67
Carson, Clayborne, 12
Carter, Brenda, 188–89, 191–92
Castle, Del, 164
Castro, Fidel, 10, 19, 34
Catholic Church, 4
Central Intelligence Agency (CIA), 249, 286n14
El Centro de la Raza (Seattle, Wash.), 80, 85, 112
Chan, Warren, 213, 220
chauvinism, male, 121–22, 150–51, 297n4. *See also* sexism
Checker, Chubby, 103
Cheney, James, 54
Chesler, Phyllis, 122
Chicago 7 conspiracy case, 25–27, 283–84nn18,23; and The Day After (TDA) demonstrations, 26–27, *27*, 56, 284n25; and "Days of Rage," 26, 55–56
Chicago Police Department, 23–25, 283nn11,12,16
Chicano Liberation Front, 37, 185
Chicanos, 4, 15, 21, 37, 80, 143, 185, 205–6, 302n13
Chile coup, 137, 206–7
Chillicothe (Ohio) federal reformatory, 46, 48
China: Chinese People's Liberation Army, 75, 206; "Little Red Book," 63; revolution in, 11, 13, 34, 63, 151, 206; Williams relocating to, 16

Chinese Americans, 15
Churchill, Ward, 137–38
Cinque. *See* DeFreeze, Donald "Cinque"
City Light public utility (Seattle): bombing of, 159–64, 196–97, 238; and Mead's trials, 216–17; strike at, 153–54, 157, 159, 163–64; women at, 158, 164
Civil Rights Act (1968), 25
civil rights movement, 3–5, 10–13, 21–22, 30, 54, 62; and American Indian Movement (AIM), 135–36; and Bertram, 114–15; and Brown, 98; in Monroe (N.C.), 9–11, 22; and prison reform, 30, 32; in Seattle (Wash.), 105, 293n2
Clapton, Eric, 284n34
Clark, Judy, 128
Cleaver, Eldridge, 23, 31, 121, 151–52, 283n9
*Close Encounters* (film), 257
Coller, Jack, 137–38
Coltrane, John, 99
Columbia University building occupations, 21
Committee to End Grand Jury Abuse, 184, 188–90, 196
communists, 3, 13, 17, 25, 64, 115, 285n3; Armsbury as, 58; and homosexuality, 154; Jackson as, 98; Left's views of, 201, 203, 206, 208; Lippman as, 58; Marighella as, 34; Mead as, 45, 48, 58, 64–65, 74, 78, 80, 201, 216, 221; and *Prairie Fire,* 77–78; and Revolutionary Union (RU), 150–53, 298n13; Sherman as, 150–53; Workman as, 55
Comprehensive Employment and Training Act, U.S. (1973), 117–18
Congress, U.S., 20, 60, 181, 294n6
Congress of Racial Equality (CORE), 54
Connery, Ray O., 243
Constitution, U.S., 11; Eighth Amendment, 57; Fifth Amendment, 184, 219; First Amendment, 203; Ninth Amendment, 57
construction worker demonstrations, 82–83, 148–49
CONvention, 112–14, 118, 148, 155
Convoy Company bombing, 265
Cook, Mark, 112, *113,* 114, 118, 293n2(ch10), 293–94n3(ch11); and GJB, 155, 161–62, 165–69, 174–77, 230, 300n4, 303n24; as prisoner, 112, 162, 165, 176, 230, 259–60, 264, 277, 293–94n3; release from prison, 277; and Sherman's jailbreak, 174–77, 250, 301nn7,8,14; trial of, 218
*C. O. P. Newsletter,* 283n16

Corbett, T. Patrick, 82
Corddry, Tom, 161
corporations, 12, 33, 35, 61, 159, 203, 235, 286n12. *See also names of corporations*
"Correctional Congress" (ACA), 72–73, 82
correctional officers: at Bedford Hills (Westchester, N.Y.) women's prison uprising, 128–29; killing of, 31–32, 98, 127; at King County Jail (Seattle), 219–21; at Raleigh (N.C.) Correctional Center for Women (CCW), 127–28; at Terminal Island penitentiary (San Pedro, Calif.), 96–100; at Washington State Penitentiary (Walla Walla), 112–13, 233–36
Coupez, Nancy (mother), 104, 228–29, 268
Coupez, Therese, 239; aliases of, 225, 255; arrest of, 274; at Attica Day demonstration, 127–28; childhood/education of, 104–5; in drag, 273; flight from Seattle, 251–52; at Holly Near concert, 171; as lesbian, 105, 118; in New York City, 128–31; in Oregon, 224–30; reading of, 123–24; release from prison, 276–77; response to Safeway bombing, 147; and Sherman, 178, 224–26, 230, 249, 260, 297n1; and Smith, Frank "Big Black," 113–14, 294n5; in Tacoma, 255–56, 258–60, 262–63, 265–66, 268–69, 273; trial of, 277; vacations of, 125–26, 230; and Women Out Now (WON), 105–6, 108–12, 117, 124
Coupez, Victor (father), 104, 228, 274
COYOTE (Call Off Your Old Tired Ethics), 111, 114, 117–18, 229
Creech, Papa John, 99
criminal justice system, 1; and Chicago 7 conspiracy case, 25–26, 55–56, 283–84n23; and class action suits, 57, 61, 64; and construction worker demonstrations, 82–83; and contempt charges, 26–27, 56, 183, 195, 284n25; and death penalty, 98; and fingerprints, 140, 182, 191–92, 194–96, 198, 236; and grand jury investigations, 50, 182–86, 188–92, 194–97, 201, 204–5, 228–29, 302n13, 303nn23,24; and insanity defense, 218–19, 221–22; and jailhouse lawyers, 44, 48–50, 52–58, 60–62, 64, 74, 219, 221–22, 288n1; motions of prejudice, 213–14, 218; and precedent, 49, 53, 61; and prison reform, 30–31, 69; and search warrants, 137, 187–88, 194–95; and Seattle Seven, 56, *57,* 60; and subpoenas, 182–86, 189–92, 194–95, 204–5, 214, 221, 252; and use immunity, 184
Croatian independence, partisan of, 37

Crooks, Carol, 128–29
*Crusader, The*, 16–17, *17*, 281–82nn26,27
Cuba: Cuban revolution, 5, 11, 13, 17–19, 34, 206; exile in, 10–11, 121; and Venceremos Brigade, 188–89
Czeisler, Robert, 218

Daley, Richard J., 23, 25, 283n14
Davis, Angela, 286n11
Davis, Miles, 99
Day, Dolores, 84
DeAntonio, Emile, 185
"Dear Sisters in the Weather Underground" (Alpert), 130
*Death Ship, The* (Traven), 257
Debray, Régis, 18–19, 282n33
DeFreeze, Donald "Cinque," 33–34, 119–20, 286n14
Dellinger, Dave, 20–22
democracy, 16, 20; participatory democracy, 4, 30, 62, 68, 70
Democratic National Convention (Chicago, 1968), 23–25, 150–51, 283nn13,14,16
Desmond, Jerry F., 290n27
Detroit (Mich.) riots, 16–17
Deutscher, Isaac, 63
Dever, Paul, 235
DeVere, Merlin L., 95
*Dialectic of Sex, The* (Firestone), 115
Dillinger (dog), 232, 250–52
direct actions, 4, 21, 59, 61, 138, 304n46
discrimination, institutionalized, 114, 117–18, 158, 235
Doherty, Ed, 60
*Doherty v. United States*, 60, 288n1
Dohrn, Bernardine, 77, 286n11, 287n22
Donovan, Robert J., 25
Douglas, William O., 53
Dowd, Jeff, 56
*Dragon* (Bay Area Radical Collective), 139, 166, 180–81, 197, 221
drug dealers, 37, 94, 103, 118
Dunaway, Mike, 220
Dunbar-Ortiz, Roxanne, 15, 151–52
dune buggy races, 125–26
Durham (N.C.) Action for Forgotten Women, 127–28, 293n1
Durruti, Buenaventura, 61
dykes, 92–93, 96–97, 100, 103, 114, 128, 258. *See also* lesbians
Dylan, Bob, 293n9

Eddie, 82–83, 154–55
Edwards, Harry, 84
Ehrlichman, John, 185
Elbrick, C. Burke, 286–87n18
Ellenbogen, Helene, 194–95, 221
Emiliano Zapata Unit, 36–37, 287n24, 296n24
Ensslin, Gundrun, 246–48
Eve, Arthur O., 291–92n31
Everett (Wash.): BIA office bombing, 138, 145, 211; Everett Community College, 143; Snohomish County Courthouse bomb threat, 143
ex-convicts: at Brighton (Mass.) bank robbery, 32–33, 286n10; Brown as, 101, 103–5, 110; Cook as, 112; DeFreeze as, 286n14; Gilday as, 32, 286n10; in GJB, 181; Mead as, 2, 34, 47–50, 72, 74; "Nick the Greek" as, 104; "Prisoners' Coalition" at SCCC, 103–4; radicals' collaboration with, 30–37, 285nn2–4, 286nn10,14; Seidel as, 2; Sherman as, 2–3, 64, 72, 152–53; Sing Louie as, 74; voting rights for, 118

Fanon, Franz, 207–8, 285n4
fascism, 25, 33, 76, 82, 124, 147, 151, 200, 207, 248, 286n13
Federal Bureau of Investigation (FBI): and Alpert, 130; arrest of Brown, 250–54; and bank robberies, 242–43; and bombings/bomb threats, 2, 138, 144–46, 162, 185, 203, 211, 239–40, 245, 265–66; and Chicago 7 conspiracy case, 283–84n23; creation of bomb plots by, 144; and GJB, 3, 176, 180–81, 185, 188, 190–92, 201, 228, 237, 239, 242–43, 250–52, 266–68, 273–75, 303n24, 310–11n4; and grand jury investigations, 185, 188, 190–92, 303nn23,24; Hoover as director of, 36, 287n21; killing of agents, 138, 302n13; and Mead, 47, 51–52; raids by, 188, 190, 303n24; and Revolutionary Union (RU), 151; and Saxe, 301n13; and Swinton trial, 130–31, 295n6; and Symbionese Liberation Army (SLA), 33–34, 119; in Tacoma, 256; "Ten Most Wanted" list, 33, 124, 286n11, 302n13; at Terminal Island penitentiary (San Pedro, Calif.), 100; wiretaps of, 227; and Workman, 55; at Wounded Knee siege, 136–38, 183, 302n13; and Wright, 230
*Federal Reporter*, 49, 53
*Feminine Mystique, The* (Friedan), 115
feminism/feminists, 33, 103, 105, 111, 115, 122–

23, 125, 130–31, 150–51; Feminist Karate Union, 110–11
Ferguson, Adele, 254
Ferris wheel bomb threat (Puyallup), 143
firearms/armed struggle, 10, 16; and Armsbury, 56; and Brown, 149, 226–27, 231, 242–43, 250; and GJB, 154–55, 164, 166–69, 172, 186–88, 202–5, 209, 216–17, 232, 237, 254, 260, 267, 273, 300n4; hollow-point bullets used by police, 81, 172; and Jackson, Wilbur "Popeye," 75; and Left Bank Collective, 139, 194–97, 203–8; and Mead, 41–44, 50–52, 64, 81, 83, 139, 154–55, 164, 166–69, 200–204, 212, 216–17, 219, 222; and Peltier, 79; and *Prairie Fire*, 76–78, 121, 123, 125, 139, 196–97; and Revolutionary Union (RU), 151–53; and Symbionese Liberation Army (SLA), 74; at Wounded Knee siege, 137–38. *See also* self-defense, armed
firebombs, 36, 54, 66, 83, 144, 243, 245, 247
Firestone, Cinda, 114
Firestone, Shulamith, 115
First National Bank Building (Seattle) protest, 79
Fish and Game Department, U.S., 47–48, 50
Florence (Ariz.) Detention Center, U.S., 50
Foley, Tom, 60
Folsom prison strike, 75, 291n17
Fonda, Jane, 59–60
Ford, Gerald, 79, 222
Ford, Ralph Patrick "Po, 25, 139–43, 145, 188–90, 204, 296n18
Fort Lawton seizures, 136
Foster, Marcus, 33, 212, 286n13
Franklin, Bruce and Jane, 151–53
Fraunces Tavern (New York City) bombing, 37
Freedom Riders, 9
Friedan, Betty, 115
Fuerzas Armadas de Liberación Nacional (FALN), 37, 185

Garry, Charles, 286n13
Gates, Daryl, 15
*Gauntlet, The* (film), 257
gay bars, 93–94, 102, 108, 293n6
gay liberation movement, 74, 116–17
gays, 74, 76, 93–94, 102, 116–18, 126, 227; as dumpster-divers, 158; in GJB, 3–4, 150, 201; grand jury investigations of, 185, 302n13; reeducation camps for, 154; and Revolutionary Union (RU), 154, 298nn13,14. *See also* bisexuals; lesbians

George Jackson Brigade (GJB): arrogance of, 204–5; bank robberies, 156, 165–71, 173–74, 204, 212, 216, 221–23, 226, 228, 239, 242–43, 250–51, 256, 260, 267, 270; bombings, 1–3, 25, 38, 86–87, 138–39, 141–43, 145–49, 153–55, 157–64, 170, 189, 194, 196–97, 203–4, 211, 216–17, 235–41, 243–48, 263–66, 287n25, 297n3; Bust the Union Busters communiqué, 265; ceasing to exist, 272, 274–77, 311–12n4; false IDs, 149–50, 166, 226, 235; flight from Seattle, 252–54; grand jury investigation of, 50, 182–86, 188–92, 194–97, 201, 204–5, 303nn23,24; ideology of, 3–5, 202; International Women's Day communiqué, 178–81, 188–89, 191–92, 201, 211–13, 264, 300n4, 301nn13,14, 303–4nn23,32; and kidnappings (proposed), 248–50, 253–54; and Left Bank Collective, 138–39, 143, 145, 180, 202–6, 238; Left's views of, 200–209, 305nn2,10; "Mayday Communiqué," 236–38, 308n13; and Mead's trials, 211, 213–15, 222–23; membership of, 2–4, 201; "Open Letter to Bo (Rita D. Brown), An," 253; in Oregon, 224–30; and police raids, 186–89, 302n19; and prison conflicts, 1–2, 85–87, 210, 235–37, 240; recruitment for, 147–50, 153–56, 225, 227–29, 297n1; and Sherman's jailbreak, 173–80, 182–83, 197, 201, 210, 213, 300n5, 301nn7,8; state liquor store robberies, 155–56, 239; in Tacoma, 252–75, 311–12n4; and Valerian Coven document, 270–71; women in, 4, 148–50, 154, 158, 166, 178–81, 191–92, 196, 201, 211, 239, 266 (*see also* Bertram, Janine; Brown, Rita D.; Coupez, Therese); "You Can Kill a Revolutionary, . . . " communiqué, 247–48. *See also* Mead, Ed
ghettos, 12, 15–16, 21, 114
Gilday, William, 32, 286n10
Gitlin, Todd, 3
Glide Memorial Church (Tenderloin, San Francisco), 75
Goff, Lawrence and Betty Sue, 151
Goins, Wanda, 84
Goodfellow, Pat, 243
Goodman, Andrew, 54
Goodwin, Guy F., 185
Gordon, Dexter, 99
Gorgons, The, 124
Gorman, Donald J. Jr., 172

grand jury investigations, 50, 182–86, 188–92, 194–97, 201, 302n13, 303nn23,24; and anti-grand jury demonstrations, 192, *193*; and Coupez, 228–29, 274; Left's views of, 204–5; in Oregon, 228–30, 239
Great Depression, 121
Great Northwestern Federal Savings & Loan robbery, 267
Green, Joseph Franklin, 85
Greene, Felix, 48
Gresham (Wis.) clinic occupation, 81–82
Grief, Tom, 115
"Guardians of the Oglala Nation" (GOONs), 136–37
*Les Guérillères*, 122–23
guerrillas: Baraldini as, 128; "Guatemalan guerrilla" approach, 14; guerrilla warfare, 14–18, 28, 67, 76, 148, 194, 206–7, 281–82n27; Guevara as, 17–18, 21, 35, 66, 74, 119, 282n33; in Quebec, 281n19; and Third World revolution, 14, 17–19, 206; urban guerrillas, 2, 15, 34–35, 139, 155, 161, 166, 175, 181, 185, 194, 229, 232, 236, 248; and urban riots, 15–17, *17*
*Guerrilla Warfare* (Guevara), 35
Guevara, Ernesto "Che," 17–18, 21, 35, 282n33; execution of in Boliva, 18, 66, 74, 119
Guinea Bissau, 208

Haber, Al, 13
Haggerty, Patrick, 117, 158
Haig, Alexander, 137
Haldeman, Bob, 249
Hall, Camilla, 119–20, 294n4
Hanson, Robert, 81, 142, 160, 181, 190–91
Harp, Carl, 69–70, 84
Harris, Bill and Emily, 124, 141, 295n15
Harris, Jerva, 142
Harvey, James, 234–35
Hastings, Sandra, 176, 303n24
Hayden, Tom, 5, 13, 25, 281n21, 283n13
Hearst, Patricia, 33–34, 73–74, 119, 124, 141, 144–46, 218, 290–91n12, 295n15, 299n8
Hearst, Randolph A., 33, 73, 119, 286n17, 290–91n12
Hearst Corporation, 33, 119, 123
Henderson, Paul, 234
Herbert, Joe, 173
heroin, 49, 83, 94, 96, 99, 101–2, 118, 176
Heydrich, Reinhard, 246
Hibernia Bank robbery, 74

hijacked planes, 36, 246–47
Hilltop Community Center (Tacoma), 114
Himmelman, Lynn P., 249
hippies, 13, 22, 24, 50, 66, 115, 284n32
Ho Chi Minh, 31, 69, 198–99
Hoffman, Abbie, 26
Hoffman, Julius, 26
homophobia, 106, 117, 277
homosexuals, 74, 76, 97, 154, 297n4, 298nn13,14. *See also* bisexuals; gays; lesbians
Hoover, J. Edgar, 36, 287n21
Horne, Gerald, 15
Horowitz, Donald, 190
Horswill, Erle W., 214
hostage-taking: by Atteberry, 83–84; at Attica uprising, 62, 112; at bank robberies, 166; at campus demonstrations, 21; by Jackson, Jonathan, 121; in prison, 62, 84, 112, 210; at Washington State Penitentiary (Walla Walla), 84
Hot Tuna (rock band), 99
Hubenet, Kathy, 189, 194
Hutton, "Li'l Bobby," 23

*Iconoclast, The* (underground paper), 114
imperialism, British, 115–16
imperialism, U.S., 18, 34, 148, 153, 202, 222; and *Prairie Fire*, 76–78
indigenous rights, 60, 136–38, 154, 289n19
International Brotherhood of Electrical Workers (Local 77, Seattle), 157, 163–64
Irwin, John, 68
"I Shot the Sheriff" (song), 29, 284n34
"It Could Have Been Me" (song), 171

Jackson, George, 1, 31–32, 62, 75, 80, 86, 188; *Blood in My Eye*, 121, 123–24, 199, 268, 292n32; death of, 62, 99, 148, 248, 293n9; and prison reform, 31–32, 62; *Soledad Brother*, 98, 148, 292n32. *See also* George Jackson Brigade (GJB)
Jackson, Jonathan (brother), 121
Jackson, Wilbur "Popeye," 75
Jackson State College killings, 35
jailbreaks. *See* prison escapes
jailhouse lawyers, 44, 48–50, 52–58, 60–62, 64, 74, 219, 221–22, 288n1
James, Jennifer, 117
jazz, 98–99, 103
Jefferson Airplane, 69
Joan Little Defense Committee (N.C.), 127

johns. *See* pimps
Johnson, Jerome, 283n11
Johnson, Lyndon B., 24
Johnson, Virgil, 174–75, 180, 226, 250
Jones, Jeff, 77, 130
Jonson, Ben, 282n29
Joplin, Janice, 93
al-Jundi, Akil, 127
"jury tax," 49
Justice Department, U.S., 26, 181, 185–86; Internal Security Division (ISD), 185, 202–3

karate classes, 24, 110–11, 129
Kelleher, Dan, 116–17, 219
Kelley, Clarence, 181
Kelly, Joseph, 56
Kennedy, John F., 5, 13, 206
Kennedy, Robert, 206
Kent State University killings, 35, 66
Kerner Commission, 281n22
Keyport Naval Torpedo Station (Bangor, Maine), 304n46
kidnappings, 33–34, 36, 73–74, 246, 248–50, 253–54, 299n8, 309n14
Kikpatrick, Dan, 216
Killien, Phillip Y., 213, 215–17
Killsright, Joe Stuntz, 138
King, Martin Luther Jr., 10, 105, 181, 269–70; assassination of, 22–24, 105, 115, 206
King County Jail: Bertram at, 274; Cook at, 230; Coupez at, 274; and GJB, 263–64; Mead at, 62–63, 81, 210–13, 219–21, 306n6; Sherman at, 173–75, 274; Whitnack at, 197–98
*King County Jail Times*, 63
KING TV (Seattle), 141
Kintapuasch. *See* Captain Jack
Kirkpatrick, Eileen, 209
Klamath Falls (Ore.), 91–92, 120–21
Kleindienst, Richard, 25
KOMO TV, 243, 245, 263
Kray, Jill, 73, 76, 85, 182–83, 186, 189
Kropotkin, Pyotr, 61
Ku Klux Klan, 10, 54, 59
KZAM radio station, 161, 180, 236, 247

Lacquer, Walter, 305n2
LaGuardia Airport explosion, 37, 160–61
Lampson, Mary, 185
Landon, Bob, 254
LaRue, Mark, 84, 210, 306n6
Lavender Country, 117, 179

law enforcement. *See* police
Leary, Timothy, 62, 288n1
Leavenworth (Kan.) penitentiary, U.S., 46, 49, 61–63
Left Bank Collective (Seattle, Wash.), 76, 79, 85, 138–40, 189–91, 296n13, 311n2; and firearms/armed struggle, 139, 194–97, 203–8, 304nn40,41; at Mead's trials, 221; views on GJB, 138–39, 143, 145, 180, 202–6, 238
Lenin/Leninists, 34, 56, 77, 152, 204, 219
Lerner, Michael, 56
lesbians, 91–97, 99, 101–3, 105–6, 108, 111, 114–18, 124–25, 225; at Amazon Women's Music Festival (Santa Cruz), 125; at Attica Day demonstration, 127–28; in GJB, 181; Leftist Lezzies, 108, 198; in New York City, 128; and Revolutionary Union (RU), 154; Saxe as, 301n13; in SLA, 119–20
"Letter from a Birmingham Jail" (King), 105
Lewis, William, 172
liberalism, 5, 12–13, 271
*Liberation* magazine, 11, 20
Lien, Janice, 240
*Life* magazine, 15
Lincoln, Abbey, 99
Lincoln Park (Chicago, Ill.), 24
Lindberg, William J., 184
Lippman, Peter, 182–83, 192
Lippman, Roger, 55–56, 58, 63, 67–69, 76, 85, 289n11; and "Black Duck Motors," 67; and GJB, 154, 182
Little, Joanne (Joan), 127, 261
Little Richard, 103
Lompoc Federal Correctional Institution (FCI Lompoc, Calif.), 46, 48–49
Long, Huey P., 151
Longshoreman's Local 52, 164
looting, 15–16, 24, 26
Los Angeles County Sheriff's Department, 33–34, 54, 119
*Los Angeles Examiner*, 44
*Los Angeles Free Press*, 33
Los Angeles International Airport, 97
Los Angeles Police Department (LAPD), 15, 33–34, 119–20
*Los Angeles Times*, 25
"lumpen proletariat," 21, 31, 68, 285nn2,4
lynchings, 10, 34

Mair, Peter, 183, 190
Malcolm X, 5, 10, 23, 31, 269–70, 281n22, 285n3

Manson, Charles, 179
Mao/Maoism, 34, 63, 75, 151, 206, 216, 253
Marighella, Carlos, 34–35, 73, 76, 208, 286–87n18
marijuana, 50, 62, 69, 73, 94, 102, 118, 150, 249–50
Marin County Courthouse hostage crisis, 121
Marion County Jail (Salem, Ore.), 264
Marley, Bob, 29, 284n34
Marshall, "Chip," 56
Marshals' Special Operations Group, U.S., 136–38, 198
Martha and the Vandellas, 103
Martí, José, 18, 282n29
martial law, 16, 28, 32, 281n19
Marx, Karl, 31, 56, 68
Marxism, 31, 34, 58, 68, 105, 116, 123, 152, 217, 219, 285nn2,4
Mathers, Helen M., 142
Mathews, Joseph L., 168, 172–73, 180, 212–17, 300n3
Mathis, Ray, 252, 274
Mauney, A. A., 10
Maxwell, Roger, 71
Maynes, Jo, 304n46
McDonald, Larry, 181
McNamara, Edmond, 33
McNeil Island (Puget Sound) penitentiary, U.S., 49–50, 53–64, 74, 288n1; "genocide complaint" in, 57–59, 63–64; and GJB, 150, 165; Men's Advisory Council (MAC), 58; and Steilacoom Prisoner Support House, 64, 67; strike in, 58–60, 69, 71
McNutt, Harlan, 234–36, 249, 254
Mead, Ed, 1–3; acknowledgment of GJB membership, 200–202, 210, 212–13, 216; as airplane inspector/mechanic, 46–49, 52, 67, 76; in Alaska, 41–42, 44–45, 47–52, 64–65; and American Indian Movement (AIM), 78–79, 291n29; arraignment of, 182; and "Bellevue Sniper," 69–70, 84; birth of, 41; as bisexual, 44, 74, 76, 150; blinded in left eye, 44, 148; and bombings, 1–2, 76, 85–87, 135, 138, 141–43, 145–46, 149, 153, 158, 161, 164, 295n1, 296nn18,19, 297n3; and Brown, 148–50; in Buffalo (N.Y.), 79, 291–92nn29,31; childhood of, 41–45, 221–22; as communist revolutionary, 45, 48, 58, 64–65, 74, 78, 80, 201, 216, 221; at construction worker demonstrations, 82, 148–49; denied right to argue before Supreme Court, 54; desire for retribution, 47, 61–62; education in prison of, 46–49; as ex-convict, 2, 34, 47–50, 72, 74; and firearms/armed struggle, 41–44, 50–52, 64, 81, 83, 139, 154–55, 164, 166–69, 200–204, 212, 216–17, 219, 222; and grand jury investigations, 192, 196, 198–99; interest in psychology, 46–47; and International Women's Day communiqué, 211–12; as jailhouse lawyer, 48–50, 52–58, 60–62, 64, 69, 74, 219, 221–22, 288n1; in juvenile detention, 41–43, 45; at Leavenworth (Kan.) penitentiary, U.S., 46, 49, 63; and New World Liberation Front (NWLF), 34, 75–76, 139, 230; parole of, 47–49, 83; petty crimes of, 42–44, 47–52, 64; as pimp, 49; political study of, 61–64, 67; and Prairie Fire Organizing Committee, 76, 85, 201; as prisoner, 41–50, 52–64, 76, 81, 150, 165, 192, 196, 198–200, 210–13, 219–23, 230, 233, 235, 238, 259–60, 264, 272, 276, 306n6; and prisoners' unions, 68–73; and prison strikes, 58–60, 62–63, 290n27; recruitment for GJB, 147–50, 153–56; release from prison, 277; response to Ford's death, 140–41; and robberies, 155–56, 165–69, 171–73, 212, 216–17, 221–23; in San Francisco Bay Area, 34, 73–76, 79, 86, 291n29; and Symbionese Liberation Army (SLA), 34, 73–74, 141–44, 201; trials of, 200, 212–19, 221–23; views on Revolutionary Union (RU), 150, 152–53; and Washington State Penitentiary (Walla Walla) conflicts, 83, 85, 218, 230; and Whitnack, 195. *See also* George Jackson Brigade (GJB)
Mead, Edward (father), 41–44
Mead, Mary Ann (sister), 42, 44, 47–48
Mead, Ramona (mother), 42–44, 73
Mead, Virginia (sister), 42, 44
*Mead v. Parker*, 61, 64, 290n30
Means, Russell, 136
Medford (Ore.), 227–29
media coverage: of anti-war rallies, 24–25, 283n14; of automotive machinists strike, 245–46; of bank robberies, 32, 173, 242; of "Bellevue Sniper," 69–70; of Berkeley demonstrations, 28; of bombings/bomb threats, 135, 140–45, 149, 163–64, 185, 202–3, 236–40, 263–65, 296n18, 297n3; of Brown's arrest, 250–54; of civil rights movement, 98; of construction workers demonstrations, 83; of GJB, 1–2, 138, 175, 178–81, 186, 188, 191–92, 200–209, 211–13, 230–31, 269, 273–74, 277, 307n1, 311n2;

of grand jury investigations, 186, 189, 198, 303–4nn23,32,34; and Hearst Corporation, 33, 119, 123; of jailhouse lawyers, 58; of Mead's trials, 200, 212–14, 218–19, 221–23; of National Guard Armory robbery, 51; in Oregon, 231, 307n1; of police raids, 188; of police use of hollow-point bullets, 81; of prison conflicts, 58, 60, 84, 99, 234–36, 238, 240; of prisoner's death at Terminal Island, 100; of prisoners' unions, 70–71; of Safeway bombings, 140–43, 149, 197, 296n18, 297n3; of Sherman's jailbreak, 175–76, 180; of SLA, 34, 76, 119–20; of Vietnam war, 20; on views of police, 202; of Wounded Knee siege, 137–38
Meinhof, Ulrike, 246–47
Melville, Sam, 130
Menominee Warrior Society (Gresham, Wis.), 81, 203
Meranto, Phil, 105
Mercado, Manuel, 282n29
Meyer, Lynn B., 144–45
Meyerson, Jack, 184, 188, 190, 218, 222
Mifflin, James W., 214–15, 217–18
military, U.S., 16–17; at anti-war rallies, 20; arson/bombing attacks against, 35; and Fort Lawton seizures, 136; insubordination in, 4, 21; and Shelter Half (Tacoma), 116, 294n6; at urban riots, 16–17; at Wounded Knee siege, 135, 137–38. *See also* Vietnam war
Miller, Gene, 84
Miller, Shelley, 128
Mills, C. Wright, 29, 235
*Mini-Manual of the Urban Guerrilla* (Marighella), 34–35, 76, 286–87n18
Minutemen, 67
missionaries, Protestant, 151
Mitchell, John, 284n25
Mitchell, Katie, 189, 191–92, 194
Mitchell, William, 141
Mitford, Jessica, 60, 72
Mitrione, Dan, 249, 309n14
Modie, Neil, 274
Möller, Irmgard, 246, 248
Monroe (N.C.), 9–11
Moore, Frank, 27
Moore, W. F., 160
Moratorium to End the War in Vietnam Day, 26, 55
Morgan, Robin, 130
Moriwaki, Lee, 203
"Mother Right" (Alpert), 131

Movement of the Revolutionary Left (M.I.R.), 207
Mtume, Cinque. *See* DeFreeze, Donald "Cinque"
Multnomah County sheriff, 54
Mussolini, 151

Narcotic Addict Rehabilitation Act (NARA) units, 97–98, 100
Nation, Shane, 141–42
National Association for the Advancement of Colored People (NAACP), 10–11, 282n33; Legal Defense Fund, 61
National Guard: at Democratic National Convention (Chicago, 1968), 24; in Gresham (Wis.), 81–82; at Kent State University, 35, 66; in Monroe (N.C.), 10; in Newark (N.J.) riots, 15; in Plainfield (N.J.) riots, 16, 281n21; at Raleigh (N.C.) Correctional Center for Women (CCW), 128; at University of California at Berkeley, 28
National Guard Armory robberies, 32, 51–52, 301n13
National Lawyers Guild (NLG), 63, 69, 79, 169, 183–84, 186; *Contempt*, 74
National Rifle Association, 10
National Strike Information Center (Brandeis Univ.), 33
Nation of Islam, 10, 31
Native Americans. *See* American Indians
Nault, Mike, 221
Nazis, 76, 138, 246–48
Near, Holly, 171
Newark (N.J.) riots, 15–16, 281n21
New Left, 12, 150, 235
Newton, Huey, 22–23, 31, 284–85n1
New World Liberation Front (NWLF), 34–37, 75–76, 139–40, 158, 185, 201, 230, 286–87n18, 296n15; People's Forces Unit IX, 139–41, 143, 145, 274, 296n13, 311n2; *The Urban Guerrilla (TUG)*, 76, 139
New Year's Eve bombings, 158, 160–65, 194, 196
New Year's Gang, The, 25, 36
New York City: Brown/Coupez in, 128–31; The Day After (TDA) demonstrations in, 26; LaGuardia Airport explosion, 37, 160–61; Stonewall riots, 74
New York Corrections Commissioner, 62, 291n17
*New York Times*, 14, 274, 311n2
Nick the Greek, 104, 108–9, 112

Nixon, Richard, 3, 25, 28, 185, 283n14; announcement of Cambodian bombing raids, 32, 35; impeachment of, 3; pardon of, 79, 222
nonviolence, 9, 21, 23, 117, 122, 304n46
Northern Regional Correction Institution (Fairbanks, Alaska), 52
*Northwest Passage*, 164, 200–209, 223, 228, 305n2
Nyerere, Julius, 115

Oakland (Calif.), 22–23, 37; killing of Superintendent of Schools, 33, 212, 286nn12,13; Police Department, 22–23, 33, 286n13; school policing proposal at, 33, 286n13
Oates, Joyce Carol, 310n2
O'Connor, Paul, 237
Oglesby, Carl, 12, 24, 283n13
Old National Bank robbery, 242
Olson, Jerald E., 95
Olson, William, 202–3
Olympia bombing. *See under* Washington State Department of Corrections
"On the Death of Bruce" (Mead and Sherman), 173, 300n3
*Open Road* (Vancouver paper), 197, 267
*Oregonian*, 231
Organized Crime Control Act (1970), 184
Otty, Shan, 111
"Our Losses are Heavy" communiqué, 275–76
*Outlaw Women* (Dunbar-Ortiz), 151
Owens, Phil, 83

Pacific Gas & Electric Company, 34, 158
Pacific Life Community, 304n46
Pacific National Bank of Washington robbery. *See* Tukwila bank robbery
*Pacific Reporter*, 49
pacifism, 11, 62, 122, 304n46
Park, Roxanne, 202–6, 208, 305n2
Parker, Jacob J., 57, 60–61, 64, 290n30
*Parker, Mead v.*, 61, 64, 290n30
Parker, Wayne, 194–95
patriarchy, 21, 115, 122–23, 150
Patriots Party (Eugene, Ore.), 56
Peltier, Leonard, 78–79, 82, 291n29
Pennington, William, 236
Pentagon, 20, 24, 137
People's Forces Unit IX (NWLF), 139–40, 145, 274, 296n13, 311n2
People's National Bank robbery, 242
Perón, Juan, 151

Perry, Nancy Ling, 120
Phil Smart Mercedes Benz and BMW car dealership bombing, 247–48
Piercy, Marge, 257
Pillon, Chuck, 194
pimps, 49, 117–18
Pine Ridge Indian Reservation (S.Dak.), 135–38, 183, 302n13
pipe bombs, 1–2, 25, 27, 37, 76, 85–87, 138, 140–41, 160, 162, 188, 198, 235–36, 240, 245, 247, 263, 296n18
Pitkin, Stan, 182–83, 185
Plainfield (N.J.), 16, 281n22
police, 1–2, 4; at anti-war rallies, 20–27, 27, 283nn11,12,16; assault on, 168, 172–73, 180, 212–18, 300n3; and Atteberry, 83–84; at bank robberies, 166–69, 171–73, 179–80, 212–17, 239, 300n3(ch17), 300n3(ch18); at Bedford Hills (Westchester, N.Y.) women's prison uprising, 128–29; Bellevue Police Department, 235–36, 246–47; Berkeley bombing of headquarters, 27–28; and Black Liberation Army (BLA), 37; at Brighton (Mass.) bank robbery, 32–33, 286n10; and Brown, 91–92, 108, 111, 126, 250–52, 254; burning of SLA Compton safe house, 33–34, 119–20, 124, 173; at campus demonstrations, 21, 28–29, 284n29; at car dealership bombings, 245–47; at construction worker demonstrations, 82; creation of bomb plots by, 144; at The Day After (TDA) demonstrations, 26–27, 27, 284n25; at "Days of Rage" riots, 26; at Democratic National Convention (Chicago, 1968), 23–25, 283nn11,12,16; and Division of Corrections (Olympia) bombing, 86; and gays, 94; in Gresham (Wis.), 81–82; killing of, 22–23, 32–33, 36–37, 78, 128, 204, 286n10; at King County Jail (Seattle), 221; Left's views of, 202, 204–6, 208; and Mead's trials, 212–17, 221; in Monroe (N.C.), 10–11; and New World Liberation Front (NWLF), 76, 139; and New Year's Eve bombings, 160–61; in Oakland city schools, 33; Olympia Police Department, 240–41; in Oregon, 226, 231, 237; and Patriots Party (Eugene, Ore.), 56; and People's Forces Unit IX (NWLF), 140; at Puget Sound Power and Light Company bombings, 240–41, 265; raids by, 186–90, 194–95, 302n19, 304nn40,41; at Raleigh (N.C.) Correctional Center for Women (CCW), 127–28; Redmond Police Depart-

INDEX   331

ment, 67, 235; Renton Police Department, 263; and Revolutionary Union (RU), 151–52; at riots in response to King assassination, 22–24; in Tacoma, 256, 259, 261–62, 265–67, 269, 273; Tukwila Police Department, 166–69, 171–75, 179–80, 212–17, 300nn3,5; at urban riots, 15–16, 22–25, 281n22; at Washington State Penitentiary (Walla Walla) conflict, 84; at Wounded Knee siege, 136–38. *See also* police brutality; Seattle Police Department (SPD)

police brutality: at anti-war rallies, 21–22, 24–28, 283n16; at bank robberies, 173; at Bedford Hills (Westchester, N.Y.) women's prison uprising, 128–29; in Newark (N.J.) riots, 15; at SLA Compton safe house, 119–20; at University of California at Berkeley, 28–29, 284n29; at Washington State Penitentiary (Walla Walla), 113

police informers, 33, 144, 151, 286n14, 287n24

Political Support–George Jackson Brigade (PS-GJB), 277

poor people/poverty: American Indians as, 135; and Brown, 91, 102, 104, 121; in Central District (Seattle), 82, 111, 144; and City Light bombing, 159–60; and civil rights movement, 11–13; and criminal justice system, 49; and GJB, 147, 159, 201, 205, 237; and Mead, 42–43, 55, 142, 216–18; and prison reform, 30, 55, 75; and Rap Center (Tacoma), 116; and Safeway bombings, 142–43, 159–60, 189; and SLA's "People in Need" program, 73, 75, 286n17, 290–91n12; and urban riots, 16, 22

Popular Movement for the Liberation of Angola (MPLA), 207–8

Portland (Ore.): and American Indian Movement (AIM), 138; Department of Public Safety, 55; and GJB, 227–31, 239; Portland Trailblazers, 85

Power, Katherine, 32–33, 301n13–2n13

Prague Spring (Czechoslovakia), 24

Prairie Fire Organizing Committee (PFOC), 76–77, 79, 85, 196–97, 201

*Prairie Fire: The Politics of Revolutionary Anti-Imperialism: Political Statement of the Weather Underground*, 76–78, 121, 123, 125, 139–40, 196–97

Pratt, Edwin, 105, 293n2

Pressmen's Union, 302n13

Pringle, Jack, 254

prisoners, 1–2, 4, 10, 16, 21, 30, 47; and anti-war movement, 54–55; Armsbury as, 56–59, 63; Atteberry as, 83–84; Baraldini as, 128; Bertram as, 276–77; and Black Panther Party, 31, 284–85n1; Brown as, 95–101, 104, 129, 148, 254–69, 272, 276–77; Clark as, 128; Cleaver as, 23, 31; Cook as, 112, 162, 165, 176, 230, 259–60, 264, 277, 293–94n3; Coupez as, 276–77; custody battles of women prisoners, 111; deaths of, 38, 55, 57, 62, 100, 290n29; DeFreeze as, 120; dehumanization of, 57–58; Dellinger as, 20; Desmond as, 290n27; in Detroit (Mich.) riots, 16; drug use of, 69, 84, 96–99, 233; Edwards as, 84; Green as, 85; Harp as, 70, 84; high recidivism rates for, 68, 70; in isolation cells, 30–31, 48, 63, 68, 73–74, 113, 128, 210–11, 213, 219–21, 232–33, 235, 240, 247–48, 264, 277, 306n6; Jackson, George, as, 31, 62, 75, 98–99, 121; Jackson, Wilbur "Popeye," as, 75; as jailhouse lawyers, 44, 48–50, 52–58, 60–62, 64, 74, 219, 221–22, 288n1; Lippman as, 55–56, 58; mace used on, 219–21; Malcolm X as, 31; Mead as, 41–50, 52–64, 76, 81, 150, 165, 192, 196, 198–200, 210–11, 213, 219–23, 230, 233, 235, 238, 259–60, 264, 272, 277, 306n6; medical neglect of, 30, 55, 68, 83, 100, 127, 198, 234; mental health treatment for, 1, 57, 234, 308n11; in Monroe (N.C.) city jail, 10; mothers as, 111; Newton as, 23; organizing for control in prisons, 70–71, 106, 112; out-of-state transfers of, 1, 43, 46, 61–63, 95, 99, 128, 293n10; political activities of, 61–64, 67–68; pregnancies of, 100; rights of, 53–54, 57, 62–64, 75, 83–84, 99, 106, 112, 165, 235; Shakur, Assata, as, 129, 159; Sherman as, 54–55, 59, 150, 165, 173–75, 276–77; Sing Louie as, 59, 62; Smith, Frank "Big Black," as, 112–14; Sostre as, 301n13; "street cred" of, 31, 284–85n1; strikes by, 58–60, 62–63, 68–69, 71, 75, 99, 150, 233–36, 238, 290n27, 291n17; and unemployment, 68, 72; unions for, 68–72, 75, 290n8; visitation rights, 58–59, 68, 111–12, 211; Whitnack as, 197–98, 221; women prisoners, 95–101, 104–6, 108–12, 125, 127–29, 197–98, 221 (*see also* names of women prisoners); Workman as, 55

prison escapes, 3, 52, 62, 64, 99, 120, 162; and Mead, 210–11, 213, 306n6; by Sherman, 173–80, 182–83, 197, 201, 210, 213, 226, 300n5, 301nn7,8

prison guards. *See* correctional officers
prison reform, 1–2, 30–32, 36, 235, 264; and abolition of prisons, 68, 106, 125; Action for Forgotten Women (Durham, N.C.), 127–28, 293n1; after "Unity Strikes," 68; and anti-war movement, 30–32, 62; and Attica uprising, 129; and Brown, 103–6, 108–12, 124–25, 127–29; and CONvention, 112–14, 118; and Coupez, 105–6, 108–12, 124–25, 127–29; "Inside Out" (organization), 69; Joan Little Defense Committee (N.C.), 127; and Mead, 50, 67–73; in New York City, 128; and participatory democracy, 4, 30, 62, 68, 70; and prisoners' unions, 68–72, 75, 290n8; and rehabilitation, 70–71, 97, 102, 110, 127, 233–35; Santa Cruz Women's Prison Project, 125; and Washington State Penitentiary (Walla Walla), 233; Women Out Now (WON), 105–6, 108–12, 114, 117, 124
Pritchard, Denise, 145
Procunier, Raymond, 286n12
Progressive Labor, 150
prostitution, 49, 111, 117–18; decriminalization of, 111, 117; and employment, 117–18
Protestant missionaries, 151
Proudhon, Pierre-Joseph, 61
psychology: and Brown, 103; Mead's interest in, 46–47; and NARA units, 97
Puerto Ricans, 4, 21, 37, 185, 202, 205–6
Puget Sound National Bank robberies, 261, 270
Puget Sound Power and Light Company bombings, 240–41, 263–65
Puppet Power, 111
Purdy women's prison (Purdy, Wash.), 105–6, 109–12, 178; Gay Activists Alliance, 106, 108; and Women Out Now (WON), 105–6, 108–12, 114

Quakers: American Friends Service Committee, 136, 165, 239–40; as pacifists, 11, 20; as social workers, 104
"Quarter Moon Tribe of the Woodstock Nation," 66
Quebec Liberation Front, 281n19
*Quotations from Chairman Mao*, 63

race war, 15–16, 17
racism/racists, 11, 91, 98, 114–16, 143, 147, 202, 219, 222, 235, 237, 264, 277. *See also* white supremacists
radicals: collaboration with ex-convicts, 30–37, 285nn2–4, 286nn10,14; identifying with revolutionaries abroad, 5, 13–15, 19, 34, 36, 48; new breed of, 13; patriotism of, 11; and prison reform, 30–32, 50, 285nn3,4; rejection of liberalism by, 5, 12–13; separatism prominent among, 3; Zilsel as, 76
Rainier National Bank: bank robbery, 239–40; bombings, 235–39
Raleigh (N.C.) Correctional Center for Women (CCW), 127–28
Ramsey Lewis Trio, 99
rape, 69–70, 127, 246–47, 261, 277
Raspe, Jan-Carl, 246–48
Ray, Dixy Lee, 234, 249, 254
Ray-Keil, Alice, 304n46
Raymond, Jill, 196–97, 301n13
Raymond, Laurie, 196–97, 304n46
Razore, Warren, 188
Reagan, Ronald, 28, 286n17, 311n6
Red & Black bookstore (Seattle, Wash.), 105
Red Cloud (Oglala Lakota leader), 135
Red Guerrilla Family, 37, 185, 286–87n18
Redmond (Wash.): J. J. Welcome Company, 82–83; Police Department, 67, 235; Rainier National Bank bombings in, 235–37
Red Star Singers, 116
Reed, John, 181, 201, 239, 245, 252, 254
Reed, Marion, 254
Remington Rand Corporation Building (Seattle) attempted bombing, 144
Remiro, Joe, 212, 286n14
Republican Convention (Miami, 1972), 185
Republicans, 286n17
"Requiem for Nonviolence" (Cleaver), 23
Reserve Officers Training Corps (ROTC), 3, 66; bombings of buildings, 66, 144
Revolutionary Communist Party, 150, 298n13
Revolutionary Union (RU), 150–54, 260, 298nn13,14
*Revolution in the Revolution?* (Debray), 18–19
"Revolution That Flopped, The" (*Seattle Times*), 144–45
Rhay, Bobby J., 68, 83–85, 233–34
Ribicoff, Abraham, 25
Richard, Marguerite, 142
Rifle Club (NRA), 10
RIOTSONG, 275
Roberto, Holden Álvaro, 207
Robinson, Kay E., 142
Robinson, Renault, 25, 283n18
Rockefeller, Nelson, 62, 79

Rosebud Indian Reservation (S.Dak.), 135–36
Ross, Diana, 103
Rubin, Jerry, 20, 26
Rudd, Mark, 130
Russian Revolution, 16, 206
Rutledge, James, 281n21

*Safe House: A Casebook Study of Revolutionary Feminism in the 1970's* (Beal), 122
Safeway bombings (Seattle), 140–43, 145–47, 149, 153, 158–62, 188–89, 197, 203, 296nn18,19,24, 297n3–98n3, 299n9
Sale, Kirkpatrick, 13–14, 249
Salvation Army store (San Pedro, Calif.), 99–100
Sam Melville-Jonathan Jackson Unit, 37
Sanders, Henry, 28
San Francisco Bay Area, 37, 68; gay liberation movement in, 74; Mead in, 34, 73–76, 79, 86, 139, 291n29; New World Liberation Front (NWLF), 34, 36–37, 75–76, 139–40, 145, 158, 185, 201, 230, 286–87n18, 296n15; Radical Collective's *Dragon*, 139, 166, 180–81, 197, 221; Symbionese Liberation Army (SLA), 33–34, 36, 73–76, 119–20, 122, 124, 173, 201, 286nn14,17, 295n15
*San Francisco Chronicle*, 37
San Francisco City Council, 36
*San Francisco Examiner*, 33
San Francisco Mime Troupe, 116
*San Francisco Phoenix*, 120
San Jose City College, 151
San Jose State University, 151
Sannes, David, 144
San Quentin State Prison (Calif.), 23, 31, 36, 75, 98, 121, 248; killing of guard, 36, 287n24; "Unity Strikes" in, 68
Santa Cruz (Calif.): Amazon Women's Music Festival, 125; Women's Prison Project, 125
Saxe, Susan, 32–33, 179, 301n13–2n13, 305n10
*Scanlan's*, 15, 281n19
Schaffer, Jim, 265
Scheyler, Robert, 249
Schlesinger, Arthur Jr., 13
Schleyer, Hanns Martin, 246, 248
Schroeder, Walter, 286n10
Schwerner, Mickey, 54
Scott, Jack, 295n15
Scott, Mary Ann, 167–68
Scott, Tyree, 82–83
Seale, Bobby, 22
Seattle (Wash.), 1–2; Association of Washington Prostitutes, 118; Beacon Hill, 148, 161; Boeing, 76, 152–53, 165, 236; Brenda's Autoshop, 224, 227, 310–11n4; Capitol Hill, 67, 76, 85, 102, 158, 177, 179, 186–91, 199, 204, 242, 275–76, 303–4n32 (*see also* Safeway bombings); Center for Addiction Services, 117; Central District, 82–84, 102–3, 111, 144; El Centro de la Raza, 80, 85, 112; Children's Orthopedic Hospital, 163; City Light public utility, 153–54, 157, 159, 161–64, 196–97, 216–17; Coffee Coven, 108; CONvention in, 112–14, 118, 148, 155; "Cooperating Community," 67; "Correctional Congress" (ACA) in, 72–73; The Day After (TDA) demonstrations in, 26–27, 27; Dragon House, 69, 82, 85, 140, 169; Federal Building attempted bombing/bomb threats, 139–40, 143; Federal Courthouse, 26, 27, 56, 57, 79, 140, 192, 212–14, 273–74; "Flako Drift" collective house, 117; Harborview Hospital, 142, 173–76, 300–301nn4,7; King County Jail, 62–63, 81, 173–75, 197–98, 210–13, 219–21, 230, 263–64, 306n6; Kingdome stadium, 118; Laurelhurst district, 160–63, 196, 216–17; Left Bank Collective, 76, 79, 85, 138–40, 143, 145, 180, 189–91, 194–97, 202–6, 208, 221, 238, 296n13, 304nn40,41, 311n2; Lesbian Resource Center, 111; Liberation Coalition, 110; North Seattle safe house, 242, 250–54; Pacific Car & Foundry, 152; People's Forces Unit IX (NWLF), 139–41, 143, 145, 274, 296n13, 311n2; Pike Place Market, 76, 180; Pioneer Square, 93–94, 118, 157, 176; Post Office, 93–96; Rainier National Bank bombings, 235; Remington Rand Corporation Building, 144; Safeway bombings, 140–43, 145–47, 149, 158–62, 188–89, 296nn18,19,24, 298n3, 299n9; Seattle-King County Bar Association, 184; Seattle Left, 110; Seattle Seven trial, 56, 57, 60, 289n8; Shelly's Leg, 108, 293n6; 10th Street Collective, 108, 113–14, 121, 123–24, 154, 158, 224; University District ("the Dub"), 66, 103–5, 108, 117, 144, 147, 161–62; Urban League, 105, 293n2; Workin' On It (underground press), 124. *See also* Seattle Police Department (SPD)
Seattle Central Community College (SCCC), 103–4, 112; Drama Department, 104, 108–9; Prisoners Coalition, 103–4, 108–9, 155
*Seattle Magazine*, 281n26

Seattle Police Department (SPD): and Brenda's Autoshop, 227; at construction worker demonstrations, 82; and grand jury investigations, 181, 189–90, 194–95, 198; hollow-point bullets used by, 81, 172; Intelligence Unit, 176, 190; and Mead's trials, 212–14; and New Year's Eve bombings, 160–62, 164; raids by, 186–88, 304nn40,41; at Safeway bombings, 140, 142–46; and Sherman's jailbreak, 176–77, 301n7; wiretaps of, 123

*Seattle Post-Intelligencer* coverage, 58, 70–71; of automotive machinists strike, 246; of bank robberies, 179–80, 230, 242; of bombings/bomb threats, 1–2, 138, 163–64, 237; of GJB, 1–2, 138, 175, 179–80, 211–13, 230, 273–74; of grand jury investigation, 188, 191–92, 196, 303–4nn23,32,34; of Mead's trials, 200, 212–14, 218–19, 221–23; newspaper owned by Hearst, 119; of prison conflicts, 234, 237, 264; of Safeway bombings, 141–43, 145, 297n3

*Seattle Sun*, 2, 253, 263

*Seattle Times* coverage: of bombings/bomb threats, 144–45, 237; of GJB, 1–2, 203, 209, 269, 309n1; of grand jury investigations, 198; of Mead's trials, 200, 212, 214, 218–19, 221; of Mead's youth, 42; of police use of hollow-point bullets, 81; of prison conflicts, 60, 84, 234–37, 264

*Second Sex, The* (Beauvoir), 115

Seeger, Pete, 59–60

Seeley, Barb, 105

Seidel, Bruce, 69, 70, 71; alias of, 169, 183–84; at anti-war rallies, 25; as bisexual, 150; and bombings, 1–2, 85–87, 135, 138, 158–59, 161, 295n1; at construction worker demonstrations, 82–83, 148–49; at "Correctional Congress" (ACA), 72; death of, 2, 168–73, 179–80, 213, 215–17, 264, 300n4(ch17), 300n3(ch18); and GJB, 25, 147–49, 154–56, 158–59, 161, 165, 167–70, 172, 204; response to Ford's death, 140–41; and Whitnack, 195

self-defense, armed: and Black Panther Party for Self-Defense, 22–23, 31; Debray's discounting of, 18–19, 282n33; and guerrilla warfare, 16, 18; and Jackson, 31–32; at Mead's trials, 212–13; in Monroe (N.C.), 10–11, 282n33; and Patriots Party (Eugene, Ore.), 56; in Plainfield (N.J.), 16; universally acknowledged in civil rights movement, 10–11; and women, 122

Sendic, Raul, 309n14

sexism, 49, 103, 115, 121–22, 130, 143, 147, 149, 154, 222, 237, 239, 274, 297n4

Shakur, Afeni, 129

Shakur, Assata, 129–30, 159

Sharp, Morell, 190, 195

Sheets, John, 173

Shelton, David, 211

Sherman, Joanne, 64, 67, 153, 227

Sherman, John, 2–3, 59, 64, 67–72; aliases of, 225, 252, 258; arraignment of, 182; arrest of, 274–75; bad relationships with, 249–51, 256, 262; and bank robberies, 165–69, 171–73, 226, 228–31, 273, 300nn3,4(ch17), 300n3(ch18); and bombings, 161, 235, 239–40, 243–45, 265–66; and Coupez, 178, 224–26, 230, 249, 260, 297n1; employment of, 152–53; flight from Seattle, 251–52; as fugitive, 191–92, 196, 239; gambling of, 225–26, 262–63; and grand jury investigations, 191–92, 196; handwriting of, 191–92, 196; jailbreak of, 173–80, 182–83, 197, 201, 210, 213, 226, 300n5, 301nn7,8; and kidnappings (proposed), 249–50; Left's views of, 204; and Mead's trials, 215–16; in Oregon, 224–30; as prisoner, 54–55, 59, 150, 165, 173–74, 276–77; recruitment to GJB, 150, 154; release from prison, 277; response to Safeway bombing, 153; and Revolutionary Union (RU), 150–54, 260; state liquor store robbery of, 155–56; and stolen cars, 258–59; in Tacoma, 255–56, 258–60, 262–63, 265–69, 273–74; trial of, 277

shoplifting, 42, 93, 159

Silvernale, Charles, 163

Simmons, Frances, 142

Sing Louie, George, 59, 62, 74

*Sir! No Sir! The Suppressed Story of the GI Movement to End the War in Vietnam* (documentary), 294n6

*Sisterhood Is Powerful* (Morgan), 130

sit-ins, 21, 28, 284n29

Skagen, Roy, 142–46

S. L. Savidge Dodge car dealership bombing, 243–45

Smith, Dick, 188–89, 303n23

Smith, Frank "Big Black," 112–14, 127, 294n5

"Socialism and Man in Cuba" (Guevara), 18

socialists, 13, 105, 125, 154, 164, 201, 206

*Soledad Brother* (Jackson), 98, 148, 292n32

Soledad Prison (Calif.), 31, 120

Soltysik, Patricia, 119–20

Sostre, Martin, 179, 301n13
*Soul on Ice* (Cleaver), 23, 31
Special Weapons and Tactics (SWAT) Units, 33–34, 119–20, 138
Spellman, John D., 263–64, 311n6
*Spook Who Sat by the Door, The* (film), 281n25
Sporleder, Annie, 84
Stanford University, 151
State Street Bank & Trust Company (Brighton, Mass.) robbery, 32–33, 286n10
state troopers, 16, 112–13; and bank robberies, 167; and bombings/bomb threats, 160, 240; and Brown's arrest, 254; at Jackson State College, 35; in Monroe (N.C.), 10; at Raleigh (N.C.) Correctional Center for Women (CCW), 128; and Symbionese Liberation Army (SLA), 33–34; at University of California at Berkeley, 28; at Wounded Knee siege, 138
Steilacoom Prisoner Support House, 64, 67
Steinlauf, Michael, 82, 169–70
Stephenson, James, 186–87
Stern, Susan, 56, 289nn8,11, 299n9
Stiere, Robert, 213
St. James, Margo, 117
Stoller, Nancy, 125
strikes, 33, 35; by automotive machinists, 243–46, 265, 270–71; at City Light (Seattle), 153–54, 157–59, 163–64; hunger strikes, 62, 198, 290n27; by Pressmen's Union, 302n13; in prison, 58–60, 62–63, 68–69, 71, 75, 99, 150, 233–36, 238, 240, 270, 290n27, 291n17; "Unity Strikes," 68; against Weyerhauser, 120–21
student movements, 3–4, 11–14; and Black Panther Party for Self-Defense, 22; at Brandeis University, 33; and Columbia University building occupations, 21; at Jackson State College, 35; at Kent State University, 35; and Lippman, 55–56, 154; and prison reform, 32, 285n4; response to Nixon's announcement of Cambodian bombing raids, 32, 35–36; and Revolutionary Union (RU), 150–52; in Seattle (Wash.), 66–67; at University of California at Berkeley, 27–29, 284n29; in West Germany, 38, 246. *See also names of student groups*
Student Nonviolent Coordinating Committee (SNCC), 11–12
Students for a Democratic Society (SDS), 3, 11–14, 24, 66, 121, 246; "Action! Action! Action!" shard of, 55–56; and Columbia University building occupations, 21; "Port Huron Statement," 13; and Revolutionary Union (RU), 150–51; and Weatherman, 3, 25–26, 55–56, 150; women in, 128
Sturgis, Autrey "Scat," 176
*Sunfighter, The,* 69, 135, 147, 295n1
Supreme Court, U.S., 53–54, 60, 288n1
*Surfacing* (Atwood), 257, 310n2
Sweigert, Phillip, 274
Swinton, Pat, 130–31, 295n6
Symbionese Liberation Army (SLA), 33–34, 36, 73–76, 124, 286nn14,17; burning of Compton safe house, 33–34, 76, 119–20, 122, 124, 173, 295n15; GJB in sympathy with, 141–44, 238, 247, 249; grand jury investigations of, 185–86; and Hearst, 33–34, 73–74, 119, 124, 141, 144–46, 290–91n12, 295n15; Left's views of, 201, 206; and male chauvinism, 150; and Mead, 34, 73–74, 141–44, 212; "People in Need" program, 73, 75, 286n17, 290–91n12; women in, 33, 119–20 (*see also* Hearst, Patricia)

Tacoma (Wash.): and Bertram, 114–16; community college in, 105; County-City Building bomb threat, 143; FBI office bombing, 138, 145, 211; and GJB, 252–75, 311–12n4; Martin Luther King, Jr. Center, 116; Rap Center, 116; Shelter Half, 116, 294n6; Sheridan House, 116; and Women Out Now (WON), 111
*Tacoma News Tribune,* 240, 254, 274
"Tania," 74, 119, 294n2
Tarang'anya (Kenya) *harambee,* 115–16
tear gas, 26, 28, 99, 119–20, 128, 136, 252
television, 34, 76, 98–99, 115, 120, 141, 212, 243, 263, 267–68
Terminal Island penitentiary (San Pedro, Calif.), 95–101, 104; Admission and Orientation (A&O) building, 96; landscape maintenance work in, 96–97; NARA units at, 97–98, 100; reading groups at, 98; work-release program at, 99–100
terrorism, 15, 37; and GJB, 200, 202–4, 240, 305n2; grand jury investigation of, 181, 185, 188, 195; LaGuardia Airport explosion as, 37, 160–61; Left's views of, 200, 202–4, 207, 209, 305n2; New Year's Eve bombings as, 160–61; by police, 173, 180, 203; Safeway bombings as, 143, 145, 160; state terrorism, 247–48

"Terrorism in Seattle: The George Jackson Brigade" (McDonald), 181
Thetford, Lois, 116
Third World revolution, 14, 17, 19, 25, 29, 77–78, 202, 204, 206–8, 284–85n1
Traven, B., 257
*Tricontinental* (Cuban journal), 286–87n18
Trident Nuclear Submarine Base, 154, 304n46
Tropp, Robert, 1–2
Trotsky, Leon, 63
Tukwila bank robbery, 2–3, 144, 156, 165–74, 176, 179–80, 237, 300nn3,4, 301n13; and Mead's trials, 212–13, 215–16, 221–23
Tukwila Police Department, 166–69, 171–75, 179–80, 183, 300nn3,5; and Mead's trials, 212–17
Tupamaros (Uruguay), 207, 248–49, 309n14
"Two, Three, Many Vietnams" (Guevara), 18, 21

Uhlman, Wes, 144
"Umbilical Corps, The," 275
*Underground* (documentary), 186
Union Bank in Tacoma robbery, 270
*Union Maids* (documentary), 258
unions: Automotive Machinists Union, 243–46, 265, 270–71; California Prisoners Union, 75; and civil rights movement, 21; for electrical workers, 157, 163–64; grand jury investigations of, 185; Longshoreman's Local 52, 164; Pressmen's Union, 302n13; for prisoners, 68–73, 75, 82, 85, 148, 150, 290n8; for prison guards, 72, 233, 235; Progressive Labor, 150; for prostitutes, 117–18; Revolutionary Union (RU), 150–54; in *Union Maids* (documentary), 258; United Construction Workers Association (UCWA), 82–83, 148–49, 169–70; United Farm Workers (UFW), 140, 142, 158–59; United Prisoners Union (UPU), 75; Washington Prisoners Labor Union (WPLU), 69–73, 75, 82, 85, 148, 150; worker-student alliances, 150–53
United Construction Workers Association (UCWA), 170
United Waste Control Corporation, 188
University of California at Berkeley: Avakian as student at, 151; and bombing of Berkeley police headquarters, 27–29; Ethnic Studies department, 28; Free Speech Movement, 28, 284n29; and guerrilla warfare, 28; "People's Park" campaign, 28–29, 284n32; sit-in in Sproul Hall, 28; "Vietnam Day," 20, 282n1

University of Illinois, 105, 147
University of North Carolina, 127–28
University of Oregon, 56, 92
University of Washington, 103–5, 112, 117, 147, 161; bombings at, 66, 144, 162; International Women's Day, 103–4
*University of Washington Daily*, 66
University of Wisconsin, 36, 128
Uptagraph, B. K., 2
urban riots, 15–17, 17, 281–82nn21,22,27; anti-war rallies as, 20–25, 282n1; in response to King assassination, 22–23
Utah State Industrial School (Ogden, Utah), 42–43

Valeri, Robert, 32
Valerian Coven document, 270–71
Vander Wall, Jim, 137–38
Vargas, Armando "Angel," 58
Venceremos Brigade, 151–52, 188–89
veterans: and Brown, 93; and burning of SLA Compton safe house, 120; and civil rights movement, 21; collaboration with radicals, 33, 37, 286n14; grand jury investigation of, 185; POWs at "Correctional Congress" (ACA), 72–73; and Revolutionary Union (RU), 151; at Shelter Half (Tacoma), 116, 294n6
Vickery, Gordon, 163
Vietnam Veterans against the War, 185
Vietnam war, 3, 14, 16–17, 20, 38; and burning of SLA Compton safe house, 120; Cambodian bombing raids, 32, 35; escalation of, 19–20, 32, 35, 62; Hearst's defense of, 119; loss of, 135; Mead's response to, 54; POWs in, 72–73; and *Prairie Fire*, 77–78; as revolution, 5, 11, 13, 17–18, 34, 206–7; and Shelter Half (Tacoma), 116, 294n6; Tet Offensive, 16–17, 281–82n27; and Williams' *Crusader* newsletter, 16–17, 281–82n27; and Women Out Now (WON) programs, 111. *See also* anti-war movement
vigilantes, 10, 81, 138
violence, 5, 86, 286n12; at anti-war rallies, 21–22, 24–27, 35, 283n16; and Bertram, 117, 229; and GJB, 173, 179–81, 200–202, 205, 211, 217, 234, 237, 265; Jackson's views of, 32, 80, 86, 292n32; Left's views of, 200–202, 205–8; mob violence, 9, 234; in Monroe (N.C.), 9–11; in prisons, 234; and radicals' collaboration with ex-convicts, 32–33,

INDEX   337

285n4, 286nn10,14; in self-defense, 10–11, 32; and student movements, 27–29, 35, 246, 284n33; and women, 122–23; at Wounded Knee siege, 137. *See also* bombings; firearms/armed struggle; self-defense, armed
Voorhees, Donald, 183, 218–19, 221–22, 304n46

Waldt, Lawrence, 221, 263–64
Walker Commission, 283n16
Wallbom, Mark, 167, 172, 215–16, 300n5
Walsh, Ruth, 263
Walton, Bill, 85
"Waltzin' Will Trilogy" (song), 117
Ward, Larry, 144
War on Poverty, 12
Washington (D.C.) anti-war rallies, 12, 20–24, 26, 284n25
Washington Bankers Association, 238–39
Washington Monument demonstration, 26
*Washington Post*, 185, 293n10, 302n13
Washington Prisoners Labor Union (WPLU), 69–73, 75, 82, 85, 148, 150
Washington State Board of Prison Terms and Paroles, 217, 223
Washington State Department of Corrections, 2, 36, 106, 108, 110; Division of Corrections bombing, 1–2, 62, 85–87, 135, 138, 145, 147–49, 210, 295n1
Washington State Department of Vocational Rehabilitation (DVR), 102–3
Washington State Penitentiary (Walla Walla), 1–2, 68, 83–85, 104–5, 112–13, 189, 233, 249; Black Panther Party chapter at, 112, *113*, 155; *Bomb, The*, 112; Intensive Security Unit, 84–85, 210, 233, 238; LaRue at, 84, 210; lockdown at, 233–34, 236, 238; Mead at, 218, 230, 233, 235, 238, 264; Pivot at, 112, 165; Resident Governance Council/Resident Council (RC), 83–85, 233–34, 236–37; strike at, 233–36, 238, 240, 270; Sturgis at, 176; "The Super Crew" at, 112; women prisoners at, 104–5
Washington State Reformatory (WSR, Monroe), 69–72, 104, 108, 114, 150, 277, 294n5
Watergate scandal/trial, 185, 218, 249
Watts riot (1965), 15, 28
Wayler, Rex, 136
Weatherman, 3, 25–26, 35–36; "armed and incompetent," 37, 287n26; and Clark, 118; Days of Rage, 26, 55–56, 128; Hoover's assessment of, 36, 287n21; and Lippman, 55–56, 289n8; "New Morning, Changing Weather" communiqué, 35–36, 287n22; and SDS, 3, 25–26, 55–56, 150; and Seattle Seven, 56, 289n8; Townhouse explosion, 35, 69, 287nn22,26; women in, 56, 77, 118, 130, 286n11, 287n22, 289n8; Workman named as, 55. *See also* Weather Underground
Weather Underground, 28, 35–37, 56, 76–77, 139, 246; and Alpert, 130; and bombings, 62, 185; and Brinks truck attempted robbery, 128; conflated with GJB, 160, 162, 299n9; grand jury investigations of, 185–86; and male chauvinism, 121–22, 150; Mead's views on, 201; and *Prairie Fire*, 76–78, 121, 123, 125, 139–40, 196–97; "Red Dragon Print Collective," 77; and Withey, 169
Weinberg, John, 251
Welcome, Leroy "Bud," 82–83
Wershow, Dan, 190
West Coast Women's Printing Conference, 124
West Germany, 36; Red Army Faction (RAF), 38, 246–48
Westinghouse, Robert, 274
Westlund, Warren, 243–44
Westlund Buick car dealership attemped bombing, 243–45
Wexler, Haskell, 185
Weyerhaeuser, C. Davis, 249
Weyerhauser, 91–92, 120–21, 236, 249
*What Is to Be Done?* (Lenin), 77
white supremacists, 5, 9, 11
Whitnack, Jeff, 190
Whitnack, Nancy "Michelle," 190–92, 194–98, 204–6, 221, 305n54
Wicker, Margo, 48–52, 64–65
Wilkins, Roy, 10–11
Williams, Cecil, 75
Williams, Mabel, 9–10
Williams, Robert, 16; association with revolutionary leaders, 11; escape to Cuba of, 10–11; exile of, 10–11, 16, 281–82n27; in Monroe (N.C.), 9–11, 22; ouster from NAACP, 11; as patriot, 11; publisher of *Crusader* newsletter, 16–17, *17*, 281–82n27; views on armed self-defense, 10–11, 18–19, 282n33
Williams, Robert Lewis III, 103
Williams, Ronald, 137–38
Wilson, Dick, 136–37
Wilson, John Arthur, 144–45, 212, 214
Wilson, Lloyd, 265

Wilson, Peter. *See* Seidel, Bruce
Withey, Michael, 82, 169, 183–84, 186, 228
*Woman on the Edge* (Piercy), 257
women: in bank robberies, 32–33, 286n11; and Brenda's Autoshop, 224, 227, 310–11n4; at campus demonstrations, 28, 284n29; at City Light (Seattle), 158, 164; custody battles of women prisoners, 111; on FBI's "Ten Most Wanted" list, 33, 286n11, 302n13; in GJB, 4, 148–50, 154, 158, 166, 178–81, 191–92, 196, 201, 211, 239, 266 (*see also* Brown, Rita D.); International Women's Day (Univ. of Washington), 103–4; mothers as prisoners, 111; as "mules," 97; as single mothers, 111, 189; in SLA, 33, 119–20; use of firearms by, 10, 119, 130; and violence, 122–23; as war workers, 42; in Weatherman, 56, 77, 118, 130, 286n11, 287n22, 289n8; women prisoners, 95–101, 104–10, 112, 125, 127–29, 197–98, 221 (*see also names of women prisoners*)
*Women and Madness* (Chesler), 122
Women Out Now (WON), 105–6, 108–12, 114, 117, 124, 224; constitution of, 105–6; Legal Defense Fund, 111–12; Survival Fund, 111
women's liberation movement, 115, 123, 130, 297n4
*Women's Press* (Eugene, Ore.), 196
Woo, Michael, 169–70
working class, 4; at anti-war rallies, 25; Armsbury as, 56; and automotive machinists' strikes, 243–44, 265, 271; Brown as, 91–93; and City Light bombing, 153–54, 157, 159; in civil rights movement, 21; and COYOTE, 117–18; and GJB, 201, 237, 239; and homosexuality, 154; Mead as, 45; and prisoners' unions, 72; and Revolutionary Union (RU), 150–52, 154; and Safeway bombings, 143, 153, 158–59; and unemployment, 72
Workin' On It (underground press), 124
Workman, Donovan, 55
World War II, 20, 29, 41–42, 164, 248
Wright, Laddie, 186–88, 302n19
Wright, Walter, 179, 191–92, 196, 211–12, 222–23, 230, 303n23
Wyatt, F. Lowry, 249

Yaplee, Danny E., 142
Yoshimura, Wendy, 141
Younger, Evelle, 160, 299n8
Young Lords (Puerto Rican youth gang), 21
Young Patriots (Chicago), 56

Zeiger, David, 294n6
Zengakuren (Japanese student federation), 24
Ziegler, John, 183, 198
Zilsel, Paul, 76, 138–39, 145, 180, 194–95, 206–7, 221, 296n18
Zirpoli, Alfonso, 74

TEXT
10/12.5 Minion Pro

DISPLAY
Minion Pro

COMPOSITOR
Integrated Composition Systems

INDEXER
Sharon Sweeney

www.ingramcontent.com/pod-product-compliance
Lightning Source LLC
Chambersburg PA
CBHW030519230426
43665CB00010B/690